CAMBRIDGE STUDIES IN LINGUISTICS

General Editors · W. SIDNEY ALLEN · EUGENIE J. A. HENDERSON
FRED W. HOUSEHOLDER · JOHN LYONS · R. B. LE PAGE · F. R. PALMER
J. L. M. TRIM

Old English Phonology

In this series

Other volumes in preparation

OLD ENGLISH PHONOLOGY

ROGER LASS
JOHN M. ANDERSON

University of Edinburgh

Cambridge University Press

CAMBRIDGE

LONDON · NEW YORK · MELBOURNE

Published by the Syndics of the Cambridge University Press
The Pitt Building, Trumpington Street, Cambridge CB2 IRP
Bentley House, 200 Euston Road, London NWI 2DB
32 East 57th Street, New York, N.Y.10022 USA
296 Beaconsfield Parade, Middle Park, Melbourne 3206, Australia

© Cambridge University Press 1975

Library of Congress catalogue card number: 74-80360

ISBN: 0 521 20531 X

First published 1975

Printed in Great Britain
at the University Printing House, Cambridge
(Euan Phillips, University Printer)

HELGE KÖKERITZ AND O. K. SCHRAM
in memoriam

Contents

III TWO PROCESSES OF VOWEL EPENTHESIS:
   BREAKING AND BACK UMLAUT

IV PALATALIZATION AND *I*-UMLAUT

V STRENGTHENING AND WEAKENING OF OBSTRUENTS:
   FRICATIVE VOICING ASSIGNMENT, CONTINUANCY
   ADJUSTMENT, AND SOME RELATED PROCESSES

List of abbreviations

acc. accusative
Aelf. Aelfric
AFB Anglo-Frisian Brightening
ant anterior
Arm. Armenian
artic articulation
Av. Avestan
C consonant
CLOS closure
cons consonantal
cont continuant
cor coronal
dat. dative
DHH Diphthong Height Harmony
Du. Durham
e- early
Finn. Finnish
Fr. French
G. German
gen. genitive
Gmc Germanic
Go. Gothic
Gr. Greek
Hung. Hungarian
IE Indo-European
INF infinitive
IPA International Phonetic Association
Ka. Kannaḍa
L. Latin
lat lateral
ME Middle English
MHG Middle High German

MnSpan.   Modern Spanish
MSC   morpheme structure condition
MS(S)   manuscript(s)
n.   nominative/(foot)note
N   nasal consonant
nas   nasal
Nb.   Northumberland
NE   New (= Modern) English
NHG   New (= Modern) High German
Nth.   Northumbrian
O   obstruent
obs   obstruent (feature)
OE   Old English
OED   Oxford English Dictionary
OFris.   Old Frisian
OHG   Old High German
OIcel.   Old Icelandic
OIr.   Old Irish
OJ   Old Japanese
ON   Old Norse
OS   Old Saxon
OSpan.   Old Spanish
PART   past (passive) participle of the OE strong verb
PD   Proto-Dravidian
pers.   person
PGmc   Proto-Germanic
phon   phonation
PIE   Proto-Indo-European
pl.   plural
PP   past participle and preterite forms of the OE strong verb
PR   Puerto-Rican
PRES   present forms of the OE strong verb
$PRET_1$ preterite indicative 1 and 3 person singular of the OE strong verb
$PRET_2$ preterite forms of the OE strong verb other than $PRET_1$
P-rule   phonological rule
PU   Proto-Uralic
R   resonant (nonobstruent) consonant
REL   release
RP   Received Pronunciation
S   segment
SC   structural change
SD   Structural description

sg./sing. singular
Skr. Sanskrit
Span. Spanish
SPE The Sound Pattern of English (= Chomsky & Halle 1968)
strid strident
SV strong verb
SW south-west(ern)
syll syllabic
V vowel
voc vocalic
WGG West Germanic Gemination
WGmc West Germanic
WS West Saxon

Preface

This book is the result of four years of wrestling with some major problems of Old English phonology. The length of time it has been in the works, as it were, is significant when one comes to look at its overall structure. Between the appearance of our preliminary mimeographed version (1970) and the present publication, there have been many new developments in phonological theory, which have – for better or worse – left their mark. In particular, the theory as a whole seems much less stable and unified than it did in the first two years or so after the appearance of *The sound pattern of English* (1968), which more or less established the shape of the 'classical' generative paradigm.

The main questions that have arisen seem to cluster around the basic problem of what we might call the 'determinacy' of phonological descriptions. To what extent, for instance, does the requirement that all non-suppletive allomorphy be referred to unique morphophonemic representations operated on by 'independently motivated' and 'phonetically natural' rules still hold? (And, for that matter, how can you tell, in cases less obvious than *go:went* or *good:better*, whether you really have suppletion?) This issue seems to be at the bottom of the whole 'abstractness' controversy (Kiparsky 1968a, Hyman 1970, etc.); and the controversy has by no means been effectively settled (cf. Harms 1973, Hyman 1973, Vago 1973).

This problem has left a structural impress on our work: the bulk of this book (with some polemical exceptions) is what might be called a 'classical' or 'standard' generative phonology of OE; but at the end (ch. VI) we have added a rather elaborate quasi-palinode. We say 'quasi-', because it is not so much a 'retraction' as a reconsideration of some of our conclusions and procedures in the light of theoretical issues that seem more important now than they did earlier, but are not yet settled enough to make us change our basic analysis. On these matters we leave the decision to the reader, and let our own uncertainty stand.

Basically this book is an attempt to discover which of those processes that the handbooks call 'sound-changes' dating to pre-OE times, and reflected in intraparadigmatic variation of various kinds, can be recovered as synchronic rules of OE. In general, then, the prime issue is the 'depth' of OE morphophonemics; how many of the variations in morpheme-shape are synchronically motivated (i.e. are alternations) and how many are relics of historical processes with no synchronic relevance (i.e. suppletions). Our general conclusion is that nearly all of them – including even the 'ablaut' alternations in the strong verbs – can be shown to play a significant part in the synchronic phonology, if this is constructed pretty much according to the requirements of standard theory. In this sense, of course, there is in this book, as in any other study of its type, a certain epistemological indeterminacy: is it an account of 'the structure of OE', or of 'the structure of standard theory', as shown by its confrontation with the facts of OE? We cannot tell at this point whether the two are 'complementary' (in the sense of 'complementarity' in physical theory) or not. But the problem of whether scientific descriptions are ontological at all, or solely epistemological, cannot be solved here: though we do think it worth mentioning.

Any generative treatment of the facts established by the older 'philological' investigations is bound to be somewhat controversial in its interpretations, vis-à-vis the older ones; this is only to be expected. And the extent to which our challenges to the older views are well founded is a matter for the reader to judge. But what is not so obvious is that almost any large-scale investigation conducted in the framework of 'standard' theory is bound – by virtue of the language-specific facts it deals with – to be controversial vis-à-vis that theory as well. So that even though our basic orientation is that of Chomsky and Halle, there are a number of points where we depart from the paradigm, and make rather different proposals. This is clearest in issues like the degree of specification required for lexical entries (the admission of 'archisegments': cf. chs. I, V, VI), and the choice of a feature inventory (cf. Preliminaries). Both types of controversial claims will be apparent throughout; but the main impulse here is exploratory rather than polemical.

It is clear that anyone working in historical linguistics and approaching the subject from a contemporary point of view will find himself in the midst of a complex network of indebtedness: to the scholars of the 'old tradition' and to those of the new, including those of his colleagues who have taken the time to exact a personal (rather than simply biblio-graphical) debt. Our bibliography will give some idea of our impersonal indebtedness; but a number of personal acknowledgements are in order. First and foremost, to the two men (now deceased) who were largely responsible for getting us interested in historical linguistics in the first place, and presided over our early training: Helge Kökeritz, late Professor of English at Yale University, and Dr O. K. Schram, late Reader in English Language at the University of Edinburgh. To their memory, with great affection and gratitude, we dedicate this work.

More directly, we would like to acknowledge the help (both con-structive and destructive) of those of our colleagues who have read parts of this book in various versions, or have generously given of their time to discuss our ideas with us. Most especially the following: David J. Tittensor, Charles Jones, Gillian Brown, Geoff Pullum, James R. Hurford, Bengt Sigurd, Robert P. Stockwell, Mary Taylor, Charles Bird, and Fred Householder.

And finally, we must mention the heroic efforts of Jane Lind in deciphering and typing our first draft; the patience of our wives, Jaime and Margaret, during our long periods of utter abstraction; and the fortitude and perceptive commentary of our students in Indiana and Edinburgh, who sat through our early expositions of much of this material.

R.L., J.M.A.

Edinburgh
November 1973

Preliminaries: the feature framework

1 Prologue

There seems at the moment to be a modicum of agreement among phonologists on certain central theoretical issues; e.g. on the (ideal) goals of phonological descriptions, the overall shape of the grammatical model, and so on. And there seems to be an equally large amount of controversy about details. The most basic outlines of the theory are fairly clear; at this point there even seems to be something approaching a 'canon'. The major rule-formalisms have been worked out in detail, and there are at least three works which in their very different ways can serve as 'texts': Chomsky and Halle (1968: henceforth *SPE*), Harms (1968), and Schane (1973). These books, together with the discussions in Postal (1968) and a host of shorter papers, can be taken to define, in broad outline, the substantive assumptions and argumentative strategies of a 'standard theory'.

Competing 'schools' have not yet arisen in generative phonology in quite the same way they have in syntax: there is no fully (or even partly) articulated 'countertheory' that stands in the same relation to the canon as say case-grammars stand to transformational grammars in the strict sense. The main counterproposals, important as they are, rather nibble at the edges than go for the centre.[1] Most of the major problems are at least statable within the standard theory.

---

[1] Some of the major controversies concern: 'abstractness' (Kiparsky 1968a vs. Hyman 1970); the admissibility of 'abstract rules' or 'metarules' (Lass 1969b, Foley 1969); the status of 'conspiracies' (Kisseberth 1969, 1970a); the role of 'hierarchies' (Foley 1969, Zwicky 1969, Lass 1971a); the proper handling of exceptions (Postal 1968, *SPE*, Kisseberth 1970b); and the admissibility of extrinsic rule-ordering (Koutsoudas, Sanders and Noll 1971). Our position on most of these issues will be clear from the exposition.

The only one we will not comment on in the body of the text is rule-ordering (but cf. p. 7 n. below). We will assume that phonological rules by and large apply in linear sequence, and that they can be ordered extrinsically. We might note also that the attack on extrinsic ordering is the most 'central' of the controversial proposals vis-à-vis the essential formalism of the theory.

One debated matter, though, is of particular importance in the initial stages of a description: and this is the choice of a feature-inventory. In a sense this is perhaps the most basic issue of all, since the features are the critical substantive entities in the metatheory, and as 'atomic' elements in a description they have major consequences for everything else.

There have been many proposals on this matter (cf. the discussions cited in Harms 1968: ch. 4); the subject has held a central place in phonological debate since the first large-scale synthesis of Jakobson, Fant and Halle (1951). The basic questions seem to be: (a) are the correct primitives acoustic (Jakobson et al. 1951) or articulatory (*SPE*), or both (Ladefoged 1971)? And (b), given a choice on this, which is the right set? Our position here will be that the primes should, overall, be articulatory (but cf. ch. v below); and that the general type of framework that should ultimately be chosen will probably be something like the one in *SPE*. But not in all details: we will propose several modifications to that inventory, including both new features and redefinitions of old ones. The discussion below will outline both our agreements and disagreements with the *SPE* framework, following its typological classification (*SPE*, ch. VII).

2   The major class features

2.1   Sonorant/nonsonorant (obstruent)

This feature distinguishes vowels, nasals, liquids, and 'glides' (see below) on the one hand from the 'true consonants' (stops, fricatives, affricates). Chomsky and Halle have defined this distinction in terms of a putative difference in vocal-tract configuration: sonorants have a setting that allows 'spontaneous voicing' (300–1), i.e. there is no major inhibition of transglottal airflow; whereas obstruents have 'non-spontaneous voicing', i.e. they require a faster airflow to produce voice. Ladefoged (1971) has shown that this supposed distinction is without experimental support; but this does not deny the importance of the categories. One can retain (as Ladefoged does) a 'parametric' definition: there is an important class-cleavage between segments characterized by a quite small output of periodic acoustic energy (obstruents) and those with a large output (sonorants). Whatever the proper criteria for the division turn out to be, there is no doubt that the specifications

[+sonorant] and [−sonorant] (or, as we will state them here, [−obstruent] and [+obstruent]) represent significant 'polar' categories in phonology.[1]

2.2 Vocalic/nonvocalic, consonantal/nonconsonantal

These two features are closely related, in that they function on the hierarchical level below [±obs] to distinguish the rest of the 'major classes' of segments. We also treat them together because one of our basic points here is that [vocalic] is not a necessary feature; its functions can be fulfilled by the well-motivated specification [+cons] for some segments assumed in standard theory not to be consonantal, and by a use of the feature [syllabic] in a special sense to be defined later.

In the *SPE* framework, the features [obs, voc, cons] interact as follows to define the major segment classes:

(1)	Obstruents	Liquids	Nasals	Vowels	'Glides'
Obs	+	−	−	−	−
Voc	−	+	−	+	−
Cons	+	+	+	−	−

The motivation for this classification hinges on the definition of 'glide': and this is a category which we claim is (at least lexically) nonexistent.

What is it that [vocalic] allows us to do? The main functions seem to be: (a) to characterize [j w] uniquely at the 'class' level, so as to make them distinct from the categories V, C; and (b) to create a class where [j w] group with [ʔ h]. We suggest that (a) never has to be done at the lexical level, and that (b) should never be done at any level.

Consider the phonetic nature of the class 'glide' as defined here: if it consists of [j w ʔ h], then it has first, both voiced and voiceless segments, and second, a range for stricture from full closure ([ʔ]) through close approximation ([h]) to open approximation ([j w]). In other words, the same phonetic range as the class 'consonant' (at least if 'stricture' is

---

[1] There are difficulties in using phonetic criteria to define certain 'parametric' categories. This is even clearer in the notorious 'consonant'/'vowel' problem. It may be that the best way to handle these would be along the lines proposed by Pike (1943). His solution is to have two *phonetic* types, 'vocoid' and 'contoid', defined in terms of stricture, and to let the other terms, 'vowel' and 'consonant', be strictly phonological (i.e. 'functional') ones. Generative phonology as presently constituted does not seem to allow this kind of solution, and we will not push it any further.

not defined solely in the *oral* cavity, but in the vocal tract as a whole; which Chomsky and Halle, apparently following Jakobson, deny).[1]

The definition of 'glide', and hence the need for [vocalic], arises from what appear to be two arbitrary decisions: one is, as we noted above, the decision to exclude 'glottal' from the range of 'points of articulation'. The other, as we will see, is the claim that initial [j w] (*SPE* [y w]) and the postvocalic elements in English diphthongs are the same kinds of segments. Our position on this second point, which we will argue below, is that the initial 'glides' should be taken as consonants (in all probability as liquids) and the diphthong finals as nonsyllabic vowels.

In a framework like this, the major class divisions are easy to make: we have only:

(2)	Obstruents	Liquids	Nasals	Vowels
Obs	+	−	−	−
Cons	+	+	+	−

Nasals are distinct from other consonantal sonorants, of course, by the specification [+nas].

Thus in English, for example, /j w/ will be lexically distinct from all other segments by virtue of the appropriate specification from (2) plus articulatory features; and postvocalic 'glides' will be specified by [−syllabic] – but not at the lexical level. The detailed arguments in support of this will be given in §§3–4 below.

If [±syll] is assigned postlexically, this can be handled by a conjunction of conventions and language-specific rules. The major convention, which would hold for most languages, is:

$$(3) \qquad\qquad [+\text{obs}] \rightarrow [-\text{syll}]$$

[1] The characterization of [ʔ h] is particularly troublesome. In addition to defining them as [−cons, −voc], *SPE* also makes them sonorants (which in view of their 'spontaneous voicing' criterion is certainly peculiar: nothing is more antithetical to transglottal airflow than [ʔ]). There are other reasons for rejecting this assignment: first, on phonetic grounds (cf. the descriptions in Gimson 1965 or any other good treatment of articulatory phonetics) they are clearly obstruents; second, if one looks at their phonological behaviour (in terms of substitution, historical development, etc.) it is clear that they are specially related to the voiceless stops and fricatives, respectively. In particular, [h] is nearly always the reflex of an obstruent, and it is tempting to visualize [ʔ] and [h] as the minimally specified (articulation-free) voiceless stop and fricative respectively. (See further the remarks on [h] in lenition hierarchies in ch. v below, and Lass, in preparation b.)

This is not strictly relevant here, however; there is no evidence for independent or substitutive [ʔ] in OE, and [h] clearly derives from an underlying voiceless velar fricative in certain positions; in which case we assume that it is a voiceless glottal fricative.

This would be suspended in those relatively rare languages (like Russian) which allow obstruents as syllabic peaks.

Assignment of syllabicity to nonobstruents would probably work this way. Suppose there is a universal rule that says that any stretch of segments between word boundaries must contain at least one element marked [+syll]: so that if all segments but one in some input string are obstruents, the sonorant will be automatically marked [+syll]. Thus the lexical form of Czech *prst* [pr̩st] 'finger' would be /prst/; /r/ would not be marked for syllabicity, but (as far as major class features are concerned) only as [−obs, +cons]. This /r/ would be converted to [r̩] by the universal rule, which might be like this:

$$(4) \qquad\qquad [-\text{obs}] \rightarrow [+\text{syll}] \ / \ [+\text{obs}]_0^n$$

(We omit the environment bar according to Bach's 'neighbourhood convention' (1968). The rule says: 'a sonorant is syllabic if in catenation with zero to *n* obstruents between word boundaries, with no other sonorant present.' The form of the rule specifies no positional constraints: e.g. in /prst/ the context is [+obs] _____ [+obs] [+obs], etc. For some further arguments for postlexical syllabicity assignment see Brown (1970).)

Now Chomsky and Halle (353–5) have also suggested that [vocalic] be replaced by [syllabic]; but in terms very different from ours. We will develop our own arguments first, and then return in §4 to theirs, and some of the problems involved.

3.   Syllabicity assignment and 'glides'

3.1   Phonological preliminaries

The basic question is whether close approximants like [j w] ever need to be specified in such a way, in any language, that they represent a *lexical* category distinct from all others. The evidence we are acquainted with suggests that this is not the case. It further suggests that segments of this type do not in fact have a 'universal' specification; their phonological characterization depends in large part on the particular language in which they occur.

Thus as Brown (1970) has shown, in Lugisu and other Bantu languages, the distinction between [i u] and [j w] is referable entirely to redundancy rules operating on underlying /i u/; these rules assign 'onset' or 'nuclear' function respectively depending on other elements in the string. Whereas in OE (as well as Modern English) it seems that phonemic /j w/ are required: though as we will see there are surface occurrences of segments like [i̯ u̯] which cannot be referred to them, but must be taken as vowels.

Let us approach this by considering what would happen if we tried to analyse OE phonetic [w] as a vowel. We will anticipate here a number of arguments which will be developed in detail in chapters I–III below. The main point is that elements like [j w], whose uncertain status is clearly shown in equivocal terms like 'semivowel' or 'glide', are 'ambiguous' because they have different sources in different languages. And an analysis that is well motivated for a Bantu language will not work for one with a Germanic type of phonology (this is not to say that Brown claims that it should: simply an illustration of the special problem).

It is traditionally assumed that OE had at least three contrasting types of syllabic nuclei: 'long' vowels, 'short' vowels, and 'diphthongs'. Most of the handbooks also propose a two-way contrast for the diphthongs as well: 'long' (historically from the original Germanic diphthongs, and 'breaking' of long vowels) and 'short' (from 'breaking' of short vowels and various other diphthongizations). This four-way contrast is unnecessary: 'long'/'short' is essentially a single vowel/ cluster distinction, and diphthongs are simply a subset of the set of vowel clusters. We will demonstrate this in detail later on (especially ch. III); for now let us assume it, and see what happens if we do. Remember that the essential fact seems to be that there are only two basic nuclear types in OE: /-V-/ and /-VV-/.

There is good historical evidence that except under certain exceptional circumstances, and in certain exceptional items, the OE diphthongs were 'falling': in the handbook term, they had their 'stress' on the first element. In terms of our discussion here, this means that only the leftmost elements of two-vowel clusters were [+syll]. The special cases of 'stress-shift' (*Akzentumsprung*) are then instances where, contrary to the norm, the rightmost member of a cluster is [+syll]. These exceptional forms show up for instance in the divergent developments of certain class II strong verbs. Thus the normal development in OE *fréosan* > ME *frēsen* > NE *freeze* (where the acute marks the 'stressed' element); and the 'exceptional' one in *céosan* > *ceósan* > *chōsen* > *choose*. Actually there are few enough of these forms at any period so that they can be treated as lexical exceptions, and the formulation of the general processes can ignore them.

Let us say then that in OE syllabicity is assigned to nonconsonants as follows: if two nonconsonants are contiguous, the leftmost one is assigned [+syll] by the rule (5):

(5) *Syllabicity assignment*

$$[-\text{cons}] \rightarrow \begin{cases} [-\text{syll}] \,/\, [-\text{cons}] \,\underline{\hspace{1cm}} & \text{(a)} \\ [+\text{syll}] & \text{(b)} \end{cases}$$

The subrules are to be taken as simultaneously applicable.[1]

---

[1] According to the currently accepted use of brace-notation in generative phonology (e.g. Harms 1968: 58–9), any schema abbreviated by braces is a sequence of conjunctively ordered rules. Thus Harms (59) gives as an example of the 'proper' use of braces the following rule:

(i)
$$[-\text{obs}] \rightarrow \begin{cases} [-\text{nas}] \\ [+\text{nas}] \,/\, \begin{bmatrix} +\text{cons} \\ -\text{voc} \end{bmatrix} \end{cases}$$

Since in brace-abbreviated schemata, higher-line expansions precede lower-line expansions, Harms describes the operation of the schema as follows: 'First, all nonobstruents are specified as nonnasal; then, by the second line of the braces, the special case reverses its nasality to "plus" ' (59).

This seems, for rules of this specific type, a wasteful and counterintuitive (if not counterempirical) interpretation. Since the schema (i) is essentially a redundancy statement ('the only sonorants that are nasal are the ones that are also consonantal and nonvocalic'), the assignment to all sonorants of [−nasal] as a 'first step' in the expansion defeats the generalization; it introduces a feature-specification which is not a real property of the segment in question in any reasonable sense, but is an artifact of the convention.

We therefore suggest that schemata like (i) be handled in a more intuitively natural way (as indeed they have often been in the past), and written:

(ii)
$$[-\text{obs}] \rightarrow \begin{cases} [+\text{nas}] \,/\, \begin{bmatrix} +\text{cons} \\ -\text{voc} \end{bmatrix} \\ [-\text{nas}] \end{cases}$$

Thus the second specification gets its intuitively natural meaning of 'elsewhere'. Since the environments of the two rules of the schema, with the exception of the factored-out [−obs], are disjoint, it seems that we can take (ii) as abbreviating a set of rules whose application has the same effect as a condition of disjunctive ordering: i.e. the rules apply to disjoint environments, and can therefore be taken as applying simultaneously.

To return to the particular case of our syllabicity-assignment schema: let us assume that we formulated it as a conjunctive schema, in the manner proposed by Harms:

(iii)
$$[-\text{cons}] \rightarrow \begin{cases} [+\text{syll}] \\ [-\text{syll}] \,/\, [-\text{cons}] \,\underline{\hspace{1cm}} \end{cases}$$

Instances of 'stress-shift' in diphthongs can now be handled this way: any form that undergoes the process, like *cēosan*, *lēosan* 'lose', in those dialects and at those times when it does, is marked with a minus-rule feature for syllabicity assignment and a plus–minor-rule feature for 'stress-shift'. This latter rule, which we call 'right syllabification', is in essence the mirror image of (5a):

(6) *Right syllabification*

$$[-\text{cons}] \rightarrow [+\text{syll}] \,/\, [-\text{cons}] \underline{\quad\quad}$$

(This will be strictly a minor rule in the formal sense of Lakoff (1965); see also Harms (1968).)

Now to the problem. If OE did not have 'glides' as a lexical category, we must find some way of accounting for the well-attested initial [w]. If we accept (a) that syllabicity is assigned according to (5), (b) that 'glides' are nonsyllabic vowels, and (c) that long vowels are clusters, we are in serious trouble.

OE has numerous forms with initial orthographic *wu-* (and presumably phonetic [wu-]): *wurdon* 'they became', *wudu* 'wood', *wucu* 'week', *wulf* 'wolf', *wund* 'wound', *wundor* 'wonder'. Now if all these forms began with lexical /uu-/, and syllabicity assignment worked as we have claimed, we would never get the right surface forms. These words by (5) would begin with initial syllabic [u], and we would get **ūrdon*, **ūdu*, **ūcu*, etc. Unless of course they were subject to (6). But this would be difficult, because there are also forms with initial *ū-*: *ūre* 'our', *ūþe* 'he granted', *ūt* 'out', etc. The first group suggests that there might be some constraint on (5) governed by word-initial position; the second group shows that this is not true. So it looks as if we may need [vocalic] after all, unless we want to mark all *wu-* forms as [+(rule 6)], and get ourselves bogged down in a mass of unmotivated exceptions.

If the rules were conjunctively ordered, then, for example, every case of diphthongization by epenthesis would involve a specification of the epenthesized vowel as [+syll], and then a reversal of that specification; and in Old English rules of epenthesis occur at quite widely separated points in the grammar.

So we will adopt the convention throughout that all schemata with content of the type 'X → Y in the context C, and Z elsewhere', where C may represent any number of sub-environments, may be represented as braced sequences of the type (ii) abovᵣ and interpreted as simultaneously applicable sets of rules. (It would be possible, o course, to impose a condition of disjunctive ordering on a schema like (ii) or (5) by fiat; but in view of the well-motivated connexion of disjunctive ordering specifically with parenthesis notation, we feel that simultaneous applicability is simpler and more natural.)

(The same difficulty will also come up in forms beginning with
w + liquid, like *wlite* 'face', *wrītan* 'write'; by rule (5) these should be
*ulite, **urītan*. We need exceptions for them as well.)

So the interpretation of [w] as [u̯] (at least as [u̯] < /u/) will not
work. It is clear that initial [w] must be assigned to some other category,
distinct from lexical /u/; and the same will hold for [j], some occurrences
at least of which must be from /j/ (distinct from /i/) – though as we will
see some [j] are from palatalized /g/ (cf. ch. IV). But there is still the
question of whether /w/ should be described as [– cons, – voc]; we will
now approach this via the equivalent segments in Modern English.

3.2 Phonetics and phonology of NE [j w]

Chomsky and Halle clearly take prevocalic [j w] and the nonsyllabic
approximants following certain syllable nuclei in English as both
phonetically and phonologically identical. Thus they identify the
second elements in the nuclei of *quite, pool*, with the syllable onsets in
new, quite, respectively: e.g. [pūwl] 'pool', [gōwl] 'goal' (186), [kwīyr]
'queer', [kwāyt] 'quite', [nyūw] 'new' (193). This is by no means radical
or unusual: it is the same assumption made *phonologically* by Trager
and Smith (1951), and indeed is almost canonical in American descriptive practice. (For further treatment see Lass, in preparation b,
ch. I.)

On phonetic grounds, to begin with, this is untenable. As we can see
for instance from the actual data cited by Trager and Smith, the pre-
and postvocalic approximants are usually quite different. It is extremely
rare in English (in any dialect) to find a postnuclear 'glide' even as
close as [i] or [u] (let alone [j] or [w]); most often *pool,* *quite* have nuclei
ending in [ɪ ɔ] or [e o], while the onsets may be as close as [j w] or
[j̣ ẉ] (the latter being what Trager and Smith represent as 'raised' high
vowels: we owe the notations [ẉ], etc. ('lowered [w]') to Sandy
Hutcheson). In other words, it seems that the prevocalic glides are
consonantal approximants or something very similar, while the postvocalic ones are just as obviously vowels – and not even high ones at
that (it is a common misconception that [ɪ ɔ] are articulatorily 'close';
they are in fact half close, i.e. more like [ë ö]).

Now Chomsky and Halle nevertheless classify both of these approximant types as nonconsonantal and nonvocalic, in accordance with these
definitions:

[−voc]: either the constriction in the oral cavity exceeds that for [i u]; or the vocal bands are not positioned for 'spontaneous voicing'. (On the basis of §2.1 above we can omit the second condition.)

[−cons]: there is no 'radical constriction in the mid-sagittal region of the vocal tract'. Further, if a segment is [+cons], 'the obstruction must be at least as narrow as that found in the fricative consonants' (302). It is worth remarking also (cf. n. 1 below) that 'in the case of the common lingual [r]-sounds, the raised tongue narrows the passage sufficiently to produce a consonantal obstruction even if it does not make complete contact with the roof of the mouth' (302–3).

Let us consider these definitions vis-à-vis the segments that actually appear phonetically. Certainly there is no doubt that all the postvocalic approximants classified in *SPE* as 'glides' are *always* by their definitions [−cons, +voc], i.e. they are never closer than [i u] and very rarely that close. On the other hand, the prevocalic approximants may be as close as [j w] (with friction) or as open as [e o] (in some dialects before low vowels, as in *yacht, watt*). So there is no phonetic evidence that the second elements of English complex nuclei can ever be nonvocalic, but considerable evidence that prevocalic approximants can be consonantal. If the postvocalic 'glides' are lexically [−cons, −voc], they must be respecified phonetically, in every nucleus and in every dialect, as [+voc]; whereas there are only certain cases where the prevocalic ones must be respecified. That is, there is evidence from variability for two possible feature specifications for prevocalic [j w], but none for the postvocalic 'glides'.[1]

So it seems reasonable to take the frictionless, 'vocalic' forms of /j w/ (those that verge on [ɪ e] or [o o]) as 'weakened' forms of a consonantal segment (see §3.3 below for details). Such an interpretation, if we extend it to OE, will get us out of the difficulties discussed in §3.1, and permit unambiguous syllabicity assignment by (5).

Before going on to some phonological matters, let us note that the consonantal interpretation of [j w] is an old one in English; no less a phonetician and phonologist than Henry Sweet made the same distinction that we are making here (1877: 31 ff.). Sweet defines consonants

---

[1] We might note that in some dialects (like those of the two authors), the *SPE* definitions at the phonetic level will specify /r/ as [−cons] and /j w/ as [+cons]; since the 'common lingual [r]' (presumably [ɹ]) is present in both, and always has an opener stricture than /j/ or /w/. This suggests that it may be best to take [+cons] as a feature which cannot be defined in any truly phonetic way, but only phonologically (i.e. /r/ is phonetically 'vocoidal').

as 'the result of audible friction, squeezing or stopping of the breath in some part of the mouth (or occasionally of the throat)' (31). He further subclassifies them according to stricture type; and his category 'open' is of particular interest here, as it includes [j w].

An open consonant, for Sweet, is one were 'the passage is simply narrowed without any contact, such as (kh) in G. "ach"...' (33). Further, 'the restriction as to contact applies only to the actual friction channel, and even then there may be slight contact, provided that the current of breath is not impeded' (ibid.).

Within the open category, Sweet describes the two relevant segments as follows. He calls [j] 'front-open-voice', and exemplifies it with English *you*, German, Dutch, Danish *ja*. He further remarks, significantly, that 'this consonant is often, as in E...weakened into a vowel' (37). As for [w], Sweet says that it is in articulation 'simply (*u*) [= [ɔ]: RL/JMA] consonantized by narrowing the lip passage' (42). He also notes the occurrence in English of 'cheek compression' in [w], and says that it 'might therefore...be described as the "high-back-round-squeezed"' (43). (Even though Sweet describes English [j] as 'weakened into a vowel' and [w] as '(*u*) consonantized', he does not appear to be claiming as it were an opposite 'direction of derivation' for the two. At least he nowhere states that 'nonconsonantized' forms of [w] exist. The claim about [w] seems to be meant as purely descriptive; that about [j] is directional.)

On the other hand, Sweet interprets the nonsyllabic post-nuclear segments in *say*, *eye*, etc. as truncated vowels, not consonants. He gives an example of how diphthongs are formed:

...If we place the vocal organs in the position for (i) [= [i]: RL/JMA], and then allow voice to sound while passing from the (i) to the (a) [= [ɑ]: RL/JMA] position, and hold the (a) long enough to give it a fixed character, we have the diphthong ([i]a). If we begin with a full (a) and then pass to the (i) position, letting the voice cease as soon as the (i) position is reached, we have (a[i]).

The important point is that ([i]a) is not to be equated with (ja). If we understand Sweet correctly, it would be wrong to transcribe *yăcht* in most cases as ([i]at), except in certain dialects where (j) is so weakened as to approach (i). The 'canonical' transcription would be (jat). See further his later comments in the same chapter (70).

From these phonetic remarks, we can pass to some matters of phonology. Consider the discussion of the two English 'semi-vowels' in Gimson (1965), where questions of 'function' (i.e. syllable-position) are brought in. Gimson says (207):

Despite the fact that semi-vowels are, in phonetic terms, generally vocalic, they are treated within the consonant class, mainly because their *function* is consonantal rather than vowel-like, i.e. they have a marginal rather than a central situation in the syllable...Their consonantal function is emphasized by the fact that the articles have their preconsonantal forms when followed by /j/ and /w/, i.e. *the yard, a yacht, the west, a wasp*, with /ðə/ or /ə/ rather than /ðɪ/ or /ən/...In addition, the allophones of /j/ and /w/, when following a fortis consonant, are voiceless and fricative, as in *cue, quick* [kju̥ː], [kw̥ɪk], i.e. they fall within the phonetic definition of a consonant.

Gimson's last argument is not compelling, because many languages have voiceless vowels which can serve as syllable nuclei (e.g. Japanese [ɯ̥]), and which have a stricture of open approximation (i.e. are 'vocalic'). But there is an interesting phonological argument related to the devoicing. That is, in English, not only do /j w/ devoice after voiceless obstruents, but so do /r l/: e.g. in *creek, sleep*. Nasals do not generally devoice here (*snow, smooth*), nor do high vowels (*keep, coop*). From this point of view, the affinities of /j w/ are with the liquids, which suggests that they might reasonably be specified as [−obs, +cons].

But what seems really significant is the behaviour of the English articles before /j w/. Let's say that we wanted to formulate the rule for deletion of /n/ from the indefinite article (assuming that it's reasonable to take the underlying form as something like /æn/). If we used the *SPE* specifications, where /j w/ are [−cons, −voc] (and there is no [+syll]), we would have to write a rule whose complexity is out of all proportion to the obvious simplicity of the process. That is: we would have to give the two-feature class [−voc, −cons] as a separate disjunction, because /n/ appears only before vowels, which are [+voc, −cons], but not before liquids, which are [+voc, +cons], or before nasals and obstruents, which are [−voc, +cons]. There is no single feature of the two ([voc], [cons]) which could trigger the deletion rule. But if 'glides' are [+cons], then the rule only has to state the obvious fact that they pattern with obstruents, nasals, and liquids (i.e. all [+cons] segments), as against vowels. The resulting rule will be intuitively more natural, as well as requiring only two features in its SD, as against eight if 'glides' are nonconsonantal, nonvocalic, sonorants. Our classification gives a 'cheaper' rule; this is not 'proof', but it certainly is in its favour.

3.3 English /j w/: summary

It is clear that OE /j w/ cannot be taken as nonsyllabic vowels; it is also clear that NE /j w/ cannot either, and that there is no motivation for representations like [wūw] 'woo', [yīy] 'ye', etc. It also seems reasonable to assume that OE and NE /j w/ may have been the same kinds of elements (though there is evidence that at least some OE [j] begin as obstruents: cf. ch. IV). We must now establish a phonological classification, and see what the rule of 'weakening to vowels' we mentioned above might look like. We propose the following feature specifications:

(7)

	j	*w*
obs	−	−
cons	+	+
ant	−	−
cor	−	−
high	+	+
back	−	+
round	−	+
cont	+	+
voice	+	+

Our decision to view /j w/ as liquids was discussed in the preceding section. One problem here is that, unlike the other liquids /r l/ and the nasals /m n/, /j w/ cannot appear as syllabics. It might be of course that if sonorants of this degree of stricture are syllabic they in fact *are* [i u]. But this requires further investigation, and we will leave it for now. The proposals made so far in this chapter are preliminary working hypotheses; their ultimate correctness or incorrectness will not affect the bulk of our discussion of OE.

If the specifications in (7) are reasonable, then the rule weakening /j w/ before vowels is easy to state. Both segments are [+high], by virtue of being respectively palatal and velar (/w/ is a labiovelar, but the back of the tongue is in high vowel position). Since English (except for Scots, most dialects of which lack the rule we are discussing) has no velar fricatives (unless the *SPE* arguments for underlying ones, 233–4, are to be taken seriously), we can safely assume that the conjunction [+cons, +high, +cont] will specify /j w/ and no other segments. The rule is then:

(8) *Prevocalic vocalization*

$$\begin{bmatrix} +\text{cons} \\ +\text{high} \\ +\text{cont} \end{bmatrix} \rightarrow [-\text{cons}] \: / \: \underline{\hspace{2cm}} \: [-\text{cons}]$$

This will turn /w/ into some kind of [u] and /j/ to [i]. Rule (8) is thus a rather common sort of lenition; more specifically, an assimilation to the feature [−cons] on following vowels. (In most dialects there would be late rules to adjust the height of the outputs to that of following vowels.)

4.   Chomsky-Halle's [+syllabic] and ours

Chomsky and Halle (353–5) suggest that there are good reasons for re-placing [vocalic] by [syllabic]. We will not go into their particular arguments here; they seem in general well founded. We are concerned mainly with the status of this feature in the grammar. They consider (if we understand them correctly) [syllabic] to be a replacement for [vocalic] at the lexical level: since they give different specifications for syllabic and nonsyllabic nasals and liquids, those marked [+syll] are presumably underlyingly different from the others. But this does not seem to be the case in the languages with which we are familiar.

Take for instance the Czech *prst* 'finger' that we referred to earlier (§2.2). If the difference between the [r̩] here and the nonsyllabic [r] in other forms were lexical, then we would have two kinds of underlying /r/, [+syll] and [−syll], with the former always being predictable from its environment. Chomsky and Halle of course realize this, and they make provision for it, by saying that 'vowels would normally be syllabic peaks, whereas the remaining sonorants – i.e. liquids, glides, nasal consonants – would normally be nonsyllabic, but could become syllabic under special circumstances...' (354).

But then they go ahead and use [syllabic] as a 'major class feature', which would imply the possibility of having syllabic vs. nonsyllabic nasals and liquids in the lexicon; even though they have already admitted that the syllabicity of nasals and liquids can be environmentally pre-dicted, which would make it a derived feature, not a lexical one. This treatment is inconsistent: there is no need to specify a 'major class' (which presumably means a lexical class) which is always the result of rules or interpretive conventions operating on another major class.

Another clear example of the derived status of syllabic sonorants other than vowels comes from one of our dialects (New York City). In this dialect, syllabic liquids and nasals occur as follows: (a) /l/ is syllabic morpheme-finally, following a stressed vowel + an obstruent or nasal: *little*, littler [lɪtl̩ɹ]; (b) /r/ is syllabic only word-finally following a stressed vowel and another [+cons] segment: *mother, littler* above (this fails only when the preceding consonant is /r/, e.g. in *mirror* [mɪɹəɹ]); (c) nasals are syllabic only when preceded by a stressed vowel and a homorganic obstruent: *button* [bətn̩] but *bottom* [bärəm].

Most importantly, however, syllabic consonantal sonorants occur almost exclusively in 'allegro' forms; in slower speech the syllable peak is not the nasal or liquid but a reduction vowel (normally [ə] before /m l r/ and [ɪ] before /n/). This suggests that the underlying forms have vowels, and that the syllabic consonants derive via a rule that deletes unstressed vowels in certain contexts. It certainly seems more natural to posit a rule deleting vowels in rapid speech than to suggest that the nasals and liquids are lexically syllabic, with svarabhakti vowels inserted in slow speech.

If [syll] is a lexical feature; and if, as we have suggested, postvocalic high 'glides' are not a separate kind of segment but are nonsyllabic vowels, another difficulty arises, this time in stating rules for vowel epenthesis (i.e. 'diphthongization'). The two positions appear to be mutually contradictory: if [+syll] is assigned lexically, then postvocalic glides cannot be nonsyllabic vowels.

The trouble arises if all vowels are assigned the feature [+syll] in the lexicon, before any phonological rules operate on them. Consider the SPE diphthongization ('glide-insertion') rule, the first stage of the central vowel-shift complex. The rule (slightly modified for this exposition) is this (*SPE*: 243):

(9)

$$\emptyset \rightarrow \begin{bmatrix} -\text{voc} \\ -\text{cons} \\ +\text{high} \\ \alpha\text{back} \\ \alpha\text{round} \end{bmatrix} \Big/ \begin{bmatrix} +\text{tense} \\ \alpha\text{back} \end{bmatrix} \underline{\hspace{1.5cm}}$$

This inserts [w] after [ū] and [y] after [ī]. Now let us say that we reformulate it, according to our claim that postvocalic 'glides', unlike prevocalic ones, are vowels. The rule will now insert, not a segment marked [−voc, −cons], but a vowel marked with the appropriate features:

(10)

$$\emptyset \rightarrow \begin{bmatrix} -\text{cons} \\ +\text{high} \\ \alpha\text{back} \\ \alpha\text{round} \end{bmatrix} \Big/ \begin{bmatrix} +\text{tense} \\ \alpha\text{back} \end{bmatrix} \underline{\hspace{2em}}$$

Now if vowels are marked [+syll] in the lexicon, and glides do not exist, the output of (10) will be:

(11)

$$\begin{bmatrix} -\text{cons} \\ +\text{tense} \\ \alpha\text{back} \\ \alpha\text{round} \\ +\text{syll} \end{bmatrix} \begin{bmatrix} -\text{cons} \\ +\text{high} \\ \alpha\text{back} \\ \alpha\text{round} \\ +\text{syll} \end{bmatrix}$$

Then we would need a special rule to desyllabify vowels after other vowels:

(12)   [−cons] → [−syll] / [+syll] _____

This means that syllabicity has to be assigned twice: once by convention to all vowels in the lexicon, and then again after the operation of any rules producing vowel clusters. This appears to be the consequence of distinguishing between pre- and postvocalic 'glides' (which we think we have shown to be necessary), and at the same time allowing syllabicity to be distributed in the lexicon.

So if we are going to treat [w-] and [-u] differently, this entails post-lexical distribution of syllabicity. We claim then that no segments are marked for this property in the lexicon; they are marked only for the other major class features, [obstruent] and [consonantal]. Syllabicity is assigned by convention (5), which is an 'everywhere' rule, i.e. it operates at any point where its proper analysis is satisfied. Syllabicity is simply a nonlexical feature; it is like stress, which *SPE* claims (for English at least) is exclusively postlexical, being assigned by rules of the cycle.

This does of course raise the problem of unspecified feature values in the lexicon; but we will defer this to the end of chapter 1, when we will have more material to work with. Let us just note that saying no segments are marked in the lexicon for syllabicity is not the same as admitting zero as a 'third value'. We are proposing not empty cells but absent features.

We can now bring together the various conditions on syllabicity assignment for vowels and consonants touched on in the preceding discussion:

(13) *Syllabicity assignment (generalized)*

A. $[+\text{obs}] \rightarrow [-\text{syll}]$

B. $[-\text{obs}] \rightarrow \begin{cases} [+\text{syll}] \,/\, [+\text{cons}] \underline{\hspace{1.5em}} [+\text{cons}] & \text{(a)} \\ [-\text{syll}] & \text{(b)} \end{cases}$

C. $[-\text{cons}] \rightarrow \begin{cases} [-\text{syll}] \,/\, [-\text{cons}] \underline{\hspace{1.5em}} & \text{(a)} \\ [+\text{syll}] & \text{(b)} \end{cases}$

(Parts (a) and (b) within both B and C are once more simultaneously applicable. To allow for the 'laryngeal' /Λ/ in OE (cf. ch. i, § 5), which is [−syll] and [+obs, −cons], the whole set must be interpreted disjunctively, so that it is [−syll] by A rather than [+syll] by C. Convention (4) above is a special case of B (a), which marks liquids, nasals and vowels syllabic between consonantal segments. Note that this formulation also assumes that boundaries like /#/ are consonants (cf. ch. v). (13) allows for distribution of syllabicity specifically for OE, though A and B are probably quasi-universal.)

5.   The stricture and resonator features

We accept most of these features in essentially the *SPE* forms; though there are certain difficulties. We list the relevant features here for convenience, with comments where necessary.

5.1   Primary strictures

1. *Coronal/noncoronal*. Coronal segments involve articulations where the blade of the tongue is 'raised from its neutral position' (*SPE*: 304). Thus [+coronal] characterizes dental, alveolar and palato-alveolar consonants. The so-called 'neutral position' is described by *SPE* as the tongue configuration for 'the English vowel [e] in...*bed*' (300), i.e. roughly half-open front position, with the front of the tongue in its 'normal' position opposite the hard palate.

2. *Anterior/nonanterior*. This is difficult, since its definition is, like many in *SPE*, based on 'ordinary English' articulations, which of course

means 'ordinary East-Coast American'. But such things are slippery at best. At any rate, they take as their defining point (304) the stricture location for 'ordinary English [š]' (=[ʃ]), and define as [+ant] all constrictions anterior to this, and as [−ant] all strictures posterior to [ʃ], including [ʃ] itself. Thus labials, dentals and alveolars are anterior, and palatoalveolars, palatals, velars, uvulars and vowels are nonanterior. From a phonological point of view there is something to be said for characterizations like the rather old-fashioned 'lingual', where labials are excluded by virtue of the tongue not being an active articulator. (On the feature 'lingual', as well as the problem of just what [anterior] means, see Lass 1973a. We will return to the problem of labials in ch. v below.) We might finally note that for many speakers the distinction between [s] and [ʃ] is not one of location but of tongue shape, 'slit' vs. 'groove'.

5.2 Tongue-body features

1. *High/nonhigh*. High sounds are those in which the body (not the blade) of the tongue is raised above 'neutral' position; thus high vowels, palatals and velars are [+high], while low and mid vowels, labials, dentals, uvulars and pharyngeals are [−high].

2. *Low/nonlow*. Here too 'neutral' position is the reference point. Low segments have the tongue body below this position, whereas nonlow sounds have it neutral or higher. In the *SPE* assignments, low vowels and pharyngeals are [+low]; all other oral articulations (except those with secondary pharyngealization) are [−low].

We take issue with this in one important respect: and this is the assignment of [−low] to uvulars, thus distinguishing them from the [+low] pharyngeals, both being [+back]. The real distinction between uvulars and pharyngeals does not seem in fact to be the lowness of the latter, but rather their greater backness: the tongue *root* is the active articulator, and it is moved into a position in the oral pharynx farther back than for that say [ɑ]. The interesting thing about the specifications [+high] and [+low] is that when they are used for vowels, they define segments which in a reasonable sense have 'cognate consonants': thus high front vowels are cognate to dentals or palatals, high back vowels to velars, and low back vowels to uvulars (or, with tongue-root retraction, to pharyngeals). But mid vowels, which are nonhigh and nonlow, do not have 'equivalent' consonantal articulations; by definition they are too far away from any 'passive' structure to form a consonantal stricture without going to [+high] or [+low] position.

So the *SPE* assignments suggest that uvulars are cognate to vowels like [o ɔ], which is simply not the case. Therefore we will treat uvulars as being [+low], and leave the issue of distinguishing them from pharyngeals alone, as it is not relevant to OE.

3. *Back/nonback*. In [+back] segments, the tongue is retracted from neutral position: thus back vowels, velars and uvulars are [+back], whereas front vowels and prevelar consonants are [−back].

Not all conjunctions of features of course are equally admissible. Thus we assume (tautologically) that no segment can be marked plus and minus for the same feature. On similar grounds, the conjunction [+high, +low] is ruled out, since the gestures involved (simultaneous raising and lowering of the tongue body from a specified position) are contradictory (*SPE*: 305). But conjunctions like [+ant, +back] are not excluded, since different parts of the tongue are involved; we can have velarized dentals and labials.

The following feature specifications are relevant for the OE consonants:

(14)	*Anterior*	*Coronal*	*High*	*Low*	*Back*
Labials	+	−	−	−	−
Dentals	+	+	−	−	−
Palatals	−	−	+	−	−
Velars	−	−	+	−	+
Uvulars	−	−	−	+	+
Velarized dentals	+	+	+	−	+
Velarized labials	+	−	+	−	+

5.3 Narrowing of the vocal tract

Round/nonround. This is the only feature of this type that we will consider here. Chomsky and Halle define as [+round] any segments which 'are produced with a narrowing of the lip orifice' (*SPE:* 309) and we will accept this definition in the usual sense of the phonetic use of the term. But we remark on a slight imprecision: that 'narrowing' might just as well refer to a top-to-bottom constriction, in which case the term would also describe very 'spread' vowels as well, e.g. many types of [ɯ]. Though, as Chomsky and Halle remark, 'all classes of sounds may manifest rounding' (*SPE:* 309), in OE only the velarized labial [w] and the rounded vowels [u o y ø] are [+round].

5.4   Secondary apertures

1. *Nasal/nonnasal.* Nasal sounds are produced with the velum lowered so that at least some of the air escapes through the nose, setting up a secondary resonance. In OE, the feature [+nasal] specifies so far as we can tell only consonants; there may of course have been contextual nasalization of vowels, as there is in many dialects of Modern English; but this kind of phonetic detail is generally not reconstructible without direct (e.g. orthoëpic) testimony.

We will not in this study approach the problem of whether the nasals [m n ŋ] are to be specified as stops or continuants. Following the evidence from Modern English, where it seems as if the nasals may be systematically noncontinuant, we will mark them as such without further discussion, though this decision will in no way affect the rest of our analysis (see further *SPE*: 316–17).

2. *Lateral/nonlateral.* In Chomsky and Halle's definition, 'lateral sounds are produced by lowering the mid section of the tongue at both sides or at only one side, thereby allowing the air to flow out of the mouth in the vicinity of the molar teeth' (317). In OE the only [+lateral] segment is the one represented in the orthography as *l*, which we will suggest in chapter III was probably (at least pre-consonantally) a velarized dental [ɫ]. In dialects where both [l] and [r] are specified as $\begin{bmatrix} +\text{anterior} \\ +\text{coronal} \\ -\text{back} \end{bmatrix}$ and [r] is not trilled, [+lateral] is presumably uniquely distinctive for [l].

As we showed in (14), a velarized dental of any kind is specified $\begin{bmatrix} +\text{anterior} \\ +\text{back} \end{bmatrix}$; the added specification [+back] will distinguish so-called 'dark' [ɫ] from 'clear' [l].

5.5   Manner of articulation

Continuant/noncontinuant. 'In the production of continuant sounds, the primary constriction in the vocal tract is not narrowed to the point where the air flow past the constriction is blocked; in stops the air flow through the mouth is effectively blocked' (*SPE*: 317). Thus vowels, liquids and fricatives are [+continuant], and affricates and stops are [−continuant].

This last point raises the possibility that in distinguishing stops from affricates the crucial feature is [±delayed release]. While it is generally true that affricates are characterized as against their cognate stops by means of release, in Germanic at least it seems that the crucial feature is [±strident]. In this study we characterize the affricates [tʃ dʒ] as essentially strident versions of [c ɟ]. The motivation for this will become clear in chapter IV.

5.6 Tense/nontense

As far as we can tell, this feature (if it exists) plays no significant part in OE phonology. In Modern English, of course, if the Chomsky-Halle analysis of the central vowel-shift rule is correct, it may be crucial (though there are other ways to handle the vowel-shift: see Lass, in preparation b, ch. 1). We assume here that there was no tense/lax distinction in the OE vowel system; and that if in fact such a distinction is true of Modern English it is a later development, the result of a major typological shift. We comment on this to some extent in chapter VI.

5.7 Voiced/voiceless

This is one of the least satisfactory features in the inventory, and paradoxically one of the oldest and most firmly established. The problem is that the classification is oversimple, since there are many possible configurations of the vocal cords, larynx and vocal tract that can be responsible for what is traditionally known as 'voice' or 'voicelessness' − not to mention the variety of phonation-types such as whisper, 'murmur' or breathy-voice, creak etc. (cf. Ladefoged 1971).

A good deal of recent work has suggested that in fact we can do without the voiced/voicelessness distinction as such, and instead characterize these qualities more finely by means of a conjunction of glottal-height and vocal-cord-attitude features. For further discussion see Bird (1969), Ladefoged (1971), Maran (1971) and our brief treatment in chapter V.

5.8   Strident/nonstrident

This is again a rather unsatisfactory feature, for two reasons. First, because alone of the whole inventory it tends to be based on perceptual rather than articulatory features. And second, because the definition given in *SPE* (329) is really parametric rather than binary in the sense of most of the other features: 'A rougher surface, a faster rate of flow, and an angle of incidence [of the air stream against some surface: RL/JMA] closer to ninety degrees will all contribute to greater stridency.'

But despite this unsatisfactory definition, and the typological difference between stridency and the other features, we retain it in this study; if for no other reasons than that it seems to help in the capturing of certain generalizations, and because we have nothing better to substitute for it. So we accept it with reservations.

6.   Some remarks on the 'universal vowel inventory', and on transcription

Given the features available for vowel characterization, according to the Chomsky-Halle inventory, there are twelve basic vowel types which require symbols in a universal phonetic inventory. The features for vowel-distinctiveness proper are [±high], [±low], [±back], and [±round]; further types can be made available by using [±tense] as a kind of dichotomizing operator. These features give us a 'universal' inventory like this (using the Chomsky-Halle symbols):

(15)

	[−back]		[+back]	
[+high]	i	ü	ɨ	u
$\begin{bmatrix} -\text{high} \\ -\text{low} \end{bmatrix}$	e	ö	ʌ	o
[+low]	æ	œ	a	ɔ
	[−round]	[+round]	[−round]	[+round]

This inventory allows only three distinctive heights and two front–back dimensions for any vowel system; any further distinctions are normally handled by using [±tense], so that e.g. a contrast of [e] vs. [ɛ], [i] vs. [ɪ]. [u] vs. [ʊ] is handled by marking the first member of each pair [+tense] and the second [−tense]. Central vowels in languages like English are handled by assuming them, in general, to be derived from unround back vowels.

In general, it seems that this inventory is too restrictive: there are many languages (e.g. Danish: cf. Ladefoged 1971, some dialects of Swiss German: Kiparsky 1968b, and in all probability even English: Wang 1969) that seem to require four distinctive vowel heights. This can easily be handled by using the features [±high] and [±mid], where the latter can serve as a 'diacritic' on the former: thus [i] is $\begin{bmatrix} +\text{high} \\ -\text{mid} \end{bmatrix}$, [e] is $\begin{bmatrix} +\text{high} \\ +\text{mid} \end{bmatrix}$, [ɛ] is $\begin{bmatrix} -\text{high} \\ +\text{mid} \end{bmatrix}$ and [æ] is $\begin{bmatrix} -\text{high} \\ -\text{mid} \end{bmatrix}$ (Wang 1969; for another proposal of a somewhat similar type see Anderson and Jones 1972).

Whatever the merits, though, of these proposals (and surely some such revision is necessary, even for English: cf. Lass, 1973b), the problem does not seem to arise in OE. Here the vowel inventories, both underlying and superficial, seem to fit perfectly naturally into a three-height framework. We will therefore use only the features specified in (15) to characterize the vowel-types we will be dealing with: though for purposes of (a) avoiding confusion with narrow IPA transcriptions cited elsewhere in this book, and (b) for maximum accessibility, we will not use the Chomsky-Halle symbols, but rather the normally accepted symbols of the IPA. The only departures we will make in vowel representation is the use of [a] for the low back vowel: since OE apparently never had an [a]:[ɑ] type of contrast, but rather [æ]:[ɑ].

The vowel-types we will be operating with, then, are:

(16)

	[−back]		[+back]	
[+high]	i	y		u
$\begin{bmatrix} -\text{high} \\ -\text{low} \end{bmatrix}$	e	ø		o
[+low]	æ		a	
	[−round]	[+round]	[−round]	[+round]

As far as other symbols used here, we will in general adhere to the conventions of the IPA, with the following addition: the symbols [c ɟ] will be used for 'palatal' (= post-alveolar, pre-velar) affricates, voiceless and voiced respectively.

I 'Ablaut' in the Old English strong verb

1 Introduction

The so-called 'strong' verbs in OE (as in the other Germanic dialects) are traditionally characterized as forming 'their preterite and past participle by means of a change in the vowel of the stem' (Moore and Knott 1955: 49). This is a rather oversimplified way of saying that these verbs (as opposed to the 'weak' verbs, which in general show uniform vocalism throughout the paradigm, and 'form their preterite and past participle' by suffixation) display considerable variation in their radical vowels. This is evident not only within the paradigm for any single verb, but in differing sets of variations which characterize different subtypes of strong verbs. This second (inter-paradigmatic) type of variation is primarily associated with the traditional division of the strong verbs into 'classes': we will discuss the basis for this below. The former (intra-paradigmatic) type of variation accounts for the alternative label sometimes given to these verbs: 'vocalic' vs. 'consonantal' (weak).

The intra-paradigmatic variations are associated with specific syntactic contexts: typically, the vowels of the present and 'past participle' are distinct both from each other and from those of the preterite; and this in turn (being of composite origin) has two different vowels, depending on person/number/mood specifications. It is these syntactically determined alternations in the radical vowel that most obviously characterize the 'strong' as against the 'weak' verb: they are usually said to represent a process called 'ablaut' or 'gradation'. The ablaut alternations involve differences both in quantity ('long' vs. 'short') and quality (of superficially various kinds).

Something of both kinds of paradigmatic variety is displayed in (1.1) below, which includes (in orthographic form) only representatives of the 'regular' members of the first six classes (i.e. those which do not display any idiosyncratic developments or deviations from the ablaut series we shall be looking at below):

(1.1) *The OE strong verb, classes I–VI*

Class	PRES	PRET$_1$	PRET$_2$	PART	
I	bīdan	bād	bidon	-biden	'wait'
II	bēodan	bēad	budon	-boden	'command'
III (a)	helpan	healp	hulpon	-holpen	'help'
(b)	weorpan	wearp	wurpon	-worpen	'throw'
(c)	bindan	band	bundon	-bunden	'bind'
IV	beran	bær	bǣron	-boren	'bear'
V	sprecan	spræc	sprǣcon	-sprecen	'speak'
VI	bacan	bōc	bōcon	-bacen	'bake'

(In this table as henceforth, for expository convenience, we follow the usual convention of marking vowel symbols representing 'long' vowels with a macron.)

We shall argue in this chapter that all the root vowel alternations represented in (1.1) – both within any paradigm and between one paradigm and another – are the result of synchronically recoverable, rule-governed processes. That is, the root vowels in the lexical representations of these verbs need not be differentially specified. We shall indeed claim that this radical vowel is lexically *un*specified (further than that it is a vowel); and that the various realizations in the 'regular' members of the first six strong verb classes are determined by phonological rules sensitive to their syntactic and phonological environments. We will attempt to formulate these rules in the immediately following sections, and we will return to the notion 'unspecified vowel' in §7.

The columns in (1.1) indicate the paradigmatic variation in the various subtypes (classes) of verbs. The label at the head of each column is a cover-term for those members of the syntactic paradigm containing a particular vowel. Thus PRES stands for all the present forms of the verb; PRET$_1$ for the first and third person singular of the preterite indicative; PRET$_2$ for all other preterite forms; and PART for the past (passive) participle. There is a further kind of variation found in the PRES forms of some verbs, with a different vowel in the second and third person present indicative, as in *helpan/hilpst, hilpð, weorpan/wierpst, wierpð*. We assume that the latter two variants in each set are associated with the presence of a high front vowel in the underlying form of the inflection (historically *-*isi*, *-*iþi*: cf. Go. -*is*, -*iþ*, OHG -*is*, -*it*). We shall later propose independently motivated rules to account for this. So we will ignore these latter variations in the immediately following discussion, and concentrate for the moment on the variations displayed in (1.1).

Historically, the vowel-alternations within the paradigms are partly reflexes of the Indo-European 'ablaut' processes (whatever they were); and partly (in the case of the distribution of [u] and [o] in PRET$_2$ and PART) of early Germanic changes, related to the metaphonic process we noted just above. Thus behind all the rather different (in OE) phonetic 'series' or *Ablautsreihen* in classes I–V is the single historical Indo-European series: [e-o-ē-ƀ/∅] (though the third term appears only in the PRET$_2$ of classes IV and V, and this is thought – cf. Kuryłowicz 1956: §40 – to have replaced an earlier [ƀ/∅]).

The Indo-European [e]/[o] alternation ([e]/[a] in Germanic) constitutes what is traditionally called the 'qualitative ablaut' or 'gradation' (*Abtönung*); and, whatever its origin, it appears to antedate the development of [ē] and [ƀ/∅] ([u/e/∅] in Germanic) – respectively the 'lengthened' and 'reduced' grades. The [e-ē-ƀ/∅] gradation is traditionally called the 'quantitative ablaut' (*Abstufung*). The whole series is most clearly represented (at a superficial level) in classes IV or V, where IE [o] has become Gmc [a] in PRET$_1$ (to give OE [æ] by 'Anglo-Frisian brightening' (henceforth AFB), a process we describe below in ch. II), and IE [ē] in PRET$_2$ has given by normal development OE [ǣ]. The 'reduced' grade of PART turns up as [u]/[o] in class IV or [e] in class V.

Thus the superficial series [ber-, bær-, bǣr-, bor-] represents an earlier, pre-OE series *[ber-, bar-, bēr-, bor-], which can be considered a direct reflex of an IE series of the type *[bher-, bhor-, bhēr-, bhƀr-]. In classes I–III, rather more drastic changes have taken place. We shall not investigate these here as historical phenomena: but their correlation with the synchronic processes we will be proposing will be evident to anyone familiar with the historical tradition.

We will not be concerned, either, with the origins of the ablaut in any detail: but it is worth noting, in view of our synchronic account, that both the *Abtönung* and the *Abstufung* are generally considered to reflect accentual differences that prevailed at different periods: thus the *Abtönung* is connected with the Indo-European 'pitch accent', and the *Abstufung* with the later (expiratory) stress. In the pre-ablaut period, all these verb forms can be considered, under this interpretation, to have had nondistinct root vowels. (For fuller early discussion, with special reference to Germanic, see Streitberg 1963:

§§45–9; Prokosch 1938: 118–31; and for Indo-European in general,
Kuryłowicz, 1956.)

So, given the common underlying vowel series, the differences
between the phonetic series that we find in the various OE classes are
due to later changes. These involve in particular modifications of the
radical vowel determined by postvocalic elements: especially the
immediately following root segments. Largely because of this, the
'canonical' classification of the strong verbs is not based (as it may at
first appear to be) on the vowel alternations, but (at least for the first
five classes) on the character of the post-vocalic radical segment(s) in
Indo-European. (See further on this Levin 1964.) Thus in Indo-
European, the first two classes have a postvocalic 'semivowel' (nonsyllabic vowel), front in I and back in II, which is in turn followed by a
single consonant. The vowel in class III precedes a liquid or nasal plus
one other consonant; and in classes IV and V there is only one postvocalic
radical segment, either a liquid or a nasal (IV) or an obstruent (V). This
is shown below in (1.2):

(1.2) *Postvocalic radical sequences in Indo-European*

Class	Postvocalic sequence	OE example
I	-iC	bīdan (cf. Go. beidan)
II	-uC	bēodan (cf. Go. biudan)
III	-RC = ⎰-lC ⎱-rC -NC	⎰helpan weorpan ⎱bindan
IV	-R	beran
V	-O	sprecan

Key: C = consonant, R = 'resonant' (liquid or nasal), N = nasal, O =
obstruent.

The phonetic differences between corresponding vowels in the various
classes can be related historically to these postvocalic sequences.
Further, differences between corresponding vowels in 'regular' members of the same class are even more strikingly dependent on the same
context. For instance, the differences between class III verbs of type (c)
in (1.1) and those of types (a) and (b) are ontogenetically a function of
the presence vs. the absence of a postvocalic nasal.

Whatever the historical processes that may have been involved, the
important claim that we intend to make in the following discussion is

that these relations are synchronically recoverable. We will propose, in particular, that the differences between the root vowels in the paradigms of classes I–V are determined by rules responsive to the postvocalic sequences. That is, a single ablaut series can be recovered not only historically, but synchronically as well.

We shall propose further that the ablaut series itself is phonologically and syntactically determined, so that the root vowel in all 'regular' members of the first five classes is specified in the lexicon only as 'V' ($= [-$consonantal]).

Such an interpretation will also be extended eventually to class VI. We will show that (whatever their historical origin) the members of this class can be regarded as displaying the same ablaut series as either class IV or class V verbs. The radical vowel here too appears lexically as merely /V/. The superficial differences between class VI verbs and the 'regular' members of classes IV and V are due to the presence in the lexical representations of the former of a particular prevocalic element, whose character we will endeavour to establish on the basis of its effect on the paradigm of these verbs. We will finally (in appendix I) explore the possibility of extending such an interpretation to many of the apparently rather heterogeneous verbs in the final strong verb class, VII (the traditional *reduplizierende Präterita*).

In the next two sections of this chapter, we consider those parts of the phonology relevant specifically to classes I–V – i.e. those rules that account for the interparadigmatic differences whose historical origins we have sketched above. The fourth section will be concerned with the ablaut rules themselves; and in the fifth section we will examine the status of class VI. In the final two sections we look at various matters of principle arising from our discussion of the strong verbs. (Some of the arguments in this chapter are discussed at greater length in Anderson 1970; but the present account differs quite notably from the proposals made there, largely because of our attempt to embed the ablaut rules in a more extensive fragment of OE phonology.)

2   Post-ablaut alternations in classes III–V

The verbs in classes II, IV and V, and two of those in III, show a (phonetically) different vowel in each column in (1.1), and might thus appear to display four different ablaut grades. However, some of these differences appear to be post-ablaut variations attributable to phonological rather than syntactic conditioning; and we claim that one must allow for at most three ablaut (i.e. syntactic) contexts. Specifically, the alternation between [u] and [o] in, for instance, class II (*budon/-boden*) is due to a rule of vowel harmony which we shall propose below. Further, the fact that we find 'long' vowels (*sprǣcon*, etc.) in the PRET$_2$ forms of classes IV–VI (where in the other classes these vowels are 'short' (*wurpon*, etc.)) is also dependent on phonological structure. (A rather different explanation is required for the presence of a long vowel in PRET$_1$ forms of class VI – as *bōc*, *fōr*, etc.) We shall formulate the appropriate rules shortly.

Notice at this point, however, that the difference between the (paradigmatically) corresponding vowels in the class III verbs (in particular) exemplified in (1.1) are even more superficial, being attributable to synchronic AFB, breaking, and 'nasal influence'. We delay discussion of these processes in detail until chapters II and III, where we examine a wider range of relevant data. We merely observe here that the difference in radical vowel between *weorpan* and *helpan* (whatever the orthographical *eo/e* may turn out to represent), and that between *wearp* or *healp* and *bær* in class IV, can be attributed (synchronically) to a post-ablaut rule of breaking. Similarly, the difference between *bær* and *band* is due to the operation and 'failure' of AFB: the back vowel in *band* is due specifically to failure of AFB before a nasal. Thus, to anticipate ourselves, the above-mentioned forms, after operation of ablaut proper, will be of the types [werpan], [helpan], [warp], [halp], [bar] and [band].

The high vowels in the PRES and PART forms *bindan/-bunden*, as compared to the mid vowels of the other verbs of this class, can also be related to the presence of the nasal. We might begin our discussion of post-ablaut processes by formulating the rule responsible for this:

(1.3) *Pre-nasal raising: first version*

$$\begin{bmatrix} V \\ -\text{low} \end{bmatrix} \rightarrow [+\text{high}] \ / \ \underline{\hspace{1cm}} [+\text{nasal}]$$

Thus [bendan] > [bindan], [-bonden] > [-bunden]. The other rules involved in producing the alternations in class III (and the differences between these and those of class IV) will, as we have indicated, be formulated in the appropriate subsequent chapters.

We can now say (albeit largely by anticipating subsequent discussion) that the vowel series of class III is at some stage of derivation representable as [e-a-o-u]. We have already suggested that the [u] ~ [o]

alternation is phonologically determined. So let us now survey the range of forms in class III in which *u* and *o*, respectively, appear. We find *u* throughout the PRET$_2$ forms, i.e. in the second person indicative singular (*wurpe*), the indicative plural (*wurpon*), and throughout the subjunctive (*wurpe(n)*); whereas *o* occurs only in PART (except of course when this form meets the condition for pre-nasal raising).

We account for this distribution by a rule which says that $\begin{bmatrix} +\text{back} \\ -\text{low} \end{bmatrix}$ vowels are [−high] before a following non-high vowel; otherwise [+high]. This presumes an underlying [u] in the preterite indicative plural inflexion, and an inflexional [i] in the other PRET$_2$ forms (cf. Go. *-um, -uþ, -un; -ima, -iþ, -ina*). We thus also assume a later rule conflating [u] and [i] in verb inflexions wth [o] and [e] respectively: [-un] > [-on], [-i(n)] > [-e(n)]. Accordingly, we find a [+high] vowel in the PRET$_2$ forms (before the [+high] inflexional vowel: *wurpe(n), wurpon*) but a [−high] vowel in PART (*-worpen*). Notice too that the distribution of [−low] front vowels is determined in the same way: thus *helpan*, with a mid vowel before the nonhigh inflexional vowel, but *hilpð* with a high vowel before the (subsequently deleted) [i] of the inflexion. The [i] is present only in the underlying forms of the second and third person present indicative. Thus we have the singular *helpe* (first person), but *hilpst, hilpð* (with later syncope in West Saxon).

There appears then to be a single rule adjusting the highness of nonlow root vowels (whether back or front) according to the highness of a following vowel. We might formulate it this way:

(1.4) *Highness harmonization: first version*

$$\begin{bmatrix} V \\ -\text{low} \end{bmatrix} \rightarrow [\alpha\text{high}] \ / \ \underline{\qquad} \ S_0^3 \begin{bmatrix} V \\ \alpha\text{high} \end{bmatrix}$$

(where 'S$_0^3$' = 'zero to three intervening segments'). The 'S^0' environment may be typified by *bīdan* (see below, §3), the 'S^1' environment by *beran*, the 'S^2' environment by *helpan*, and the 'S^3' environment by *berstan*. Prior to the operation of (1.4), the root vowel in both *helpan* and *hilpð* is $\begin{bmatrix} -\text{low} \\ -\text{back} \end{bmatrix}$, but not specified for highness (this will be discussed in §4). But since the root vowel in *helpan* is followed by a nonhigh inflexional vowel it is specified as [−high], whereas the nonlow nonback vowel in *hilpð* (< [hVlpiþ]) becomes [+high]. Similarly, *hulpon* with a vowel specified only as back and nonlow before an inflexional [-un], vs. *holpen*. 'Highness harmonization' must precede pre-nasal raising (1.3), since the latter can 'undo' the highness assignments resulting from (1.4) – as in PART *-bunden* (which should be *-*bonden* by (1.4) or PRES *bindan* (which would be *bendan).

Observe now, however, that we do not find evidence in present subjunctive forms for a radical -*i*-, which we might expect if the present subjunctive inflexions were identical to those we posited for the preterite subjunctive, where an inflexional [-i(n)] raises the preceding root vowel. We do not have **hilpe(n)*, but rather *helpe(n)*. We can allow for this by proposing a partially distinct set of inflexions for the present subjunctive, which do not contain a high vowel and are perhaps only superficially identical with those for the preterite, which are collapsed with them by the rule conflating inflexional [i u] with [e o] mentioned above. (This is in accord with their history – cf. Campbell 1959: §731.)

An alternative to the account we have just proposed would be to allow for the distribution of [u] and [o] in $PRET_2$ and PART forms in terms of this very syntactic information: i.e. [u] is the vowel found in $PRET_2$ forms and [o] that for PART (in the absence of a following nasal). The raising of the vowel in *hilpð* (cf. *helpan*) might be accounted for by an extension of *i*-umlaut (cf. ch. IV). The inflexions for the present and preterite subjunctives need not then be differentiated (to allow for *hulpe*, with raising, but *helpe*, without). The inflexional vowel is in both cases [e], and the high vowel in *hulpe* is associated with the syntactic context. This has certain attractions (and may indeed be correct for a later period), but the evidence for the operation of highness harmonization elsewhere (as in *bīdan* < [beidan] and *brūcan* < [briukan] < [breukan] – see below) appears to favour the former proposal. Moreover, we have in this case, and elsewhere (as in the formulation for quantitative ablaut proposed below), preferred rules invoking 'natural' phonetic conditions, where available, to formulations based directly on syntactic contexts. Our proposals will require re-formulation to the extent that this principle proves illusory. However, we shall discover other motivations below for somewhat modifying the formulation suggested above in (1.4).

Let us sum up the preceding discussion. We have proposed that certain differences in the series of root vowels associated with members of class III be attributed to synchronic rules of highness harmonization, pre-nasal raising, AFB, and breaking. We have already formulated highness harmonization (1.4) and pre-nasal raising (1.3). AFB and breaking will be discussed in detail in chapters II and III. In class III, then, if the phonology contains such post-ablaut processes, there is at most only a three-way distinction which we can associate with ablaut – viz. the differences between the vowels of PRES, $PRET_1$ and $PRET_2$/ PART forms.

This is true also of classes IV and V (though, indeed, in the latter we find the same vowel in PRES and PART), except for the presence of what is traditionally called a 'long' vowel in $PRET_2$ forms. Compare with *hulpon* and *bundon*, the $PRET_2$ forms of *beran* (IV) and *sprecan* (V): *bǣron* and *sprǣcon*. We claim that once again this is a reflexion of a rule of OE that takes into account the phonological context rather than, say, some ad hoc morphological feature like [+ long $PRET_2$] associated with these verbs. Observe, in the first place, that classes IV and V both differ from class III in that they have only one postvocalic root segment: *ber-*, *sprec-*, vs. *help-*. This suggests that the presence of a 'long' vowel in the $PRET_2$ of the former might be due to the fact that in these cases only one segment separates the root vowel from the inflexion. The analysis we will propose for classes I and II in the next section – such that they also have two lexical postvocalic root segments – accords with this suggestion; for they too lack a 'long' vowel in $PRET_2$.

As a first attempt to capture this, we propose a rule which lengthens the vowel in $PRET_2$ forms with only one postvocalic radical segment (i.e. a syntactically constrained 'lengthening in open syllables'):

(1.5) *$PRET_2$ lengthening: first version*

$$V \rightarrow \begin{cases} [-\text{long}] & \text{(a)} \\ [+\text{long}] \ / \ \left[\dfrac{\quad\quad}{[\text{PRET}_2]}\right] \ C \ V & \text{(b)} \end{cases}$$

(where '$PRET_2$' is a cover symbol for the feature specifications representing the syntactic situations we have discussed above). The subparts of (1.5) are conjunctively ordered: the output of (a) is available as input to (b). Thus all vowels are marked [− long] by (1.5a), but those in the context in (b) are converted to [+ long]. (We shall have reason to reconsider the notion 'length' in the light of the following discussion: see §6 below. It should be observed here that [+ long] was not included in the inventory of features discussed in the Preliminaries; we claim no theoretical status for it, for reasons which will become clear later on.)

The vowel in the $PRET_2$ of classes IV and V, [æ], is superficially [+ low]. But if it represented merely a lengthening of the vowel we find in PRES it should be mid. So we propose a tentative rule of Lowness Assignment for long vowels (to be modified later in the light of our discussion of class VI):

(1.6) *Lowness assignment: first version*

$$\begin{bmatrix} V \\ +\text{long} \end{bmatrix} \rightarrow [+\text{low}]$$

(This rule obviously must follow (1.5).) If we were using current markedness theory as a constraint on rule outputs, we would have to specify [−back] in the SC of this rule, to override the marking convention for low vowels (*SPE:* 405, X), which would otherwise be presumed to operate. But we reject universal markedness in its strong form; for some discussion, see appendix IV, and Lass (1972).

With respect to classes III–V, we must now propose rules for the ablaut alternations themselves; we must also account for the difference between class V and the others, where we find an *e* rather than the *u ~ o* of the former: *-sprecen* vs. *-boren*. This latter distinction seems to be associated with the character of the following segment. In class V it is an obstruent, whereas in III and IV it is a sonorant. But before trying to formulate rules for this and the ablaut alternation, we will extend our present analysis to classes I and II. We will show that essentially the same vowel alternations that we have proposed for classes III–V underlie the relevant parts of their paradigms also.

3. Post-ablaut alternations in classes I–II

Superficially, as is clear from (1.1), the vowel-series of classes I and II are unlike both each other and, more markedly, those of the other three classes we have considered. The examples from I and II are alike in having in PRES and $PRET_1$ nuclei of the types traditionally regarded as 'long' vowels or diphthongs, and 'short' vowels in the rest of the paradigm. Historically, these latter are derived from the second vowel in an originally divocalic nucleus, the first one having been deleted. There is no such deletion in the PRES and $PRET_1$ forms; they represent the end-point of developments from complex nuclei with second element [-i] (class I) or [-u] (class II). Compare the Gothic forms below in (1.7):

(1.7) *Classes I and II in Gothic*

	PRES	PRET$_1$	PRET$_2$	PART
I	beidan	baiþ	bidum	bidans
II	-biudan	-bauþ	-budum	-budans

(We realize that the *ei* in the PRES of Gothic class I verbs is not usually considered to be diphthongal; but given the massive difficulties of Gothic orthography we consider these spellings to be at least suggestive; cf. Braune-Ebbinghaus 1966: §16.)

The first element is historically [e] in PRES and [a] in PRET$_1$: i.e. the same vowels that underlie (synchronically and historically) the corresponding forms in classes III–V. It therefore seems worth considering to what extent underlying representations of the type the history suggests might reasonably be recoverable synchronically.

The spellings in the PRES and PRET$_1$ forms of class II are usually thought to have represented, respectively, a mid and a low front-to-back 'falling' diphthong, so that *ea* is a writing for *æa* = [æa] (see further ch. III, especially p. 74 n.) and *eo* = [eo]. Let us suppose this to be reasonably accurate. If it is, we can easily derive nuclei of this kind from underlying sequences of the type we envisage (i.e. [eu], [au]) by independently motivated rules. Thus we need to provide for shifts from [eu] to [eo] and [au] to [æa]. (We assume that the second element in such sequences is simply a nonsyllabic vowel: cf. the discussion in Preliminaries, §2.2.) That the second element in each case is in fact an underlying [u] is suggested by the presence of a *u* in the PRET$_2$ and PART forms, where, as we will propose, the initial element has been deleted.

The presence of [æ] in the [æa] (*ea*) of the PRET$_1$ is provided for by fronting under AFB (ch. II), which converts [a] to [æ] and is blocked (or undone) only if a consonant intervenes between the [a] and a following back vowel (and in other circumstances not relevant here).

We also need a further rule which will harmonize the height of the second (nonsyllabic) element of a diphthong with that of the first, so that for example [eu] > [eo] and [æu] > [æa], thus giving us a mid 'diphthong' in the PRES (e.g. *bēodan*) and a low one in PRET$_1$ (e.g. *bēad*). This rule is also required elsewhere. It applies for example to the two-vowel sequences resulting from breaking, e.g. *wearþ* < [wærp]. The derivation of the breaking nuclei is discussed in detail in chapter III, and we delay until then the precise formulation of this rule, which we will call diphthong height harmony (henceforth DHH).

Now we have argued that *bēodan*, *bēad*, phonetically [beodan], [bæad], are at some stage in their derivation [beudan], [baud], respectively. And we have suggested a second element [u] in the diphthongs on the basis of the *u* in PRET$_2$ and PART. We have also observed (though of course this is merely suggestive and not evidential), that there is historical corroboration: cf. Go. *biudan*, *bauþ*. Now let us apply these arguments to class I. We notice that the PRET$_2$ and PART of these verbs have, not *u* but *i*, which would suggest, if the two cases are parallel, that the PRES and PRET$_1$ forms of *bīdan* should be derived from diphthongal nuclei in [-i], e.g. respectively [beidan], [baid]. And once again the historical evidence (cf. Go. *beidan*, *baiþ*) points in the same direction. But the OE forms show 'long' monophthongs: *bīdan*, *bād*.

Let us concern ourselves first with *bād*. Since historically it is quite common for diphthongal nuclei to 'monophthongize' and yield 'long' vowels (OE *ī* < PG*ei is a case in point), it seems reasonable to suggest that derivations of this sort may also occur synchronically. I.e., that whatever 'long *ā*' may turn out to mean phonetically, for example, it is possible that at some point in their derivations at least some *ā* may derive from a sequence [aa], which in turn may derive from [ai].

And we already have, in fact, nearly all the rules we need to account for just such a derivation. Let us begin with [ai]. Once again, [a] becomes [æ] by AFB, giving a sequence [æi]. Since the second element does not match the first in height, DHH applies, giving [ææ]. What we need now is a rule that will make this sequence [+back], i.e. [aa]. And in fact it seems that we may very well need a rule of this kind for other purposes: and moreover, an *α*-switching rule which will also convert [aa] to [ææ] – i.e. that will reverse the backness value on any [+low] divocalic cluster.

But before we get to this we must say a few words about the possible implications of this proposal. Because of the obvious similarities between classes I and II, we have argued that just as *bēad* may derive from a representation like [baud], so *bād* may derive from [baid]. If this is so, it opens the way to the possibility that other 'long' vowels may have their sources in divocalic clusters as well. For instance, let us suppose that there are 'long' vowels (other than those derived from diphthongs) that start out as geminate vowels, i.e. clusters whose members are identical. If it is reasonable that $\bar{a}$ in some instances may derive via [aa] from [ai], then there seems no reason in principle why at least some $\bar{a}$ (or some other 'long' vowels) should not derive from a geminate sequence like [aa] directly, i.e. without having passed through a stage like [ai]. So we open the way to the possibility of a second class of 'long' vowels, one derived not from PRET$_2$ lengthening (1.3), but from a diphthong or geminate.

Now recall that in the course of deriving $b\bar{a}d$ from [baid] we passed (after DHH) through a stage [ææ]. If there are some superficial $\bar{a}$ that derive from [aa], might there not also be some superficial $\bar{æ}$ that derive from [ææ]? Historically, we know that at least one class of $\bar{æ}$-forms in WS have a source in WGmc $\bar{a}$, e.g. $h\bar{æ}r$ 'hair' (cf. G. *Haar*). Now if a derivation of this sort were, let us say, to operate synchronically also, with forms like $h\bar{æ}r$ deriving from [ææ] via [aa], we would have to keep their derivations separate from those of surface $\bar{a}$-forms which pass through a stage [ææ], and from $\bar{e}$-forms like $h\bar{e}r$ 'here' (putatively < [ee]). If indeed the vowel in $h\bar{æ}r$ is to be kept distinct in derivation from vowels originating in [ai] and developing by independently motivated rules to [ææ] and by a further rule to [aa], it would be advantageous if $h\bar{æ}r$ did not contain an underlying [ææ]: otherwise it would have to be blocked in some arbitrary way from shifting to [aa].

But why (apart from this need to keep it distinct) should $h\bar{æ}r$ at any point in its synchronic derivation have a nucleus which is not some form of [æ]? There is in fact a reason: in discussing AFB we will provide evidence that there is no independent motivation for an underlying segment of the type [æ] at all in OE: that it occurs always as one member of some alternating pair. Specifically, it occurs so frequently as a member of an [æ]/[a] pair that we can show that given those two vowels, one of them must be derived. We reach a situation then where the only motivation for a choice of the single necessary low vowel will be the preferability of one of the two vowel systems /i e æ u o/ or /i e u o a/. And on grounds of universal system naturalness we prefer (in the absence of strong counter-evidence) a system whose only low vowel is /a/ to one whose only low vowel is /æ/.

So if there is, as we will try to show, no systematic /æ/ in OE, the geminate [ææ] in words of the $h\bar{æ}r$ class must have some other source: and if these are not derived from an underlying low back vowel, they constitute the only exceptions to an otherwise valid generalization. This can be avoided if we assume that in the lexicon the $\bar{æ}$-forms fill the empty 'long' /a/ slot, and are shifted to [ææ] by the same rule that moves other (derived) [ææ] from [ai] to [aa]. A full treatment must await both the discussion of AFB and the proposals we will make in chapter VI on the OE vowel system and the derivation of 'long' vowels (which we will also consider in a preliminary fashion in §6 of this chapter). But assuming (a) that the [aa] in *bād* is derived via [ææ] from [ai], and (b) that the [ææ] in *hǣr* is derived directly from [aa], we shall provide at this point a formulation of the 'backness switching' rule:

(1.8) *Backness switching*

$$
\text{SD:} \quad
\begin{bmatrix} V \\ +\text{low} \\ \alpha\text{back} \end{bmatrix}
\begin{bmatrix} V \\ +\text{low} \\ \alpha\text{back} \end{bmatrix}
\qquad
\text{SC:} \ [-\alpha\text{back}] \ [-\alpha\text{back}]
$$

$$
 \quad\quad 1 \quad\quad\quad\quad 2 \quad\quad\quad\quad\quad\quad 1 \quad\quad\quad 2
$$

Thus we can derive even the PRET_1 of class I from the common ablaut series without great additional cost.

We can now give plausible derivations for the PRES and PRET_1 forms of class II, and the PRET_1 form of class I, which take as their starting point the same vowel grades as in classes III–V. Thus at one level class III [werpan, warp] and class IV [beran, bar] will be paralleled by class II [beudan, baud], and [warp], [bar] and [baud] will be paralleled by [baid]. There remains class I PRES. If, once more, this is interpreted as involving a sequence of two vowels, then it must be at some stage [ei], so that we have [beidan] parallel to [beudan] (and of course also to [werpan, beran]). If our preceding analysis is correct, then we must at some point have a shift of [ei] to [ii] (parallel to [ai] > [aa]). And in fact this is already provided for by highness harmonization (1.4), which specifies that a nonlow vowel takes on the height value of a following vowel if zero to three segments intervene. And in this case the vowels are contiguous, and the second is [+high], so that [ei] > [ii].

But observe that the first vowel in the sequence in class II PRES, i.e. [eu], is not affected by (1.4): we do not get *[iu]. We can account for this if DHH precedes highness harmonization: by DHH [eu] becomes [eo], to which highness harmonization applies vacuously. But then the question arises: why is the class I PRES [ei] not susceptible to DHH, giving [ee]? In these circumstances it would appear that DHH must be constrained to apply only to divocalic sequences whose elements *differ* either in backness or lowness. Or, alternatively, suppose that DHH is an 'anywhere (redundancy) rule' (cf. Stanley 1967), i.e. one that can operate at any point in a derivation where its proper analysis is met. Then it can apply to PRET$_1$ in class II after AFB, and to PRET$_1$ in class I before AFB. So:

(1.9)   au → æu (AFB) → æa (DHH)

                         ai → aæ (DHH) → ææ (AFB)

In this case DHH need only be constrained to apply to sequences where the two vowels differ in backness – which is a more natural constraint than the 'backness or lowness' disjunction. It will fail in the case of [ei].

A third alternative is to suggest that highness harmonization does precede DHH. Under this interpretation it is unnecessary to introduce a constraint on DHH which excludes [ei], since it will already have become [ii]. However, we would also expect [eu] to have become [iu] by highness harmonization. But this need not be excluded as a possible step in the derivation. For observe that we shall perhaps need a rule to lower to [eo] the [iu] that results from breaking of [i]; as in *meox* 'excrement', with *eo* from [i]. This could also apply to [iu] from ablaut. Further, if DHH were to operate as supposed under the other two alternatives, the vowel in PRES forms would have had to be marked as [−high] even before highness harmonization; and this would mean that the ablaut rule we will propose in §4 would have to be made more complex. However, it is not certain that we need to allow in West Saxon for synchronic breaking of [i]; it might be possible to regard all such forms as containing underlying /e/, regardless of the fact that they had historical /i/ (but see the discussion in ch. III, §7 and ch. VI below). And we shall be discussing below some motivations for reinterpreting highness harmonization in a way that is compatible with the former two alternatives. It looks then, on balance, as if the second alternative – that DHH applies to any divocalic sequence where the vowels differ in backness – receives the most support from the West Saxon evidence. However, some important considerations of a rather different kind will arise in chapter VI, §2; and we shall review the situation at that point.

We have also now proposed in outline an account that would relate classes I–V to a single underlying ablaut series; and we are almost in a position to discuss the rules producing the ablaut alternations themselves. There remain only the PART and PRET$_2$ forms of classes I–II to account for. We presume that these result from the deletion of the first vowel in the radical sequence; though why these vowels are deleted can best be considered in relation to a discussion of the source of the ablaut series.

However, we must take note at this point of certain evidence suggesting that our interpretation of highness harmonization is oversimple. Observe first of all that the [i] in PART of class I is not lowered to [e] in the appropriate environment for lowering under highness harmonization, whereas the [u] in PART of class II is lowered to [o] (-*holpen* vs. -*biden*). This suggests that lowering before a [−high] vowel affects only vowels marked [+back]. Similarly, if we take into account, say, nouns as well as strong verbs, it is clear that we find [o]'s that are not raised before [-i] or [-u], as in *dehter* 'daughters' which shows *i*-umlaut of [o] (cf. sing. *dohtor*), i.e. an [o] that must precede an [i]; cf. also *hofu* 'dwellings'. Accordingly, we propose a modified version of (1.4), whereby it is split into two parts. One of these applies only to syllabic vowels in strong verbs (and certain related forms) and precedes the operation of the rule deleting the first vowel in the PRET$_2$ and PART forms of classes I and II. We give this as (1.10):

(1.10) *Strong verb highness assignment*

$$
\begin{bmatrix} V \\ +\text{syll} \\ \alpha\text{back} \\ -\text{low} \end{bmatrix} \rightarrow [\alpha\text{high}] \, / \, \begin{bmatrix} \underline{\quad\quad} \\ [\text{SV}] \end{bmatrix}
$$

I.e. in strong verbs, the front and back nonlow vowels are respectively [−high] and [+high]. ([SV] is not to be understood as a feature present in the lexical entries for strong verbs; but rather as a morphological cover symbol; strong and weak verbs are morphologically distinct, in that weak verbs develop a pre-inflexional suffix throughout the paradigm.) So, *helpan* but *hulpon*.

The second part of the rule need not precede the deletion of the syllabic vowel in PRET$_2$ and PART of classes I and II. It lowers a back vowel before a [−high] vowel and raises a front vowel before a [+high] vowel. So, -*holpen* but *hilpð*. There is no lowering in *hulpon* because of the high vowel in the inflexion ([-un]), and no raising in *helpan* before [-an]. This rule can be stated as follows:

(1.11) *Highness harmonization: second version*

$$\begin{bmatrix} V \\ \alpha back \\ -low \end{bmatrix} \rightarrow [-\alpha high] / \underline{\quad} \; S_0^3 \begin{bmatrix} V \\ -\alpha high \end{bmatrix}$$

If both (1.10) and (1.11) precede deletion of the syllabic vowel in classes I and II, then they can be collapsed as:

(1.12)

$$\begin{bmatrix} V \\ \alpha back \\ -low \end{bmatrix} \rightarrow \begin{cases} [\alpha high] / \begin{bmatrix} \underline{\quad} \\ +syll \\ [SV] \end{bmatrix} & (a) \\[2em] [-\alpha high] / \underline{\quad} S_0^3 \begin{bmatrix} V \\ -\alpha high \end{bmatrix} & (b) \end{cases}$$

But the interpretation of the development of the divocalic sequences in classes I and II that we adopted above suggests that (1.12a) (i.e. (1.10)) be ordered before the operation of DHH and (1.12b) (i.e. (1.11)) after; that is, they are separate processes. So despite the fact that the rules look as if they are collapsible by brace-notation, they turn out to be non-adjacent, and we adopt the following ordering: (1.10), DHH, AFB, DHH, (1.11).

We thus envisage the following derivations for the nuclei of the PRES and PRET₁ forms of classes I and II:

(1.13)

	Class I		Class II	
	PRES	PRET$_1$	PRES	PRET$_1$
After ablaut and (1.10)	ei	ai	eu	au
DHH		aæ	eo	
AFB		ææ		æu
DHH				æa
Highness harmonization (1.11)	ii	ææ	eo	æa
Spelling	*bīdan*	*bād*	*bēodan*	*bēad*

The PRET₁ [ææ] in class I becomes [+back], i.e. [aa], by the backness switching rule that we gave earlier on, as (1.8).

We now observe that a number of verbs that seem otherwise to belong to class II show *ū* in the infinitive, instead of the expected *ēo*. Thus *brūcan* 'enjoy', *brēac*, *brucon*, *-brocen* (in this class are also *lūcan* 'lock', *būgan* 'bend', *sūcan* 'suck', and various others). We propose that because of the restriction of the irregularity to one part of the paradigm, these verbs be allowed to undergo the majority of the ablaut rules as if they were in fact 'regular' class II verbs. This will provide the correct forms for PRET$_1$, PRET$_2$ and PART. But they will be marked in the lexicon with an exception-feature, let us say [−DHH], which will have the following effect. First, DHH is blocked in the PRES forms of these verbs; they remain as [eu] rather than moving to [eo]. This means that by highness harmonization (1.11) they will become [iu]. At this point, a special rule assimilating the first vowel to the second will operate:

(1.14) *Class II monophthongization*

$$\text{SD:} \quad \begin{bmatrix} \text{V} \\ +\text{high} \\ -\text{back} \end{bmatrix} \quad \begin{bmatrix} \text{V} \\ +\text{high} \\ +\text{back} \end{bmatrix} \quad \text{SC: } 1 \ 2 \to 2 \ 2$$

$$\phantom{\text{SD:} \quad} 1 2$$

This rule (involving 'regressive' rather than 'progressive' monophthongization – cf. ch. III, §8) is a 'minor rule' in the technical sense. That is, no form may be subject to it unless it is specifically marked for it, i.e. [+(1.14)]. This minor rule feature, and the [−DHH] exception feature apply only to the PRES forms; they are presumably deleted from the other parts of the paradigm after lexical insertion.

Thus *brūcan* would be derived by a sequence like: /-Vu-/ > [eu] > [iu] > [uu]; and the surface *ū* is presumably another instance of a 'long' vowel derived from an underlying two-vowel sequence.

4 Ablaut

Now to the actual synchronic processes which produce the basic ablaut series. The phenomena associated with *Abstufung* ('quantitative gradation') are perhaps the more complex. We have to allow in the first place for the various modifications of the vowel in the PRET$_2$ and PART forms. We have already suggested (in §2), that a lengthening rule, provisionally given as (1.5), is involved in the derivation of the vowel in the PRET$_2$ of classes IV and V, and that this is in part dependent on the nature of the following sequence. Also, in the other PRET$_2$ and PART forms the development of the vowel once more depends on the following environment. Before a vowel, the PRET$_2$ vowel is deleted; before a sonorant consonant we find u (or o by height harmonization); before an obstruent we find e. We can summarize these alternations this way:

(1.15) *Quantitative ablaut: preliminary version*

$$
\begin{bmatrix} V \\ [PP] \end{bmatrix} \rightarrow
\begin{cases}
[+\text{long}] \ / \ \ \underline{} \begin{bmatrix} \overline{[PRET_2]} \end{bmatrix} C\ V & \text{(a)} \\[2ex]
[\alpha \text{back}] \ / \ \underline{} \begin{bmatrix} C \\ -\alpha\text{obstruent} \end{bmatrix} & \text{(b)} \\[2ex]
\varnothing \ \ / \ \underline{} V & \text{(c)}
\end{cases}
$$

'PP' is a cover symbol which represents the union of the paradigmatic sets represented by 'PRET$_2$' and 'PART'.

If this is the rule for the synchronic *Abstufung*, then it is a rather strange process. There is a variety of developments whose motivation (in terms of 'natural' processes) is, to say the least, obscure. We suggest rather that underlying all the *Abstufung* phenomena is the distribution of the (stress) accent. That is, we propose that all the forms in which lengthening takes place are [+accent], whereas elsewhere in PRET$_2$ and PART the vowel is [−accent]. The rest of the paradigm is un-marked for accent at this stage. The unaccented vowel is deleted before a following vowel, which then becomes syllabic. Historically, it is usually suggested that deletion takes place after sonorant consonants also, and that the [u]/[o] represent a later epenthesis. But it is doubtful whether this can be shown to be relevant synchronically. Restated in terms of accent distribution, the *Abstufung* can be shown to be more of a unitary phenomenon, and (at least in part) more natural:

(1.16) *Quantitative ablaut* (Abstufung): *revised version*

$$
\text{A.} \quad V \rightarrow
\begin{cases}
[-\text{long}] & \text{(a)} \\[1.5ex]
[+\text{long}] \ / \begin{bmatrix} \underline{} \\ +\text{accent} \end{bmatrix} & \text{(b)}
\end{cases}
$$

$$
\text{B.} \quad V \rightarrow
\begin{cases}
[\alpha\text{back}] \ / \ \underline{} \begin{bmatrix} C \\ -\alpha\text{obstruent} \end{bmatrix} & \\[2ex]
\varnothing \ / \ \underline{} V &
\end{cases}
\Bigg/ \begin{bmatrix} \underline{} \\ -\text{accent} \end{bmatrix}
\begin{matrix} \text{(a)} \\[2ex] \text{(b)} \end{matrix}
$$

Thus, lengthening occurs if the vowel is [+accent]; all other vowels are

[−long]. Deletion of the vowel before another vowel occurs if the first vowel is [−accent].

This restatement presupposes a rule assigning accent in the appropriate way. We assume that it includes at least the following subpart:

(1.17) *Pre-Germanic accentuation*

$$
\begin{bmatrix} V \\ [PP] \end{bmatrix} \rightarrow \begin{cases} [-\text{accent}] & \text{(a)} \\ [+\text{accent}] \, / \, \underline{\qquad} \text{C V (C)} \,\#\, & \text{(b)} \end{cases}
$$

The rule places accent on a vowel in a PP form if it is followed by one consonant plus one vowel (plus one consonant) plus word boundary. If we assume (in accordance with its history) a disyllabic inflexion for PART, then only $PRET_2$ forms in classes IV and V meet the condition for accentuation. All other PP forms are [−accent]. The rest of the paradigms are unspecified with respect to accent. At some point after the operation of these rules we assume the application of the Germanic accent rule, which places the primary accent on the syllabic vowel of the root.

The *Abtönung* ('qualitative gradation') appears to rely much more simply and directly on the syntactic information embodied in our cover-symbols. It involves the development of a $\begin{bmatrix} +\text{back} \\ +\text{low} \end{bmatrix}$ root vowel in $PRET_1$ forms and a $\begin{bmatrix} -\text{back} \\ -\text{low} \end{bmatrix}$ vowel elsewhere (unless otherwise modified). So we give this rule provisionally as:

(1.18) *Qualitative ablaut* (Abtönung): *first version*

$$
\begin{bmatrix} V \\ +\text{syll} \\ [SV] \end{bmatrix} \rightarrow \begin{cases} \begin{bmatrix} -\text{back} \\ -\text{low} \end{bmatrix} & \text{(a)} \\ [+\text{low}] \, / \, \underline{\big[\overline{\qquad}\big]} [PRET_1] & \text{(b)} \end{cases}
$$

The [+low] vowel resulting from part (b) is [+back] by convention.

One effect of stating the *Abstufung* as we did in (1.15) is to eliminate specification of one of the syntactic distinctions we have relied upon in our discussions so far, viz. $PRET_2$/PART; these are now conflated under a single cover-symbol, 'PP'. It is further possible to reformulate (1.18) so as to eliminate reference to $PRET_1$:

(1.19) *Qualitative ablaut: revised*

$$\begin{bmatrix} +\text{syll} \\ [\text{SV}] \end{bmatrix} \rightarrow \begin{cases} \begin{bmatrix} -\text{back} \\ -\text{low} \end{bmatrix} & \text{(a)} \\ [+\text{low}] \ / \ \begin{bmatrix} \overline{[\text{PP}]} \end{bmatrix} \text{(S) C } \# & \text{(b)} \end{cases}$$

This relies on the fact that the $\begin{bmatrix} +\text{back} \\ +\text{low} \end{bmatrix}$ vowel is found only in the inflexionless forms of the preterite paradigm. Thus, only one syntactic cover-symbol is necessary for the statement of the ablaut, viz. [PP], which is to be interpreted as 'preterite and past participle'.

There is indeed a further, perhaps more significant way, in which reference to syntactic contexts, and particularly the content of the cover symbols, can be simplified. However, we can do this – i.e. interpret '[PP]' as referring not just to $PRET_2$ and PART forms, but PART and all preterite forms (not excluding $PRET_1$ = 1 and 3 pers. sing. preterite indicative) – only if qualitative ablaut (1.19) precedes Pre-Germanic accentuation (1.17), and we add [−low] to the specification of the vowel on the left-hand side of (1.17). It will then affect only the necessary parts of the paradigm, since the $PRET_1$ forms are excluded by their [+low] specification. We propose then that the only syntactic reference that need be made in the rules (though see appendix I for a further possibility) is to 'preterite and past participle', which we will abbreviate as '[PP]'. (However, for convenience of exposition, we shall continue to employ the cover-symbols PRES, $PRET_1$, $PRET_2$, PART.) Accordingly, [−low] must be added to the left-hand side of (1.17).

It seems likely that we could extend the ablaut rules we have just formulated in a straightforward way to encompass ablaut alternations manifesting themselves not in the strong verb paradigm proper but rather in related forms, e.g. *byrþen* 'burden', (*ġe*)-*byrd* 'birth' (cf. *beran*); but we will not attempt to make this explicit here. However, we would like to note that the regularities of the ablaut system operate clearly even in certain seemingly anomalous verbal forms. For instance, the so-called 'weak presents' – the strong verbs showing umlaut and gemination in the present paradigm, but 'normal' ablaut elsewhere – are in fact not really exceptional. Paradigms like *sittan – sæt – sǣton – ġeseten* 'sit' and *biddan – bæd – bǣdon – ġebiden* 'ask' are generated by the ablaut rules in the normal way; the only exceptional property is the presence of a /-jan/ suffix in the present system. Thus these verbs emerge from the ablaut rules as [sitjan], [bidjan], etc., (with root [i] by highness harmonization), and do not get their proper surface forms until they have passed through gemination. (On the synchronic formulation of the gemination, and the ordering relations between gemination and umlaut, see appendix II.)

This concludes our basic discussion of the ablaut rules as such. Clearly the rules we have proposed in this section all precede the rules formulated in previous sections – and indeed elsewhere in this study. We have tried so far to make one basic point: that the intra- and inter-paradigmatic variations in the root vowel of the strong verbs of classes I– V are governed by synchronic phonological processes which take as their starting point an unspecified vowel. Thus, the vowel in *bǣron*, for instance, is lexically simply /V/. It is $\begin{bmatrix} -\text{back} \\ -\text{low} \end{bmatrix}$ by qualitative ablaut a (1.19), [+accent] by pre-Germanic accentuation (1.17), [+long] by quantitative ablaut A (1.16), [−high] by strong verb highness assignment (1.10), [+low] by lowness assignment (1.6) and [−round] by universal convention.

5 Class VI

Consider now the question of the analysis of class VI strong verbs, which (as shown in (1.1)) involve a phonetically rather different series of vowels. In particular, the series displays only two vowels (excluding the umlauted forms), both of them back, a short one occurring in the PRES and PART and a long one in the preterite forms:

(1.20) PRES	PRET$_1$	PRET$_2$	PART
bacan	bōc	bōcon	-bacen

The quality of the vowels and their intra-paradigmatic distribution is unlike anything in the first five classes. In the analysis of these latter we are able to suggest derivations from a common [e-a-ē-ъ/∅] series. And these involve, for the most part, rules which have their independent motivations elsewhere in the phonology (as we show in the following chapters). It would appear, then, that we must posit for class VI a second ablaut series, such that the vowels in these verbs are marked distinctively in the lexicon and undergo a special series of ablaut rules (which will nevertheless take into account in part the same syntactic and phonological contexts as do the rules for classes I–V). This would involve us not only in additional rules, but also in additions to the rules we have already formulated in order (where necessary) to exclude verbs of class VI.

In view of these added complexities, we might ask if we could not interpret the root forms of class VI as being derived via the common ablaut series. Let us review what there is in common with classes I–V. We have already observed that the same syntactic and postradical phonological environments are relevant in the respective derivations. In terms of the structure of the root itself, the members of class VI are like the verbs of classes IV and V in containing only one postvocalic segment, either a sonorant consonant (like class IV: *faran*) or an obstruent (like class V: *bacan*). Further, like classes IV and V, class VI shows a 'long' vowel in the $PRET_2$ form and a 'short' one in PRES and PART. The only discrepancy with regard to 'length' is in $PRET_1$, where the vowel in class VI is 'long'. The major differences are in the quality of the root vowel throughout the paradigm. So if we propose that class VI verbs do not display a distinct ablaut series, we need a plausible explanation of why they do not show the same superficial series as, in particular, classes IV and V. This should ideally involve accounting for the differences throughout the paradigm in a uniform way. We are going to suggest further that the distinctiveness of class VI can be allowed for in terms of natural processes. That is, we do not propose that the members of class VI are like verbs of either class IV or class V, except for the presence of a diacritic feature which in some way overrides the consequences of the ablaut rules, etc. The phonetic character of the process is reflected in the homogeneity of the results: all the vowels in class VI are $\begin{bmatrix} +\text{back} \\ -\text{high} \end{bmatrix}$; the only quality difference involves $[\pm \text{low}]$. We turn now to a consideration of these processes, and the way in which members of class VI differ lexically from verbs of classes IV and V.

Let us assume that the verbs of class VI undergo the same ablaut rules, under the same conditions, as those in classes I–V – i.e., in particular, pre-Germanic accentuation (1.17), quantitative ablaut (1.16) and qualitative ablaut (1.19). With respect to these the verbs of class VI 'behave' like members of class IV (*faran*, etc.) or class V (*bacan*, etc.).

Thus, the PRET$_1$ vowel is assigned $\begin{bmatrix} +\text{back} \\ +\text{low} \end{bmatrix}$ and all the others $\begin{bmatrix} -\text{back} \\ -\text{low} \end{bmatrix}$ (1.19) and the PRET$_2$ vowel is lengthened. We must now determine what operations convert the outputs of these rules into the surface forms with [a] and [ō]. Consider first the vowels in PRES, PRET$_2$ and PART, which do not involve any change in quantity.

The PRES and PART forms both contain a radical [a] – *bacan*, *-bacen*; a $\begin{bmatrix} -\text{back} \\ -\text{low} \end{bmatrix}$ vowel has become $\begin{bmatrix} +\text{back} \\ +\text{low} \end{bmatrix}$. The vowel in PRET$_2$ (which is [+long] by (1.16)) is superficially also [+back] but [−low]: *bōcon*. We have apparently two processes, one affecting the [+long] vowel, the other vowels which are not [+long]. However, there are motivations for regarding the shifting of the [+long] vowel as involving two steps, the first one being identical to the process affecting the vowels which are not [+long]. That is, in the first place, the vowel in *bōcon*, which emerges from the ablaut rules as $\begin{bmatrix} +\text{long} \\ -\text{back} \\ -\text{low} \end{bmatrix}$, becomes $\begin{bmatrix} +\text{back} \\ +\text{low} \end{bmatrix}$ by the same rule that affects other nonlow vowels in class VI verbs. We need not, in this case, restrict its operation to vowels which are not [+long]. At this stage, we have a $\begin{bmatrix} +\text{long} \\ +\text{back} \\ +\text{low} \end{bmatrix}$ vowel in forms like *bōcon* and *fōron*. However, we shall now need a rule to make such vowels [−low], thus apparently dissipating the economy just achieved by treating long and nonlong vowels together. But notice at this point that the desired switch, in lowness, is the mirror-image of a rule which we have already formulated with regard to the [+long] front vowel in *bæron*, *sprǣcon*, etc. We proposed in § 2 a rule (1.6) assigning [+low] to the only [+long] vowel envisaged at that time – which was $\begin{bmatrix} +\text{long} \\ -\text{low} \\ -\text{back} \end{bmatrix}$ after the operation of the ablaut rules. We now have a second set of [+long] vowels which also emerge from the ablaut rules with such a specification but which are then shifted to $\begin{bmatrix} +\text{long} \\ +\text{low} \\ +\text{back} \end{bmatrix}$. By (1.6) the [−low] value in the first set of [+long] vowels was switched to [+low]. We would have to modify the rule anyway to refer only to [−back] vowels. But it is clear that we can modify it in such a way as to accomplish the final step in the derivation of the vowel in *bōcon*, which involves a switch from [+low] to [−low]. We need merely incorporate a variable over + and − into the modified rule:

(1.21) *Lowness assignment: revised*

$$
\begin{bmatrix} V \\ +\text{long} \\ \alpha\text{back} \end{bmatrix} \rightarrow \begin{bmatrix} -\alpha\text{low} \\ \alpha\text{back} \end{bmatrix}
$$

This must follow the rule which assigns $\begin{bmatrix} +\text{back} \\ +\text{low} \end{bmatrix}$ to the PRES, PRET$_2$ and PART forms of class VI. Compare the derivations for *bǣron* and *fōron*:

(1.22)

	Class IV	Class VI	
Qualitative ablaut (1.19)	e	e	1
Pre-Germanic accent (1.17)	′e	′e	2
Quantitative ablaut (1.16)	′ē	′ē	3
(To be given)		′ā	4
Lowness assignment (1.21)	′ǣ	′ō	5

We must now consider the rule which accounts for stage (4) in class VI verbs.

But before we can do this, we must consider another factor relevant to the character of such a rule – on the assumption that it involves a natural process rather than a diacritic feature. And this is the development of the vowel in the PRET$_1$ forms in class VI. Observe that in its case there is not only a difference in quality but also a 'length' distinction; we find indeed the same vowel as in PRET$_2$ – *bōc/bōcon*. Presumably, this vowel has, like the vowel in PRET$_2$, undergone lowness assignment, as just revised in (1.21), whereby its lowness value has been switched. We have, then, to account for the presence in PRET$_1$ forms of a vowel which is $\begin{bmatrix} +\text{long} \\ +\text{back} \\ +\text{low} \end{bmatrix}$ where we would expect from the output of the ablaut rules the corresponding short vowel (cf. *bær*, which has been fronted under AFB). In class VI overall, we have the following situation: the vowels in PRES, PRET$_2$ and PART are shifted from their post-ablaut values of $\begin{bmatrix} -\text{back} \\ -\text{low} \end{bmatrix}$ to $\begin{bmatrix} +\text{back} \\ +\text{low} \end{bmatrix}$; the vowel in PRET$_1$, which is already by the ablaut rules $\begin{bmatrix} +\text{back} \\ +\text{low} \end{bmatrix}$, is not changed in quality, but lengthened.

We propose the following account of these phenomena. Class VI verbs are the same as either class IV or class V in their postvocalic root structure: i.e. the vowel is followed by a single (sonorant or obstruent) consonant. They are like all the 'regular' verbs in classes I–V in that the root vowel is specified merely as a vowel. But they differ from the other classes, in particular from classes IV and V, in containing an immediately prevocalic segment which at some stage in its derivation is $\begin{bmatrix} +\text{back} \\ +\text{low} \end{bmatrix}$. After this segment, a vowel which is not itself $\begin{bmatrix} +\text{back} \\ +\text{low} \end{bmatrix}$ becomes so – as in *bacan, bōcon* (the latter becoming [−low] by lowness assignment (1.21)). The prevocalic segment is then deleted. However, before a vowel which is $\begin{bmatrix} +\text{back} \\ +\text{low} \end{bmatrix}$ already (as in PRET$_1$ forms, by qualitative ablaut), the segment is vocalized. This results in a sequence of two $\begin{bmatrix} +\text{back} \\ +\text{low} \end{bmatrix}$ vowels, the first from vocalization of the prevocalic segment, the second via qualitative ablaut. We thus have a geminate ('long') vowel, which becomes [−low] by (1.21) or its equivalent: *bōc* (cf. below).

The prevocalic element itself, which is alternatively vocalized or deleted, we interpret as a 'laryngeal' or 'glide' – by which we mean a segment with the major class features $\begin{bmatrix} +\text{obstruent} \\ -\text{consonantal} \end{bmatrix}$. We assume that although [+obstruent] normally predicts [+consonantal], the conjunction we propose is possible under the standard definition of 'consonantal' (cf. Preliminaries, §2.2). That is, [±obstruent] refers only to glottal configuration, and [+consonantal] implies an obstruction in the midsagittal region of the vocal tract. So a configuration in which the vocal cords are positioned so as to inhibit large-scale output of acoustic energy (i.e. in a configuration equivalent to full closure or close approximation), and in which there is nonetheless no supraglottal obstruction, is not impossible. This is in fact a reasonable characterization of segments of the (general) type [ʔ h]. On these grounds we provisionally argue for an underlying nonconsonantal obstruent in the position in question. Vocalization accordingly will involve only a change from [+obstruent] to [−obstruent]; and the resulting conjunction, $\begin{bmatrix} -\text{obstruent} \\ -\text{consonantal} \end{bmatrix}$, is unambiguously interpreted as a vowel, as we have claimed in Preliminaries, §2. The naturalness of these processes – assimilation of the quality of a vowel, deletion of a glide, vocalization of a glide – gives some support to our proposal for class VI verbs.

We claim then, to sum up so far, that class VI verbs have a post-vocalic root structure like class IV or class V, but also contain a pre-vocalic glide. They therefore undergo, like other strong verbs, qualitative and quantitative ablaut. However, the presence of the glide accounts for the difference in quality in PRES, PRET$_2$ and PART forms and the difference in quantity in PRET$_1$. The following rules are required. In the first place, a rule vocalizing the glide before a low back vowel:

(1.23) *Glide vocalization*

$$\begin{bmatrix} +\text{obs} \\ -\text{cons} \end{bmatrix} \rightarrow [-\text{obs}] / \underline{\hspace{2cm}} \begin{bmatrix} V \\ +\text{low} \end{bmatrix}$$

Then we need a rule to assimilate a vowel which is not $\begin{bmatrix} +\text{back} \\ +\text{low} \end{bmatrix}$ to the glide, ordered after (1.23):

(1.24) *Vowel-glide assimilation*

$$V \rightarrow [+\text{low}] / \begin{bmatrix} +\text{obs} \\ -\text{cons} \end{bmatrix} \underline{\hspace{2cm}}$$

(Again – cf. qualitative ablaut – the low vowel is [+back] by convention.) Finally, the glide must be deleted (where it has not been vocalized):

(1.25) *Glide deletion*

$$\begin{bmatrix} +\text{obs} \\ -\text{cons} \end{bmatrix} \rightarrow \emptyset$$

We therefore propose the derivations below (1.26) for the vowels in the various forms of *faran*. We use 'A' as a symbol for the glide. This ignores the placement of syllabicity and the Germanic accent.

In suggesting such a synchronic analysis for class VI, we are of course aware that 'laryngeals' have been invoked in attempts to explain the historical development of the members of classes VI and VII (cf. the interpretation of class VII we outline in appendix I) – see e.g. Lehmann

(1.26)

	PRES	PRET$_1$	PRET$_2$	PART
Qualitative ablaut (1.19)	Ae	Aa	Ae	Ae
Pre-Germanic accent (1.17)	Ae	Aa	A'e	A'e
Quantitative ablaut (1.16)	Ae	Aa	A'ē	A'e
Glide vocalization (1.23)	Ae	aa	Aē	Ae
Vowel-glide assimilation (1.24)	Aa	aa	Aā	Aa
Glide deletion (1.25)	a	aa	ā	a
Lowness assignment (1.21)	a	oo	ō	a

(1955: 69–70). However, this remains controversial (and may continue to be so within the frame of reference in which the debate has thus far been conducted), and the details are uncertain. It may be that the historical placement in the root of the 'laryngeal' and aspects of its phonetic character (there is a variety of views on this) differ from the relevant parts of our analysis. We have attempted to argue for the presence in the lexical representations for these verbs of a segment of the kind we have outlined on the basis of the synchronic evidence alone. Such historical developments and reinterpretations as might have occurred in this case are quite usual, given the appropriate conditions. In view of the complexity of the issues involved, we shall not dwell here on the relation between these parts of the synchronic phonology and their history. But we do find it interesting, and potentially significant, that historical and comparative investigations and our examination of the synchronic phonology of OE have led to the positing of a segment of a certain phonetic character (or at least of a certain 'phonetic effect') in this group of items.

However, it should be noted that the analysis we have proposed for class VI (and for class VII – see appendix I) is in violation of the strong form of Kiparsky's (1968a) 'alternation condition', which says that 'absolute neutralization' – the occurrence of a segment in underlying representation which never appears in surface forms – is impermissible. The prevocalic laryngeal in classes VI and VII undergoes absolute neutralization; it never appears phonetically, since it is either deleted or vocalized. We have based our analysis on the naturalness of the processes involving the glide. In particular, it provides a source for the 'colouring' of the following vowel in PRES, PRET$_2$ and PART of class VI, and it provides the first element in a bimoric vowel sequence (by vocalization before a vowel agreeing in lowness) in PRET$_1$. If it can be shown that these phenomena can be allowed for, without loss of explanatory power, in terms of some 'rule feature' (or in some other way not requiring a neutralized glide), then we must withdraw our laryngeal.[1] Otherwise, it would appear that the 'alternation condition' should not be retained in its strong form.[2]

[1] One possibility that suggests itself to us runs as follows. Suppose we adopt the alternative for lexical representation of the root vowel in strong verbs suggested in §7, whereby it is specified as $\begin{bmatrix} u \text{ high} \\ u \text{ low} \\ u \text{ back} \\ u \text{ round} \end{bmatrix}$. By the marking conventions this becomes $\begin{bmatrix} -\text{high} \\ +\text{low} \\ +\text{back} \\ -\text{round} \end{bmatrix}$.

Qualitative ablaut (1.19) can now be modified in two ways: part (b) can be eliminated, and part (a) can be replaced by a formulation by which all root vowels are $\begin{bmatrix} -\text{low} \\ -\text{back} \end{bmatrix}$ if they are not [$\overline{\text{PP}}$] or if they come before an inflexional vowel (i.e. throughout the paradigm with the exception of PRET_1, which remains [a]). Consider now class VI. We can enter them in the lexicon as 'normal' class IV or V verbs but associated with an exception feature [−(1.19)]. Throughout the paradigm the root vowel will thus remain [a]. However, we now encounter difficulties in deriving the long vowels in the preterite forms. Even the PRET_2 vowels will fail to meet the conditions for PRET_2 lengthening which requires that the vowel be [−low]. Some minor rule with the desired consequences would apparently have to be introduced. It is quite likely that the degree of irregularity suggested by this characterizes class VI eventually. Its members certainly show historically the instability Kiparsky notes for cases of absolute neutralization. But presumably this development starts from a stage at which neutralization has been introduced but not reinterpreted (in terms of exception features, for instance). It is not certain that OE has left this stage behind. We therefore hesitate to abandon the laryngeal analysis for class VI, and even class VII.

[2] Kiparsky's unwillingness to allow absolute neutralization (which in cases like the one we are dealing with he rather contemptuously calls 'diacritic use of phonological features') ends up, paradoxically, as something very like the Saussurean dichotomy. For instance, he shows in his paper that it is possible to analyse the harmonic properties of the so-called 'neutral' /e:/ in Hungarian: cf. héj-am 'my rind' but kés-em 'my knife' by deriving those é that show back harmony from an underlying unround back vowel /ə:/, which is then neutralized in surface representation, and collapses with é < /e:/. He notes further that there is in fact evidence for this vowel historically. But he rejects the analysis (a) because it can be handled by means of an exception feature, and (b) apparently because of the history. That is, he claims in essence that knowledge of history is a crutch for the synchronic linguist, which in effect as we said above is equivalent to the strong form of Saussure's dichotomy.

There are several oddities about this kind of claim. First, it seems rather perverse to assume that a solution requiring a rule-feature is in any way more 'natural' than one based on so universal a phonetic phenomenon as assimilation. Second, there are degrees of historical depth, and not all analyses which use segments of the same type as happened to occur historically are equally to be faulted on these grounds. Thus the unround back vowel in the Hungarian examples seems reasonable, in a way that an analysis of NE that derived right, regular, ruler and rectum from /rekt-/ would not be.

Finally, the ultimate consequence of this claim would be a rejection of the notion that underlying representations can persist. The gains we have made through such demonstrations as Chomsky and Halle's of the central role of vowel-shift and trisyllabic laxing would be undone. As just one example, Chomsky and Halle's treatment

6 Long vowels

Before concluding, we must return briefly to the question of the two sources for long vowels exemplified in the last line of (1.26). The nucleus in *fōr* is developed as a sequence of two $\begin{bmatrix} +\text{back} \\ +\text{low} \end{bmatrix}$ vowels which are then shifted to [−low] by some modification of rule (1.21) (lowness assignment). However, as formulated immediately above, the rule affects [+long] vowels only, i.e., in particular, those vowels which result from the operation of part A (b) of quantitative ablaut (1.16), which lengthens the accented vowel in the PRET$_2$ forms of classes IV–VI (*bǣron, cwǣdon, fōron, bōcon*). But we also have to allow for a similar shift (from low to mid) in the case of the geminate vowel developed in PRET$_1$ of class VI (*fōr, bōc*) by vocalization of the glide. The original lowness assignment rule was formulated at a stage in the present argument when we had not yet considered interpreting 'long' vowels as geminates. The developments of the nuclei in PRES and PRET$_1$ of classes I and II appear to require such an interpretation. Similarly, it seems clear that the 'long' vowel in PRET$_1$ of class VI, which is derived by vocalization of a prevocalic glide, involves a geminate at some stage. But this geminate undergoes a process (lowness assignment) which we have restricted to [+long] vowels. This suggests that we now reinterpret the A part of quantitative ablaut, which is the source for the [+long] vowels. If we regard this as involving epenthesis of an identical vowel (forming a geminate nucleus), then the rule for lowness assignment can be formulated as a unitary process, and 'long' vowels can be interpreted in a uniform way as involving a divocalic sequence with identical members.

Accordingly, we propose the following revision to part A of the quantitative ablaut:

(1.27) *Quantitative ablaut A: revised*

$$\text{SD:} \qquad [+\text{accent}]$$
$$\text{I}$$
$$\text{SC:} \qquad \text{I} \rightarrow \text{I} \quad \text{I}$$

of *right/righteous, paradigm/paradigmatic, sign/signify*, makes these forms totally regular as a result of assuming the velar fricatives [x ɣ] (*SPE*: 233–4). It would seem that to rule out the regularities simply because of a rather poorly supported principle would cost more – even in terms of phonetic naturalness – than it would save. (For further arguments of this kind, cf. Hyman 1970. And for some tentative reversals of the position we take here, see ch. VI.)

The structural change is simply a copying of the complete specification for any vowel that meets the SD. However, the right member of the geminate will be marked as [−syll], by the syllabicity conventions discussed in Preliminaries, and [−accent] by the Germanic accent rule. If we assume that vowel-glide assimilation (1.24) precedes quantitative ablaut, then the 'copy' in the case of class VI PRET$_2$ forms will be assigned the appropriate $\begin{bmatrix} +\text{back} \\ +\text{low} \end{bmatrix}$ specification.

Lowness assignment can now be interpreted as referring to appropriately specified geminates. We reformulate it once more:

(1.28) *Lowness assignment: second version*

$$\text{SD:} \quad \underset{\text{I}}{\begin{bmatrix} \text{V} \\ -\text{high} \\ \alpha\text{back} \end{bmatrix}} \quad \underset{\text{2}}{\begin{bmatrix} \text{V} \\ -\text{high} \\ \alpha\text{back} \end{bmatrix}}$$

$$\text{SC: I } 2 \rightarrow \underset{\text{I}}{\begin{bmatrix} -\alpha\text{low} \\ \alpha\text{back} \end{bmatrix}} \quad \underset{\text{2}}{\begin{bmatrix} -\alpha\text{low} \\ \alpha\text{back} \end{bmatrix}}$$

But this now raises some problems relating to the fact that only certain of the vowel geminates that meet its SD do in fact undergo (1.28). For lowness assignment fails, for instance, with respect to the vowel in *hēr* 'here', if we assume that it has underlying /ee/, and also in *h r* 'hair' if we assume underlying /aa/ (cf. §3). In the second instance we could relate this to the prior operation of backness switching (1.8) for long vowels, but in that case we must explain why lowness assignment fails in *bād*, which goes from [ææ] to [aa] by backness switching.

What seems to be involved here is a (global) derivational constraint on the application of (1.28) lowness assignment (on such constraints see Kisseberth 1969). This constraint says basically that lowness assignment applies only to the results of phonological rules producing a sequence of two vowels where lexically there is only one. That is, original (lexical) divocalic nuclei are excluded from lowness assignment; on the other hand, derived divocalic nuclei are excluded from backness switching (1.8). Compare the derivations in (1.29) below.

The original divocalic nuclei (*hēr, hǣr, bād*) do not undergo lowness assignment (even if they meet the SD) but do, where they meet the SD, undergo backness switching. We will return to this in chapter II, where we will also consider these rules in relation to interconnected processes like 'retraction' of [æ] before nasals and AFB.

(1.29)

Input	/ee/	/aa/	/Vi/	/V/	/AV/	/AV/
Qualitative ablaut (1.19)			ai	e	Ae	Aa
Glide vocalization (1.23)						aa
Vowel-glide assimilation (1.24)					Aa	
Pre-Germanic accent (1.17)				'e	A'a	
Quantitative ablaut (1.27)				ee	Aaa	
Glide deletion (1.25)					aa	
Lowness assignment (1.28)				ææ	oo	oo
DHH (to be given)			aæ			
AFB (to be given)			ææ			
Backness switching (1.8)		ææ	aa			
Output	ee	ææ	aa	ææ	oo	oo
Example	*hēr*	*hǣr*	*bād*	*cwǣdon*	*fōron*	*fōr*

7   Apologia for unspecified vowels

We claimed above that the root vowels in strong verbs (and presumably also in related forms) are unspecified except for the major class features (which do not include [vocalic] or [syllabic], for reasons discussed in the Preliminaries above). Now, having reviewed the processes affecting these vowels – in particular the quantitative and qualitative ablaut – we can discuss the motivations for this claim in more detail, and formulate in a preliminary way the kind of lexical entry that might be appropriate for such vowels.

Our major motivation is the fact that the complete set of alternations in the strong verb paradigms can be specified by rules which take into account the syntactic and phonological environments of the radical vowels. These rules, it is clear, are of such a type that they offer no very strong support for one particular (articulatorily specified) lexical representation as opposed to any other. The various articulatory specifications are distributed in such a way that the most natural account would seem to be a lexically unspecified segment.

Let us say, however, that we want to choose a specific vowel, in order to avoid partially unspecified phonemic matrices. The general distribution seems to be such that the particular vowel that could be best supported would probably be [e]. We might look at this first in terms of lexical 'complexity', i.e. those evaluative judgements that would be arrived at on the basis of say the theory of marking. In this case we could, for instance, remove the first part of qualitative ablaut (1.19), which specifies the vowels in strong verbs as $\begin{bmatrix} -\text{back} \\ -\text{low} \end{bmatrix}$, and rather enter such verbs in the lexicon with the specifications $\begin{bmatrix} -\text{back} \\ u\ \text{low} \\ m\ \text{high} \\ u\ \text{round} \end{bmatrix}$. In terms of a sim-

plicity metric based on markedness, however, such a representation would be more 'costly' than the lexical entry for say *dæġ* 'day', which would be $\begin{bmatrix} u\ \text{back} \\ u\ \text{low} \\ u\ \text{high} \\ u\ \text{round} \end{bmatrix}$. This would be indeed paradoxical, since the most

obvious fact about the strong verbs, if our analysis holds up, is that the quality of the vowel in any part of the paradigm for a regular verb of classes I–VI is predictable by rule. This is obscured if the entries for strong verb radical vowels are more complex than some of the entries for the root vowels of items where specification of the nonmajor class features is essential for distinguishing them from other possible items, and determining which phonological rules will apply. Moreover, the inclusion of [−back] in the specification for each strong verb would seem (insofar as we can specify things like this) to outweigh the cost of rule (1.19), part (a).

But, still within the markedness and cost-assignment framework, one might counter this argument in the following way. Suppose we enter the root vowel of strong verbs in the lexicon as $\begin{bmatrix} u\ \text{high} \\ u\ \text{low} \\ u\ \text{back} \\ u\ \text{round} \end{bmatrix}$.

Qualitative ablaut can then either be retained as in (1.19), or indeed simplified. Specifically, part (b) can be eliminated and part (a) reformu-lated to assign $\begin{bmatrix} -\text{low} \\ -\text{back} \end{bmatrix}$ to any root vowel that is not [$\overline{\text{PP}}$] or is followed in the same word by another vowel, i.e. in parts of the paradigm that bear an inflexion. Thus, only the vowel in the PRET$_1$ forms will retain the [+low] specification resulting from the application of the marking conventions. However, this proposal has the rather strange consequence that the 'basic' forms in the strong verb paradigm are now the preterite indicative singular first and third persons: other parts of the paradigm have their vowel specifications derived by phonological rules. And the basic objection is still not met. The fact that strong verbs are not distinguished from one another in terms of the specification of the root vowel remains uncharacterized. Their uniform lexical representation as 'unmarked' for [high, low, back, round] (or whatever) is apparently fortuitous.

So if we try to assign cost to lexical representations of the root vowels of strong verbs on a markedness basis (which we do not think is correct, anyhow), we find that these verbs, whose vowels are clearly dependent on rules operating on postvocalic segments, must have more complex entries than other items where vocalic distinctiveness is idiosyncratic. Or we find that we are forced to choose as 'basic' forms counterintuitive parts of the paradigm. And if we use some other kind of criterion for choosing the 'basic' vowel, the decision is arbitrary. As far as we can see, then, either the strong verbs all have radical /V/, with no further specification, or we give up the idea of rule-governed predictability, assign the six classes to six taxonomic categories with purely morphological markers, and enter all the tense-forms as lexical suppletions.

We must now attempt to clarify what we mean by 'unspecified'. We intend by this that the articulatory features of the nuclear vowel in strong verbs are not marked as + or − or *u* or *m*. We have argued that any representation of this kind is undesirable because it fails to capture the essential fact concerning these vowels, i.e. that their articulatory specification is completely determined by synchronic rules of OE. How then are such vowels represented in the lexicon? We do not propose that for each feature apart from the major class ones there is simply an empty cell. Rather we introduce a convention for unspecified articulation based on the notion of bi-parametric matrices discussed in appendix II. There we argue for the relative independence of the phonatory and articulatory gestures, so that it is natural for a rule to refer to either (in its entirety) and leave the other unchanged. For instance, there are rules whose SDs or SCs require identity between segments of articulation-as-a-whole. We propose a notation whereby this can be represented by variables outside the bracket for the articulatory (or phonatory) gesture – for example:

(1.30)
$$\begin{bmatrix} +\text{consonantal} \\ \alpha[\text{artic}] \end{bmatrix}$$

With regard to the notion 'unspecified vowel', we extend this convention to allow for lexical entries of the form, roughly:

$$(1.31) \qquad \begin{bmatrix} \text{V} \\ \text{o [artic]} \end{bmatrix}$$

i.e. V with unspecified articulation. We return to such questions concerning the lexicon in ch. VI. We observe only that [o [artic]] is not merely another way of representing empty cells that are filled by 'blank-filling' rules. A vowel like (1.31) is a *systematic phoneme* (call it an 'archi-vowel') which has independent status as a member of the lexical inventory, along with the set of vowels that happen to have specified articulation.

II *The Anglo-Frisian brightening*

1 Introduction

In this chapter and the next we will examine the phonological processes reflected in the OE graphic alternations *æ* ~ *ea* ~ *a*, and *e* ~ *eo*. The alternation *a* ~ *æ* is traditionally said to be due to the 'Anglo-Frisian brightening' (*Aufhellung*) or 'fronting'; and the alternations *æ* (*a*) ~ *ea*, *e* ~ *eo* to 'breaking' or 'fracture' (*Brechung*), or in some cases to 'velar umlaut'. We will deal only with the first of these in this chapter; but first we will sketch out the contexts for both of them, as an aid to historical and synchronic orientation as we proceed.

We find both breaking and AFB represented in the paradigms of (non-nasal) class III strong verbs like *helpan, healp, melcan, mealc* (historically **helpan, *halp > *hælp* [AFB] > *healp* [breaking] or *weorþan, wearþ* (historically **werþan > weorþan* [breaking], **warþ > *wærþ* [AFB] > *wearþ* [breaking]). The historical **a* in the 'broken-æ' forms is well-motivated: it represents in most cases an IE *o*-grade perfect, as against an *e*-grade present (cf. Gr. *léipō, le-lóipa*, etc.).

Now we saw in chapter 1 that there seems to be good reason for accepting as output of the synchronic ablaut rules paradigms which show [a] as the vowel of the preterite singular of class III verbs, e.g. [helpan, halp], [werÞan, warÞ] (for the representation [Þ] here see ch. VI, §2.2.3). So if we want to explain the apparently 'irregular' forms (cf. *bindan, band*) even within a synchronic grammar, we are going to have to have a rule somewhere that looks very like what the handbooks call the 'sound-change' breaking.

Now we observe that in the strong verbs there are two sets of alternations that breaking must account for: *a* ~ *ea* (cf. *band, wearþ*) and *e* ~ *eo* (cf. *helpan, weorþan*). And we further observe that the ablaut rules have supplied us with [a] in those places where *ea* appears in the written forms. This, plus the historical evidence, and the clearly morphophonemic nature not only of the alternation of *ea* with *æ*, but of both of these with *a*, suggests that our synchronic grammar is going to need a rule or set of

[59]

rules generating [æ] from [a]: in other words a synchronic parallel to the (historical) AFB.

The AFB gets its name because it is supposed to characterize an isogloss setting apart an 'Anglo-Frisian' subgroup within the so-called 'Ingvaeonic' (North-Sea Germanic) subgroup of West Germanic: it shows up in such contrasts as OE *dæġ*, OFris. *deg* 'day' vs. ON *dagr*, Go. *dags*, OHG *tag*, etc. Before discussing the synchronic rule, let us sum up the historical evidence, as generally described in the handbooks. Since the AFB is crucial to breaking, as the [æ] produced by it serve as input to the breaking rule, we will discuss the developments of both processes, following the standard accounts, e.g. Campbell (1959), Wright (1925), Brunner (1965), Lehnert (1965).

(a) *Anglo-Frisian brightening.* Pre-OE **a > æ* except in certain contexts, e.g. before *w*, before a nasal cluster, and before a consonant plus a back vowel. (We will discuss these contexts in detail below.)

(b) *Breaking and retraction.* At a later stage, *æ*, being a nonback vowel, 'broke' or diphthongized before certain back consonants or clusters, especially [x] (*h*) or [r l] plus a consonant. Where breaking did not occur, as in Anglian dialects before [l], the [æ] was 'retracted' to [a]: thus WS *eald*, Angl. *ald* < **ald* (cf. G. *alt*).

(c) *Late OE mergers.* First *ea* from breaking (and other sources, such as 'back umlaut': cf. ch. III) was monophthongized to *æ*, and this *æ* 'fell in with' other OE *æ* (i.e. those that had not undergone breaking). At a later period, in most OE dialects, all *æ* 'from whatever source' merged with 'original' OE *a*.

The historical developments are shown schematically below in (2.1):

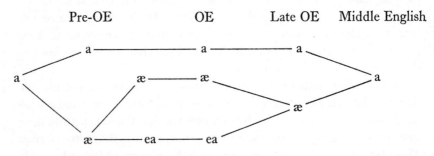

| Pre-OE | OE | Late OE | Middle English |

Leaving aside 'exceptional' forms and dialect variations, it does seem that the virtual identity of (historical) input and output argues strongly for development and gradual loss of a set of related rules affecting low vowels: that in fact all OE forms showing *a*, *æ*, *ea* have the same underlying vowel from pre-OE through (early) Middle English. (In Middle English, the low vowel, judging from comparative and other evidence, was not back but front: see the discussion in Lass 1973b.)

At any rate, if the development shown in (2.1) is substantially correct, we seem to have a series of 'splits' and 'mergers' that can be characterized overall as 'elaboration' followed by 'simplification' of the grammar. The early development, up to OE, can be characterized as 'elaboration', and the later ones as 'simplification' (cf. Kiparsky 1968b; Traugott 1969). That is, over time a set of rules develops, and after a period of maximum diversification in rules and outputs, the variety becomes increasingly restricted until all outputs but one disappear. The overall process then looks like this:

(2.2)

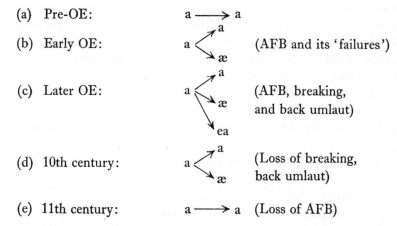

(a) Pre-OE: a ⟶ a

(b) Early OE: a ⟨ a / æ   (AFB and its 'failures')

(c) Later OE: a ⟨ a / æ / ea   (AFB, breaking, and back umlaut)

(d) 10th century: a ⟨ a / æ   (Loss of breaking, back umlaut)

(e) 11th century: a ⟶ a   (Loss of AFB)

(Note that we have omitted here any consideration of the segment represented in some OE dialects as *o* < pre-OE **a* before nasals. This seems to be merely a variant of *a*, that is a non-AFB form of some kind that we cannot specify any further.) We shall take up again various considerations having to do with the 'loss of diphthongs' in §8 of the following chapter. We turn now to the AFB in detail, both historical and synchronic.

2   Anglo-Frisian brightening as a 'sound-change'

The vowel system on which AFB operated was probably of the type shown below in (2.3):

(2.3)   i   u
                                e   o
                                        a

That is, a three-height, five-vowel system of an extremely common type.

The AFB in outline (but in more detail than given above) seems to have worked as follows:

(a) WGmc *a > $æ$ in closed syllables, and in open syllables if the following vowel was nonback. Thus the paradigm *dæġ/dæġes/dæġe* 'day, n. acc. sing., gen. sing., dat. sing.', but *dagas/daga/dagum* 'id. pl.', *bæc* 'back', *snæġl* 'snail', *hræfn* 'raven'.

(b) WGmc *a remains a in open syllables where the following vowel is back: or where the following vowel was back historically but where there is a synchronic front vowel: *faran* 'go', *nacod* 'naked', *lagu* 'water', the plural forms of *dæġ* cited above, *staþelian* 'establish' < *$staþulōjan$, *macian* 'make' < *$makōjan$. (In the class II weak verbs like *macian*, *stician* 'stick', *prician* 'prick', etc. the lack of palatalization in the surface forms suggests some reflex of the historical pre-inflexional vowel in the synchronic underlying forms. This is further borne out by the OHG cognates, e.g. *salbōn* 'anoint', OE *sealfian*. Cf. ch. IV, §8.)

WGmc *a also remained before *w*: *clawu* 'claw'; before nasals: *mann* 'man', *hand* 'hand'; and before geminate consonants of whatever origin, if before a back vowel: *habban* 'have' (vs. pret. *hæfde*), *abbod* 'abbot', *mattoc* 'mattock'. Some cases of $æ$ for expected a, e.g. *hnæppian* 'nap' beside *hnappian* are supposed to be due to 'analogy', as (inversely) are forms like *paþes*, *paþe* (gen. sing., dat. sing. of *pæþ* 'path'): but of course if the variation $a \sim æ$ is predictable from underlying representations in /a/, then these sporadic inconsistencies in the orthography need not represent 'analogy' or sound change, or anything phonetic. They are rather the same sort of thing we will discuss in chapter IV with reference to the graphs *c* and *g*: a capitalization on the possibility of using a single character to represent any member of the set of possible phonetic realizations of an underlying segment. If the alternations of the phonetic equivalents of *a*, *æ*, *ea* are predictable by environment, then the graphs may be equivalent (even if all possible equivalences are not sanctioned by tradition), since only one value could possibly be represented in a single environment. (And of course values much further apart can be represented by single graphs, e.g. [ɪ], [ai] by *i* in NE *divinity/divine*, and so on.) Thus, one cannot conclude that 'lapses' from the traditional rather 'phonetic' orthography into a more morpho-phonemic type have either systematic or phonetic significance; in cases like those we have been looking at, the writer's (or reader's) knowledge of the language dictates the necessary value for any given environment.

(c) WGmc **a* appears as *æ* when it is followed (or was followed historically) by an umlauted vowel in the next syllable, e.g. *æþele* 'noble' < **aþali* (cf. OS *aðali*), *mægden* 'maiden' (cf. OHG *magatīn*). This is synchronically of course simply one or the other of the cases listed under (a), i.e. the open-syllable environment where the following vowel is nonback, or the closed-syllable environment.

There is one problem, however, which is raised by the behaviour of the output of AFB under *i*-umlaut. And this is that historically the *i*-umlaut of WGmc **a* is apparently normally *e* in OE, not *æ*; whereas the umlaut of long **ā* is *ǣ* (cf. *hāl* 'whole', *hǣlan* 'heal' < **hailjan*). Now if as we will show in chapter IV the umlaut normally operates stepwise along any given parameter (back vowels go to front, low front vowels go to mid), then the vowel whose umlaut is [e] must be [æ] or [o]: but certainly not [a], whose umlaut is [æ]. Where AFB is operative, the development is straightforward: in *nerian* (with WGmc **a*) the *e* is from [æ] by *i*-umlaut, the original [a] having been fronted by AFB. But cases like *mann/menn*, etc., unambiguously show umlaut of WGmc **a*, not *æ* (since in particular AFB fails before a nasal).

So we are forced to the conclusion that the input to *i*-umlaut must be [æ]; and at the same time, as we saw in (b) above, the presence of a following nasal blocks AFB, so that there cannot be any [æ]. There are various ways of handling this, but we will postpone the discussion until we have formulated the rule in more detail. At that point we will show how we can accommodate in a synchronic grammar of OE the two conflicting facts: (a) that AFB 'fails' before nasals, and (b) that the umlaut of WGmc *a* before nasals in OE is [e], not [æ]. And we will show further that it is possible to do this in a quite natural way.

3   The rule for Anglo-Frisian brightening

If we want to work the AFB into the synchronic phonology of OE, we must account for two sets of forms which might reasonably be said to involve it:

(2.4)   (a) 'unchanged' short [a]: *mann, dagas, macian, abbod.*
   (b) [æ] from [a]: *bæc, dæġ, hræfn.*

Forms showing 'velar umlaut' like *ealu* 'ale' will (like the 'broken' forms) be discussed in the next chapter; they will, however, be of some relevance to the discussion in §4 of the present one. But before formulating a rule to cover any forms conceivably resulting from AFB, we must consider one preliminary question: whether the long vowels (including diphthongs) are to be subject to it. The forms which have phonetic [ææ] and [aa] derive from various sources, as we have shown in chapter I. For instance, the strong verb $PRET_1$ forms *bād* and *drāf* have their source in [ai], the low back first vowel being due to qualitative ablaut (1.19). Forms with [ææ] have two sources (aside from those derived from [aa] via *i*-umlaut, to which we will return in ch. IV): [ee] from quantitative ablaut (1.27) as in *cwǣdon, bǣron,* etc.; and [aa], which we have suggested as a synchronic as well as a historical source for the vowels in *hǣr* 'hair' etc. However, the appropriate superficial distribution of [ææ] and [aa] in these forms is provided for without assuming AFB for long vowels. The nucleus of *bād* is derived via DHH (which we formulate in ch. III (3.15)), with AFB acting on the first vowel and backness switching (1.8) operating on the resulting geminate. This last rule also derives [ææ] in *hǣr* from underlying /aa/. The shift from [ee] to [ææ] in *cwǣdon* is accomplished by the lowness assignment rule for derived geminates (1.28), i.e. geminates which come from original simple vowels. We can summarize these derivations as follows:

(2.5)

Input	/Vi/	/aa/	/V/
Qualitative ablaut (1.19)	ai		e
Quantitative ablaut (1.27)			ee
DHH (to be given)	aæ		
AFB (to be given)	æx		
Backness switching (1.8)	aa	æx	
Lowness assignment (1.28)			æx
Example	*bād*	*hǣr*	*cwǣdon*

Given these processes, and in particular backness switching of low geminates, we assume that those instances of [aa] that are not derived from [ai] as an output of qualitative ablaut are to be interpreted as containing lexical /ai/. We extend a similar interpretation to those instances of *ēa* (i.e. [æa]) which are not produced by quantitative ablaut. Thus, the nucleus in *bēad* comes from the [au] which results from quantitative ablaut in strong verbs class II; whereas the [au] in, say, *bēam* 'tree' is lexical. Their subsequent derivations involve AFB ([au] → [æu]) followed by DHH ([æu] → [æa]). Clearly, then, we must allow for AFB to affect the first members of clusters like [ai] and [au]. However, the long vowel corresponding to [a] does not itself undergo AFB but is rather subject to backness switching.

AFB thus fails to affect [a] in a geminate: we shall call this 'failure environment (a)'. We have already observed that it also fails before a single or geminate consonant plus a following back vowel, as in *dagas, macian* < /makojan/: we shall call this 'failure environment (b)'. AFB also fails before a nasal (*mann, camb*), except in an umlaut environment (*sendan* < [sændjan] < /sandjan/); this will be 'failure environment (c)'. As a first approximation, we now formulate the rule as one which assigns [+back] to a [+low] vowel in certain environments, but which otherwise marks it as [−back]:[1]

(2.6) *Anglo-Frisian brightening: first version* ('Short low vowel backness assignment')

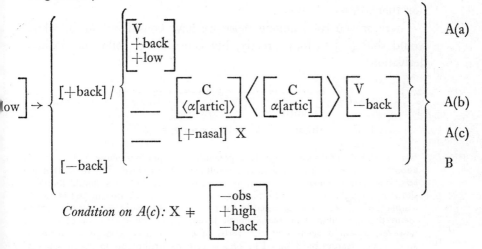

[1] There are however certain 'failures' of AFB which must apparently be attributed to an exception feature. Consider the singular present indicative paradigm for *faran*:

3   LOE

The angled parentheses in A(b) allow for geminate consonants before the back vowel. The subrules are to be taken, according to Preliminaries, p. 7 n., as simultaneously applicable, not conjunctively ordered.

We turn now to consider some evidence which suggests that for certain environments (under A), the process of retraction should not be collapsed as we have done in (2.6) with the fronting; i.e. that fronting and retraction, in some instances, are not adjacent rules.

4   Doubts and retractions

Now let us consider a form like *nōmon*, the PRET$_2$ of *niman* 'take'. We have allowed, under our ablaut rules, for [oo] only in strong verbs of class VI; but *niman* is class IV (cf. its other forms: *nam* (beside 'analogical' *nōm*), *-numen*), in which the vowel of PRET$_2$ is normally [ææ] (< [ee] by lowness assignment (1.28)). Historically the distinctiveness of *nōmon* is considered to be associated with the nasal consonant immediately following the radical vowel, – as is (cf. ch. I, §2) the occurrence of [i] rather than [e] in PRES and [u] rather than [o] in PART. It seems worth considering whether some regular synchronic process underlies the [oo] in *nōmon* (and in its counterpart *c(w)ōmon*, PRET$_2$ of *cuman* 'come'). Otherwise verbs like this will have to be specified in the lexicon as exceptional. True, they are not numerous, and this would represent no great cost; but there is an independently motivated derivation that will handle them.

There are no rules among those we have considered so far which would shift [ee] to [oo] directly; but consider the following possible derivation:

(2.7)   e———→ ee———→ ææ———→ aa———→ oo

                 Quantitative   Lowness
                 ablaut   assignment

---

fare/færst/færð. The second and third person forms appear to show AFB, but it is absent from the first person despite the following front vowel. But recall that the second and third person inflexions contain an underlying /i/; they should therefore show not only AFB but also *i*-umlaut, as in *nerian*. What we find in fact is merely *i*-umlaut of [a], AFB having failed in their case also. In traditional historical treatments this is attributed to 'paradigmatic levelling'. In the synchronic phonology, however, it would seem that the verbs of class VI have associated with them an exception feature blocking AFB. This is perhaps attributable to the presence of the prevocalic laryngeal; it could then be framed as a 'readjustment rule' for laryngeal verbs. But see ch. VI, §6.

The first two stages are the same as for the PRET$_2$ form of any verb in classes IV–VI. The last stage appears to be a second operation of lowness assignment; and this can be allowed for if we formulate this rule as being applicable to any derived geminate that meets the SD. The crucial stage is [ææ] → [aa]. Now, we have associated with lowness assignment (1.28) and backness switching (1.8) a constraint that says that they are applicable only to derived and original divocalic sequences, respectively. Thus, the shift from [ææ] to [aa] in the case of *nōmon* cannot be interpreted as the result of backness switching. This is accomplished instead by a process of retraction before nasals.

We have already provided for retraction of [æ] to [a] as one of the 'failures' of AFB (A(c)). Also, it was necessary to exclude from A(c) in (2.6) nasals in an *i*-umlaut environment which appear to show AFB followed by *i*-umlaut, as in *sendan*:

$$(2.8) \qquad\qquad a \longrightarrow æ \longrightarrow e$$

$$\qquad\qquad\qquad\quad \text{AFB} \quad \textit{i}\text{-Umlaut}$$

However, suppose that we now remove case A(c) from (2.6), and have instead a later rule retracting short and long [æ] before nasals. This can also be ordered after *i*-umlaut, thus accomplishing what the condition on A(c) was intended to ensure by allowing retraction to apply only to those vowels which have not been umlauted to [e]: the vowel in *sendan* will have been umlauted before retraction applies, thus removing the need for any analogue to the condition on case A(c) required by our original formulation.[1] So we can eliminate case A(c) from (2.6), and

The historical facts seem to be as follows. In early OE, the AFB rule collapsed both fronting and retraction as adjacent: that is, the fronting failed in all pre-nasal environments, so that the *i*-umlaut of WG *a was quite uniformly *æ*, not *e*, i.e. there is no umlaut of [æ] before nasals. The *æ*-forms are quite common (even uniform in some cases) in older texts like the *Epinal Glossary*, the *Leiden Riddle*, Bede's *Historia* (in Germanic names in the Latin text, like *Hængist*), and so on. In later texts these are fairly uniformly replaced by *e*-forms, though some *æ*-spellings persist as late as the *Rushworth Glosses* (Campbell 1959: 74).

Campbell explains the *æ* > *e* change (74) as due to a kind of 'secondary' umlaut: 'the palatalized consonant or consonant group early caused a further change of *æ* to *e*'. But (except in the case of velars, which are palatalized by preceding as well as following vowels anyhow) there is no evidence for palatalization of the segment or group between the umlauted vowel and the umlauting suffix as an integral part of the umlaut; or even for its having taken place at all. The umlaut looks like a simple case of metaphony, and the historical facts can be explained just as easily on the assumption that nasal retraction was at some point reordered to follow AFB and umlaut. This way – synchronically – the earlier forms show *æ*, i.e. the umlaut of *a* add a rule that retracts low vowels before nasals. We will not formulate this rule now, since we intend, in the section that follows, to handle this process by means of a general convention for nasal influence.

To conclude this section, we take note of an argument put forward by Campbell (1959: §§157–8), that the notion of 'retraction' or 'restoration' is more generally applicable. He provides support for this only with regard to case A(b) in (2.6), and he cites in particular pairs like *slēan* (PGmc **slaxan*) and *dragan*. However, this alternation deserves our attention. We will show below (ch. III) that the diphthongs in 'contracted' verbs like *slēan* and *sēon* are as elsewhere derived from divocalic sequences containing as first elements respectively [æ-] and [e-]. They originate in the 'breaking' of [æ] and [e] before a (subsequently deleted) voiceless velar fricative. This would appear to show then, that the vowel in *slēan* did undergo part B of AFB followed by breaking (and loss of [x]), and that 'retraction' before back vowels (as exemplified in *dragan*) is not to be collapsed with AFB, part B as a single rule. (Retraction fails in the case of *slēan*, etc. because of the removal of the intervening consonant by 'loss of h': cf. ch. III, §6, and rule (3.26).)

We can therefore now reformulate AFB this way:

(2.9) *Anglo-Frisian brightening: revised*

$$
\begin{bmatrix} V \\ +\text{low} \end{bmatrix} \rightarrow
\begin{cases}
[+\text{back}] \;/\; \begin{bmatrix} V \\ +\text{low} \end{bmatrix} & \text{A} \\[2ex]
[-\text{back}] & \text{B}
\end{cases}
$$

We also introduce a new rule of retraction of [æ] before back vowels:

(2.10) *Retraction of æ before back vowels*

$$
\begin{bmatrix} V \\ +\text{low} \end{bmatrix} \rightarrow [+\text{back}]/\underline{\qquad}
\begin{bmatrix} C \\ \langle\alpha[\text{artic}]\rangle \end{bmatrix}
\left\langle \begin{bmatrix} C \\ \alpha[\text{artic}] \end{bmatrix} \right\rangle
\begin{bmatrix} V \\ +\text{back} \end{bmatrix}
$$

because AFB failed before all nasal groups; and the later forms show the umlaut of *æ*, i.e. *e*, because after reordering nasal influence did not affect AFB.

We assume further that the scattered later examples of *æ*-spellings are merely lexical exceptions, or perhaps in some cases 'fossil' spellings. There is certainly no principled reason to assume that any new rule affects *tout à coup* all lexical items meeting its proper analysis; we must allow for diffusion of rules through the lexicon, and indeed for the possibility that certain items may never be 'reached' at all by certain rules (cf. Wang 1969, Chen 1972).

As formulated, rule (2.10) would affect the second element in [ææ]. This could be avoided by inserting [+syllabic] in the specification on the lefthand side. However, there is an alternative, and generalizable, possibility. That is, a convention for geminates which says that no rule applies to one member unless the other member is also mentioned in the SD. This means that we can retain (2.10) as formulated. Further, we can now eliminate part A(a) from the revised rule (2.9) for AFB that we have just proposed. This subpart was intended to ensure that geminate [aa] was not affected by AFB, since the distribution of [ææ] and [aa] is provided for by another rule, backness switching. We can thus revise AFB even further:

(2.11) *Anglo-Frisian brightening: final version*

$$\begin{bmatrix} V \\ +low \end{bmatrix} \rightarrow [-back]$$

This revision presupposes what we shall refer to as the 'geminate SD convention'.

We must now turn to the characterization of 'nasal retraction', which introduces certain wider considerations. But there is one further possible 'retraction' environment that we must consider before moving on; and this is before *w*. We did not include 'before *w*' as one of the contexts for failure of synchronic AFB. But, historically, we find an [a] for WGmc *a before [w] even when a front vowel follows: thus *awel* 'hook' as well as *clawu* 'claw' (with following back vowel). Synchronically, one might suppose that some such words (which are moreover not numerous) contain an underlying back vowel (with which we can associate retraction of *æ* (2.10)). There are certain instances where this would be difficult to justify, as in the PART form of *sēon, ġesawen*. However, these could be marked with an exception feature (as are verbs like *faran*). Similarly, the historical retraction of [ææ] to [aa] in *ġetāwe* 'armour' need not be interpreted as such synchronically, but rather as a regular development from /ai/. This kind of explanation is not open to us in the case of *sāwon*, the PRET$_2$ form of *sēon*; but this verb is clearly idiosyncratic under any interpretation. We accordingly refrain from proposing a nonminor rule of retraction before [w] for West Saxon. (Similarly, cases of historical 'breaking' of [e(e)] or [i(i)] before [w] are also perhaps to be regarded synchronically as lexical (*þēow* 'servant') or as instances of *u*-umlaut (*hweowol* 'wheel') (cf. ch. III).)

5   A convention for 'nasal influence'

We suggested in §4 that the phonology of OE includes a process retracting a [+low] vowel immediately before a nasal consonant. In chapter I, §2, we formulated a rule (1.3) of pre-nasal raising, which specifies any [−low] vowel as [+high] immediately before a nasal. Thus we find *bindan* vs. *helpan*, and *-bunden* vs. *-holpen*. Now why should nasals have two such disparate but regular effects on immediately preceding vowels? These changes can scarcely be taken as 'assimilations' in any obvious sense.

Let us consider these two rules first in terms of their distributional effects. We observe that the vowel system contains, at the point where pre-nasal raising applies, at least the vowels [i e u o a], and at the point where pre-nasal retraction applies, [i e æ u o a]. After pre-nasal raising, the system contains, in the relevant environment, only the proper subset [i u a], since [e] has been raised to [i] and [o] to [u]. And after pre-nasal retraction, which retracts [æ] to [a], the system is again, in that environment, [i u a]. So the effect of the two rules, which at the outset appear not to have anything really in common, is that of a 'functional conspiracy' in the sense of Kisseberth (1970a, c; see also Lass 1973c). In pre-nasal environments, one rule in essence deletes all occurrences of [e o], and the other all occurrences of [æ]. And the combined effect of the rules is to produce, in that environment, the exceedingly common and perhaps 'optimal' (or at least certainly minimal) three-vowel system /i u a/. The proper subset of the whole vowel system that is allowed to occur before nasals is in fact the minimal vowel system that is apparently allowed in a natural language (see further on this Jakobson 1941).

There are various ways of handling this phenomenon. One way is in terms of the theory of markedness, specifically the version proposed in *SPE*. Thus we might begin by noting that, in the first instance, [−low] vowels are assigned the value [+high]: and in the second, [+low] vowels become [+back]. That is, within the Chomsky-Halle theory, the vowels are in each case assigned their 'unmarked' values for the feature in question. If the marking conventions proposed for vowels are correct, then the following ones seem to operate in this case (*SPE*: 405, conventions VIII, X):

(2.12)   VIII. $[u \text{ high}] \to [+\text{high}]$
                 X. $[u \text{ back}] \to [+\text{back}] \; / \; \left[\underline{\hspace{2em}} \atop +\text{low}\right]$

Thus these conventions define the minimal three-vowel system as noted above:

(2.13)   i   u $\begin{bmatrix} +\text{high} \\ -\text{back} \end{bmatrix}$ $\begin{bmatrix} +\text{high} \\ +\text{back} \end{bmatrix}$

   or

   a $\begin{bmatrix} +\text{low} \\ +\text{back} \end{bmatrix}$

Let us assume, for the sake of argument, that the OE vowels (except in the strong verbs – cf. ch. 1) have in the lexicon 'unmarked' values for lowness and roundness. We will follow Chomsky and Halle's marking convention VI (405):

(2.14)

$$\text{VI.} \quad [u \text{ low}] \to \begin{cases} [+\text{low}] \;/\; \begin{bmatrix} \rule{1.5em}{0.4pt} \\ u \text{ back} \\ u \text{ round} \end{bmatrix} \\[2em] [-\text{low}] \end{cases}$$

Vowels would thus be entered in the lexicon as either [+back] or [−back] or [u back]. A [u back] vowel which is [u low] will be [+low] and [u high]; the value of this is specified by convention VII which requires that [+low] vowels are [−high]. Thus the vowel in *dæg̣* will be lexically $\begin{bmatrix} u \text{ high} \\ u \text{ low} \\ u \text{ back} \\ u \text{ round} \end{bmatrix}$; all the (plus and minus) values are supplied by the marking conventions. The vowels which are specified as [−low] by VI – i.e. those which are marked as [+back] or [−back] – will also be specified as either [m high] or [u high]. The values of '*m*' and '*u*' are specified by VIII. Thus lexically the root vowel in *wlite* 'face' is $\begin{bmatrix} u \text{ high} \\ u \text{ low} \\ -\text{back} \\ u \text{ round} \end{bmatrix}$, that in *helm* 'helmet' is $\begin{bmatrix} m \text{ high} \\ u \text{ low} \\ -\text{back} \\ u \text{ round} \end{bmatrix}$, that in *god* 'God' is $\begin{bmatrix} m \text{ high} \\ u \text{ low} \\ +\text{back} \\ u \text{ round} \end{bmatrix}$, and that in *lust* 'pleasure' is $\begin{bmatrix} u \text{ high} \\ u \text{ low} \\ +\text{back} \\ u \text{ round} \end{bmatrix}$. These values may of course be altered by particular rules of OE (like highness harmonization).

What happens before nasals is that the unmarked values for highness in nonlow vowels and for backness in low vowels are assigned to the vowel in question, whatever its source. We propose therefore that both pre-nasal raising and pre-nasal retraction can be removed as rules from the synchronic phonology of OE, since they follow from a general convention governing pre-nasal vowels. This says that unmarked values are assigned to these vowels in accordance with conventions VIII and X (2.12), if they are [−low] and [+low] respectively. We shall refer to this as the 'nasal influence convention', and we give it below as (2.15):

(2.15)

$$\begin{bmatrix} V \\ \langle \alpha[\text{artic}] \rangle \end{bmatrix} \rightarrow \left\{ \begin{array}{l} [u\ \text{high}]/\ \begin{bmatrix} \overline{\quad} \\ -\text{low} \end{bmatrix} \\[2ex] [u\ \text{back}]/\ \begin{bmatrix} \overline{\quad} \\ +\text{low} \end{bmatrix} \end{array} \right\} /\!\!-\!\!- \left\langle \begin{bmatrix} V \\ \alpha[\text{artic}] \end{bmatrix} \right\rangle [+\text{nasal}] \quad \begin{array}{l} \text{(a)} \\[2ex] \text{(b)} \end{array}$$

The angled brackets allow for nasal influence to affect both geminates and single vowels. By the maximum expansion the first of two identical vowels undergoes nasal influence. The alternative expansion allows for nasal influence on the second of a two-vowel sequence or on a single vowel. Thus, both the shift of [ææ] to [aa] in the derivation of *nōmon* and the assignment of [+high] to the root vowel in *bindan* and *-bunden* are predictable from this convention. We suggest that not only [ee] from quantitative ablaut (as in *nōmon*) but also lexical /ee/ is subject, when before a nasal, to convention (2.15): accordingly, *mōna* 'moon' and *mōnaþ* 'month' have underlying /ee/ (once more their historical source in IE). This means that the nasal environment must also override the derivational constraint associated with lowness assignment (1.28) whereby the rule applies only to derived (not lexical) geminates. The alternative in the case of *mōna* etc. is to enter them lexically with, say, /oo/. But they would then have to be specifically excluded from the first part of (2.15), to prevent a shift to [uu].

It is, however, necessary to indicate for the grammar of any language in which the nasal convention (as opposed to nasalization, which has rather different results – see p. 73 n.) is applicable, the points at which each subpart of (2.15) is operative, since, for instance, [e] from *i*-umlaut (*sendan* etc.) is not subject to (a), though the unumlauted [æ] in *band* undergoes (b) (> [a]). Thus, subpart (a) must apply before *i*-umlaut, and subpart (b) after. Note also that the marking convention for round-ness does not appear to apply in this environment, since vowels like [y] in *cyning* 'king' are not blocked. However, in this particular case, this need not be associated with the convention, given the a subpart (affecting nonlow vowels) operates before *i*-umlaut, since front round vowels are produced only by that rule and later ones (cf. ch. IV). Never-theless, the 'optimization' of the vowel system, i.e. its reduction to the 'triangular' [i u a], occurs with reference only to the dimensions of highness, lowness, and backness.[1] Further, it must perhaps be restricted to stressed nuclei (cf. present subjunctive plural inflexion *-en*, preterite indicative plural *-on*).

The formulation in (2.15) is explicit enough to work; and within the framework of the theory of marking it seems to be the correct way to state it. But we have strong reservations about the theory, and feel that a formulation in perhaps less rigorous and more 'functional' terms – i.e. a 'metarule' in the sense of Lass (1969b) would be more appro-priate: i.e. a formulation that states the goal of the conspiracy first, and allows any rules implementing the goal to be later, derivative pheno-mena. The alternative statement might be something like this:

(2.16) *Metarule:* Reduce vowel system to [i u a] before nasals.

       Implications: Raise mid vowels.

                 Retract low front vowels.

       Implementation: (2.15), or two individual rules referring only to plus and minus values.

---

[1] It may be of some interest to inquire why this convention should operate at all. What reason is there for reducing the size of a vowel system in this environment? We suspect that the ultimate motivation may be related to the motivation for other examples of system reduction in specific environments: e.g. the reduction of vowels to [ə] or [ɨ] under low stress in English. That is, there may be cases in which for some reason a full set of distinctions might, at output, create too heavy a perceptual load for the receiver. Thus under low stress the speed of articulation and relative lack of sonority function effectively as channel noise; and similarly, perhaps, the extra formants in the transition to a nasal have an analogous effect. Alternatively or perhaps subsequently to the nasal convention, nasalization occurs, as in Old Norse, the effect of which is to merge nonlow front vowels as [e], cf. OE *rinc*, ON *rekkr* 'man' (see Prokosch 1938: §42). Either way, the number of height distinctions is reduced from 3 to 2. And from the point of view of comprehension, of course, the loss of distinction makes no difference if it is recoverable (i.e. rule-governed): cf. *professor* vs. *professorial*.

III *Two processes of vowel epenthesis: breaking and back umlaut*

1 Introduction

We turn now to two processes – one of major and the other of rather minor scope – which show up in the alternation of certain single-graph and digraph spellings in OE. The first is the phenomenon traditionally known as 'breaking' or 'fracture'. This correlates with the appearance of the 'digraph' spellings *ea*, *eo*, and *io*, where we would expect to find (respectively) *æ*, *e* and *i*. Compare:

(3.1)   *Broken*   *Unbroken*

        wearp 'he threw'   bær 'he bore'

        weorpan 'throw'   beran 'bear'

        miox 'excrement'   witan 'know'

In WS, *eo* and *io* are often interchanged, with (historical) broken [i] usually spelled *eo* in later texts (cf. Campbell 1959: §§148, 153; Sweet 1871: xxi–xxix). Primarily on this basis, and because of identical subsequent development, the reflexes of broken [e] and [i] are assumed to have fallen together.

The digraph spellings for these (short) vowels are traditionally associated also with changes other than breaking, and we shall briefly consider one of these ('back umlaut') in §7 of this chapter. The spellings *ea* and *eo/io* are assumed to represent breaking (rather than some other change) only in certain environments. Breaking is a 'combinative' change effective before the consonant groups [l] + C, [r] + C and [x](C). These are traditionally considered to be 'back' consonant groups, and breaking is interpreted as epenthesis of a 'protective' back 'glide vowel' ('*Gleitelaut*', '*Übergangsvokal*') between the preceding front vowel ([æ], [e] or [i]) and the 'back' segment or cluster. (Thus the spelling *ea*, from breaking of [æ], is a way of writing *æa*.)[1] The height of the

---

[1] Spellings of the type *æa* do in fact appear in early texts: thus (for WGmc *au*, not the breaking of *æ*) we find the names *Aean-*, *Æata* in Latin MSS of Bede; and in later texts what Campbell calls 'occasional survivals', e.g. *geræafie*, *Vespasian Psalter*, and

glide vowel is considered by and large to be determined by the height of the preceding vowel.

In the traditional handbook analysis, breaking has some interesting consequences for the OE phonological system. OE starts out with a series of diphthongs, traditionally called the 'original long diphthongs', deriving from Proto-Germanic diphthongs: thus *þēod* 'nation' (cf. Go. *þiuda*), *ēacian* 'increase' (cf. Go. *aukan*). Breaking of the short vowels is assumed to have produced a new series of 'short diphthongs', parallel to these in segmental structure but differing in 'length'. But the long vowels too were subject to breaking, and in this case the diphthongs produced fell together with the 'original long diphthongs': thus *lēoht* 'light (in weight)' < **līxt*, *nēah* 'near' < **nǣx*. These latter nuclei would be identical with the diphthongs in *þēod*, *ēacian* respectively, and would contrast with the 'short' diphthongs in *weorþan*, *wearp*. (Note that throughout this discussion we use the traditional editorial macron to identify the 'long' diphthongs: this does not represent, as we will show, a theoretical claim, but is merely for convenience in identifying forms.)

Thus, within this tradition, OE has been considered to possess a four-term vowel system: long and short monophthongs, and long and short diphthongs. This view, and the interpretation of breaking outlined above, have recently been the subject of considerable controversy. We will try in the following two sections to clarify the main issues involved; we will then outline our own proposal.

2 The 'digraph controversy'

In 1939 Marjorie Daunt published a paper which was the first important challenge to the traditional claim that the *ea*, *eo* spellings in OE represented diphthongal developments of vowels in certain environments. The argument begun by this paper has gone on since then, and this chapter will be our own contribution. The controversy is quite well known, so we will not enter into a detailed discussion. But we will review briefly the major points in the controversy, so as to set our own efforts in some kind of historical perspective. We outline below the major positions that have been taken.

(A) The 'traditional' view, outlined in the previous section:

þæah, *Cura Pastoralis* (1959: § 135). From breaking we find *bæurnæ*, probably dat. sing. of *bearn* 'child' (Campbell 1959: §276), on the Urswick Cross.

essentially that *ea*, *eo* represent 'short' diphthongs parallel to 'long' *ēa*, *ēo*. (For some remarks on the history of this view see Hockett 1959, Samuels 1952.) The assumption is that front vowels before back consonants were 'protected from the following consonant by the development of a vocalic glide' (Campbell 1959: §139).

The writers who hold this view are not in general concerned with the status of the 'long' and 'short' diphthongs in the phonological system as a whole, though it is clear that they consider them to be in origin the results of some kind of assimilatory process. (We postpone for now discussion of other processes which have been said to result in similar diphthongs, i.e. back umlaut (cf. §7 of this chapter) which gives *heorut/ heorot* 'hart' < *herut*, and 'palatal diphthongization' (cf. appendix III) which gives WS *ġiefan* 'give' < *ġefan*.)

We might add here that no one, to our knowledge, has challenged the view that one set of digraph spellings (e.g. in *earm* 'arm', *eald* 'old', *heorte* 'heart', *seolf* 'self') is 'related to' the short vowels, while another set (e.g. in *bēam* 'tree', *bēad* 'he commanded', *bēon* 'to be', *bēodan* 'command') is 'related to' the long vowels. These relations are clear from historical sources, synchronic patterning, variant spellings, and historical developments (see further §8 of this chapter). The important fact is that in one way or another all the scholars concerned have insisted that there are two different kinds of entities involved. At the risk of being slightly paradoxical we will anticipate our argument and say that we both agree and disagree that they were different; it depends upon the level of abstraction.

(B) The second major position is that the long digraphs represent true diphthongs, but the short ones represent front vowel + diacritic, and this diacritic reflects the quality of the *consonantal* environment, but says nothing about the vowel. Thus *ea* represented the same segment in *earm*, *eall* as *æ* did in *æcer*: but the *ea* indicated the following consonant had a velar colouring that one did not normally expect in consonants after [æ]. The main exponent of this position was Daunt (1939); and it seems that her view can be taken as a claim that OE had multiple liquid phonemes: so that the alternations *æ* ~ *ea*, *e* ~ *eo* represented adjustments in writing to indicate for instance which of two contrasting /r/- phonemes was meant in a given word. (Cf. the discussion of her position in Samuels 1952: 17, 23.) This view was picked up again by Mossé (1945: 31), but without systematic reference. Mossé merely says that 'le premier élément vocalique après une consonne palatale et le second devant une consonne vélaire sont des signes diacritiques destinés à indiquer la prononciation palatale, vélaire, ou arrondie de la consonne'. He suggests, following this statement, that this particular diacritic technique is of Irish origin; a point which was central to Daunt's thesis.

(C) A third position is taken by Hockett (1959), who claims that the long and short digraphs represent distinct (taxonomic) phonemes, the long ones historical diphthongs of a /Vw/ type, the short ones monoph-thongal vowels, in many cases of morphophonemic origin: all monoph-thongized in historical OE. A somewhat similar view, which nonetheless has affinities also with position (D) below, is held by Wagner (1969).

(D) Finally, it has been argued that the long digraphs represent (phonemic) diphthongs, and the short ones monophthongal allophones of short vowels, paired *æ* ~ *ea, e* ~ *eo*. In each case the digraph repre-sents a 'backed' or velarized allophone of a front vowel, due to assimila-tion to a following back consonant (breaking) or metaphony with a follow-ing back vowel (back umlaut). This claim was first put forward by Stockwell and Barritt (1951), and was subsequently refined and restated by Stockwell (1958), and Stockwell and Barritt (1961) *contra* Hockett (1959).

Stockwell and Barritt's 1951 study not only provoked Hockett's 1959 paper (and in this case the argument was in large part a methodo-logical one, about biuniqueness, etc.), but also a series of attempts on the part of more 'philologically' oriented scholars to defend the tradi-tional view. The monuments in this discussion are Kuhn and Quirk (1953), Stockwell and Barritt's answer (1955), and Kuhn and Quirk's answer to that (1955). The entire controversy makes instructive reading at this point, as it furnishes an excellent example of the interpenetration of metatheoretic presuppositions and the claims of data in historical study. Essentially Kuhn and Quirk in the earlier papers, and Kuhn again (1961) in a final restatement, tried to defend the traditional position (A) against other kinds of analyses. The 'linguist–philologist' debate is now mainly of historical importance; but what is interesting, looking back over the claims and counterclaims, is the nature of the evidence appealed to, and the actual shape of the vowel systems proposed.

Position (A) posits a vowel system consisting of a set each of long vowels, short vowels, long diphthongs and short diphthongs. Since this view as it is stated in the handbooks does not distinguish the status of elements within the system, it is difficult to state it in terms of any dichotomy like 'phonemic'/'allophonic' or 'underlying'/'derived': but it does look as if all the surface segments are meant to have equal status – and Kuhn's restatement (1961) in explicitly taxonomic-phonemic terms does suggest this. The inventory proposed by position (A) would then look like this:

(3.2)   ī   i   ȳ   y   u   ū
           ē   e   ø̄   ø   o   ō
           ǣ   æ   a   ā
                        ēa, ea; ēo, eo; īe, ie

(In our discussion we will henceforth omit the front-round vowels, as we show in chapter IV that they are derived from underlying back vowels; and we will also postpone until that chapter a consideration of *ĭe*. These segments are at any rate not crucially involved here, as [y ø] do not figure in breaking, and *ĭe* arise by other processes.)

Position (B) would, as far as we can tell, produce an inventory like (3.2), but with the short digraphs not representing anything different from the short vowels /i e æ/. Position (C), on the other hand, gives a quite different picture, as follows: we omit the other vowels, and just give the digraphs (after Hockett 1959):

(3.3)   ea   /a/   eo   /ə/
                ēa   /a·/   ēo   /ə·/

Hockett does not give the symbols in diagonals an explicit phonetic characterization: though the implication is of course that the phonetypes are in some way represented 'naturally' by the symbols chosen. (It might be noted that the /a a·/ do not coalesce with the 'phonemes' represented in spelling by *a*, since these are assumed by Hockett – as well as by Stockwell and Barritt – to have been rounded vowels of the type [ɔ]. We shall return to the evidence provided by the later developments of the various diphthongs in §8.)

Position (D), that of Stockwell and Barritt (1951) and Stockwell (1958), sees the digraphs and their phonetic reflexes as in (3.4). As far as we can tell, all treatments of the digraph-diphthong question can be assigned to one of the four classes we have described, with minor differences of detail (e.g. Moore and Marckwardt 1964, assign length in 'long' diphthongs to the first element, so that *ea* and *ēa* contrast as [æa] vs. [æ:a], and Kuhn 1961 assigns it to the second, e.g. [æa] vs. [æa:]).

(3.4)

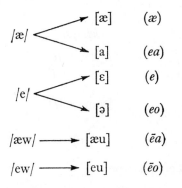

3 Phonetic character of the 'long' and 'short' digraphs

The whole controversy about what the OE digraph spellings represented seems to be based on the following facts and assumptions:

(3.5) *Facts.* The historical developments of the entities represented by the long and short digraphs suggest that they belonged respectively to the same classes as the long and short vowels: e.g. the reflexes of *ēa*, *ēo*, participate in the Great Vowel-Shift (*beam* < ME *bēm* < OE *bēam*; *bee* < ME *bē* < OE *bēo*), while the reflexes of short *ea*, *eo* do not (*hard* < ME *hard* < OE *heard*; *earl* < ME *erl* < OE *eorl*).

Assumption. Therefore the reflexes were different in Middle English, the long digraph entities giving long vowels and the short ones short vowels.

Assumption. Therefore the long and short digraphs must have represented entities of respectively the long and short vowel type in OE.

Meta-assumption. Since sound change is irreversible, the two above assumptions are borne out by the facts.

Now one of the more important changes that generative phonology has permitted us to make in the standard assumptions about historical change is the rejection of the meta-assumption about irreversibility. Once we consider the possibility of both rule-addition and rule-loss as factors in change, we are no longer constrained to accept that sound changes – even 'splits' and 'mergers' – are necessarily irreversible.

It is quite simple (given the proper conditions for recoverability) to assume that a merger can be 'undone', for example, by loss of the rule that produced it. Thus schematically we can have processes of this type:

(3.6)

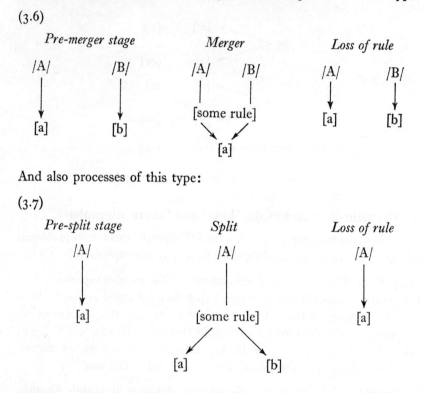

And also processes of this type:

(3.7)

As long as lexical representations remain stable there is no reason in principle why such phenomena cannot occur. And since it is clear that sound changes do not proceed with uniform speed across the lexicon (cf. Wang 1969), it is quite likely that situations of both these types can be shown to have occurred in languages by virtue of the presence of 'relic' forms.

A case in point, concerning the reversal of a split, is the history of the Middle High German obstruent-devoicing rule in Yiddish (cf. King 1969: 46–8). In this case the rule devoicing obstruents in word-final position was apparently added to most German dialects somewhere c. 900–1200, and was later lost from most Yiddish dialects: thus *hɔbm* 'to have' vs. *ix hɔb* 'I have', *liyd* 'song' vs. *liyder* 'songs' etc. But there are still relic forms such as *avek* 'away', *hant/hent* 'hand/hands', *gelt* 'money' which show the devoicing. The simplest explanation for the voiced-final forms in Yiddish – given the sporadic voiceless ones – is not that there never was a rule devoicing final obstruents, but that the rule was at one point a part of the grammar of Yiddish, and was lost except in certain sporadic items, where it remained for a time as a 'minor' rule in the phonology, presumably followed by restructuring in the lexicon. Thus the situation with early Yiddish /d/ is as follows:

(3.8)

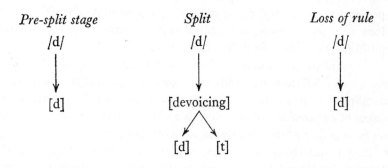

| *Pre-split stage* | *Split* | *Loss of rule* |

Since we are not concerned with biuniqueness, we do not have to 'assign' these [t] resulting from terminal devoicing to /t/, and they can therefore be recovered from underlying representations as /d/ when the rule is lost: they have never, that is, 'become' /t/ (i.e. by lexical restructuring), but have merely been realized for a time as (derived) [t], predictable by rule from underlying /d/. (For a similar example, see Kiparsky 1968a, and cf. our discussion of AFB and the loss of this and related rules in ch. II, §1.)

It seems then that there is no principled reason why the long and short digraphs (which were after all orthographically identical) had to represent entities that were *phonetically* different at all: so long as their underlying representations remained stable. (The problem of the relation between reversibility of merger and the stability of underlying representations is discussed p. 108 n.) Once we drop the irreversibility requirement, it seems reasonable at least to suggest that the two classes of sounds were spelt the same because (in surface phonetic representation) they were the same, and were both diphthongal. The 'original diphthongs' are, as the term suggests, historically non-identical divocalic nuclei; subsequent developments (§8) support this view. So breaking (along with the associated conventions and later rules discussed below) results in the elimination for certain environments of the 'length' distinctions characterizing the input vowel segments: an instance that is of the middle term of (3.6).

This assumption, which we will justify historically as we proceed, thus leads to a surface vowel system which has the advantage of not being typologically unlike any living Germanic vowel system.

So in our formulation *nēah* 'near' represents the breaking of a 'long' (i.e. geminate) vowel, whereas *seah* 'he saw' results from the breaking of short [æ]; but the two sequences are phonetically identical. Thus *ea* represents the same diphthong whether it is derived (via breaking) from a long or a short vowel; and indeed if it descends from an 'original' diphthong, as in *bēad*. And the same for *eo*.

As we said above, it has traditionally been claimed that only the broken long vowels fell together with the original diphthongs; we propose extending this to include the short vowels as well. The former two sources of *ea* (breaking of long vowels and original diphthongs) do however go together *phonologically*, as deriving from divocalic (diphthongal or 'long') underlying sequences, and this accounts for their similar historical developments, as against the divergent ones of the diphthongs whose underlying source is a 'short' (single) vowel.

This account will however give us, as output of breaking, two classes of diphthongs contrasting in length *at that level*: bimoric sequences resulting from epenthesis after a short vowel – schematically /VX/ > [VVX]; and trimoric sequences resulting from epenthesis after a long vowel – /VVX/ > [VVVX]. This distinction is ironed out later by a general (and independently motivated) convention for the simplification of trimoric nuclei.

Our position has the following advantages over the positions (A)–(D) discussed above: (1) as we said above, it does not lead to a phonetic system which is radically different from the phonetic systems of living Germanic languages; (2) it does not contradict the orthographical evidence; (3) it does not contradict the historical evidence, but in fact enables us to account simply and naturally for the later developments; and (4) it enables us to account for later (Middle English) developments in certain dialects that cannot be reconciled with a monophthongal interpretation of even *some* of the breaking forms (cf. positions (B)–(D) outlined in §2), as described in §8.

In essence we adopt the traditional view that breaking is epenthesis of a back vowel between a front vowel and a back (continuant) consonant, with the addition that the two derivational classes of breaking diphthongs yield phonetic sequences identical both to each other and to the diphthongal nuclei derived from an underlying (pre-breaking) source.

Before trying to formulate the rules that accomplish all this, we must look in some detail at the relevant environments. We have described them collectively as involving a front vowel before a back consonant; following a view such as that of Lehnert (1965: 51–2), who describes the process (for the short vowels) in this way:

Zwischen den kurzen palatalen Vokalen *æ, e, i* (< WG. *a, e, i*) und folgenden gedeckten velaren Konsonanten *X* (geschrieben *h*), *r, l* oder einfachem *h*... schob sich ur-ae. ein Übergangslaut *u* ein, so dass die Kurzdiphthonge *æu, eu, iu* entstanden, die sich wie die WG. Diphthonge *au, eu, iu*...und wohl gleichzeitig mit ihnen zu *ęa* (= *æa*), *ęo, io*...entwickelten. Doch sind die aus dem WG. entwickelten Diphthonge ae. lang (*ę̄a, ę̄o, īo*), die ae. Brechungs diphthonge dagegen kurz (*ęa, ęo, io*).

But it is not obvious in what sense *r* and *l* can be said to represent 'velaren Konsonanten', and we turn now to this problem.

4   Excursus: the nature of OE /r l/ and the notion 'back environment'

The tradition (and the historical evidence) suggests that breaking is epenthesis of a 'protective' back vowel; and further that the segments before which this epenthesis takes place are [r l x]. But why these three? The only one, on the face of it, that seems likely to require that a preceding front vowel be 'protected' from it is [x] since it alone is unambiguously [+back]. This is certainly so if, as we assume, the display in (3.9) below is a reasonable characterization of these segments.

Of the three segments supposedly causing epenthesis of a back vowel between a front vowel and themselves, two are marked [+anterior, −back], which does not suggest any useful generalization. The only point-of-articulation feature that all three have in common is [−low]; but since it seems (cf. Preliminaries, §5.2) that all pre-uvular consonants are [−low], this feature is redundant for all the nonvowel segments of OE.

The problem becomes doubly difficult when we consider breaking before such groups as *rl, rm, rn, rd*, where both members of the cluster

(3.9)

	r	l	x
obstruent	—	—	+
consonantal	+	+	+
anterior	+	+	—
coronal	+	+	—
high	—	—	+
low	—	—	—
back	—	—	+
lateral	—	+	—
continuant	+	+	+
voice	+	+	—

are apparently [+anterior]. If we follow this to its logical conclusion, we must assume two separate (and essentially unrelated) processes involved under the general heading of breaking:

(3.10) (a) *Dissimilatory epenthesis*:

$$\varnothing \rightarrow \begin{bmatrix} V \\ +\text{back} \end{bmatrix} / V \underline{\hspace{2cm}} \begin{bmatrix} -\text{obs} \\ +\text{ant} \\ +\text{cor} \end{bmatrix}$$

(b) *Assimilatory epenthesis*:

$$\varnothing \rightarrow \begin{bmatrix} V \\ +\text{back} \end{bmatrix} / V \underline{\hspace{2cm}} \begin{bmatrix} +\text{obs} \\ +\text{back} \end{bmatrix}$$

This leaves us with three possible assumptions to work on:

(A) If breaking did occur, and was unitary (i.e. there was epenthesis in these two unlike environments), then it was a bizarre and 'unnatural' process, and it is not possible to construct a reasonably general rule. This amounts to a null hypothesis.

(B) It is a historical error, based largely on an overcredulous acceptance of orthographical evidence, that makes us assume that there was only one kind of breaking. There were actually two, but unlike the formulation in (3.10) they were both assimilatory, only the epenthesized segments were of different types in the two environments. We discuss this (not entirely unattractive) possibility at the end of this section.

(C) The strongest hypothesis: this says that the process was entirely natural, i.e. assimilatory; and that all three of the postvocalic segments causing it did have some common specification, which has so far escaped us.

We will begin by considering the implications of position (C). One way, of course, is to assume some kind of 'back-coloured' [r] and [l] to explain just those cases where we need such segments. Thus let us say all /l/ become [ɫ] in preconsonantal environments, and all /r/ become something equivalent, let us say a velarized [rᵚ]. In the case of /l/ this is not unreasonable, as for instance most (non-Irish, non-Northumbrian) dialects of English have [ɫ] preconsonantally, even before labials and dentals; but this is certainly not the case with NE /r/. This solution has other drawbacks as well, particularly as it verges on the rather hard-to-motivate 'multiple liquid' analysis, and in addition requires the operation of a low-level type of phonetic rule at a quite distantly prephonetic stage of the grammar (though this in itself does not disqualify it).

In addition, this analysis does not help us in the solution of another problem also tied up with OE /r/: the odd facts about its behaviour in relation to the 'West Germanic gemination'. In this change, it will be recalled, any consonantal segment following a short stressed vowel and preceding /i j/ was doubled – just in case the segment in question was not /r/. Thus *tellan* 'tell' < **taljan* (cf. ON *telja*), and so on: but class ɪ weak verbs *nerian* 'save', *herian* 'praise' < **narjan, *harjan*. (These are of course the class ɪ weak verbs in *-ian* < /-Cjan/, unlike the class ɪɪ weak verbs with the same ending < /-Cōjan/.) See further the detailed treatment of gemination in appendix ɪɪ.

So we now find that the specifications for /r l/ in (3.9) will not work under assumption (C); and we do not want to invent special features for just those cases where we need them. So what are the alternative possibilities? And given these possibilities, is there any evidence to support them? We think that there is some suggestive evidence from Modern Scottish and northern English dialects for what these segments might have been like in OE; and accordingly we propose the following tentative characterizations of OE /r l/, which under the hypothesis (C) above will help give us a better account of breaking, and also perhaps will explain some of the peculiarities of the gemination:

(3.11)   (a) OE /r/ was a uvular continuant

               (b) OE /l/ was a velarized dental lateral

(Whether /r/ is to be specified as a trill [ʀ] or a fricative [ʁ] is obviously a surface matter, beyond historical recoverability; but we are now arguing for a phonological characterization, i.e. uvular point of articulation, without fine manner specification. So we will use the symbol [R] in discussion of OE as a cover-symbol for some kind of uvular continuant.)

These two sound types, while by no means the commonest in Modern English, have a fair distribution: according to Orton and Halliday (1962), [ʁ] or the variant [ʁʷ] were characteristic of all nine areas surveyed in Northumberland, and two (areas 1 and 2) in County Durham. A uvular [ʁ] also occurs, according to our own observations, in a number of western Scots dialects, and (usually in alternation or free variation with an apico-alveolar trill or approximant) in a fairly wide selection of eastern dialects, including areas as far to the east and south as Edinburgh and Peebles and as far north as Aberdeen. (Though in these Scots instances it is more often an idiosyncratic 'stylistic' variant than a property of a regional dialect proper.)

The distribution of segments of this type in the Germanic *Sprachgebiet* outside of Britain is extremely wide. There are uvular *r*'s as far as we know in at least some dialects of every Germanic language except Icelandic; some form, either trill or fricative, is found in Danish, SE Norwegian, S Swedish (especially Skåne), Standard Dutch, Standard German, and most dialects of Yiddish. (It is usually assumed – cf. Malmberg 1963: 46–7 – that uvular *r* is an 'urban' phenomenon, possibly of Parisian origin, which entered German and travelled north in the 18th century; but this is difficult to square with the existence of such segments in dialects of Yiddish which have been isolated from German since the Middle Ages, and are surrounded by apical-*r* languages: e.g. the case of eastern Yiddish where the 'adstratum' languages are Russian, Polish, Hungarian, Rumanian, etc. Further, there is apparently (Frank Banta, personal communication) some orthoëpic evidence suggesting a posterior *r* in some types of German as early as the 14th century.)

As for [ɫ], some form of dental/alveolar lateral with velar coarticulation occurs in most dialects of Modern English (with the notable exception of Northumbrian and N Irish), both British and American, contiguous to back segments, preconsonantally, and word-finally; in many dialects (e.g. Cockney: cf. Sivertsen 1960: §4.41) it is in fact a 'vocoid glide' of the type [ǫ] or [ɤ̯] in final position – which seems to be a case of the velar articulation overriding the other. A slightly 'dark' /l/ is standard in all positions in most American dialects, and a heavily velarized [ł], with a very clear [ɯ]-, [ɤ]-, or [o]-resonance is the sole realization of /l/ in many Scottish dialects, as well as in parts of Northern England.

So we can now specify – tentatively – the segments crucially involved in the OE breaking as follows:

(3.12)

	ł	x	R
obstruent	−	+	−
consonantal	+	+	+
anterior	+	−	−
coronal	+	−	−
high	+	+	+
low	−	−	+
back	+	+	−
lateral	+	−	−
continuant	+	+	+
voice	+	−	+

So all the segments causing breaking are characterizable at least as $\begin{bmatrix} +\text{cons} \\ +\text{cont} \\ +\text{back} \end{bmatrix}$. And further, the one segment of the three, /x/, that is capable of causing breaking if no other segment follows, is [+obs]: i.e. the

conjunction $\begin{bmatrix} +\text{obs} \\ +\text{back} \end{bmatrix}$ will trigger breaking alone, supported by no following segment; whereas [+back] alone is insufficient if not in conjunction
either with [+obs], or a following segment with the specification [+cons].
This suggests that breaking before single /x/ and not before /ɫ R/
but only /ɫC RC/ (i.e. some consonantal segment, either sonorant or
obstruent) is a function of some kind of strength hierarchy, in which
/sonorant+sonorant/ or /sonorant+obstruent/ 'equals' one obstruent,
as far as the power to induce a particular change is concerned (see further
ch. v, and Lass 1971).

Under the 'common-feature' assumption (C) we can now characterize the conditions for breaking as follows:

(3.13)

(a) All segments causing breaking are at least

$$\begin{bmatrix} +\text{cons} \\ +\text{back} \\ +\text{cont} \end{bmatrix}$$

(b) Anteriority, coronality, laterality and voicing are not significant;
and obstruency is not either, except insofar as one segment marked
[+obs] is 'as strong as' two marked [−obs] or a catenation [−obs]
[+obs].

This analysis, however, is a consequence of our choosing to argue
along the lines suggested by (C); and we have selected [+back] as the
trigger-feature according to the traditional notion that breaking (as
claimed by Lehnert in the passage quoted at the end of §3) is in fact
epenthesis of a back vowel. We are thus claiming that the three rules
– those epenthesizing back vowels before /rC/, /lC/ and /x/ – are significantly 'related', i.e. are potentially collapsible into an abbreviatory
schema. So we have argued that if there is one process called 'breaking',
then /r/ must be [+back] in order to enable us to generalize the environment (again assuming that the most 'typical', because simplest,
environment is that before /x/), and that a back /r/ is uvular.

We must note here, however, that there is still another way to salvage
position (C), without going so far as we have in claiming uvular articulation for /r/ (though we would need a velarized /l/): it might very well
be, that is, that our 'problem' in characterizing this environment is not
a problem at all, but rather an artifact of the current feature-inventory,
which does not permit us – in a non ad hoc way – to characterize as

[+back] any segment which might be a reasonable exponent of OE /r/ except a uvular. We will merely note this possibility here, as the space required to discuss it in detail would be disproportionate, and we have at the moment no very firm ideas on the matter.

But let us consider another possibility: that, as we suggested above might be the case, assumption (C) is not the right one, and we should instead choose (B). This says that the spelling and the scholarly tradition have misled us into thinking that all three rules refer to the same thing, whereas actually there are two processes: breaking before /x/, and breaking before /r l/. Under this view the two processes may have nothing more in common than the fact that they involve diphthongization; the epenthetic vowels may be different in the two cases, and the environments (in terms of specific features triggering a rule) disjoint. If we argue this way, then we might suggest two unrelated processes: (a) backness assimilation of front vowels to /x/, with back-vowel epenthesis as the means of obtaining feature-agreement; and (b) something like sonorancy assimilation before liquids plus a consonant, with some feature of the liquid being copied out or segmentalized as a vowel (cf. Harms 1968: 70–1), not necessarily back.

This sort of analysis would be suggested by dialects like Lass's (New York City), where there is epenthesis of a 'glide' vowel of the type [i] between front vowels and (apical) /r/, and of [ə] between back vowels and /r/, and all vowels and (velarized) /l/. There are also cases in other American dialects where phenomena very much like breaking occur before clearly apical liquids (cf. the detailed study in Sledd 1966).

But we have adopted our particular analysis – albeit tentatively – because of two factors: (a) a general desire to make the grammar maximally 'simple' in cases where no compelling counterevidence seems to be available; and (b) the fact that an analysis of /r/ as a segment of the type [R] seems to be useful not only in regularizing the environment for breaking, but in explaining some of the peculiarities of the West Germanic gemination.[1]

---

[1] Fred Householder (personal communication) expresses a considerable scepticism about [R] in OE, and suggests that the facts can be handled in other ways. He says first that according to the distribution 'it looks as if all uvular *R* areas in Europe are in contact (ignoring the water between Britain and the mainland) [this is true except for Yiddish: RL/JMA], i.e. are a single area. This is normally the case with innovations, not archaisms.' Further, in reference to the breaking argument itself, he makes the following comments: 'As for the argument from breaking, one need only suppose that the *r*, though apical, was somewhat retracted or retroflexed (as most American *r*'s are today)... The occurrence of dark *l* before another C is evidently Indo-European,

5 Breaking and diphthong height harmony

We interpret breaking as epenthesis of a back vowel between a front vowel and a back continuant consonant which either is an obstruent, or if not is followed by another consonant. In the preceding section we have examined the character of this environment in some detail. We turn now to a formulation of the breaking rule and a discussion of its place in the phonology. We propose the following characterization:

(3.14) *Breaking: first version*

$$\varnothing \rightarrow \begin{bmatrix} V \\ +\text{back} \end{bmatrix} \Bigg/ \begin{bmatrix} V \\ -\text{back} \end{bmatrix} \underline{\quad\quad} \begin{bmatrix} +\text{cons} \\ +\text{back} \\ +\text{cont} \\ \langle -\text{obs} \rangle \end{bmatrix} \langle +\text{cons} \rangle$$

The epenthetic back vowel is then accommodated to the highness and lowness coefficients of the preceding vowel by a rule of DHH, which we have already alluded to (§1.3) in connexion with the development of diphthongs. Thus *weorþan* but *wearþ* – cf. *bēodan, bēad*. We suggest that after DHH, the diphthongs resulting from breaking are identical to those derived from lexical divocalic sequences. Thus DHH will operate both on the [-i] and [-u] of the lexical complex nuclei, and the

being attested not only for Germanic but also for Italic and Greek. The epenthetic vowels which develop before *r* in Greek (especially Aeolic) and Latin (and this *r* is indubitably apical) all tend to be more open, or back, or rounded. Note also the Sanskrit fluctuation between *r̥* and *ur* in many roots (including -*mur*- 'die') where we know the *r* was apical...Retracted apical -*r*- also occurs in many Turkic languages, and is apparently much more widely distributed in the world than uvular *R*...And retracted *r* and dark *l* have very similar articulator shapes and similar acoustic properties as well.'

If this is so, and if OE /r/ was a retracted apical [r], we are still left with the problem of why /r l/ should pair with /x/ and no other segment. And even more, the problem of why /r/ alone should be excluded from the gemination. It may well be that Householder's objections are well-founded, in which case the problem is (as we suggested earlier) that the present feature-framework gives us no feature that will characterize the three segments in common. For even if a velarized [l] is [+back] it does not seem that even a 'retracted [r]' has the requisite tongue-*body* retraction to qualify as [+back] under the standard definition: it seems that the 'retraction' is of the blade of the tongue.

But even the difficulty with gemination may not be insuperable, under an analysis of /r/ as non-uvular: cf. Householder's comments quoted in appendix II. Against our own position we might add one further objection: Charles Jones (personal communication) has pointed out that those areas that now show uvular *r* are precisely those that in OE had the least productive breaking, i.e. the dialects that descend from Old Northumbrian.

back vowel from breaking (which is probably [u]): see below. In both these cases it will assign highness and lowness values agreeing with those of the preceding vowel. We now give a first statement of this rule:

(3.15) *Diphthong height harmony: first version*

$$
\begin{bmatrix} V \\ \alpha back \end{bmatrix} \rightarrow \begin{bmatrix} \beta high \\ \gamma low \end{bmatrix} \Big/ \begin{bmatrix} V \\ -\alpha back \\ \beta high \\ \gamma low \end{bmatrix} \underline{\qquad}
$$

The reason for requiring backness disagreement between the two vowels was discussed in §1.3. Among other things, it prevents us from predicting that the vowel in *bīdan* is [ee] (from [ei]) by DHH without the backness restriction. Strictly we should add [αback] on the right of (3.15) to override the convention whereby [+low] vowels are [+back].

The assumption that the epenthesized vowel produced by the breaking rule is [u] is actually not forced on us by the synchronic data: though historically, judging from early spellings, it seems to have been. As far as the synchronic grammar is concerned, since DHH operates automatically on two-vowel sequences the result of breaking could just as well be a vowel unspecified except as [+back], since its other features are automatically supplied by DHH. It would probably be better, in fact, to consider this to be the case, as it would then prevent our having to resort (as was the case also in our ablaut analysis) to excessive phonetic specification at a pre-phonetic level. But in our exposition we will use, where necessary, the value [u], in order to avoid representations like 'þi [V, +back] xan' (cf. (3.27)). Since DHH automatically supplies the proper articulatory characterization for the epenthesized vowel, both for phonetic purposes and for the requirements of other rules, we will use this device as an expository convenience.

In the case of geminate ('long') front vowels in the breaking environment, the operation of (3.14) will give a trimoric sequence – two front vowels followed by one back. We assume that any such sequence will be simplified by a general convention to a bimoric sequence identical to that produced by breaking of the corresponding short vowel. We shall return to this in the next section, where we will propose a formulation embracing these and other instances of trimoric sequences. (We will also discuss the implications of such a convention for the history of the language – in particular in the interpretation of the events involved in the rise of the 'new' Middle English diphthongs, in chapter VI.)

But let us return to some of the points arising from our discussion of breaking itself. We have already observed that in West Saxon the reflexes of broken [e] and [i] apparently fall together. This suggests that we can interpret those instances of *eo/io* that result historically from the breaking (etc.) of [i] as having [e] as their synchronic source in WS. That is, /i/ does not appear before breaking clusters in the synchronic phonology of WS. The historical /i/ in *meox* is restructured at some point after the collapse of the *eo/io* distinction to /e/. (The situation in the other dialects is apparently somewhat different, and the interpretation of the evidence difficult; we will not discuss this any further here. (For a general survey see Campbell 1959: §§146, 148, 153.) We will, however, have occasion to return briefly to the general matter of 'the diphthongization of [i]' in §7 below, and finally in chapter VI, §2.)

More problematic are the apparent restrictions on the operation of breaking, particularly of [e] before /l/ + C, suggested by spellings like *melcan* 'milk', *delfan* 'dig'. It would seem at first possible to formulate a quite natural characterization of this restriction – viz. that breaking fails before [l]-clusters other than [lx]: cf. *eolh* 'elk'. We could indeed perhaps reformulate the breaking rule in such a way as to eliminate breaking of [e] before [l] + C; and to include instances like *eolh* under the shorter expansion of (3.14), if we allow for an optional liquid before the [x]. But there are difficulties here, because the generalization is not really that breaking fails before [l] + C except when C = [x]. For we find as well as *self* 'self' spellings like *seolf*, and the spelling *aseolcan* 'become languid' is quite usual (cf. Campbell 1959: §146). So that breaking apparently takes place before -*lf* and -*lc* if *s*- precedes. If spellings like *seolf*, *aseolcan* represent genuine occurrences of breaking, then we must add to rule (3.14) a restriction which says that breaking of [e] before [l] + C occurs just in case C = [x], or C = [f] or [k] and [e] is preceded by [s]. But we will not try to formalize this, as quite frankly we do not understand it: we have no idea of what (if it is in fact a genuine condition) its motivation could possibly be, or even how to formulate it.

We note finally here that when the sequences resulting from breaking appear in an *i*-umlaut environment, the reflexes of both [æ] and [e] (/ _____ [i]) – and of the corresponding long vowels and diphthongs – are spelt *ie* in West Saxon. We will propose an interpretation for these spellings and the developments underlying them in the following chapter.

6 Hiatus and contraction

The well-known alternation of forms with and without medial *h* (= [x])
in certain strong verb paradigms and noun and adjective forms is
commonly ascribed to a 'sound-change' involving among other things
loss of intervocalic [x] and 'contraction' – i.e. 'absorption' of post-
hiatal vowels after the loss into the original nuclear vowels, thus
causing 'lengthening'. Characteristic forms illustrating this can be
found in the infinitive and preterite singular of strong verbs with
historical stems of the type /...Vx/. For example:

(3.16)

Class	INF	PRET$_1$	Cognates showing [x]
I	lēon	lāh 'lie'	cf. OHG *līhan* (class I)
	wrēon	wrāh 'cover'	cf. OHG *rihan*
II	tēon	tēah 'draw'	cf. Go. *tiuhan*
V	gefēon	gefeah 'rejoice'	cf. OHG *-fehan*
VI	flēan	flōh 'flay'	cf. OFris *flecht*, n.
	lēan	lōh 'lend'	cf. OHG *lahan*

The preterites suggest clearly that these verbs undergo 'normal' ablaut,
so that we must account for the *ēa/ēo* forms of the infinitive so as to
permit us also to derive the rest of the forms in the usual way. Consider,
too, second and third person present indicatives like *siehst* and *siehþ*
from *sēon* 'see', which show *i*-umlaut of the breaking of [e], the vowel
we would expect in the PRES forms. (Historically the [x] is not lost
here because of the prior loss of the inflexional [i] after *i*-umlaut.) If
we consider the loss of [x] to be historical only, and not recoverable
in the synchronic grammar, then we must analyse these verbs as having
exceptional PRES forms (though the second and third person indicative
are regular) in the lexicon; and aside from the fact that this relieves us
of having to make a stronger claim about them, it does not accord with
the regularity of the alternation. If [x] shows up in surface forms just
where we would expect it – given an infinitive with medial [x] and a
late deletion rule; and if, further, the infinitive forms seem to show
breaking, which depends on the presence of [x]; then it seems only
reasonable to suggest that this so-called sound change, like others we
have discussed and will discuss, is a synchronic property of the OE
grammar.

If we assume that the ablaut rules as they stand are substantially correct, then the presence of [x] in the verb-forms cited is necessary, as in each case it will stand in a place that must be filled by some consonantal segment in order for the SD of the ablaut rules to be met. Thus the post-ablaut structures of representative verb-forms from (3.16) would be:

(3.17)	Class	INF	PRET$_1$
	I	lēon	lāh
		[leixan]	[laix]
	II	tēon	tēah
		[teuxan]	[taux]
	V	gefēon	gefeah
		[-fexan]	[-fax]
	VI	flēan	flōh
		[flaxan]	[flaax]

The root vowel in class II is already diphthongal, and it will become [eo] by DHH. Thus, in this case, after loss of [x], we appear to find only loss of the 'inflexional vowel'. Observe too that diphthongs will also be developed in classes V and VI by breaking (preceded by AFB in class VI); [-feoxan], [flæaxan]. So once more we arrive at the surface forms merely by loss of [x] followed by loss of the inflexional vowel:

(3.18)			
Input	teuxan	-fexan	flaxan
DHH (3.15)	teoxan		
AFB (2.11)			flæxan
Breaking, DHH		-feoxan	flæaxan
(3.14)			
Loss of [x] and 'contraction'	teon	-feon	flæan

Notice that such a development for *flēan* presupposes an interpretation of AFB and retraction before back vowels as separate processes (cf. ch. II, §4) such that retraction is obligatory for class VI (rather than AFB blocked) before any V.

In these derivations we observe once again the absence of superficial 'length' differences between the diphthongs of the sort that has traditionally been ascribed to say [teoxan] vs. [-feoxan]. Further, contraction does not result in any change in the ultimate length of diphthongs, which

are all bimoric before and after loss of [x]. (There is very little orthographic indication of length of diphthongs, and the metrical evidence
is at best equivocal. Further, it is quite likely that orthographic (and
perhaps even metrical) practice was morphophonemic. We consider
the third major source of evidence concerning length – later developments – in §8.)

Leaving aside, for the moment, the question of *lēon*, etc., we turn
to 'contraction'. If we presume loss of [x] in these forms, what
happens to the resulting sequence of vowels?

After loss of [x], the following sequences would result:

(3.19)   [teoan]   [-feoan]   [flæaan]
            tēon   gefēon   flēan

Now we have already proposed above that the sequences of three vowels
that result from the breaking of long vowels are simplified by a convention that in some way turns a trimoric sequence into a bimoric one.
Thus, [æaa] in the derivation of *hēah* 'high' < [hææx] is simplified to
[æa]; and [eeo] in *lēoht* 'light' < [leext] to [eo]. So to begin with, we
could frame the convention in such a way that it simply eliminates
one of the two identical segments in such derived trimoric sequences.
And clearly, this same convention is applicable in the case of verbs
like *flēan*, at the stage in their derivation where we have a sequence
[æaa]. This will be simplified to [æa]. (We assume, of course, that any
anomalies in the distribution of syllabicity caused by the convention
are eradicated by a reapplication of the syllabicity assignment convention: Preliminaries, §3.3.)

But this version of the simplification convention is not powerful
enough. For observe that the trimoric sequences underlying *tēon* and
gefēon contain three distinctively specified vowels. This suggests that
if the same convention is to apply, it must be less narrowly constrained.
Rather than simply removing one of two identical vowels, trimoric
simplification must eliminate the second of two vowels which agree in
backness, just in case they appear in a trimoric sequence. This accounts
for all the instances we have noted:

(3.20)   [e e o] → [eo]   lēoht
                [æ æ a]→ [æa]   hēah
                [æ a ⓐ] → [æa]   flēan
                [e o ⓐ] → [eo]   tēon, gefēon

In each case the circled segment meets the conditions sketched out above, and is deleted. We might formulate the convention as follows:

(3.21) *Trimoric nucleus simplification: first version*

$$
\begin{bmatrix} V \\ \alpha\text{back} \end{bmatrix} \rightarrow \emptyset \ / \begin{bmatrix} V \\ \alpha\text{back} \end{bmatrix} \underline{\hspace{1.5cm}} / \ V
$$

In stating the second environment we use Bach's (1968) notation for 'mirror-image' or 'neighbourhood' environments: deletion of the second of two vowels agreeing in backness takes place when they precede or follow another vowel.

Observe however that, in addition to infinitives like *slēan* 'slay', *sēon* 'see', we also find singular subjunctives like *slēa* and *sēo*, in which the underlying inflexional vowel is front (cf. *bace, cweþe*). The sequence of vowels resulting from loss of [x] – [æae] or [eoe] – does not therefore meet the SD for (3.21). But we can allow for the loss of the final [e] in both cases if we extend trimoric nucleus simplification to apply to two vowels in a trimoric cluster which agree in backness but are not necessarily adjacent. We suggest the following notation:

(3.22) *Trimoric nucleus simplification: revised*

$$
\begin{bmatrix} V \\ \alpha\text{back} \end{bmatrix} \rightarrow \emptyset \ / \begin{bmatrix} V \\ \alpha\text{back} \end{bmatrix} \underline{\hspace{1.5cm}} / / \ V
$$

Which may be expanded as:

(3.23)

$$
\begin{bmatrix} V \\ \alpha\text{back} \end{bmatrix} \rightarrow \emptyset \ / \left\{ \begin{array}{ll} \begin{bmatrix} V \\ \alpha\text{back} \end{bmatrix} \underline{\hspace{1cm}} V & \text{(a)} \\[2ex] V \begin{bmatrix} V \\ \alpha\text{back} \end{bmatrix} \underline{\hspace{1cm}} & \text{(b)} \\[2ex] \begin{bmatrix} V \\ \alpha\text{back} \end{bmatrix} V \underline{\hspace{1cm}} & \text{(c)} \end{array} \right\}
$$

That is, the '//' context specifies that there must be a third vowel present which is contiguous to at least one of the two vowels to the left of the double slash. Case (a) is represented by *flēa* ([-æae]), case (b) by *flēan* ([-æaa]) and case (c) by *hēah* ([-ææa]).

Let us return now to contracted forms in class I, as instanced by
wrēon. Since it is a class I verb, *wrēon* must have a derivation of the
following type for its nucleus:

(3.24)

/Vi/   ———→   ei   ———→   ii

     qualitative   highness

       ablaut   harmonization

At this point, breaking of the long [ii] would occur before [x], giving
[iiu], simplified to [iu]. Once again, we find spellings with both *eo* and
io. Must we then in this instance introduce a rule collapsing the *eo* and
io diphthongs? We have already suggested that this is probably unnecessary for West Saxon for the diphthongs from breaking, in that it would
simply seem to be the case that forms which derive historically from
underlying /i/ by breaking are reinterpreted synchronically (after the
collapse of the 'broken' forms of /i/ and /e/) as deriving from underlying /e/. But, one might anticipate, verbs like *wrēon* should provide
counter-instances to this, in that the vowel that forms the second
element of the [ii] that is broken would turn up as [i] in the PRET$_2$ and
PART forms (*wrigon, gewrigen*) clearly pointing to an underlying [ei]
(→ [ii]) sequence. However, in fact, in WS such verbs are frequently
reinterpreted synchronically as belonging to class II (Campbell 1959:
§739), so that *wrēon* shows the alternations *wrēah, wrugon, gewrogen*,
rather than *wrāh, wrigon, gewrigen*. Thus in these instances too there is
no compelling reason for positing (in WS) synchronic breaking of
[i(i)] followed by collapse with the broken reflexes of [e(e)]. (Of course,
the 'reinterpretation' of these verbs as class II does not occur in all
cases: there are for example two instances of *wrāh* in the *Exeter Book*
riddles in Sweet (1969); extracts XXVIII b/5 and d/11. But these and
similar class I 'versions' of *wrēon* can be represented simply as
'exceptional' in the technical sense, as suggested below, §7.

Thus far we have not attempted to formulate the actual rule deleting
[x]. From the cases we have looked at, all we appear to need is a simple
intervocalic deletion rule. But now consider alternations like these:

(3.25)   *seolh* 'seal' – gen. sing. *sēoles*

          mearh 'horse' – gen. sing. *mēares*

The oblique form in each shows loss of [x] between a liquid and a

4   LOE

vowel. Thus the rule deleting [x] is more general – i.e. it refers to immediately adjacent sonorants, not merely vowels. So:

(3.26) *Loss of h*

$$\begin{bmatrix} +\,\text{obs} \\ +\,\text{back} \\ +\,\text{cont} \end{bmatrix} \rightarrow \varnothing \ / \ [-\text{obs}] \underline{\hspace{3em}} [-\text{obs}]$$

This rule must be ordered before the rules to be discussed in chapter v which voice fricatives between sonorants, and which convert inter-vocalic [g] to [ɣ]. Otherwise [x] would become [ɣ], and we would have to specify that only those [ɣ] whose source is [x] are deleted, so that we can get the proper representation for *āgan* 'own', [aaɣan], and so forth. Alternatively, we could specify [−voice] in (3.26) and order it simply before fricative voicing; but if we can save a feature by relying on ordering, this seems the better solution.

The application of (3.26) to forms like those in (3.25) is usually once more considered to have been associated with 'compensatory lengthening' of the root vowel (Campbell 1959: §241), but the historical evidence for this is at best contradictory. Certainly NE *seal* has undergone vowel-shift, and presupposes a ME long vowel; and *mare* probably does also (cf. *mar*). But *fearh* 'pig' (cf. NE *farrow*) and *holh* 'hollow' show a short vowel. In the cases of *seal* and *mare* the NE forms apparently developed not from the n. sing. but from n. pl. or oblique forms, and so show 'lengthening in an open syllable'. But it is doubtful whether an earlier lengthening can be substantiated.

One more point: no boundaries must appear to the left of [x] if (3.26) is to operate: thus *behindan* 'behind' without loss of *h*. Alternatively, the rules could be so ordered that [x] had already become [h] in such positions before (3.26); or the rule could specify that the vowel before [x] must be stressed. As we will see in chapter VI, the first solution seems to be the most likely.

Observe too that it is not necessary to exclude nasals from the environments in (3.26). Historically, in fact, a nasal preceding [x] had already dropped in Proto-Germanic. But there are alternations in OE which seem to depend on the fact that nasals do drop before [x] but are preserved before [g]. Thus *þēon* 'thrive' with PRET$_2$ and PART forms *þungon, geþungen*. (The alternation between [x] and [g] is due to Verner's Law – we will return to this below.) If both nasal loss and

loss of *h* are synchronic processes, then underlying *þēon* is /þVNx-/ –
which would have the following derivation:

(3.27)

Input	þVNxan
Highness harmonization:	þeNxan
Nasal influence:	þiNxan
Loss of nasal (plus lengthening?):	þixan
Breaking:	þiuxan
Collapse of eo/iu < breaking (see §7):	þeoxan
Loss of *h*:	þeoan
Trimoric nucleus simplification:	þeon

It might seem that from the viewpoint of the synchronic phonology of
OE a less abstract lexical representation, involving suppletion, would
be preferable. Further, we also find the following paradigms for *þēon*,
suggesting reinterpretation as a class I or a class II verb (on the movement of class I contract verbs to class II, see above p. 97): *þēon/þāh/*
þigon/-þigen, þēon/þēah/þugon/-þogen. There are, however, alternations
in a few other forms which seem to point to synchronic loss of nasal
in OE. These involve roots with pre-nasal [a] rather than [i]. Such
are *fōn* 'take' and *hōn* 'hang'. These are historically class VII verbs
with postvocalic nasal + [x]: cf. the preterite forms *fēng, hēng*. They
thus belong to the group of class III verbs with prevocalic laryngeal
(cf. *blandan/blēnd*, and discussion in appendix I). If a rule of nasal loss
before [x] is included in the synchronic phonology of OE, then the
derivation of *fōn* and *hōn* can be allowed for by rules which have
already been proposed. Thus: [faNxan] (post-ablaut) → [fæNxan]
(AFB) → [faNxan] (nasal influence b) → [faxan] (loss of nasal) → [faan]
(loss of *h*) → [foon] (lowness assignment). We appear to find loss of
nasal before [x] also in the 'weak' preterites *þōhte* (cf. PRES *þenčan*)
and *þūhte* (cf. PRES *þynčan*), from underlying /þaNx-/ and /þuNx-/
respectively. However, these also show 'compensatory lengthening'
of the preceding vowel (cf. e.g. Campbell 1959; §119). Consequently,
we interpret the process involved in these derivations as nasal vocalization rather than nasal loss. We suggest the following rule:

(3.28) *Nasal vocalization*

$$[+\text{nasal}] \rightarrow \begin{bmatrix} -\text{cons} \\ -\text{nas} \\ \alpha[\text{artic}] \end{bmatrix} / \begin{bmatrix} V \\ \alpha[\text{artic}] \end{bmatrix} \underline{\hspace{2cm}} \begin{bmatrix} +\text{obs} \\ +\text{back} \\ +\text{cont} \end{bmatrix}$$

The number of forms affected by this rule is small; but since the addition of this single rule provides a straightforward derivation for them, and since the other parts of the paradigm require the presence of a nasal (and are themselves quite 'regular'), it would seem that the addition of this rule is less costly than suppletive lexical entries.

We might add here that verbs like *penċan, pynċan* and certain others like *tǣċan* 'teach', pret. *tǣhte, lǣċċan* 'catch', pret. *lǣhte, sēċan* 'seek', pret. *sōhte*, also seem to require a synchronic rule spirantizing [k] to [x] before [t]. And this rule also operates – though in a more complex derivation – in forms like *bycgan/bōhte* 'buy', *bringan/brōhte* 'bring'. In other cases, spirantization apparently must be extended to apply before word-boundary as well, and be ordered after a rule that devoices final [g] to [k]: cf. *āgan*, pres. sing. *āh* (this is one of the so-called 'preterite-present verbs', with an ablauted present and a 'weak' past, like *dugan/dōhte* 'avail', pres. sing. *dēah*). The spirantization, however, is limited, either as a minor rule affecting only devoiced /g/, or perhaps to environments following stressed back vowels (cf. *bæc, blæc* with lexical /k/ following a front vowel, and no spirantization). If *tǣhte, lǣhte* are 'legitimate' forms, i.e. if the *æ* really represents [æ], then spirantization must come after breaking. Tentatively, the two rules are:

(3.29) *Devoicing and spirantization*

(a) $\begin{bmatrix} +\text{obs} \\ +\text{back} \\ -\text{cont} \end{bmatrix} \rightarrow [-\text{voice}] / \underline{\hspace{1cm}} \#$

(b) $\begin{bmatrix} +\text{obs} \\ +\text{back} \end{bmatrix} \rightarrow [+\text{cont}] / \begin{bmatrix} \text{V} \\ +\text{back} \end{bmatrix} \underline{\hspace{1cm}} \left\{ \begin{matrix} \begin{bmatrix} +\text{obs} \\ +\text{cor} \end{bmatrix} \\ \# \end{matrix} \right\}$

Again, these two rules represent added cost; but this must be weighed against the cost of suppletive consonantism in the lexical representation.

Another difficult decision about what to include in the synchronic grammar arises in the case of Verner's Law (cf. ch. v, §1). We have observed that this sound change is responsible historically for the [x]/[g] alternation in *pēon*. This is also the case with the other contract verbs:

(3.30)

wrēon	wrēah	wrugon	wrogen
tēon	tēah	tugon	togen
gefēon	gefeah	gefǣgon	—

(But note that in class VI the spelling *flōg* is normal for the PRET$_1$ of *flēan*, and the other contract verbs of this type are similar in this respect.) However, such forms are not very numerous, and there are few other examples of alternations in OE due to Verner's Law, like:

(3.31)

Class

I	snīþan	snāþ	snidon	-sniden	'cut'
	līþan	lāþ	lidon	-liden	'travel'
II	cēosan	cēas	curon	-coren	'choose'
	lēosan	lēas	luron	-loren	'lose'
	sēoþan	sēaþ	sudon	-soden	'seethe'
III	weorþan	wearþ	wurdon	-worden	'become'
V	cweþan	cwæþ	cwǣdon	-cweden	'speak'
'irregular'	wesan	wæs	wǣron	—	'be'

The list of forms is not impressive; but we decided to accept nasal vocalization on the basis of a rather less impressive body of evidence. Are the two cases similar? Let us examine first how we might in fact set up the synchronic environment for Verner's Law, and then examine the consequences.

First, we observe that certain of the necessary conditions could be easily achieved by means of rules we already have.

In particular, if we separate the two rules collapsed as pre-Germanic accentuation (1.17) as (3.32) and (3.33):

(3.32) *Pre-Germanic accentuation I*

$$\begin{bmatrix} V \\ -\text{low} \\ [\text{PP}] \end{bmatrix} \rightarrow [-\text{accent}]$$

(3.33) *Pre-Germanic accentuation II*

$$\begin{bmatrix} V \\ -\text{accent} \end{bmatrix} \rightarrow [+\text{accent}] \,/ \underline{\hspace{1cm}} \text{C V (C)} \; \#$$

then Verner's Law, which voices any continuant between vowels if the vowel preceding it is [−accent], can be allowed to apply after (3.32) and before (3.33). It will thus operate on certain segments following an unaccented vowel, and correctly affect the PRET$_2$ and PART forms of the verbs in question.

But the consequences of this will be quite far-reaching. First, there is the admittedly rather trivial fact that we will need a rule of rhotacism to turn the [z] resulting from Verner's Law in e.g. *curon* < [kuzun] < [kusun] to [r]; second, we will need a rule turning the [ɣ] and [ð] resulting from voicing of /x/ and /þ/ in [wruxun] and [wurþun] into the cognate stops [g] and [d], thus giving us a very dubiously motivated recapitulation of an early Gmc sound-change, which has left behind it alternation evidence much sparser than that for the major changes like breaking (for details, cf. ch. v). And this will have very serious consequences for later rules in the grammar, since the environment in which this strengthening takes place is in fact the one which normally causes weakening (see the detailed discussion in chapter v). It looks as if a decision to include Verner's Law as a synchronic process will entail far-reaching complications in the rest of the grammar; and these complications will force us to abandon otherwise valid generalizations: generalizations supported by far more wide-ranging evidence than that for Verner's Law. Whereas the decision to accept synchronic nasal vocalization, for example, is a different matter: it explains the set of forms involving it, and has no undesirable consequences elsewhere in the grammar. So, on balance, we think it preferable to exclude Verner's Law as a synchronic process, and to enter the verbs in question as suppletive, with /-g-/ (or /-d-/ or /-r-/) in $PRET_2$ and PART, and /-x-/ (or /-þ-/ or /-s-/) in PRES and $PRET_1$.

7   Back umlaut

Ea, eo and *io* spellings also appear in various forms (and to varying extents in the different dialects) as a reflexion of a process that appears to be similar to breaking, in that it involves epenthesis of a back vowel after a front vowel followed by a back segment; but in this case the following segment is a vowel, rather than a consonant. The historical process or 'sound change'; is traditionally referred to as 'back/velar umlaut' or 'back/velar mutation'. Thus in the Mercian *Vespasian Psalter* gloss (Kuhn 1965), we find spellings like *cweoðað* 'dicunt' (Ps. 3, 1), *gesteaðulades* 'fundasti' (Ps. 8, 4), *feadur* 'patris' (H. 1, 1), *spreocu* 'loquar' (H. 7, 1), *ongeotað* 'intelligite' (H. 7, 12), etc. And in Kentish (*The Kentish Psalm*, Cott. Vesp, D. vi: Dobbie 1942: 88–94), we find *weorada* 'troop, gen. pl.' (17), *weoruda* 'id.' (30), *feola* 'many' (48), *breogo* 'leader' (49), *sioððan* 'after' (103), *weoloras* 'lips' (116).

A number of forms in this text (and others) show what looks like back umlaut before nonback vowels, e.g. *hiofenum* 'heaven, dat. pl.' (4), but these are probably due to low-level neutralization of the unstressed vowel. It seems to be at least underlyingly back in all these forms.

The West Saxon evidence is much less satisfactory. There is very little spelling evidence in the West Saxon prose texts for back umlaut of [æ]. This is not surprising, since [æ] (from AFB) is presumably retracted before all back vowels prior to the operation of back mutation. Back umlaut of [e] and [i] (once more perhaps reinterpreted synchronically as [e]) is more common, but strangely distributed. It is indicated more regularly in spelling before [u] and [o] (both from underlying /u/) than before [a], and is quite general before the liquids and labials *f, p, w, m, l, r*, though 'paradigmatic levelling' (at least in spelling) is frequent. However, after [w], *u*-umlaut appears quite regularly even before non-liquid non-labial consonants like *g, t* etc. Thus the following are quite 'normal' spellings:

(3.34)

heofon	'heaven'	medu	'mead'
heorot	'hart'	regol	'rule'
hweogol	'wheel'	helan	'conceal'
		weras	'men'

Notice that back umlaut before velar consonants is not usual (indeed in some Anglian dialects this is the context par excellence for its failure), and we thus cannot interpret a [+back] specification for /r l/ like that discussed above (§4) as responsible for their non-inhibitory effect. We find it very difficult here to formulate any reasonably natural restrictions on this rule in WS. Or rather, we find it possible to state (with at least fair accuracy) the conditions under which the rule fails to operate, but impossible to explain them. With this in mind, we can offer, very tentatively, a formulation of the following type; we will call the rule '*u*-umlaut':

(3.35) *u-Umlaut*

$$\varnothing \rightarrow \begin{bmatrix} V \\ +back \end{bmatrix} / X \begin{bmatrix} V \\ -back \end{bmatrix} \underline{\hspace{1.5cm}} C \begin{bmatrix} V \\ +back \\ -low \end{bmatrix}$$

$$\textit{Condition: } C = \begin{Bmatrix} [-obs] \\ \begin{bmatrix} +ant \\ -cor \end{bmatrix} \end{Bmatrix} \text{ or } X = Y [w]$$

(where X and Y are variables over any substring, possibly null).

The main problem with this rule (aside from its basic obtuseness) is the sporadic application we find: even the commonest *u*-umlaut forms like *heofon* are not invariable, and the regularities of occurrence are nowhere near as consistent as those for breaking. This leads us to suspect that the rather odd conditions may reflect something like the distribution of a minor rule; the actual conditions for its application, that is, may be formative-specific, rather than (strictly) phonologically motivated. (It may in fact be a sound change 'just beginning', that somehow got aborted: this pattern is typical for the early stages of a change: cf. Chen 1972.)

This rule is obviously very similar to breaking (3.14); enough so that it is at least mechanically possible to collapse the two into one schema, which we will call 'back mutation' or 'back umlaut', reserving the term '*u*-umlaut' for (3.35). If this conflation does represent a real generalization about OE, then the two back-environment epenthesis rules can be abbreviated as follows:

(3.36) *Back mutation (including breaking)*

$$
\varnothing \to \begin{bmatrix} V \\ +\text{back} \end{bmatrix} \;/\; X \begin{bmatrix} V \\ -\text{back} \end{bmatrix} \underline{\quad} \langle +\text{cons} \rangle \atop 1 \quad 1 \begin{bmatrix} +\text{back} \\ +\text{cont} \\ \left\langle \begin{array}{c} -\text{cons} \\ -\text{low} \end{array} \right\rangle \atop 1 \quad 1 \\ \langle -\text{obs} \rangle \atop 2 \quad 2 \end{bmatrix} \begin{array}{c} \langle +\text{cons} \rangle \\ 2 \qquad 2 \end{array}
$$

$$
\text{Condition: } \langle +\text{cons} \rangle \atop 1 \qquad 1 \; = \; \left\{ \begin{array}{c} [-\text{obs}] \\ \begin{bmatrix} +\text{ant} \\ -\text{cor} \end{bmatrix} \end{array} \right\} \text{ or } X = Y \,[w]
$$

(applicable only to $\langle \ldots \rangle$, i.e. case (a) in (3.37) below).
          1   1

The schema (3.36) collapses the following three rules:

(3.37)

$$
\text{(a)} \quad \varnothing \to \begin{bmatrix} V \\ +\text{back} \end{bmatrix} \;/\; X \begin{bmatrix} V \\ -\text{back} \end{bmatrix} \underline{\quad} [+\text{cons}] \begin{bmatrix} V \\ +\text{back} \\ -\text{low} \end{bmatrix}
$$

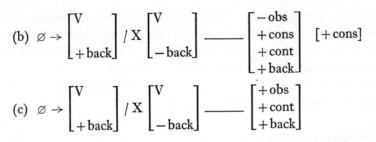

Case (a), i.e. the expansion involving '⟨...⟩', is *u*-umlaut, case (b),
                                          ₁ ₁
involving '⟨...⟩', is breaking before /r l/ + C, and case (c) is breaking
           ₂ ₂
before [x]. In the light of the above discussion, we propose case (a),
and in particular the condition on its applicability, with considerable
diffidence. We do feel, however, that with all its problems, (3.36) does
express a generalization about OE phonology. And even if, let us say,
u-umlaut turned out to be a minor (lexically specified) rule, the
similarity in type would still be striking. What we are really saying is
(a) that we are unsure of the status of (3.37a), but (b) that if it turns out
to be significant, it 'belongs' in a schema with breaking, under the metatheoretical assumption that such schemata are 'higher valued' than
pairs of non-abbreviable rules. Further, if this is the case, then it would
tend to support our analysis of /r/ and /l/ as [+back], since not only
our ability to formulate breaking as a unitary process, but also the
collapse with *u*-umlaut ('breaking before a back vowel') embodied in
(3.36) depends on this specification.

It is worth noting in passing that the entire argument for collapsing
the two processes hinges on our claim that the outputs of both breaking
and *u*-umlaut are diphthongal. If we were to accept an interpretation
like that of position (D) in §2, where the digraph spellings for the
'short' diphthongs represent back monophthongs, then *u*-umlaut would
appear to collapse, not with breaking, but with *i*-umlaut (cf. ch. IV).
This has in fact been proposed (e.g. by King 1969), as the correct interpretation: the two rules constitute a pair of metaphonic processes
(fronting before front vowels, retraction before back vowels) which
can be collapsed by variables; i.e. a case of 'alpha-generalization'.
But the arguments for diphthongal output seem too strong to permit this.

However, the following dilemma arises if we collapse breaking and *u*-umlaut. To explain the alternation between *slēan* and *dragan*, retraction of [æ] to [a] must follow loss of *h*. But loss of *h* must follow breaking. Thus, we cannot explain the absence of *u*-umlaut of [æ] as being due to prior retraction, if breaking and *u*-umlaut are collapsed. So, we must order breaking before retraction and *u*-umlaut after; or, if we retain the collapsed version in (3.35), then the $\begin{bmatrix} V \\ -\text{back} \end{bmatrix}$ in the environ-

ment must be further specified as $\begin{bmatrix} V \\ -\text{back} \\ \langle -\text{low} \rangle \\ 1 \qquad 1 \end{bmatrix}$. In view of the obvious

similarities in both SD and SC between breaking and *u*-umlaut, we adopt this modified version of (3.36).

Observe now that forms like *smeoru* 'grease' in West Saxon appear to raise again the possibility that we may have to allow for synchronic back umlaut (in the wider sense) of [i], and thus for a rule conflating the result of this in WS with [eo] (from back umlaut of [e]). This arises here because the root vowel in such forms appears in the proper environment for highness harmonization (1.11). Thus, even if we suggest lexical /e/ in *smeoru*, we would expect the radical vowel to raise to [i] before the following [+high] vowel. We seem then to have to derive the nucleus in those words via back umlaut of [i], with subsequent conflation. However, alternatively, these words could be marked as exceptions to highness harmonization. Certainly, we find [e] in nouns with inflexional -*u* which have not undergone back umlaut: *medu* etc. These seem to require that we mark them with an exception feature; or, perhaps preferably, that we restrict highness harmonization to certain morphological categories. Highness harmonization is not limited to strong verbs (cf. *gold/gylden* etc.), but it may be that the restriction is morphological, in that it is principally before -*u* in nouns that the [e] → [i] shift fails. Particularly in this latter case, the motivation for synchronic back umlaut of [i] in such forms is considerably attenuated. Clearly, such examples do not crucially require such a derivation.

This is also true, as we have observed, with regard to two other circumstances in which a rule conflating [iu] and [eo] might have been proposed. We noted (§5) that, though historically in *meox* 'excrement' there is an [i], there is no reason to suppose that it and similar words do not contain synchronic /e/. Similarly, in the derivation proposed for *bēodan* (ch. I §3) one need not invoke a stage [biud-] with a subsequent shift to [beod-], if the operation of DHH precedes highness harmonization.

However, the contract verbs of class I and class II discussed in §6 do appear to involve back umlaut of [i]. We observed in §6 that contract verbs belonging historically to class I are characteristically reinterpreted as class II. However, there are instances of class I PRET₁ forms like *wrāh* (beside *wrēah*), from *wrēon* 'cover', suggesting 'dual membership' in such cases. In that case [ei] from ablaut in the PRES forms would become [ii] by highness harmonization, with subsequent breaking of [ii] before [x] and then conflation of [iu] and [eo]: [ei] → [ii] → [iiu] → [iu] → [eo]. Similarly, the derivation proposed in (3.27) for *þēon* (/þVNxan/) involves a rule collapsing [eo] and [iu], since the [e] from the ablaut rules is raised to [i] by nasal influence (a). This can be avoided if such a verb has associated with it an exception feature [− nasal influence (a)]. Also, if the PRES forms of *wrēon* are excluded in a similar way from highness harmonization, then the radical sequence will remain as [ei] and the sequence [eia] will result in the infinitive from loss of *h*. This will be reduced to [ea] by trimoric nucleus simplification (3.22) (case (a) in (3.23)), which will shift to [eo] by DHH (3.15). Thus, even in these cases involving loss of *h*, there is no crucial motivation for the presence in the grammar of a rule collapsing [iu] and [eo]. In view of the extreme paucity of the examples requiring the exception features noted above (which are all associated with the presence of radical postvocalic [x]), we conclude that no such synchronic rule exists in the phonology of WS. However, we shall have to return to this subject again in chapter VI, §3.

8   Subsequent development of the diphthongs

We observed earlier in this chapter (§3) that those vowel clusters deriving from 'original' Germanic diphthongs, or from the breaking of long vowels, show the characteristic later histories we would expect from long vowels: they are affected (unless shortened in certain environments) by, for instance, the Great Vowel-Shift. In Middle English, these entities fall together with the front long vowel of the same height (though there are some complications due to dialect divergence). Thus both OE *hǣlan* (NE *heal*) and OE *hlēapan* (NE *leap*) show ME 'open *ē*' (becoming NE [ii] by vowel-shift), and OE *dēman* (NE *deem*)

and OE *dēop* (NE *deep*) have ME 'close ē' (once more giving NE [ii]).
The breaking diphthongs from short vowels, on the other hand, fall
together with the corresponding short vowels (unless they are lengthened
in certain contexts). Thus OE *eorþe* becomes NE *earth*, with the
typical development of ME /erC/, and OE *heard* gives NE *hard*,
with the typical development of ME /arC/ (/a/ from 'loss of breaking'
and 'loss of AFB'). These forms show developments without vowel-
shift.

Now we have proposed above that the 'long' and 'short' diphthongs
were phonetically identical. Under the assumption that 'sound change',
in particular split or merger, is irreversible, this claim cannot be reconciled in any natural way with the facts we have just outlined. But, as we
argued in §3, we are not constrained to accept this assumption, as it is
normally understood, within the framework of generative grammar.
We shall now sketch out a possible interpretation of the ME
developments.

We suggest that the post-OE histories of the diphthongs followed
a course of this type:

(3.38)

Stage I. A rule is added late in the phonology which assimilates the
second element of a divocalic nucleus to the first. We shall call this
'monophthongization'. Accordingly we see the following derivations
for the *eo* diphthongs after this rule has been added:

$$
\begin{array}{ll}
\text{bēodan:} & \text{Vu} \rightarrow \text{eu} \rightarrow \text{eo} \rightarrow \text{ee} \\
\text{dēop:} & \text{eu} \rightarrow \text{eo} \rightarrow \text{ee} \\
\text{lēoht:} & \text{ee} \rightarrow \text{eo} \rightarrow \text{ee} \\
\text{heorte:} & \text{e} \rightarrow \text{eo} \rightarrow \text{ee}
\end{array}
$$

Stage IIa. Breaking is lost. The rule of monophthongization would
now be applicable only to 'original' diphthongs, the breaking diphthongs, long and short, having 'reverted' to their underlying (/e/ or /ee/)
sources.[1] However, breaking diphthongs – even if 'short' – appear to

---

[1] This 'reversion' might seem to pose something of a problem. Where the breaking context is preserved or recoverable (phonetically or morphophonemically) then the
determination of which diphthongs are to be lost is straightforward: only those which
do not at any stage occur in a breaking environment will remain. But how is it decided
which breaking diphthongs go back to a short vowel and which to a long (geminate) –
since (we have claimed) they are phonetically identical and occur in the same crucial

be reinterpreted as 'original' if, for instance, the [x] precipitating breaking has been lost. Thus the reflex of *sēon* undergoes vowel-shift to give NE *see*. (This is on the assumption that 'compensatory' lengthening is not to be related in some more intimate way – as is suggested by the tradition – to the loss of [x].)

Stage IIb. The monophthongized 'original long' diphthongs are reinterpreted as lexical long vowels, and monophthongization is lost. Perhaps at first this affected only the original diphthongs that do not have their source in ablaut; but eventually there is associated with this and other developments a disruption of the ablaut relationships described in chapter 1. It may be that stage IIa and at least part of the implementation of IIb were simultaneous. (Note that we have used *eo* as our example in (3.38): the same general pattern holds for *ea*, but it is complicated by the loss of AFB.)

There are certain areas, however, particularly in SW England and the West Midlands, in which *eo* spellings for at least some reflexes of the OE diphthongs persist into the Middle English period. Moreover, beside these we find spellings with *u(e)*, *o(e)*, as well as *e*. These spellings have traditionally been construed as attempts at representing a front rounded vowel (cf. Jordan 1934: 86–8; Luick 1964: 333). Observe also that we find spellings like *u*, *ui*, *uy* for the OE high front rounded vowel in those dialects where it survived. No doubt such spellings continued to be used after the vowel had ceased to be round (and indeed, *eo* is borrowed into Anglo-Norman as a representation for a mid front

(breaking) environment? This raises the whole question of how the vocalic lexical representations in e.g. *hēah* and *heard* remain stable and distinct ('long' vs. 'short') when phonetically they are identical and, further, they occur in the same context – i.e. why, for instance, is the vowel in *hēah* not reinterpreted as lexically single? In short, how are such lexical differences recovered? This would appear to throw doubt on our claim that all the diphthongs spelt in the same way are identical. However, recoverability would appear to depend on the fact that it is not strictly true to say that the 'long' and 'short' breaking diphthongs occur in the same postvocalic environment. On account of morpheme-structure constraints, breaking of 'long' vowels is restricted to the position before [x]. Thus, diphthongs before /rC/, /lC/, will revert unambiguously to 'short' vowels. Before a final [x], only 'long' diphthongs occur, except where a 'short' one is dictated by the paradigm – as in *gefeah*, which as the PRET$_1$ form of a class v verb, must have a short vowel. Moreover, before [x], finally or before another consonant, is a context for the development of the new Middle English diphthongs (cf. ch. VI, §1.2), which wipes out any length difference in the preceding vowels. Thus, this source of evidence is absent. Accordingly, there seems no reason to suppose that there was any short/long distinction before [x] in OE, except where dictated paradigmatically. We shall assume that otherwise the lexical vowel immediately preceding [x] is long.

unrounded vowel – just as, conversely, *ie* appears to be borrowed from Anglo-Norman into Middle English to represent a similar sound). But in the areas mentioned it seems likely that at some point the reflex of the *eo* diphthong was a mid front round vowel. (This is especially clear from *eo* spellings for OE *ē* after *w*, where rounding assimilation of [e] is involved, not diphthongization: cf. *weori* 'weary' < OE *wēriġ*. *Piers Plowman A*, MS v, Mossé 1952: selection XXI. 1.7.) And such a development of *eo* can be accounted for quite naturally in terms of our interpretation of the OE *eo* spellings.

We suggested immediately above that in most dialects the first stage in the process whereby the OE diphthongs were lost was the addition to the grammar of a rule of monophthongization, which assimilates the second element of any vowel cluster to the first. Thus:

(3.39) *Progressive monophthongization schema*

$$\text{SD: V V} \qquad \text{SC: 1 2} \rightarrow \text{1 1}$$
$$\phantom{\text{SD: }} \text{1 2}$$

This is a general schema; the particular process involved can be formulated this way:

(3.40) *Monophthongization I: frontness attraction*

$$V \rightarrow [\alpha\text{back}] \; / \; \begin{bmatrix} V \\ \alpha\text{back} \end{bmatrix} \underline{\hspace{3em}}$$

(This will apply vacuously – as would any rule derived from (3.39) – to a sequence of identical V's.) Unrounding of the second vowel – so that [eo] > [ee], not [eø], would be provided for, presumably, by a dialect-specific morpheme-structure condition, in those dialects where front round vowels are not well-formed segments.

In the dialects of the SW and SW Midlands, however, the *eo* diphthong develops rather differently: it becomes a mid front round vowel, presumably by a mutual assimilation of the two elements, rather than by progressive monophthongization plus a MSC specifying unrounding. The first vowel acquires the roundness of the second, and the second the frontness of the first. This process differs from (3.40) in the rounding-agreement requirement:

(3.41) *Monophthongization II*

$$\text{SD:} \begin{bmatrix} V \\ \alpha back \end{bmatrix} \begin{bmatrix} V \\ -\alpha round \end{bmatrix}$$
$$\quad\quad\quad 1 \quad\quad\quad 2$$

$$\text{SC:} \; 1 \; 2 \rightarrow [-\alpha round] \; [\alpha back]$$
$$\quad\quad\quad\quad 1 \quad\quad\quad 2$$

It seems that (3.41) actually conflates two separate processes: frontness attraction (3.40), preceded by a simple roundness attraction (3.42):

(3.42) *Roundness attraction*

$$V \rightarrow [\alpha round] \; / \; \underline{\quad\quad} \begin{bmatrix} V \\ \alpha round \end{bmatrix}$$

This can all be simplified somewhat by building a condition of roundness agreement into the original frontness attraction rule (3.40), so that it serves to characterize the basic monophthongization in all the dialects:

(3.43) *Frontness attraction: revised*

$$V \rightarrow \begin{bmatrix} \alpha back \\ \beta round \end{bmatrix} \; / \; \begin{bmatrix} V \\ \alpha back \\ \beta round \end{bmatrix} \underline{\quad\quad}$$

Then the two types of dialects will differ only in the presence vs. the absence of (3.42) in their grammars. Compare the derivations outlined below in (3.44):

(3.44)

	with (3.42)	*without* (3.42)
Input	eo	eo
Roundness attraction (3.42)	øo	
Frontness attraction (3.43)	øø	ee

We assume that a similar process underlies the development of the diphthong resulting from *i*-umlaut of a broken or back-umlauted vowel, which is spelled *ie* (cf. ch. IV). Roundess attraction applies vacuously to other divocalic clusters.

These developments are interpretable in a straightforward manner in terms of the analysis of the diphthongs we have proposed. This is not the case if all the diphthongs or merely the 'short' ones are interpreted as back or retracted monophthongs (cf. positions (C), (D) outlined in §2 above). These subsequent developments therefore tend to support the traditional view of breaking and *u*-umlaut that we have argued for. Cf. further chapter VI, §§1, 2.[1]

[1] Further evidence for the diphthongal nature of both the 'long' and 'short' diphthongs is cited by Samuels (1952). As far as OE (even early) is concerned, Samuels notes that the runic symbol ᛦ (*ēor, ēar*) as in the Ruthwell Cross inscription, 'could be used for an original long diphthong (as in (*bih*)*ea*(*l*)*dun*), for a "Breaking" (as in *fearran*) and for a "Back-Mutation" (as in *heafunæs*)' (1952: 25). As far as ME developments go, Samuels cites the 'sporadic, but fairly numerous cases of a stress-shift to rising diphthongs [ja] and [jo]' (1952: 27). He gives as examples Kentish *yealde* 'old' < *eald*(*e*), *hyealde* 'hold' < *hēaldan*, and the name of the letter Ʒ *yogh, yok* < *eoh*. Further evidence is to be found in place-names (see Samuels 1952, 27, n. 7), and even perhaps in some OE spellings like *eorn* for *ġeorn* or *gearfoðe* for *earfoðe* 'where rising diphthongs and [j] have been confused at the beginning of words' (1952: 28).

For further illustration of the Middle English developments we have outlined, see Jones (1972), chapter VI.

IV *Palatalization and i-umlaut*

1 The alternation of velar and palatal *c* and *g*: preliminaries

The handbooks, as well as the standard grammars for beginners (e.g. Sweet 1957; Moore and Knott 1955) agree that OE had two segment types which were represented in the orthography by *c*: a velar, as in *catt* 'cat', *cynn* 'kin', *cēne* 'keen', and a palatal, as in *ċinn* 'chin', *ċiele* 'chill', *ċēn* 'torch' (G. *Kiene*). (The palatals are traditionally represented by a superscript dot, and we continue the practice here for clarity.) The authorities further agree that we can identify *c* before vowels as one or the other as follows:

(a) *c* represents a palatal before all 'original' front vowels, i.e. vowels that were front in Proto-Germanic or that were subject to early fronting (e.g. AFB: cf. ch. II).

(b) *c* represents a velar before all original back vowels, and before front vowels deriving (historically) from the *i*-umlaut of original back vowels.

The same solution, more or less, is suggested for the segments represented by *g*, but with complications that we will deal with below: for general information see Luick (1964: §§637.1); Campbell (1959: §§426–7); Wright (1925: §§309–11); and Brunner (1965: §§207–10).

This analysis is of course useful for the student learning to 'pronounce' OE, and is borne out, in general, by the historical evidence: suspected palatals give Modern English [ʧ] as in *chin*, and suspected velars give [k] as in *kin*. But how does this relate to the properties of the (synchronic) grammar of OE? Is the etymological evidence synchronically relevant? Are the underlying representations for forms with surface velars and palatals different with respect to the lexical segments they begin with (i.e. /k/ in one case and say /c/ in the other); or is the [k]/[c] alternation derivable by rule from a single underlying segment? We must, of course, not discount the possibility of both types of conditions holding for the same set of items at different points in the history of a language: since grammars can be restructured so that formerly distinct underlying forms are neutralized, or formerly nondistinct forms become distinct: cf. Kiparsky (1968b: 174–6).

We begin with the following working assumption: if two segment types are in morphophonemic alternation in at least some contexts; and if a certain proper subset of the set of all contexts in which the segments appear does not seem to provide the conditions for such alternation; then it is at least possible that the segments are in fact in alternation in this subset, too, but on a more abstract level of representation. In order to demonstrate this, we will examine the consequences of one argument that interprets the data as showing two lexical segments ('phonemes') /k/ and /k'/, and show that this solution fails to capture certain important generalizations about OE phonology. And further, that these can be captured in a quite simple and natural way, using the above assumption as a heuristic. We will show that the two-phoneme solution (first proposed, as far as we know, by Penzl 1947, and by now nearly 'canonical') posits as distinctive two segments that can be derived by otherwise necessary rules.

In his paper, 'The phonemic split of Germanic *k* in Old English', Penzl claims that the *i*-umlaut in pre-OE was responsible for a 'split' in the original Germanic /k/ phoneme. His account, which is essentially a 'structuralist' revision of the handbook consensus, may be paraphrased as follows:

(a) Germanic /k/ in pre-OE had two major allophones, a velar [k] and a palatal [k'], which were in complementary distribution: [k] before back vowels and [k'] before front vowels.

(b) The *i*-umlaut, which fronted original back vowels before /i j/, upset the former complementary distribution, by causing front vowels to stand after velar [k]. The palatalization process was no longer operative at the time of the umlaut (being an 'earlier sound change'), so that there was no 'secondary' palatalization of [k] when it came to stand before the new front vowels – even when these were identical in quality to the original ones that had caused palatalization in the first place.

(c) Subsequent loss of the suffixed formatives which caused the umlaut then caused a 'phonemic split', as the occurrences of [k] and [k'] were no longer predictable by environment, and therefore constituted separate 'phonemes'.

Within the taxonomic framework this solution is virtually self-evident; it does not however explain anything, and as we will see it leaves a great deal of clearly productive alternation in OE to be explained as virtual suppletion (though of course with an historical origin). The basic question is this: can we explain the fact that we get palatal and velar segments before the 'same' vowel, as in *cēne* 'keen' and *čēn* 'torch' in any other way? It seems to us that we can, and at the same time clarify some important related processes, if we take this apparent 'contrast' as derived, i.e. involving in part contrasting lexical vowels whose distinctiveness has been neutralized in certain environments.

Let us take as an example the pair of forms cited in the previous paragraph:

(4.1)   *cēne* 'keen' < *kōni-*
         čēn 'torch' < *kēnaz*

(For etymological information see Holthausen (1963) s.v. *cōene, čēn*.) Following Penzl's account, we would assume the state (4.2) before the *i*-umlaut:

(4.2)   [kōni] phonemically /kōni/
         [k'ēnaz] phonemically /kēnaz/

After umlaut, which fronts [o] to [ø], and after various processes which lower final [i] to [e], delete affixes, and in most cases unround [ø] to [e], we have the state (4.3):

(4.3)   [kēne] phonemically /kēne/
         [k'ēn] phonemically /k'ēn/

Thus history seems to demand a palatalization rule that was lost after operating on representations like those in (4.2). But as we shall see, there is no reason to imagine this rule being lost – and some good evidence for retaining it in the synchronic grammar, but having two different types of underlying representations pass through it, one of which fails to meet its proper analysis.

The simplest form for such a rule would seem to be one merely specifying the assimilation in backness of a stop to a following vowel, i.e. a rule of the sort that accounts for the variation in the initials of MnE *cool/keel, goose/geese*. We give a first approximation of this rule:

(4.4)   *Backness accommodation*

$$[+\text{cons}] \rightarrow [-\text{back}] / \underline{\hspace{2em}} \begin{bmatrix} -\text{cons} \\ -\text{back} \end{bmatrix}$$

This is not, however, enough; the rule given here is only the beginning point of the process. We must account for at least two other aspects of the OE palatalization: (a) the fact that [k'] ends up as [c], and (b) the fact that the palatalization of /g/ does not have symmetrical results. Since the output of palatalized /g/ is not an affricate but a palatal fricative [j], we need a way of getting an affricate from /k/ but not from /g/ in the same environment, while leaving open the possibility for (4.4) affecting /g/. The rule must in its final form have at least a differential voicing specification – and more, as we will see. Our final statement of the palatalization rule will capture more than merely the generalizations about palatalized [k g]; it will show up some other interesting facts about OE obstruents in general.

Now if the (synchronic) lexical representations for *cēne* and *ćēn* had the same nuclear vowel but different initial consonants, the palatalization rule would not be necessary in OE; and if there is no palatalization rule, there cannot be an umlaut rule either; and as we will show in the next section, there is morphophonemic evidence suggesting that umlaut was productive in OE. But what if we were to posit, as underlying representations for those forms showing (historical) umlaut, sequences in which the formatives causing umlaut are synchronically present: in this way we could motivate both the front vowel and the back consonant. We would then have derivations like the pair shown below in (4.5), representing the origins of *cēne* and *ćēn*. (Note that we return here to the practice of representing the 'long' vowels as geminates, in accordance with the claims made in chapter 1 – though we continue to mark 'length' in the citation of orthographic forms, for ease in identification.)

(4.5)

Input	kooni	keen
(4.4)		k'een
Umlaut	køøni	
Affix change	køøne	
Unrounding	keene	
Output	keene	k'een

Here backness accommodation (palatalization) applies only in the case of the following nonback vowel in input /keen/ and is blocked by the following back vowel in /kooni/.

If we start from underlying representations of this type, we need at least three more major rules to achieve the correct phonetic output: an umlaut rule, a rule which lowers [i] to [e] in certain suffixes, and a rule that unrounds nonhigh rounded front vowels in those dialects

which lack phonetic [ø]. (We specify 'nonhigh' because of the undoubted presence in all dialects of OE (except Kentish) of high rounded
front vowels of the type [y], written *y*.)

Thus we get a sequence of rules in the grammar which not only
produce the required surface forms in a simple way, but which also in
their sequence reflect the (putative) historical order of the 'sound
changes' they originated in. Of course it actually does not matter,
strictly speaking, whether they do or not; without adhering to the
Saussurean dichtomy one can still realize that diachronic evidence does
not crucially determine choices for synchronic ordering. We are
simply suggesting that the mere phonetic loss of the formatives causing
umlaut was probably not sufficient to result in a restructuring of the
grammar; throughout the OE period it seems reasonable to assume
what look very much like 'protoforms' as lexical representations in
many cases. And considering the arguments advanced e.g. in *SPE* for
the relative stability of underlying representations over time, this
should not be too surprising. (See also Kiparsky 1968b: 186–7.)

2   The *i*-umlaut: general considerations

Before discussing the palatalization in more detail, we must describe
the umlaut, and attempt to formulate the rules which govern it. The
historical evidence is well known, and the results in the various dialects
have been amply documented: see for example Prokosch (1938: 107–12);
Brunner (1965: 95–107); Campbell (1959: 190–204). In this treatment,
however, we will concentrate on the synchronic evidence in OE,
specifically those morphophonemic alternations which show the
operation of what is historically called *i*-umlaut. A table of examples
follows, drawn from evidence available for the 'long' and 'short' vowels.
We postpone discussion of the umlaut of the diphthongs until §3, as
this poses a number of problems.

(4.6)   *Alternation*   *Example*

ū	ȳ	*cūþ* 'known':*cȳþan* 'make known'
u	y	*burg* 'city':*byrig* 'id. dat. sing.'
ō	ø̄(ē)	*dōm* 'judgement':*dēman* 'judge'
o	ø(e)	*ofost* 'haste':*efstan* 'hasten'
ā	ǣ	*hāl* 'whole':*hǣlan* 'heal'
a	e	*mann* 'man':*menn* 'men'
a	æ	*faran* 'go':*færst* 'id. pres. 2 sing.'

These alternations are of obvious and productive types: formation of denominal verbs (*ofost:efstan*); of deadjectival verbs (*cūþ:cȳþan*); pluralization (*mann:menn*). There are other processes, too, not represented specifically in (4.6), such as formation of certain comparatives (*lang* 'long': *leng* 'longer'), and causativization (*drāf* 'drive', $PRET_1$:*drǣfan* 'herd').

The data in (4.6) require a few comments before they can be sorted out. First observe that the alternation of short [a]/[æ] is extremely restricted, compared with that of [a]/[e]. This preponderance of raised forms seems odd, as the other back vowels (including long [aa]) seem to be fronted only, and not raised. But recall that in our discussion (ch. II) of AFB, we showed that even though the historical evidence suggests 'failure' of AFB before nasals (hence *mann*, not **mænn*), the synchronic evidence suggests that the [e] in *menn* is in fact the umlaut of a derived [æ]. There is no 'double umlaut' of an underlying low back vowel, but low vowels unspecified for backness are assigned the feature [−back] even before nasals, when /i j/ follow the nasal. Thus what looks on the surface like an alternation of [a]/[e] is in fact an alternation of [æ]/[e] – only the [æ] never shows up as graphic *æ* or phonetic [æ]. A low vowel before a nasal can only be [a] if the environment is not an umlaut environment, or it can eventually come out as [e] if umlaut occurs.

Second, observe that there is an apparent irregularity in that [o] gives [e] from umlaut, while [u] gives [y]. This is due, as we mentioned above, to a late unrounding rule, which we will give in §4. We might, however, note here that there are basically two kinds of motivation for positing a stage [ø] for the umlaut of [o], even for those dialects which do not usually show such a vowel in surface forms. The first is historical: even in West Saxon, in early texts, there are traces of forms showing what is undoubtedly a front round vowel from the umlaut of [o]. For example, in *Cura Pastoralis* (Sweet 1871), we find *oeðel* 'native land' 2.7 (cf. OS *oþili*), *oele* 'oil' 368.11 < L. *oleum*, and *doe* 'do', pres. subj. 8.2. Second, even if there were no historical verification within WS for a stage [ø], the output [y] of umlauted [u] would suggest it very strongly, since a rule that mutated [u] to [y] and [a] to [æ] while converting [o] to [e] would be more complex and less intuitively natural than one that also changed [o] to [ø]. (We will discuss this further below.)

Another point to be noted is the apparent absence of any umlaut of [e]. This may seem strange, if we go by our criterion of using morphophonemic alternations as evidence, in the light of such obvious pairs as *helpan* 'help', and *hilpð* 'he helps', etc. But forms like this, which are the only real evidence for such a process, occur only in strong verb paradigms; and they are taken care of by the same rule that accounts for the high/mid back vowel alternations in these verbs (ch. I, rule (1.11)). This rule also accounts for some apparent diphthong umlauts, as in *cēosan* 'choose', *ciesð* 'he chooses'. The raising of [e] to [i] before [i] is of course technically an umlaut, and is very similar to the process we are discussing here; but it is not the same, and nothing would be gained by trying to subsume it under the same heading. It is simply an example of the fact that a language may be characterized by certain recurrent types of rules, that operate with similar effects at different points in the grammars (and historically, at different points in time, as we will see in chapters V and VI).

The basic effects of the umlaut may be summed up as follows: in a certain context, back vowels front, and if round retain their rounding. This means that in the case of the nonlow vowels /u o/ the umlaut produces new vowel types that are not present in the lexical inventory, i.e. [y ø]. When low back unround /a/ is umlauted, it coalesces with the [æ] already present from AFB (though non-lexical). If the vowels undergoing umlaut are nonback and low, they raise. Long (i.e. double) and short vowels are affected the same way, except that there are no forms showing umlaut of [ææ] to [ee]. (There is a certain complication for 'diphthongs', i.e. non-identical two-vowel clusters, but this will be treated later.)

The environment of the rule, judging from all the forms, is this: the vowel in question is followed directly by the high front vowel or palatal fricative causing the change (as in *drȳ* 'magician' < OIr. *drui, dēþ* 'he does' < **doiþ*), or one or more consonants intervene (as in *cyning* 'king' < **kuning, ende* 'end' < **ændi*).

In attempting to formulate the rule, we must keep the following facts in mind:

(a) Any cluster of the form /VV/ must be acted on by the rule in the same way as any single /V/ if it is marked [+back].

(b) The subrule raising low front vowels to mid must not be allowed to affect the output of the subrule which fronts low back vowels: otherwise [ææ] from umlaut of [aa] would be raised to [ee]. This can be accomplished by restricting the raising to short (i.e. single) vowels. However this will not prevent the raising of [æ] from [a] in *færst*, which must depend on ordering.

(c) A back vowel must retain its roundness when fronted. If we assume a marking convention for vowel roundness operating on the lexicon, and specifying all front vowels as nonround, then the retention of roundness must be specified in the rule. However, we assume that although it is probably a fact about the OE lexicon that it did not contain front round vowels, the reason for this is not markedness, but simply an idiosyncratic and language-specific property of Germanic languages at this stage of their evolution (see further appendix IV). So we will assume that there is no particular reason for a rule operating on a segment marked $\begin{bmatrix} +\text{back} \\ +\text{round} \end{bmatrix}$ to turn it into anything but a segment marked $\begin{bmatrix} -\text{back} \\ +\text{round} \end{bmatrix}$, if the structure change is $[+\text{back}] \rightarrow [-\text{back}]$. That is, rules will be assumed to operate in the 'normal' way, changing only features which are specified as changing.

We now make a first approximation to the umlaut rule – or at least to that part affecting long and short back vowels and short low front vowels. We omit, as we have said, the diphthongs, which we take up in the next section, after which we will present the complete rule.

(4.7) I-*umlaut: first approximation*

$$
\begin{bmatrix} -\text{cons} \\ \left\{ \begin{matrix} [+\text{back}] \\ \begin{bmatrix} -\text{back} \\ +\text{low} \end{bmatrix} \end{matrix} \right\} \end{bmatrix} \quad \left(\begin{bmatrix} -\text{cons} \\ +\text{back} \end{bmatrix} \right) \rightarrow \left\{ \begin{matrix} [-\text{back}] \\ [-\text{low}] \end{matrix} \right\} \quad ([-\text{back}]) / \underline{\quad} C_0 \begin{bmatrix} -\text{back} \\ +\text{high} \end{bmatrix}
$$

The usual conventions for disjunctive ordering may be assumed to apply here, with the longest expansions (and the higher-line) being made first, i.e. those including the parenthesized segments, which include the long vowels. To clarify, the expansions of (4.7) are:

(4.8)

(a) $\begin{bmatrix} -\text{cons} \\ +\text{back} \end{bmatrix} \begin{bmatrix} -\text{cons} \\ +\text{back} \end{bmatrix} \rightarrow \begin{bmatrix} -\text{cons} \\ -\text{back} \end{bmatrix} \begin{bmatrix} -\text{cons} \\ -\text{back} \end{bmatrix} / \underline{\quad} C_0 \begin{bmatrix} -\text{back} \\ +\text{high} \end{bmatrix}$

(b) $\begin{bmatrix} -\text{cons} \\ +\text{back} \end{bmatrix} \rightarrow [-\text{back}] / \underline{\quad} C_0 \begin{bmatrix} -\text{back} \\ +\text{high} \end{bmatrix}$

(c) $\begin{bmatrix} -\text{cons} \\ -\text{back} \\ +\text{low} \end{bmatrix} \rightarrow [-\text{low}] / \underline{\quad} C_0 \begin{bmatrix} -\text{back} \\ +\text{high} \end{bmatrix}$

It may seem at first that there are no occurrences of [a] as input to the *i*-umlaut; hence one case of (4.8b) will be vacuous. But there are in fact forms whose derivations very likely include umlaut of [a]. These are the few items like *færð* (3 sing. pres. ind. of *faran*) which are exceptions to AFB (cf. 1 pers. *fare*) but meet the conditions for umlaut (see further ch. 11.)

3 The umlaut of the diphthongs

There are morphophonemic alternations which suggest that both (derivational) classes of diphthongs – those from underlying /au/, /eu/ clusters and those from breaking of /e/ and [æ] – are subject to umlaut. These are exemplified by the following forms:

(4.9) (a) *Umlaut of lexical diphthongs*
        bēacn 'beacon': *bīecnan* 'signal'
        lēaf 'permission': *līefan* 'allow'
        þēod 'nation': *underþīedan* 'subject'

    (b) *Umlaut of breaking diphthongs*
        beald 'bold': *bieldan* 'encourage'
        eald 'old': *ieldra* 'older'
        feorr 'far': *afierran* 'make distant'
        beorht 'bright': *bierhto* 'brightness'

It seems clear that the forms without umlaut may in all cases be taken as 'basic' – since these pairs show the characteristic derivational processes that account for so many of the umlaut variants involving non-diphthongal nuclei: formation of deadjectival verbs (*beald: bieldan*, cf. *cūþ: cȳpan*); formation of comparatives (*eald: ieldra*, cf. *lang: leng*) and so on. So the grammar must contain a synchronic umlaut for the diphthongal nuclei also.

But a number of difficulties arise when we try to make the umlaut rule (4.7) cope with the diphthongs, and we face some serious questions. For instance:

(a) The umlauts of both *ea* and *eo* (where the first element is in one case [æ] and the other case [e]) appear to be identical; so either we must exempt the diphthongs from (4.8) and formulate a special rule for them, or we must change the rule so that *eo* is raised, and then have a second umlaut of *ea* to bring its first element up to [i]. Actually, there is, as we will see, a more reasonable solution to this.

(b) Since *ea* begins as [æu] and then becomes [æa], and *eo* begins as [eu] and then becomes [eo] (see ch. i, §3, ch. iii, §5), we must decide whether umlaut precedes or follows DHH (or whether it does both).

(c) Does the umlaut, however we finally formulate it, operate on both members of the cluster involved, or only on the leftmost, i.e. syllabic, member?

(d) Most important of all: what is the phonetic nature of the sequence represented by the spelling *ie*?

Obviously (d) is the first matter that must be clarified, since our answers to (a), (b), and (c) will depend crucially on what we eventually decide about (d).

One obvious way to attack the problem would be historically: what are the reflexes of *ie* in Modern English, and what kinds of Middle English and OE values do the modern reflexes lead us back to? And here we begin to have trouble: because virtually none of the forms with umlauted diphthongs have survived in an unambiguously recognizable way into Modern English. This lack of survival is apparently due to a conjunction of two factors: first, the number of forms with diphthongal nuclei was smaller than the number with either long or short vowels, so that the normal loss of lexicon over time had more striking results. And second, the majority of cases in which the umlauted diphthongs appear are instances of derivational processes which early became unproductive, so that through various processes of grammar simplification they tended to get lost: e.g. comparatives based on vowel-change. So that most of the relics of umlaut that are left to us are in contexts like noun/denominal verb pairs (e.g. *food:feed, blood:bleed*), or the plurals of the old monosyllabic consonant stem nouns (e.g. *foot:feet, man:men*) – whose nuclei are uniformly nondiphthongal.

We are also faced with another difficulty, which has not caused us any trouble up to now: and this is that the spelling *ie* is characteristic only of West Saxon – which is not the ancestor of any widely spoken form of Modern English (if indeed it is, strictly speaking, of any form at all). With processes like ablaut, palatalization, and umlaut of the monophthongs, which are widespread throughout the OE dialects, we could (although perhaps a bit dangerously) talk of WS [k] as if it were 'OE [k]', and draw direct lines of descent. But with *ie* the problem is different, as it appeared to our knowledge in no other dialects (cf. Sweet's remarks on this, 1871: xxix).

Because of the historical discontinuity between West Saxon and

Modern English, we will have to approach the analysis of *ie* less directly. We will look at two matters: first, the items other than *i*-umlaut of diphthongs that were spelt with *ie*; and second, the fate of *ie* in late OE, and in those Middle English dialects that we can trace with some certainty back to a West Saxon base, i.e. those of the SW and SW Midlands.

First, we observe that the spelling *ie* is very common in West Saxon texts, and in addition to umlaut it appears, in early texts, to reflect at least the following other sources (we follow in general Campbell 1959: 126–8):

(a) 'Contraction of *ĭ+e*' as in *sīe* 'be, pres. subj.'. Campbell says (1959: n. 2) that 'W-S naturally contracts *ĭ+e* to *īe*, but the other dialects had not such a diphthong, and hence their *ĭe* is disyllabic.' He cites as evidence for this a supposed metrical example where *sīe* 'fills a lift and a drop': but in the state of our present knowledge of OE metrical practice this cannot be considered compelling. Further just because West Saxon 'has' a diphthong *ie* does not mean that it must use that digraph only for a diphthong. We therefore assume that forms like *sīe* tell us nothing; their nuclei could be either diphthongs or two vowels in hiatus.

(b) 'Palatal diphthongization' of *ĕ*. As we show in appendix III, there is no very good evidence for such a process in OE; we assume (following Stockwell and Barritt 1951) that *ġie-*, *scie-* represent consonant symbol +palatalization diacritic+*e*, and not diphthongs at all. So forms like *ġiest* 'guest' (if it is in fact from [gæsti] synchronically) are probably not to the point.

(c) Back umlaut of *i*. Campbell cites cases in which '*ie* apparently replaces *io* from *i* by back umlaut in eW-S under circumstances not clear, e.g. *tielung* "effort", and related forms...various forms and derivatives of *witan*, *gewrietum* dat. pl. writings, *geflietu* pl. disputes...' (1959: 172). Campbell admits to being uncertain whether or not these forms are merely 'graphic variants of *i*', but suggests that they are too frequent to dismiss as such. He sums up by suggesting that 'it may be that where back umlaut of *i* failed to take place, there was a later tendency for *i* to become *ie*'. We are not sure what this means – it may be that in fact *ie* is simply a later spelling in these cases for the same process that led to *eo < io*; but it is interesting that these *ie* spellings do show up in environments that could not possibly be *i*-umlaut environments.

(d) 'When *i* was followed by *r*+another consonant, if the group had arisen too late to cause breaking, we find very often that *i* appears as *ie* in eW-S, though *i* frequently remains, e.g. *bierð* he bears, *iernan* run...' (1959: 126). These cases are difficult, but we suggest tentatively that they are due to a 'secondary' and rather poorly distributed breaking rule; or rather an expansion in some subdialects of the original breaking rule to cover clusters after /i/ that arose from syncope of the vowels in verbal endings. If this is so, it is simply an example of rule simplification of a common sort, and requires no further comment.

If we take all these types, plus the types we were originally concerned with, where the *ie* spellings represent the umlaut of diphthongs, and examine their later developments, we find the following pattern. In late West Saxon, the reflexes of the early *ie* forms develop as follows:

(4.10)

(a) *ĭe* > *ĭ* before palatals: *miht* 'might', *niht* 'night', *sihð* 'he sees', *hĭġ* 'hay', earlier *mieht, nieht, siehð, hĭeġ*.

(b) *ĭe* > *ў̆* elsewhere: *yldra* 'older', *yrmþu* 'poverty', *hȳran* 'hear', *frȳnd* 'friends', earlier *ieldra, iermþu, hĭeran, friend*.

That the consistent late *y*-spellings are not 'merely graphical' is shown by the developments in the Middle English dialects of the SW and SW Midlands, where the reflexes of original *y* and *y* < *ie* fall together in a vowel distinct from the reflex of OE *i*: thus the reflexes of OE *y, ie*, are fairly consistently spelt *u, ui, uy* as against *i, y* for the reflexes of *ī*: e.g. *fuir* 'fire' < OE *fȳr*, *huyren* 'hear' < *hȳran* < *hĭeran*, as against *suiþe* 'greatly' < OE *swīþe*, *þine* 'thine' < OE *þīn*.

This twofold development strongly suggests that whatever *ie* was, at least one of its elements was [+high] (since both of its reflexes are); that at least one of its elements was [+round] (since one of its reflexes is), and that at least one of its elements was [−back] (since both of its reflexes are). In one crucial respect then, it is at least possible that the structure of *ie* is the same as that of the other diphthongs: the above description would make it not unreasonable to posit a phonetic shape in which the two elements agree in height, but disagree in roundness and/or backness. The two most likely candidates then would seem to be [iu] and [iy]. We see no motivation for proposing sequences like [ui] or [yi], since the structure of the other diphthongs suggests that when rounded or back elements occur in diphthongs they will always be the nonsyllabic (i.e. rightmost) members.

If the structure of *ie* is in fact [iu] or [iy], then the late West Saxon and Middle English developments are quite clear and easy to account for. If for example the correct form is [iu], we have the following set of historical operations, parallel to (4.10):

(4.11)

(a) [iu] → { [ii] before palatals (if from umlaut of a lexical diphthong).
[i] before palatals (if from umlaut of a short diphthong).

(b) [iu] → { [yy] elsewhere (if from umlaut of a lexical diphthong).
[y] elsewhere (if from umlaut of a short diphthong).

That is, where breaking of a short vowel is concerned the nuclei undergo the development discussed in chapter III, where if the breaking rule is lost the nucleus 'reverts' to its underlying form, whether single or double.

If on the other hand *ie* is [iy], the processes are just the same as those in (4.11), except that there is no backness assimilation, but simply roundness assimilation in either direction. The choice of [iu] or [iy] is constrained by various other factors, which we will discuss below.

Let us first look at two other questions we raised at the beginning of this section: (a) whether the umlaut should apply before or after the height of the second element of the diphthong is adjusted by height harmony; and (b), whether the rule should apply to both segments of the diphthong, or only the first. We set out the consequences of all four choices below in (4.12). Since as we have observed the result of umlaut of the diphthongs is a neutralization of height-distinctions to [+high], we will for the moment separate this process as 'umlaut II', reserving 'umlaut I' for the schema (4.7):

(4.12) A. *Before height harmony*

	(a) Both vowels		(b) Left vowel only	
Input	æu	eu	æu	eu
Umlaut I	ey	ey	eu	—
Umlaut II	iy	iy	iu	iu
DHH	—	—	—	—
Output	iy	iy	iu	iu

B. *After height harmony*

	(a) Both vowels		(b) Left vowel only	
Input	æu	eu	æu	eu
DHH	æa	eo	æa	eo
Umlaut I	eæ	eø	ea	—
Umlaut II	iæ	iø	ia	io

It is clear that it will be harder to get a reasonable output if umlaut applies after DHH than before. But observe that if DHH is an 'everywhere rule', then it can apply to the [iæ iø] produced in (4.12 B(a)) or the [ia io] produced in (B(b)), with the same results as the outputs in (4.12 A(a) and A(b)) respectively. So in effect the second option simply requires an otiose set of diphthongs. Thus we can assume at least that umlaut operates before DHH.

We must now decide which is the better alternative: to have both vowels subject to umlaut, or only the first. It seems possible to make this decision only on the basis of the rest of the system, and the behaviour of the other segments under umlaut: but this leads to an apparent contradiction. The following appear to be the facts: first, the umlaut rule as it affects items other than diphthongs operates on both elements of two-vowel clusters. That is, for example both short /u/ and long /uu/ are mutated in the same way, to [y] and [yy] respectively. This would suggest that the part of the rule operating on the diphthongs should behave in that way too, affecting both segments.

But there is, second, a clear non-parallelism in the way that the diphthong umlaut works: both the diphthongs [æu] and [eu] have the same output. So in one respect the diphthongs are clearly different from the long vowels: regardless of the height value of the first element, the output is [+high]. And since this contradicts the structure change of the rule, there must be some specification to single out the diphthongs as being different in some crucial way from the long vowels. And within the framework adopted here for describing the OE vowel system, the difference between a long vowel and a diphthong is that the two elements of a long vowel are identical, while those of a diphthong are not.

So let us assume that the presence of a non-identical vowel after a nucleus with no segments intervening constitutes a differential environment that blocks the 'normal' type of umlaut, and causes the preceding vowel to become high. This leaves us only with the problem of making a choice between [iu] and [iy] as the value of *ie*, the output of the rule.

We choose [iu] (also suggested, incidentally, by Stockwell 1958), primarily because of congruity with the rest of the diphthongs. All the others, whether before or after DHH, have second elements which are [+back]; and in fact, we found it necessary to constrain the application of DHH to diphthongs whose elements differed in backness (in order, in particular, to block the shift of [ei] in *bīdan* < /beidan/, etc., to [ee]). And since two-vowel sequences which do not meet the SD for DHH in this respect are realized as surface monophthongs, we feel that the rule applicable to all nuclei (other than the source of *ie*, for the moment) which are capable of appearing as surface monophthongs should as it were 'select' the form of this third diphthong. So congruity in terms of the other diphthongs in the system, and the nature of DHH, suggest that this third diphthong be typologically similar, i.e. with a back nonsyllabic vowel following a front syllabic. We find no particular reason for positing a special secondary type of diphthong with the two elements agreeing in backness.

If [iu] is the output value, there must be a subrule in the umlaut schema which will mark the first element of a non-identical vowel cluster [+high] – no matter what its other features are. That is, we must account for the neutralization:

(4.13)

Now since the only forms that meet the non-identical cluster description at the time of the umlaut rule have a [+back] second element, and either a low or mid vowel first element, which in both cases is nonback, we need specify the height coefficient only on the output vowel – so long as we add a condition on the subrule that it applies only if the members of the cluster are not the same. So we need a rule of this type:

(4.14)
$$V \rightarrow [+high] / \underline{\hspace{2em}} VC_0 \begin{bmatrix} -back \\ +high \end{bmatrix}$$
Condition: V ≠ V

This rule is the same as the regular umlaut, except for the following: first the environments are partially disjoint, in that all /VV/ clusters undergoing the regular umlaut have both vowels the same; and second, the structure change is different, in that this is the only case, if it can be properly incorporated into the rule, in which the specification [+high] appears. But (4.14) and the other cases of umlaut do share a great many features, both in terms of environment and in terms of the kinds of grammatical alternations that they produce; enough so that if we simply made this a separate rule we would lose an obvious generalization. Judging from the paradigmatic effects, at least, the similarities are not accidental.

We now give the complete umlaut rule, with the substance of (4.14) in angled parentheses; and we note further that according to the convention stated in Preliminaries, p. 7 n., the front and back vowel umlauts are to be taken as simultaneously applicable.

(4.15) I-*umlaut: final version*

$$\left\langle\left\{\begin{matrix}\begin{bmatrix}-\text{cons}\\ [+\text{back}]\\ \begin{bmatrix}-\text{back}\\ +\text{low}\end{bmatrix}\end{bmatrix}\end{matrix}\right\}\left(\begin{bmatrix}-\text{cons}\\ +\text{back}\end{bmatrix}\right)\right\rangle \longrightarrow \left\{\begin{bmatrix}-\text{back}\\ -\text{low}\\ \langle+\text{high}\rangle\end{bmatrix}\right\} ([-\text{back}]) \, /\!\!-\!\!- \; \langle-\text{cons}\rangle \; C_0 \begin{bmatrix}-\text{back}\\ +\text{high}\end{bmatrix}$$

Condition: $\langle-\text{cons}\rangle \neq \langle-\text{cons}\rangle$

For convenience we give the full set of expansions below:

(4.16)

(a) $[-\text{cons}] \rightarrow [+\text{high}]/\!\!-\!\!- \; [-\text{cons}] \; C_0 \begin{bmatrix}-\text{back}\\ +\text{high}\end{bmatrix}$

(b) $\begin{bmatrix}-\text{cons}\\ +\text{back}\end{bmatrix}\begin{bmatrix}-\text{cons}\\ +\text{back}\end{bmatrix} \rightarrow \begin{bmatrix}-\text{cons}\\ -\text{back}\end{bmatrix}\begin{bmatrix}-\text{cons}\\ -\text{back}\end{bmatrix} \, /\!\!-\!\!- C_0 \begin{bmatrix}-\text{back}\\ +\text{high}\end{bmatrix}$

(c) $\begin{bmatrix}-\text{cons}\\ +\text{back}\end{bmatrix} \rightarrow [-\text{back}]/\!\!-\!\!- C_0 \begin{bmatrix}-\text{back}\\ +\text{high}\end{bmatrix}$

(d) $\begin{bmatrix}-\text{cons}\\ -\text{back}\\ +\text{low}\end{bmatrix} \rightarrow [-\text{low}]/\!\!-\!\!- C_0 \begin{bmatrix}-\text{back}\\ +\text{high}\end{bmatrix}$

Thus let us say that the input to (4.15) is a form [læuɪjan], lexical /laufjan/. Since the position before [fj], the environment of the rule, is occupied by a cluster whose members are not identical, case (a) of (4.16) applies, giving [liufjan], which is ultimately spelt *līefan* 'permit'. Similarly an input form [bloodjan] will meet case (b), giving [bløødjan], later spelt *blēdan* 'bleed'. And an input [mænni] will meet case (d) and give [menni], later spelt *menn* 'men'. (The rules responsible for the further modifications of the umlauted forms will be discussed later.)

One final point should perhaps be brought up here. Granted that the historical developments as outlined in (4.10) support an analysis of *ie* as [iu], why is it spelt the way it is? The answer seems to be, like the answer to why [æa] is spelt *ea* and not *æa*, a matter of graphic convention. Roughly, just as *æa* or *aea* is ruled out in all but the very earliest spelling traditions by a prohibition of 'graphic triphthongs' (see appendix III), *iu* (and generally *io*) are ruled out by a similar nonphonetic constraint: no vowel-graph may appear after *i* except *e*; unless the *i* represents [j] and the vowel is syllabic, as in some traditions which permit spellings like *iung* 'young' (usual WS *geong*). The letter *e* is in a sense the OE 'neutral' graph: it is used as a palatalization diacritic, as a replacement for *æ* when another vowel follows, and according to our analysis, here as a replacement for *u* when *i* precedes. And this is quite plausible on phonological grounds; since if *i* represents a syllabic, the only other nonconsonant segment that can follow it (except of course itself) is [u], by the provisions of DHH. A similar case can be seen in the East Anglian ME spellings of [ʃ] as *x* in modals: since ME had no initial [ks], a form like *xal* 'shall' (e.g. in *Ludus Coventriae*) must begin with something else; and if the syntactic context is something like [$_{VP}$ [x̄] x [$_V$]$_V$]$_{VP}$ then the string bracketed as 'x' must be an auxiliary, and if *xal* is an auxiliary it is the modal *shall*, so *x* is [ʃ]. Thus whatever the exact reason for the choice of *ie* rather than *iu* to represent [iu], the result is unambiguously interpretable.

4 Affix modification and nonhigh unrounding

Since the segments [i j] which cause *i*-umlaut do not in general appear as such in surface forms, there must be rules which in most cases either neutralize (lower) or delete them. We are not basically concerned in this study with these morphological rules, which would properly form part of a monograph on derivational and inflexional morphology in OE (for some fairly detailed formulations and discussion see Wagner 1969). But we will sketch out some of the typical effects of these rules here, and group them without further analysis under the cover term 'affix modification'.

(But see appendix II for some discussion of one of them.) The most typical treatments of the umlauting formatives are of the following types:

(a) A [j] is deleted when it is the initial of the verb-forming suffix /-jan/: *dēman* 'judge' < /doomjan/, *sendan* 'send' < /sandjan/. But if the preceding segment is /r/ and the vowel before /r/ is single, it remains (or is perhaps vocalized), and is spelled *i*: *nerian* 'save' < /narjan/.

(b) Word-final [i] is deleted when it is preceded by a single vowel and a geminate consonant: *cynn* 'kin' < /kunni/ < /kuni/. If the [i] is in a suffix (i.e. if a morpheme-boundary intervenes between it and its preceding consonant), it is always deleted: *fēt* 'foot, dat. sing., n. acc. pl.' < /footi/.

(c) A final [i] is lowered to [e] after a long vowel and a single consonant: *cēne* 'keen' < /kooni/.

(d) An [i] remains when it is 'protected' by a following consonant: *cyning* 'king' < /kuning/.

The total picture is of course much more complex than these four selected types would suggest, but they will serve to indicate the kind of things that the rules, when formulated, will have to account for. It is clear from the above examples that they have in part something to do with general constraints on syllable and morpheme structure (we discuss some of these matters in appendix II). We will not deal with this any further here.

We now turn our attention to the rule that unrounds the [ø] resulting from umlaut in those dialects which lack phonetic segments of that type. It may be formulated as follows:

(4.17) *Nonhigh unrounding*

$$[-\text{cons}] \rightarrow [-\text{round}] \ / \ \begin{bmatrix} \underline{\qquad} \\ -\text{high} \\ -\text{back} \end{bmatrix}$$

We tentatively order (4.17) after the processes of affix modification rather than before them: though synchronically it does not appear to make any difference. The rule actually seems, in any given subdialect grammar, to be crucially ordered with respect to no other rule, except of course umlaut, which serves as its input (and of course also, in those dialects that have it, the rule that assimilates an [e] to a preceding [w], when that rule is lost: e.g. Nth *woeġ* 'way', WS *weġ*).

We defend our ordering decision as follows. Let us say that at some level the grammar of a given dialect of a language should, if possible, represent something like an underlying 'dialect-free' common core, a shared body of rules common to all dialects (a 'pan-dialectal phonology' in the sense of Bailey 1969, *q. v.* for discussion). If we accept this, and its corollary that it is the existence of some such common core that in part accounts for the relative ease (in most cases) of interdialectal comprehension, then we would in general want the *differentia* to appear at the lowest level in the grammar consonant with the facts.

In the light of this proposal we note the following: with the exception of a few archaic forms in some of the early texts, the attested OE corpus shows us the results of the processes of affix modification in a quite similar form for all the dialects. But the dialects show a much more varying treatment of [ø]-type vowels, which suggests by the above criterion a lower level in the grammar. And in many dialects there is strong evidence for the presence of such vowels in Middle English, which further supports our decision.

In this connexion we might also mention one related fact, which may tend to confirm the low-level status of nonhigh rounding. And this is that it is in precisely those dialects of Middle English that descend from the West Saxon OE dialects in which the rule operated, that vowels of the excluded type appear. They are not, it is true, from the same source (they are mostly from OE *ĕo* and Fr. /ø/), but they are of the same type. This pattern of absence followed by occurrence followed by absence again (in later Middle English) surely suggests a late point in the grammar. (On the general history of front round vowels in Middle English see Luick 1964: §§ 357, 374–5, 412, and Mossé 1952: §§ 29–30.)

It should be clear from this discussion of ordering that (4.17) is a phonological rule proper (P-rule), not a redundancy rule or segment structure condition (Stanley 1967). Front round vowels, as we said above, do not appear in lexical representations; but they may appear in derivations as the output of any rules that specify them. So that front round vowels appear at some stage in all the dialects, and are lost in some by the addition of rules like (4.17).

5 The palatalization in detail

We return now to the further development of [k'] and [g'] from /k/ and /g/ before non-umlaut front vowels. We address ourselves first to [k']. The Modern English [tʃ], and the Middle English spellings (from c. 1200 on, pretty uniformly of the type *ch*, *cch*) suggest that at some point the original [k'] (perhaps [c]) must have become an affricate. Indeed,

5-2

inverse spellings in OE such as *orceard* 'orchard' for original *ortgeard* would confirm a value like [tj], if not even [tɕ] or present [tʃ]. (Such NE assimilations as [tj] to [tʃ] in *congratulate* make the orthographical equalization of [tj] and [tʃ] quite likely. For further examples and discussion, Campbell 1959: §§426–39.) Whatever the exact details, the change to affricate did occur. But the interesting question is: how did this come about? Or more to the point, what is the most natural way to get from [k'] to [tʃ] in a synchronic grammar? (We omit from consideration the purely historical question of whether the final assimilation results from a 'gradual sound change' like [k] > [k'] > [c] > [tj] > [tʃ], or whether there was an immediate shift from [k'] to [tʃ]. It is clear that whatever the actual historical process was, there is no synchronic justification for the 'gradual' formulation. Because of our uncertainty about phonetic detail, we will represent the OE 'palatal *k*', which we suspect was an affricate of the type [tɕ] or [tʃ], with the rather 'neutral' symbol [c], which is to be taken as specifying no more than 'prevelar, postalveolar stop with strident release'. When we come to deal later with its voiced congener, we will use the symbol [ɟ] in a similar way.)

Now if we assume that the synchronic process is a one-step shift, we might formulate the rule simply as one that automatically turns any voiceless palatal stop into an affricate. And assuming that palatal or alveopalatal affricates may be specified as basically strident stops, we make a first approximation as follows:

(4.18) *Assibilation*

$$
\begin{bmatrix} +\text{obs} \\ -\text{cont} \\ -\text{voice} \end{bmatrix} \rightarrow [+\text{strident}] \ / \ \begin{bmatrix} -\text{back} \\ +\text{high} \end{bmatrix}
$$

Observe that a rule of this type would also convert a palatalized dental to [c], which might explain spellings like *orceard* referred to above. Also, the specification for voicing is important, because of the previously mentioned dissymmetry in the developments of palatalized /k/ and /g/: recall that the output of palatalized /g/ is [j], not the voiced congener of [c], i.e. [ɟ]). (The voiced [ɟ] did in fact develop in OE, as we will see in §8; and in later periods both [c ɟ] could be generated at a low phonetic level by assimilation from [tj dj] as in *Christian, soldier*, much in the same way that [ʃ ʒ] may derive from [sj zj] as in *issue, vision*. For details, see Jesperson 1961: 1.12.2–12.5.)

But the rule (4.18) applies to palatalized /k/ only; and since /k g/ are both transformed (albeit differently) it seems worthwhile to try and capture both these processes in one rule. We will return to this shortly, after a brief recapitulation of the claims so far made about the relations of palatalization and umlaut as they affect forms containing (initial) underlying /k/. To sum up: full specification of palatal and velar realizations of underlying /k/ depends on a set of rules operating on sequences beginning /kV/. If /V/ is back, and the umlaut analysis is not met, the result is a phonetic velar. If /V/ is front, the result is palatal whether or not umlaut occurs. But if /V/ is back and the umlaut environment follows, then the result is a velar, since umlaut is ordered after palatalization. Finally, any [ø] resulting from umlaut may be unrounded in many dialects; and the [k'] produced by backness accommodation (4.4) will be acted on by some rule like (4.18), and become [c]. We will take this last point up again shortly, and show how the final results of the palatalization of /g/ can be handled by the same rule.

Returning for a moment to our point of departure, which was Penzl's taxonomic account of these matters: we see now that the so-called 'phonemic split' of /k/ is essentially a methodological or metatheoretical artifact, since the occurrences of velars and palatals are in fact predictable by rule from representations containing an underlying velar. Only an analysis which does not permit synchronic ordering of rules, but operates solely on the segmentation of surface-phonetic forms, fails to predict the alternation correctly. Penzl claimed that a 'split' had occurred, because the former allophones were no longer in complementary distribution, but had become contrastive: they could, after (historical) umlaut, appear 'in the same environment', i.e. before the same (phonetic) vowel. But as we have seen, the environments still contrast, but on a more abstract level of representation. That is, the [ee] in *cēne* and the [ee] in *čēn* are 'the same environment' only if we do not consider their derivational history – specifically the input segments.

So an analysis that gives palatal and velar stops as elements of equal status is incorrect. The evidence suggests the relationships shown below:

(4.19)

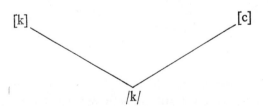

(It is of some interest here that of two recent generative studies of OE that we have seen, one, Howren 1967, fails to take account of this, and posits underlying /k k'/ as well as /g g'/. The other, Wagner 1969, also makes a case for a synchronic palatalization and umlaut.)

We now address ourselves to the development of palatalized /g/. Since OE had a voicing contrast in its labial and dental stop series – /p t/ vs. /b d/ – we might expect that the velars would be symmetrical with the others, giving voiceless and voiced triples, /p t k/, /b d g/. But the symmetry seems to be challenged by the differential palatalization, and also by an influential part of the scholarly tradition.

Thus Campbell speaks for one well-represented school of thought in claiming that *g* did not represent a stop initially – at least, not until too late for the historical origin of the rules we are discussing here. He says (1959: 21) that 'single *g* is a stop only in the group *ng* = [ŋg]', and that 'velar *ʒ* became a stop initially by the end of the OE period' (175). Others disagree: thus Moulton (1954: 24 n.58) assumes stop articulation 'because that is what we find as far back as we can trace the pronunciation from modern times'.

We will discuss the various processes of weakening and strengthening that affected the OE stops in chapter v; but for now we will merely say that there seems to us to be no very strong evidence for fricative articulation (presumably Campbell's *ʒ* = [ɣ]) in OE anywhere except in environments between back vowels. And in fact the [ɣ] between back vowels, which all scholars seem to agree on, develops into NE [w]: cf. *bow* < *būgan*. Whereas initial *g* always becomes [g] or [j]. We assume then that *g* represented an underlying stop, the voiced congener of /k/ (except when it represented Gmc /j/: see §5), and that [ɣ] existed only as the result of continuancy assimilation of /g/ in back vowel environments. To anticipate, we see the realizations of underlying /g j/ as follows:

(4.20)

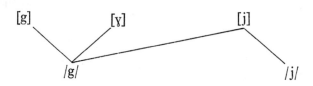

But even if we assume that /k/ and /g/ differ only with respect to the feature [±voice], we must still account for the developments [k'] >

[c], [g′] > [j] in the same environment. Clearly (4.18) was too fully specified, and did not capture the generalization we wanted: namely that in palatalized velars there is a specific relationship between voicing and continuancy; and if we assume that [+strident] is distinctive for [c], between voicing and stridency. For convenience we now give the earlier backness accommodation rule again, followed by the new rule, which acts on its output, and which we will call 'palatal softening'.

(4.21) *Backness accommodation (palatalization): first version*

$$[+\text{cons}] \rightarrow [-\text{back}] \ / \ \underline{\hspace{1.5cm}} \begin{bmatrix} -\text{cons} \\ -\text{back} \end{bmatrix}$$

(4.22) *Palatal softening: first version*

$$\begin{bmatrix} +\text{cons} \\ \alpha\text{voice} \end{bmatrix} \rightarrow \begin{bmatrix} -\alpha\text{strident} \\ \alpha\text{cont} \end{bmatrix} \ / \ \begin{bmatrix} \underline{\hspace{1cm}} \\ -\text{back} \\ +\text{high} \end{bmatrix}$$

The variables specify that the voiceless [k′] will remain noncontinuant and become strident; and that voiced [g′] will become a nonstrident continuant. This captures the interesting fact that all palatalized velars are to be characterized as [αvoice, αcontinuant]; and this is illustrative of a more general fact about velars, since it is true in intervocalic environments as well. Thus /k/ remains between vowels (e.g. *æcer* 'acre', *lōcian* 'look'), while /g/ goes to [j] between front vowels and [ɣ] between back vowels (*pleġan* 'play', *āgan* 'own'). Just as the voiceless stop remains noncontinuant in palatalization environments, it fails to undergo intervocalic lenition. The same kind of nonparallelism shows up in two contexts at least. In a sense of course this merely reflects the obvious fact that the 'stronger' a segment is (and presumably voiceless segments are stronger than voiced ones), the less likely it is to undergo lenition in some given environment. (We will discuss this in some detail in chapter v, where we consider the behaviour of the whole obstruent series under assimilation to 'weak' and 'strong' features.)

The situation in Modern English is different: we still have a backness accommodation rule, but only at low level – the rule operates on pairs like *cool/keel, goose/geese*. And now both /k/ and /tʃ/ < OE [c] are lexical segments. Actually, of course, it is possible that backness accommodation applied twice in OE, once before palatal softening and umlaut, and once after: so that no pure (unpalatalized) velar could stand before a front vowel. The difference between the two classes of forms with initial *c, g*, then would be not that there was no palatalization in the ones with umlauted vowels, but rather that only backness accommodation operated on them, and not palatal softening. Thus backness accommodation would be a redundancy rule, applying at any point in a derivation where its proper analysis was met. Then forms with underlying back vowels that were not umlauted would be subject to neither rule; forms with back vowels subject to umlaut would be subject only to (post-umlaut) backness accommodation; and forms with underlying front vowels would be subject to both rules. So ordering is crucial only insofar as the relation backness-accommodation/palatal softening is concerned, and as far as the relation umlaut/palatal softening is concerned: softening must not be allowed to act on the output of umlaut, whereas backness accommodation may.

The basic historical developments of /g/ are more or less as expected on the model of /k/, but there are a few apparent anomalies that bear some comment. First, however, the 'normal' developments:

(a) [j] before original front vowels: *ġeolu* 'yellow', *ġieldan* 'yield'.
(b) [g] before original back vowels: *gōs* 'goose', *gāst* 'ghost'.
(c) [g] before umlauted back vowels: *gēs* 'geese', *gyrdels* 'girdle'.
Some of the major anomalies are these:

(a) [g] before original front vowels: *give, get, gate, gallows*, OE *ġ(i)efan, ġ(i)etan, ġeat, ġealga*. The simplest answer here is the traditional one of 'Scandinavian influence' – however that may have operated. The most likely way would seem to be by direct borrowing of forms, i.e. ON *gefa, geta, gata, galgi*. Since Old Norse did not at that time have a palatal softening rule, these forms, if they were borrowed as is, would be 'synchronically foreign' in OE dialects that had palatal softening: an OE form beginning with the 'impermissible' sequence [ge] would then be the equivalent of a form like *Dvořak* or *Vladimir* in Modern English. That the OE forms did indeed have [j] is borne out by survivals like *yett* in place names from OE *ġeat*, and by the Middle English spelling distributions: basically non-northern forms like *yeve, yive*, as against northern ones like *gyve, give, gyff*.

(b) [ʤ] before original front vowels: *gem*, OE *ġimm* < L. *gemma*. The answer here, as in *angel* (OE *engel*) is undoubtedly reborrowing from French after the Conquest.

(c) [j] before original back vowels. We know of only one clear case of this type, which is *yawn*. The vowel suggests OE *gānian* 'gape, yawn', rather than the apparently synonomous verb *ginian* (*gynian, gionian*). The consonantism, however, suggests the latter. The *OED* (s.v. *yawn*) proposes, perhaps correctly, a sort of 'conflation': [j]-forms 'influenced by' (whatever that means) the vowel of now obsolete [g]-forms. (A similar situation holds in *shriek, screech*, which seem to be 'mixtures' of this sort also: we would expect only the (nonstandard) [skri:k] and [ʃri:tʃ].)

Aside from forms of this type, however, the developments in Modern English give us no cause to doubt the value [j] for palatalized /g/.

6 The second source of [j]: Germanic /j/ in OE

The preceding discussion has suggested that the handbook accounts are basically correct; the underlying velar stops are realized as palatals before front vowels only when those vowels are lexical (= 'etymological') front vowels and conversely as velars before lexical back vowels, regardless of their eventual (derived) backness specification. The alternations [k] ~ [c], [g] ~ [j] represent morphophonemic developments of underlying /k g/.

But there are complications. There was another class of forms beginning with phonetic [j] (and usually spelt with *g*) that clearly (on the basis of both comparative and developmental evidence) had this [j] before both front and back vowels. These forms derive historically not from Gmc /g/, but from Gmc /j/. Words of this type are spelt most often with initial *ge-* plus *u, o, a*; but it seems likely that the *e* in these cases, as in the so-called 'palatal diphthongization', is a palatalization diacritic, and does not represent a segment. Since in normal OE spelling the sequence *goc* would be read as [gok], something would have to be done if the word to be represented were [jok] 'yoke'. And the way usually chosen was to use an *e* after the *g*, i.e. *geoc*, to indicate that contrary to the usual situation a *g* before a back-vowel graph was to be read as palatal, not velar.

Many of the authorities, e.g. Campbell (1959: 171), regard this *e*, or as it is occasionally written, *i*, after *g* from Gmc /j/ as representing a 'glide' (in the sense of *Gleitelaut*, not current American usage), but the evidence for this is far from conclusive. Campbell says:

After *i̦* there was a strong tendency to develop a glide front vowel to facilitate the passage from front consonant to back vowel. The main accent of the word remained on the back vowel, so that no diphthong of the typical OE kind with an accented front vowel as its first element was formed. The usual subsequent history of the sounds under consideration is loss of the glide and development of the back vowel in ME. Thus OE *ġeoc* becomes ME *yok*, just as if the glide vowel never existed. It has, therefore, sometimes been argued that the symbol...which is generally supposed to be a glide, is merely a diacritic to indicate the palatal nature of the preceding consonant. The existence of the glide vowel is, however, proved by cases in which the accent is transferred to it.

Aside from the fact that Campbell cites none of these cases (and even if he did, the assumption would be proved only for them), the range of OE spelling variation suggests that it was certainly possible to have sequences like [jo], [ju] without epenthesis of a nonsyllabic vowel to facilitate 'transition'. We find for instance spellings with *i* followed directly by *u, o* in quite a large scatter of texts: to take a few examples, *iugie* 'I yoke', *geiukodan* 'yoked', *Aelfric's Colloquy* 24, 25 (Garmonsway 1947); *iu* 'formerly', *Seafarer* 83, *iuwine* 'friend of former days', *Seafarer* 92 (Gordon 1960), *iu* also in *Dream of the Rood*, 87 (Dickins and Ross 1954), *Phoenix* 41 (Blake 1964), *Beowulf* 2459, *iu-monna* '(of) men of old', *Beow.* 3052 (Klaeber 1950), *iugoð* 'youth', *Aelf. St Oswald* 3 (Needham 1966), *iogoðe, Beow.* 1674, *iung* 'young', *Aelf. St Edmund* 7 (Needham 1966).

In the texts cited above, the *i*-spellings alternate quite freely with the more traditional *ge-, gi-* spellings; and this would seem to support the possibility of direct transition from [j] to a back vowel, and the notion that the 'glide' vowels are simply diacritics.

The comparative evidence also points clearly to both an initial [j] and a following back vowel in forms like these: thus we have cognate sets like *ġeoc* = Go. *juk*, Gr. *zugón; ġeoguð* = OFris. *jogethe* (cf. L. *juventu-s*); *ġeong* = OFris. *iung* (cf. L. *juveni-s*); *ġeond* 'yond' = Go. *jaind*. If this is true, then the question of the formulation of the grammar might again arise. Are these forms, along the lines of the arguments presented earlier concerning umlaut, to be analysed as having underlying front vowels, so that they can be derived from underlying /g/? Surely in this case we have no evidence for any context that could account for a backness switch. The answer must be that the situation here is in fact the inverse of the [k] ~ [c] situation – these forms have underlying /j/. And it seems that the reflexes of underlying /j/ in OE overlap completely with those of palatalized /g/, so that we get the situation diagrammed earlier in (4.20).

The Modern English evidence also suggests that in all probability palatalized underlying /g/ and underlying /j/ had the same phonetic representation, and that at some point both of these phonetic [j] lost their friction in certain environments and became, in general, 'glides': see discussion in Stockwell (1962). This must have occurred quite late in the OE period and is in fact intimately connected with the so-called 'vocalization' of OE [j] < /g/ which was such a fertile source of the 'new' Middle English diphthongs (e.g. *dæġ* 'day', phonetically [dæj] becomes eME *dai*, phonetically [dai]). See further Mossé 1952: 31, and chapter VI below.)

7 An excursus: the testimony of alliterative practice

If the palatal and velar alternants of underlying /k/ and /g/ were as different as both the historical developments and the consensus of scholarship suggest, then the alliteration of *g*- and *c*-forms in much of the extant OE verse creates some difficulties. The principle behind alliterative choice, that is, seems to be neither phonetic likeness nor identity of lexical origin. Take for example the following lines from *Beowulf* (Klaeber 1950):

(4.23) Hwæt we *G*ar-Dena in *g*eardagum (1)
*g*omban *g*yldan; þæt wæs *g*od cyning (11)
*g*eong in *g*eardum, þone *G*od sende (13)
ne hyrde ic *c*ymlicor *c*eol gegyrwan (38)
ond þa *c*earwylmas *c*olran wurðaþ (282)
*c*easterbuendum *c*enra gehwylcum (758)

(The alliterating segments are italicized.)
    The lexical membership and phonetic representation of the segments involved are as follows:

(4.24)

Lexical	Phonetic
/g/ – /j/	[g] – [j]
/g/ – /g/ – /g/	[g] – [j] – [g]
/j/ – /g/ – /g/	[j] – [j] – [g]
/k/ – /k/	[k] – [c]
/k/ – /k/	[c] – [k]
/k/ – /k/	[c] – [k]

The alliterative practice seems here to deny the distinctions that both history and theory demand. There are as far as we can tell only two possible explanations: either the alliteration is based on the orthography, and is purely conventional ('eye-alliteration'), or there is some deeper systematic motivation. The assumption of mere conventional matching of letters is of course an easy one to make, but it seems doubtful considering the date of the text (Klaeber 1950: cvii ff.). And further, the deviance of this practice from what was current in other alliterative situations, e.g. the severe restriction of *s*-cluster alliteration to identical clusters, makes this more unlikely. It would be interesting if we could find a phonological explanation: and in fact one which also explains why there is no attempt to make the spelling represent the phonology in detail. We suggest accordingly that the following principles may be taken as representing in a rather crude form the primary identity-based constraints on both alliteration and spellings:

Principle I. Any variants of an underlying segment may alliterate, since they are all predictably derived from a single underlying form by phonological rules that are part of a speaker's competence. Thus [c] and [k], [j] and [g] may alliterate because the speaker knows that each of the two pairs is a possible output of one underlying segment. *Corollary:* for 'may alliterate' substitute 'may be spelt alike'.

Principle II. Any two segments may alliterate, if they are types that *can* be derived from one underlying segment – even if their sources in a particular case (e.g. *Beowulf* 1, 13) are different. Thus [g] can alliterate with *any* [j] regardless of origin, since both segments are *possible* outputs of underlying /g/: even if the actual input for a given occurrence of [j] happens to be /j/ and not /g/ at all. *Corollary:* for 'may alliterate' substitute 'may be spelt alike'.

In this way the alliterative (and orthographical) practice can be seen to depend not on phonetic likeness, nor even on underlying identity, but on the *possibility* of identity at some abstract level of representation.

Let us make the rather obvious assumption that orthography is in fact rule-governed, and that there is in the grammar of a literate speaker of a language a 'graphic component' which is interpretive vis-à-vis the phonology (actually the syntax too: but this does not concern us here) in much the same way that the phonology is interpretive vis-à-vis the syntax. (We borrow this term from U. Teleman's 'Grafisk Komponent' 1970. See this study for some suggestions about the kind of rules that are necessary for a model of 'orthographical competence'.) Now one of the conditions that may operate on this component is a general schema for graph-choice in the case of overlapping reflexes of underlying segments, which we think may make use of certain elementary set-theoretic operations. We suggest a general condition of the type shown below:

(4.25)   Let $A = \{x|x$ is a manifestation of $/a/\}$
            Let $B = \{y|y$ is a manifestation of $/b/\}$

(a) If A and B are disjoint, then no $x \in A$ and $y \in B$ may have the same graphic representation. Or to put it another way, if the intersection of A and B is empty $(A \cap B = \varnothing)$, then no members of either set can have the same spelling.

(b) If, however, the intersection of the two sets is non-empty $(A \cap B \neq \varnothing)$, then *any* member of either A or B may be represented by the same graph, i.e. there is a common representation for the *union* of the sets, $A \cup B$, regardless of whatever entities may occur in $A \cup B$.

The controlling factor is thus some aspect of a speaker's competence, as yet undescribed, and here only conjecturally posited, that permits knowledge of the type described in (4.25); an 'overview' of morphophonemic processes that can recognize the class of possible outputs for any underlying segment, and can perform elementary set-theoretic operations on these classes, in such a way as to select a possible unitary representation for the outputs of two otherwise disjoint sets.

8 Some further refinements: apparent vs. actual palatalization after front vowels: palatalization in clusters

We have so far considered the palatalization of underlying velar stops only in its relation to *i*-umlaut; and more specifically, only when the velar stop is before a stressed vowel. But we now turn to forms in which the /k g/ follow such a vowel: and these show a rather different pattern. Let us begin with cases where a front vowel precedes a velar stop, and observe the distribution of palatalized and nonpalatalized velars:

(4.26)

Palatalized	*Nonpalatalized*
ić 'I'	prician 'prick'
pić 'pitch'	stician 'stick'
dīć 'ditch'	
bēće 'beech'	brecan 'break'
	sprecan 'speak'
blǣćan 'bleach'	æcer 'acre'

(4.26) (cont.)   *Palatalized*   *Nonpalatalized*

        tǣċan 'teach'   bæc 'back'

                                              blæc 'black'

        stīġrap 'stirrup'

        īfiġ 'ivy'

        dæġ 'day'

        cǣġ 'key'

        weġ 'way'

        byrġan 'bury'

First, and perhaps most important, there are a number of instances in which /k/ appears not to palatalize after a front vowel, but /g/ does. We return to the significance of this below. First, however, let us sort out the classes of environments where /k/ fails to palatalize:

(a) In class II weak verbs, like *prician, stician*. The sequence /-iki-/ looks like a palatalization environment that can hardly lose; but consider the preterite and participial forms of these verbs: *pricode, -odest, -odon, -pricod; sticode, -odest, -odon, -sticod*. The sequence [-iki-] in these verbs is clearly superficial; they appear in fact to have a thematic /-o/ in their underlying forms, which precedes the inflexional endings (historically -ō: cf. OHG *salbōn* 'anoint' = OE *sealfian*). Thus we can assume underlying infinitives /prikojan/, /stikojan/, etc. We assume that palatalization is inhibited here by the back vowel immediately following the /k/, which is deleted from the infinitive and present system after the palatalization rules apply.

(b) The analysis of *prician*, etc., suggests an explanation for *brecan, sprecan* and the like: the crucial factor here too is the following back vowel – in this case not deleted, since it belongs to the infinitive suffix itself, and is not a thematic 'extension' of the root. (The only cases where the vowel of the infinitival suffix is deleted are those in which it is the deletable member of a trimoric sequence resulting from deletion of [x] in the 'contract' verbs like *sēon*, etc. Cf. ch. III.)

(c) Cases like *blæc, bæc, æcer*. Here we will suggest that low front [æ] is not by itself capable of causing palatalization of /k/ – though it is of /g/: cf. *dæġ*. If [æ] precedes, there must be something else in the environment, if palatalization is to take place. We return to this immediately below.

Consider now two forms, which though differing in one respect from the group in (4.26) are nonetheless important, as they come close to furnishing a (superficial) minimal pair for the palatalization of /k/: *belćan* 'belch' vs. *melcan* 'milk'. In both cases the environment at first appears to be /-elk/; but in *melcan* there is no palatalization, whereas in *belćan* there is.

The cause of the difference is quite simple, and suggests an explanation for a number of other cases: *melcan* is a strong verb (class III), and *belćan* is a class I weak verb. So that *melcan* has the lexical form /mVlkan/, while *belćan* is /balkjan/ (cf. modern dialectal *bolk* 'belch'). Thus the derivation of *belćan* has the stages /balkjan/ > [bælkjan] by AFB, then [bælk'jan] by backness accommodation, then [bælcjan] by palatal softening, [belcjan] by *i*-umlaut, and finally [belcan] by affix modification. The same holds true then for *blǣćan*, whose underlying form is /blaikjan/ > [blaakjan].

So it looks as if two classes of palatalization of /k/ which appear to be postvocalic – those like *belćan* and those like *blǣćan* – are not after all cases of palatalization after vowels, but of the normal operation of backness accommodation (4.21) and palatal softening (4.22). The crucial environment is not /-V(l)k-/ but rather /-Vkj-/. It is not *BELcan* that concerns us, but *belCAN*, and so on. We did not specify in our formulation of backness accommodation that the segment following the velar stop had to be an accented vowel; we left both /i j/ open as possibilities.

We note further that this same explanation accounts for the palatalization we find after nasals in certain cases, and not in others: thus *sincan* 'sink', *drincan* 'drink', *stincan* 'smell' have the nonpalatalizing sequence /-ka-/; whereas *finć* 'finch', *benć* 'bench' have the underlying representations /fenki/, /banki/, with derivations /fenki/ > [finki] (nasal influence) > [fink'i] (backness accommodation) > [finci] (palatal softening) > [finc] (affix modification); and /banki/ > [bænki] (AFB) > [bænk'i] (backness accommodation) > [bænci] (palatal softening) > [benci] (*i*-umlaut) > [benc] (affix modification). Derivations of the same general type can easily be constructed for /blaikjan/ > [blææcan], etc.

Now we must consider the differential developments of /k/ and /g/, and those cases which are real, not apparent, postvocalic palatalization. We observe first of all that both /k/ and /g/ palatalize in all cases after /i/, if no back vowel follows: *ić*, *dīć*, *īfiġ*. Further, whereas /g/ palatalizes after all front vowels, /k/ does not palatalize after nonhigh ones: *dæġ*, *weġ*, but *blæc*, *æcer*. And all these cases are unambiguous instances of postvocalic (underlying) /k g/: there is no way of motivating an environment that would make them prevocalic. This suggests that we can revise backness accommodation (4.21) to include this context as well; and also that we should indicate that if the segment involved is /k/, postvocalic fronting will occur only if the following segment is [+high]. This can be expressed quite naturally by means of angled parentheses. We now give the revised rule:

(4.27) *Backness accommodation: revised*

$$
\begin{bmatrix} +\text{obs} \\ +\text{back} \\ \langle -\text{voice} \rangle \end{bmatrix} \rightarrow [-\text{back}] / \left\{ \begin{array}{ll} \underline{\quad\quad} \begin{bmatrix} -\text{back} \\ \left\{ \begin{array}{l} [-\text{cons}] \\ \begin{bmatrix} +\text{cons} \\ +\text{high} \end{bmatrix} \end{array} \right\} \end{bmatrix} & \text{(a)} \\ \begin{bmatrix} -\text{cons} \\ -\text{back} \\ \langle +\text{high} \rangle \end{bmatrix} \underline{\quad\quad} \langle X \rangle & \text{(b)} \end{array} \right\}
$$

$$
\text{Condition: } X \neq \begin{bmatrix} -\text{cons} \\ +\text{back} \end{bmatrix}
$$

(Note also that we have stated the environment for prevocalic accommodation more precisely, in (4.27a): the nonbackness of the following segment is taken as crucial, and the disjunction specifies that the only nonvowel capable of representing that environment is /j/.) The condition is restricted to /k/, since as far as we can tell the presence of a following back vowel does not prevent palatalization of /g/: cf. *stīgan* 'ascend', ME *stye(n)*.

It is interesting that to judge from the rule, the more resistant, less 'palatalizable' of the two velar stops is /k/; this suggests, as we said above, that palatalization is a kind of lenition, and it is expectable that the voiceless member of a voiceless/voiced pair will show more resistance to any such process. It is also noteworthy that this stronger segment palatalizes only after nonlow vowels; and it is often the case that if only one vowel is capable of causing some kind of assimilation, it will be [i] (see the discussion of word-final spirantization in German in Lass 1971a).

One of the points we have stressed in the preceding section is the dissymmetry in the outputs of palatalized /k/ and /g/: /k/ gives an affricate [c], and /g/ a fricative [j]. But there are two classes of environments in which the palatalization outputs are not asymmetrical:

(a) Where /k/ and /g/ are preceded by another /k/ or /g/, respectively, and followed by /i j/: that is the environments where the West Germanic gemination has taken place (see appendix II).

(b) Where /k/ and /g/ are preceded by a nasal and followed by /i j/.

In both these contexts /k/ gives the expected [c], but /g/ gives an affricate [ɟ]. Consider the following instances of type (b):

(4.28)   (a)   (b)

drincan 'drink'   drenċ(e)an 'drench'
singan 'sing'   senġ(e)an 'singe'

The forms in (a) are derived like the other class III strong present singulars with a root sequence /VN/ in a series /VN/ > [eN] (qualitative ablaut) > [iN] (nasal influence (a)); the forms in (b), on the other hand, being weak verbs, derive from stems followed by a /jan/ suffix. This is especially clear in *drenċ(e)an*, which is a causative (i.e. 'cause to drink') formation on the PRET₁ stem of *drincan* (i.e. *dranc*): thus /drankjan/ > [drænkjan] (AFB) > [drænk'jan] (backness accommodation) > [dræncjan] (palatal softening) > [drencjan] (*i*-umlaut) > [drencan] (affix modification). And by the same token we might propose a base form /sangjan/ for *senġ(e)an* (cf. *menġ(e)an* 'mingle', *on ġemang* 'among'), and a similar derivation – except for some rule that gives us [ɟ] instead of [j].

Now consider the class of forms exemplified by *streċċan* 'stretch', *secgan* 'say'. These exhibit in their lexical representations the characteristic environment for gemination: short vowel + C + /j/. The *-cc-* forms clearly have underlying /k/ – cf. pret. *streahte*, where *h* (= [x]) derives from /k/ before /t/ (cf. ch. III §6); and the *-cg-*forms have underlying /g/: cf. pret. *sæġde*, and the related noun *sagu* 'saying'. (For historical information see Campbell 1959: §753.9.) These forms are merely exemplificatory: there are many more, and not only weak verbs, which show *-cg-* (and NE [dʒ]) for geminated and palatalized /g/, and *-cc-* (and NE [tʃ]) for geminated and palatalized /k/: e.g. *cycgel* 'cudgel', *brycg* 'bridge', *cryċċ* 'crutch', *þæċċ* 'thatch'. What counts is the parallelism between *-cc-* and *-cg-* spellings; the expected *-gg-* appearing in West Saxon texts normally only for geminates in nonpalatalizing environments, there parallel to *-cc-*: *frogga* 'frog', *dogga* 'dog', *bucca* 'buck'. (For further information and examples of 'inverse' spellings see Campbell 1959: §§51, 64.)

Now what is there about the environments we have discussed that would tend to produce a symmetrical, rather than an asymmetrical palatalization of /k/ and /g/? Observe that in both cases, the post-nasal and geminate, the context is unlike the prevocalic one – even though the segment in question is contiguous to the cause of the palatalization. It is different in this crucial respect: that the velar stop is 'protected' by being preceded by another – consonantal – segment. So that while /k/ weakens one step to an affricate, /g/, even though voiced and thus 'weaker' than /k/, does not go the further step to a continuant (see further ch. v).

Let us assume now that gemination follows AFB and breaking (for evidence for this apparently nonhistorical order see appendix II), but precedes palatalization and *i*-umlaut, so that the forms in question enter the palatalization-umlaut complex with geminate medial consonants. Thus /sagjan/, /strakjan/ are already [sæggjan], [strækkjan]. Now if we keep in mind the fact that /g/ > [ɟ] only if it is the second element of a geminate, or is preceded by a nasal, we can account for this change within the palatal softening rule. We accordingly revise (4.22) as (4.29) below, with the symmetrical palatalization for /g/ specified in angled parentheses:

(4.29) *Palatal softening: revised*

$$
\begin{bmatrix} +\text{obs} \\ \alpha\text{voice} \\ \\ \langle +\text{voice} \rangle \end{bmatrix} \rightarrow \begin{bmatrix} -\alpha\text{strid} \\ \alpha\text{cont} \\ \\ \left\langle \begin{matrix} -\text{cont} \\ +\text{strid} \end{matrix} \right\rangle \end{bmatrix} / \begin{bmatrix} \underline{} \\ -\text{back} \\ +\text{high} \end{bmatrix} / \langle +\text{cons} \rangle \underline{}
$$

This will give us derivations of the following types:

(4.30)

Input	sagjan	strakjan	drankjan	sangjan
AFB	sægjan	strækjan	drænkjan	sængjan
Gemination	sæggjan	strækkjan	—	—
Backness accommodation	sægg'jan	strækk'jan	drænk'jan	sæng'jan
Palatal softening	sægɟjan	strækcjan	dræncjan	sænɟjan
i-Umlaut	segɟjan	strekcjan	drencjan	senɟjan

The [j] in the suffixes will be deleted by one of the process of affix modification (§4). It remains now to formulate a rule which will convert the [kc] and [gɟ] sequences resulting from palatal softening to [cc] and [ɟɟ] respectively. We propose the following:

(4.31) *Stridency assimilation*

$$[-\text{cont}] \rightarrow [+\text{strid}] / \underline{\hspace{2cm}} [+\text{strid}]$$

To sum up, we now give a set of derivations including at least one member of each significant class of forms undergoing palatalization and umlaut – plus forms with velar stops which are subject to neither.

(4.32) A. *Initial velars*

1.	kuni	kini	katte	guldjan	gildan	gold
2.	—	—	—	—	—	—
3.	kunni	kinni	—	—	—	—
4.	—	k'inni	—	—	g'ildan	—
5.	—	cinni	—	—	jildan	—
6.	kynni	—	—	gyldjan	—	—
7.	—	—	—	—	—	—
8.	kynn	cinn	—	gyldan	—	—
9.	*cynn*	*ćinn*	*catte*	*gyldan*	*ġieldan*	*gold*

B. *Medial velars*

1.	pik	dag	strakjan	sagjan	drankjan	mangjan
2.	—	dæg	strækjan	sægjan	drænkjan	mængjan
3.	—	—	strækkjan	sæggjan	—	—
4.	pik'	dæg'	strækk'jan	sægg'jan	drænk'jan	mæng'jan
5.	pic	dæj	strækcjan	sægɟjan	dræncjan	mænɟjan
6.	—	—	strekcjan	segɟjan	drencjan	menɟjan
7.	—	—	streccjan	seɟɟjan	—	—
8.	—	—	streccan	seɟɟan	drencan	menɟan
9.	*pić*	*dæġ*	*streććan*	*secgan*	*drenćan*	*menġan*

Key

1. Input
2. AFB (2.11)
3. Gemination (appendix II, 13)
4. Backness accommodation (4.29)
5. Palatal softening (4.29)
6. *i*-Umlaut (4.15)
7. Stridency assimilation (4.31)
8. Affix modification
9. Spelling

V Strengthening and weakening of obstruents: fricative voicing assignment, continuancy adjustment, and some related processes

---

1 Introductory: theoretical background

1.1 On 'naturalness' and 'strength'

Throughout this study we have appealed to two types of notions in justifying or describing rules: one type involves judgements like 'natural' or 'unnatural'; the other concepts like 'strength of a segment', 'weakening of articulation', etc. Both, though traditional and in a sense even obvious, require more explicit formulation: especially in a chapter dealing with the history of a series of (more or less) 'natural' sound changes in Germanic which involve 'changes of strength', and their relevance to the synchronic phonology of OE.

Let us begin with 'naturalness'. It is a commonplace in both synchronic and diachronic linguistics that certain kinds of rules or sound changes are 'natural', and others less so. And in practice this conviction has sufficient force for us often to opt for a particular underlying form or reconstruction on the ground that – given the observable output, and a choice of say two processes for getting it – one alternative seems 'highly valued', and the other less so. To take a historical example: if a pair of cognate languages show respectively structures of the types /VpV/ and /VbV/, we take the former as more likely representing the protoform than the latter: since intervocalic voicing is 'natural' and the opposite is 'unnatural'. In order to justify a transition /VbV/ → /VpV/, that is, we need more evidence than to justify the opposite. In this sense, since voicing seems more natural in the sense of being more probable, we take 'naturalness' as a constraint on the products of inferential processes.

But what is the status of 'naturalness' in a domain where the 'unnatural' is also possible? Clearly we cannot equate 'natural' with 'attested', and 'unnatural' with 'unattested': this is a trivial and unrewarding distinction. And it is so because it lumps together as 'natural' two quite different kinds of processes: (a) those that occur with overwhelming frequency, and are, given their contexts, virtually predictable; and (b) those that are rare, but documented in at least some cases. And it disjoins from these a third category: (c) those which have never been observed at all.

It is clear that if (a, b) are a single class disjoint from (c), we cannot distinguish (a) from (b); and it is this distinction, not that of (a, b) vs. (c), that is of linguistic interest: since this is what must ultimately constrain reconstructed historical processes and synchronic derivations. The class (c) contains an infinity of processes, limited only by the power of imagination; whereas the content of (a, b) is a proper subset of all imaginable rules, and is of interest insofar as it defines the notion 'possible rule'. The content of (a) vs. that of (b), however, is of at least equal (if not greater) interest, since it defines 'probable rule' vs. 'possible but improbable rule'. Certainly (c) must be invoked as a metaconstraint on all linguistic inference; but the really interesting question is why – given the distinction between possible and impossible – some possibles should be more probable than others.

In one sense, obviously, the definition of 'probable rule' is simply a taxonomic observation statement, an extrapolation from observed statistical distributions. But it can also be the basis for explanation. That is: given a statistical distribution of a certain type, we can legitimately ask why it should be so. (Note that invoking 'markedness' does not help: to call a certain rule-type 'marked' is about as explanatory as calling it 'Fred'. The real question is why the property we choose to call 'M' or 'Fred' behaves the way it does: the mere fact that we can give it a name is meaningless. See further appendix IV, and Lass 1972.)

In other words, it seems reasonable to assume that statistical frequencies will have some kind of (nonstatistical) empirical correlates, i.e. that there are observable facts, like the anatomy of the vocal tract, the mode of formation of various segments, their feature-composition, properties of the cortex or cochlea, etc., that will at least help to explain why the observed distributions hold. We suspect that these facts will always, in fact, be strictly 'phonetic' (in a broad sense of that term). That is, they will ultimately have an articulatory or acoustic basis (or, more generally, when we discover how to define this intelligibly, a neurophysiological one). It does not seem obvious that there are any other kinds of 'phonological generalizations'.

In this chapter we do not set out to develop a full-fledged theory of phonological naturalness, or even of our immediate subject-matter, phonological strength (our *hubris* is insufficient). But rather, we will try to sketch out some kind of formal (and hopefully explanatory) framework for a particular class of rules: rules involving, in traditional terms, changes of articulatory strength. That is, processes of weakening (lenition), and strengthening, and certain corollary notions, like 'strong environment', 'weak environment', 'protection', etc. We will also attempt to define what might be called 'preference' for these processes: a specification of the environments favouring and disfavouring certain ones. With this done, we can proceed to a discussion of these processes in Germanic, and specifically in OE.

1.2   Articulatory strength and 'natural sound changes'

There are certain sequences of change that tend to repeat themselves again and again in the histories of languages: two common ones are given (schematically) below:

(5.1) (a) (intervocalic) voiceless stop
     (b) voiceless stop $\rightarrow$ voiced
     (c) voiced stop $\rightarrow$ voiced fricative
     (d) voiced fricative $\rightarrow$ approximant consonant
     (e) approximant $\rightarrow$ vowel
     (f) vowel $\rightarrow$ ∅

(5.2) (a) (word-initial) voiceless stop
     (b) voiceless stop $\rightarrow$ aspirated stop/affricate
     (c) aspirate/affricate $\rightarrow$ voiceless fricative
     (d) voiceless fricative $\rightarrow$ h
     (e) h $\rightarrow$ ∅

It is not overwhelmingly common to find the whole of either (5.1) or (5.2) for a given segment in one language: but portions of these sequences, highly predictable in terms of input-point on either scale, are frequent and familiar. We will examine some of these in detail later, when we have established a descriptive framework. For now let us just observe that lenition (broadly) may be defined as descent down either of the scales, or a movement from a higher point on one to a lower point on the other: e.g. from (5.2c) to (5.1d) or something of the sort. And conversely, any ascent is strengthening.

We can now begin to give some phonetic content to these notions. Initially, we define the two poles, 'strength' and 'weakness', as follows: basically, strength is equated with resistance to airflow through the vocal tract, and weakness with lack of such resistance. The more the airstream is impeded in the production of a segment, the greater its strength; the less it is impeded, the less its strength. In this framework, then, the strongest segment is a voiceless stop, and the weakest a vowel (or to go to extremes, zero). But this is oversimple, because there is another factor involved: the greater the resistance to airflow, the smaller, ceteris paribus, is the output of (periodized) acoustic energy. Our eventual scale of strengths, as we will see, will have to be a complex one, incorporating both of these factors.

For a first approximation, however, we will take the basic content of 'strong' to be 'resistant to airflow': the expansion will come later. So we can say that the stronger a segment is, in this sense, the more likely it will be to resist lenition. (We will also see that the strength of a segment correlates with its ability to trigger the structure change of a rule: a weaker segment may require the 'support' of another segment to effect the same change that a stronger segment can produce by itself.) We will see then that lenition and resistance can be defined, and the stages of lenition (broadly) predicted, in terms of a probably universal set of hierarchies for segment types.

Before proceeding, we should note that the use of 'predict' here is probabilistic, not algorithmic. That is, to say that some change is 'natural' in some environment is not to say that it will occur. Given an environment E, and the sound changes (C_i, C_j), we will use the probability of $C_i:C_j$ as defined by empirical experience as a measure of 'naturalness'. Since we do not know enough to draw up a genuine quantification, based on sound changes in an adequate sample of languages, we can say only that given a pair of changes (C_i, C_j), it will usually be the case that our experience suggests one of the following possibilities: (a) C_i, C_j occur with equal frequency; (b) C_i is more common than C_j; (c) C_j does not occur.

In case (a), C_i, C_j are equally 'natural', i.e. equiprobable; in (b), C_i is more natural (more probable) than C_j; and in (c), naturalness judgements are vacuous. But since these judgements are probabilistic, they cannot 'predict' in the usual sense for any given instance of E which of C_i, C_j) will occur: or indeed, if either (or any other change) will occur. Since the domain of a statistical generalization is an aggregate, it is nonpredictive for any given member. (On the necessity for and validity of probabilistic explanations in 'irregular subjects' like the human sciences or historical biology, see Scriven 1959.) Thus once we have established an event, its naturalness can be determined by our table of frequencies, and we can 'retrodict' it as having been of the expectable type. And conversely, if we have (through lack of evidence) an open choice of (C_i, C_j) having occurred in E, and case (b) above holds, then we can assert that C_i occurred. Thus naturalness judgements are not only retroactive taxonomic identifications: they are a decision-procedure which yields knowledge of unobservables. (This is of course obvious historically; but the same thing holds a fortiori for synchronic rules, since they are even less observable. The deeper levels of grammars are by definition observationally opaque, whereas history is – potentially at least – transparent.)

We are now prepared to discuss the lenition hierarchies. We begin with the strongest segment type, a voiceless (unaspirated) stop, and its most common transformations.

1.3   Articulatory strength and its modifications

1.3.1.   *Opening: weakening of occlusion, no change of glottal gesture.* The formation of any segment (except in general [ʔ h ɦ]) involves two gestures: a glottal configuration or phonatory gesture, i.e. 'voice' or 'voicelessness', crudely speaking, and a supraglottal gesture – an occlusion or approximation within the oral cavity. The first type of lenition we will consider involves a change in the nature of this supraglottal articulation, without change in the glottal gesture. Thus in this set of processes the vocal bands remain in 'voiceless position' (i.e. abducted), while the supraglottal articulation changes to permit increased airflow. We begin for convenience with a voiceless stop without simultaneous glottal closure, then, i.e. the configuration for a typical English initial (rather than final) /p t k/ (we are not concerned here with stops with 'supporting' [ʔ] or ejectives).

The least radical lenition of a voiceless stop involves timing: the closure is released, not at the moment of voice-onset on a following vowel, but before it, so there is some kind of voiceless continuant articulation between the release of the closure and the onset of vocal-band vibration. There are two basic types of such partial release, traditionally called 'aspiration' and 'affrication'. In aspiration, the stop is released into a period of (essentially unarticulated) breath before the next segment begins. If however the release is only partial, then we have an 'affricate', i.e. a stop released as its (relatively) homorganic fricative. Thus an aspirate is a stop released as an '[h]', i.e. with a following period of voicelessness which may have the acoustic properties of the following vowel; while an affricate is a stop whose continuant release has at least some of the articulatory properties of the primary closure.

This kind of lenition is especially common in syllable-initial position: in English, for instance, we find dialects that have synchronic rules of both types. So in some dialects prevocalic /t/ is [tʰ], while in others it is [tˢ]; and in still others (mainly Irish) where /t/ is dental, we find [t̪θ]. In terms of position on a strength scale it is difficult to decide whether aspirates or affricates should be taken as stronger: the evidence is inconclusive, so we will interpret them as belonging to the same strength rank (see below).

Both cases have a certain amount in common: crucially, what is in the absence of either of these forms of lenition essentially a unitary occlusive gesture is 'split' into two parts, the second 'opener' (less occluded) than the first. Let us say then, in a rather traditional way, that any stop articulation has two phases, in temporal sequence: one of closure, and one of release. If the release is abrupt (i.e. direct transition to a vowel), then both phases have the same articulation; if the release is continuant, then the release phase has some differential feature specification. (We might observe also that this kind of lenition can also occur finally or before a consonant: the gestural split does not require a vowel. We will return to this later.)

To exemplify, let us take the lenition possibilities so far mentioned for a particular segment: in this case a voiceless alveolar stop. In diagram (5.3) below the X-axis represents time and the Y-axis decreasing strength, or increased opening.

If weakening proceeds further, it may do so, in this kind of process, by extending the continuant phase back over the first 'mora' of the articulation, i.e. by total spirantization. Thus any stop will pass to its homorganic fricative – ceteris paribus. By adding this condition we take into account various systemic matters, such as the likelihood that [p] will go to [f] rather than [Φ] in a language that has (prior to this) only labiodental fricatives, and no bilabials; or that if there is some prior constraining factor, such as an 'output condition' prohibiting merger, the language might innovate.

It is further to be noted that this discussion – and what follows – does not presuppose anything like a theory of 'gradual' sound-change; we do not claim a necessary stepwise progression through a series like (5.3) for any segment in any language (though it is of course possible). What we are doing is setting up the degrees of the weakening scale, without claiming that any particular lenition must pass through all the phases.

(5.3)
Occlusion

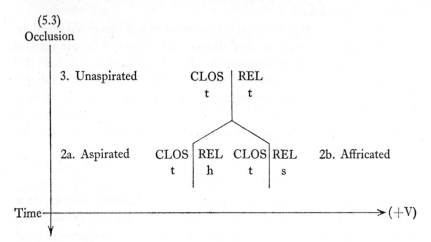

Thus for instance, as we will see shortly, there are environments in which weakening of stops may bypass the whole voiceless-weakening scale, and begin with voicing. Such differentiations are in part language-specific, and in part constrained (though never absolutely) by conditions on primary change expectable in some given context. To take an illustrative example, the Proto-Dravidian (henceforth PD) voiceless stops were spirantized intervocalically in Toda, and voiced in Kannaḍa; though they remained unchanged (lexically) in Literary Tamil. Thus (data from Burrow and Emeneau 1961):

(5.4)	*PD*	*Tamil*	*Toda*	*Kannaḍa*	*Gloss*
	*-k-	akal	oxet	agalu	'spread'
	*-t-	mutu	muθ	mudu	'old'

There is no reason to suppose that Toda ever went through a voicing phase, or that Kannaḍa ever spirantized.

Returning to scalar progression, let us add spirantization to the display in (5.3), again using [t] as an example: see (5.5) opposite.

Any segment, further, may completely lose its supraglottal articulation, and retain only a voiceless glottal configuration, i.e. the state characterizing a continuant efflux. This is especially common both with aspirated stops and with fricatives, which show a tendency to pass to [h]. Thus IE *s becomes [h] in Greek word-initially (cf. L. *septem* vs.

(5.5)

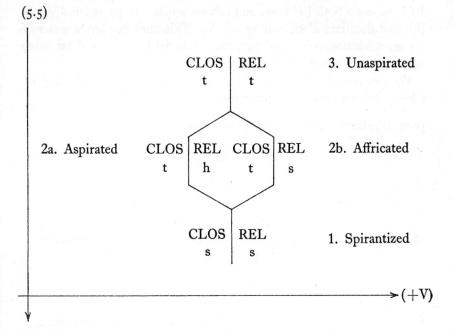

Gr. *hépta*). We assume that [h] in these cases represents the minimal 'unarticulated' fricative, i.e. the step between a fricative with full supraglottal articulation and zero. Some of the possibilities involved here may be seen in the developments of certain Proto-Uralic (henceforth PU) stops, affricates and fricatives in the modern Uralic dialects (after Collinder 1960):

(5.6)

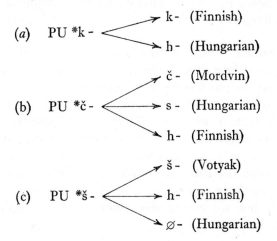

In these cases both PU stops and affricates may end up as fricatives or [h]; but fricatives alone end up as zero. This both displays a series of common lenition types, and suggests a hierarchy in terms of (at least) susceptibility to loss.

We can now complete the exposition of this type of weakening by adding the possibilities we have just explored to (5.5):

(5.7) *Weakening of closure: no glottal change*

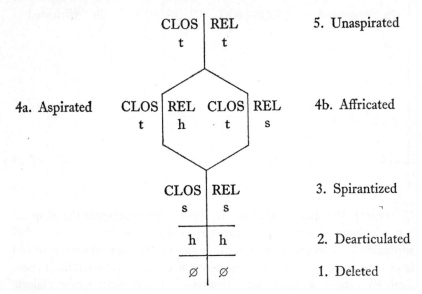

It is to be noted that this hierarchy does not presuppose input at the top: if the input is a fricative it begins at position (3), etc.

1.3.2   *Sonorization: onset of periodic output, plus opening.* Up to now we have been talking about lenition processes as if they were, by and large, context-free; as if our primary concern was with what might be called 'spontaneous weakening', like the [p t k kʷ] > [f θ x xʷ] part of Grimm's Law, or the initial [f θ s] > [v ð z] shift in southern OE and Old Low Franconian (cf. Bennett 1955). We shall in fact make a case later on (as might be expected) for an intimate connexion between certain environments and certain lenition (or strengthening) types, such that some process or processes can be singled out for some context as 'preferred'; but we are at this point concerned with types, not conditions.

If a voiceless stop weakens, it may as it were 'select' none of the options in (5.7), but begin by voicing, i.e. pass directly from a voiceless to a voiced stop, like PD *p *t *k in Kannaḍa. In this case the hierarchy for weakening will be different, as there are essentially more articulation types available with the glottis in voicing configuration than in voice-lessness configuration (voiced and voiceless obstruents, vs. nasals, liquids, semivowels, vowels).

It seems clear that under the airflow-resistance definition, voicing must be a form of lenition (as indeed it is traditionally taken to be). That is, voiced articulations are characterized by a lessened (transglottal) resistance vis-à-vis the cognate voiceless ones. For in order for voicing to occur, there must be some adjustment (whether increased supra-glottal volume or increased subglottal pressure) so that there is an up-ward pressure-gradient across the glottis. That is, there must be con-ditions favourable to the creation of a pressure-drop between the vocal bands by the outflowing air, which sets up periodic vibration.

After voicing, a segment may then undergo opening: that is, a voiced stop may affricate, then spirantize. Beyond this, once the voiced route has as it were been taken, progressive opening may supervene. This gives rise to other voiced (sonorant) categories, i.e. liquids, consonantal approximants, and (usually nonsyllabic) vowels. Finally, as in the voice-less weakening scale, deletion may occur.

We will call the kind of lenition that occurs after voicing by the general term 'sonorization': i.e. we have weakening here in the sense of decreasing resistance, but an increase in the output of acoustic energy, specifically in the form of periodic vibration. In this scale the two-phase interpretation extends only part-way down: since the 'liquid' segments ([r l], etc.), approximants (e.g. [ɹ j ʋ w]) and vowels do not have any distinct closure and release. (We are indebted to Mary Vaiana for suggestions leading to the notion of 'sonorization' as a distinct process: see especially Vaiana 1972.)

A typical lenition scale for voiced segments, parallel to (5.7), can be given as follows (again starting with [t]):

(5.8) *Sonorization and opening*

	CLOS	REL
8. Voiceless	t	t
7. Voiced	d	d
6. Affricated	d	z

	CLOS	REL
5. Spirantized	z	z
4. 'Liquid'	r	
3. Approximant	j, ɹ	
2. Vowel	i	
1. Deleted	∅	

It is probably not possible to find, in any given language, a sequence that starts at the beginning of (5.7) or (5.8) and continues all the way to zero; but various progressions within the two hierarchies, and movement from one to the other, are easy to demonstrate. Here are some cases involving the two scales:

(5.9) *Lenition by opening (schema (5.7))*

(a) 5 → 4a/4b: /t/ → [tʰ]/[tˢ] in English; affrication of voiceless stops in OHG obstruent shift ('Zweite Lautverschiebung').

(b) 5 → 3: spirantization of PIE */p t k/ in Grimm's Law; PD */t c k/ in Toda (5.4, 5.13).

(c) 4b → 3: PU */č/ → Hung. /s/ (5.6).

(d) 4b → 2: PU */č/ → Finn. /h/ (5.6).

(e) 5 → 3 → 2: PIE */k/ → PGmc */x/ → OE [h].

(f) 3 → 2 → 1: L. /f/ → OSpan. /h/ → MnSpan. ∅ (*filius → hijo*).

(5.10) *Lenition by sonorization and opening (schema (5.8))*

(a) 8 → 7: PD */t ṭ k/ in Kannaḍa (5.4, 5.13).

(b) 7 → 6: OE /-d-/ → [d̪ð] in Cumberland, Westmorland, e.g. [mo̞d̪ðə] 'mother', OE *mōdor* (Orton and Halliday 1962, VIII.I.I).

(c) 7 → 5: intervocalic /b d g/ → [β ð ɣ] in Span.

(d) 8 → 7 → 5 → 3: L. /-k-/ → OSpan. /-g-/ → MnSpan. [-ɣ-] → Puerto-Rican [w] (e.g. in L. *aqua* → Span. *agua* → PR [awa] (R. Joe Campbell, personal communication).

(e) 7 → 5 → 3 → 1: pre-OE /-g-/ → OE [-ɣ-] → ME /-w-/ → ∅ (perhaps via [u]): e.g. pre-OE *[aagan] 'own' → OE [aaɣan] → ME [ɔɔwen] → late ME [ɔɔn] (NE/oun/).

Input to (5.10) may be made, of course, from any point on the voiceless scale (i.e. a voiceless fricative, whether weakened from a stop or original, can go to a voiced fricative). In general we assume that a shift from pure opening to sonorization will be made at the appropriate point, that is that segments will not 'restrengthen' and start again.

To sum up: in lenition processes there are two basic options (assuming a hierarchical ranking where we start with a voiceless stop as the strongest type): opening, i.e. progressive continuantization without change of glottal attitude, and sonorization, i.e. voicing and then progressive opening, with increasing output of acoustic energy. The last stage in any lenition is deletion: though this is not to say that all deletion is the result of lenition.

The possibilities can be shown schematically this way:

(5.11)

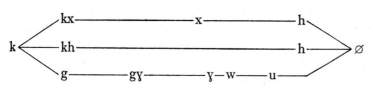

(For a preliminary treatment along somewhat different lines, see Lass 1971a; on the problem in general, Foley 1969, Zwicky 1969, Vaiana 1972.)

1.4   Preferential environments for weakening and strengthening: the concept of 'protection'

Any dogmatic statement of a 'universal' (beyond certain basic ones, such as 'all languages have vowels', or 'if a language has one fricative it is [s]') will probably have holes in it; certainly the characterization of an environment as (exclusively) a strengthening or weakening one will not hold across the board for all languages; or even if the characterization holds, that is no guarantee that any change will occur. As we said earlier, judgements of this sort are essentially probabilistic; the notion we want is something like 'preferred environment for change X'; or given some environment, 'the preferred change in environment Y is X'. We take 'preferred' here as 'statistically probable, for phonetic reasons', etc. To put it another way, for any environment that can be so characterized, some type of change is 'unmarked', and some other type is 'marked'.

For instance: a reasonably wide acquaintance with sound-changes in various language families, and with the properties of feature-changing rules in synchronic grammars, will suggest that intervocalic position,

where one vowel bears a primary accent, is a prime weakening environment. So that a set of correspondences like those below seems eminently
reasonable:

(5.12) *Latin*	*Italian*	*French*	*Spanish*
crēdere	credere	croire	creer
legere	legere	lire	leer
habēre	habere	avoir	haber

That is, we expect intervocalic stops, if they do anything, to affricate,
like the Latin velars in Italian, to spirantize (Fr. *avoir*, Span. *haber*,
where *b* = [β]), or to delete, as the Latin nonlabials do in both French
and Spanish. And if we did not have, in this case, what is in essence
(roughly: cf. Hall 1950) an 'attested protolanguage', but were to
reconstruct solely on the basis of the modern dialects, we would
certainly take Italian as representing the more 'primitive' type of the
three.

But against this we also have correspondences like L. *maior*: It.
maggiore, where in this environment what was apparently a nonsyllabic vowel has become an affricate (and in Fr. *majeur* a fricative).
And even more striking as a violation of the 'preferred' change is the
well-known Germanic *Verschärfung*, where intervocalic approximants
(or perhaps nonsyllabic vowels) turn up as stops. Thus we have
correspondences like Skr. *dváyōs* 'of two' = Go. *twaddjē*, ON *tveggja*;
Skr. *priyā́* 'wife' = ON *Frigg*, etc. (See further Streitberg 1963:
60–1; Prokosch 1938: 92–3; Braune-Ebbinghaus, 1966: 50–3.) And
there may be, as suggested by S. Anderson (1968), some evidence for
a synchronic *Verschärfung* in Faroese.

Further, there is a striking case of intervocalic strengthening in Icelandic, where original geminate sonorants have become clusters of stop
plus sonorant, and both have devoiced: OIcel. *ǫllum* 'all' > [œd̥lʏm],
Hreinn 'Proper name' > [hr̥ei̯d̥n̥] (Hreinn Benediktsson, personal
communication).

All of which goes to show that though intervocalic position is *the*
prime weakening environment, it is certainly possible (a) for segments
in that position to undergo no change at all (cf. Italian vs. French, the
PD voiceless stops in Literary Tamil); or (b), as shown above, for segments to strengthen, even to the point of vowels becoming stops. The
exceptions are exceptions, and they 'prove the rule'. If one had to

choose between Verner's Law and the *Verschärfung* in terms of likelihood, Verner would win. Which is to say that in any context we expect
assimilation rather than dissimilation. But given enough evidence we
must accept the dissimilation as a fact; and accepting it in no way
impairs our characterization of intervocalic environments as – pre-
ferentially – weakening environments.

So much for exceptions; we turn now to preferred developments.
To continue with intervocalic position: there are some interesting facts
about the typical changes in this environment which will go some way
towards laying the groundwork for our study of OE obstruent lenition
and strengthening. The examples we now turn to will enable us to
define our categories more precisely, and to determine what is in fact
to be taken as 'typical' in this context. We begin with a more detailed
view of some of the Dravidian developments sketched in (5.4):

(5.13)	PD	Tamil	Toda	Kannaḍa	Gloss
	*-k-	akal	oxet̲	agalu	'spread'
	*-kk-	akka̲n̲	okn	akka	'elder sister'
	*-t-	mutu	muθ	mudu	'old'
	*-tt-	muttu	mut	muttu	'pearl'
	*-c-	kacaṭu	kosf	kasa	'rubbish'
	*-cc-	kaccai	kots	kacce	'loincloth'

(Underlined segments are alveolar rather than dental.)

These forms appear to show the following developments: (a) PD nongeminate voiceless stops voice intervocalically in Kannaḍa and spirantize in Toda; (b) geminate stops remain geminate in Kannaḍa, without
voicing, and degeminate in Toda; (c) PD palatal stops, if single,
spirantize in Kannaḍa and Toda to [s]; and (d) geminate palatals
degeminate in Toda and remain unchanged in Kannaḍa. The palatals
are clearly an idiosyncratic class, since they spirantize in Kannaḍa,
which is a 'sonorizing' language with respect to other classes of stops in
this environment, whereas Toda is the 'opening' language of the group.
But in both cases one thing is clear: whatever process affects the single
stops does not apply (at least in the same way) to geminates. Thus
*-cc- > [ts] in Toda, but remains unchanged in Kannaḍa, just as
*-kk- > [k] in Toda but remains in Kannaḍa.

Now consider some typical developments of the PU voiceless stops
in selected environments (after Collinder 1960: 45–51, 77–88):

(5.14)

		Finnish	Hungarian	Vogul	Ostyak
1.	*k-	k	h	h	k
2.	*-k-	kk	k	g	g
3.	*-kk-	kk	k	k	k
4.	*-kt-	ht	t	kt	t
1.	*t-	t	t	t	t
2.	*-t-	t	z	t	t
3.	*-tt-	tt	t	t	t
4.	*-tk-	tk	kk	t	t
1.	*p-	p	f	p	p
2.	*-p-	p	v	p	w
3.	*-pp-	pp	p	p	p
4.	*-pt-	ht/tt	tt	t	wt

Key 1. word-initial, 2. word-medial nongeminate, 3. word-medial geminate, and 4. word-medial in a cluster.

Some implications of the Dravidian forms are made clearer here. First of all, if we take intervocalic position, it seems that by and large single stops, if anything happens to them, tend to voice, and then to spirantize; whereas geminates either remain or simplify; and intervocalic (non-identical) clusters either remain, simplify, or spirantize one element. In initial position, stops tend to remain, or in one case (Hungarian) to spirantize if nondental, with a further dearticulation of velars. Leaving aside word-initial position for the moment, we can certainly say, on the basis of the material we have looked at so far, that:

(a) Intervocalic position is a preferred lenition environment.

(b) More often than not (but cf. Toda) this environment will prefer sonorization to (simple) opening; though opening often appears to follow sonorization (cf. Hungarian [z] < *-d-, etc.).

(c) Ceteris paribus a geminate in this environment will not undergo lenition in the same way (to the same degree) as a nongeminate; it will resist. If it weakens, it will do so in the specific sense (see below) of degeminating, rather than opening or laxing.

(d) By and large medial nongeminate (non-identical) clusters tend to behave like geminates.

The moral seems to be: intervocalic is a weak position, or better a weakening position, and two segments are stronger than one. That is, we now identify strength in a segment or sequence as ability to resist a preferred lenition in a given context. So that if an environment promotes weakening, geminates and clusters will resist. And this latter point seems to carry further: not only is it true in preferred weakening environments, but in any case of weakening, regardless of whether it occurs in a preferred environment or not. Thus IE **s* was in general weakened to [h] in prevocalic position in Avestan, Armenian, Greek, and Brythonic Celtic: Skr. *sánaḥ* 'old', Av. *hanō*, Arm. *hin*, Gr. *hénē*, etc. But there are two places where IE **s* was not dearticulated: in initial **st-*, **sp-* clusters, or between a vowel and **t* (Meillet 1964: 95). Thus Skr. *sthiti-* 'position' = Gr. *stásis*, OE *spornan* 'spurn' = Gr. *spaínō*, L. *est* = Gr. *estí*. And in Grimm's Law, the one context-sensitive rule is the failure of the IE voiceless stops to spirantize after **s*: thus OE *steorra* 'star' = L. *stella*, OE *spīwan* 'vomit' = L. *spuō*.

So in addition to the notions of strengthening/weakening and 'preferred environment', we can now define 'protection': given a weakening environment, or a process of lenition independent of some specific environment, the most likely condition under which lenition will fail is if the segment (otherwise) affected is contiguous to another strong segment. Thus for example a voiceless stop protects IE **s* from dearticulation in Greek, and **s* protects the IE voiceless stops from spirantization in the Germanic consonant shift, and gemination protects the PD and PU stops from intervocalic weakening.

Before proceeding to a brief look at some other environments, we might pause to ask why intervocalic position is the sort of weakening environment we have suggested that it is, and just what the mechanisms are by which weakening takes place. Let us consider the rules responsible for intervocalic weakening in Dravidian (all segments in Toda, and nonpalatals in Kannaḍa):

(5.15)   *Toda*

$$\begin{bmatrix} +\text{obs} \\ -\text{cont} \\ -\text{voice} \end{bmatrix} \rightarrow [+\text{cont}] \; / \; V\underline{\qquad}V$$

Kannaḍa

$$\begin{bmatrix} +\text{obs} \\ -\text{cont} \\ -\text{voice} \end{bmatrix} \rightarrow [+\text{voice}] \; / \; V\underline{\qquad}V$$

(The structural analyses are more fully specified than necessary, for expository reasons.) In both cases, the input segments are the same,

6-2

and so is the environment; but the structure changes in the rules are different. The changes, however, can quite reasonably be considered to be assimilatory: since all vowels are specified as $\begin{bmatrix} +\text{voice} \\ +\text{cont} \end{bmatrix}$, the primary difference between the two cases is that the assimilatory response in each one is to a different feature; we might consider that perhaps the features of voice and continuancy are hierarchically ranked in different orders for the two languages. But it is clear that in both cases the fact of weakening – though not the particular form of the weakening – is explicable in terms of the feature-specifications of the environment.

This leads us to another point, which is relevant to the formulation of some of the rules we have already proposed for OE. We approach this again by way of a Dravidian example, in this case using the same three languages we have previously considered. Up to now we have spoken only of intervocalic position: but what about intersonorant position, i.e. cases in which the environment is not 'V_____V', but perhaps 'VN_____V', or 'V_____NV'? Consider these Dravidian forms:

(5.16) *PD*	*Tamil*	*Toda*	*Kannaḍa*	*Gloss*
*-Np-	ampu	ob	ambu	'arrow'
*-Nc-	añcu	oj	añju	'fear'
*-Nk-	tāṇku	tōg-	taṇgu	'support'
*-Nṭ-	anṭai	aḍ-	aṇḍe	'pot'

In Toda, where the preferred lenition modality in intervocalic position is opening, we get voicing (apparently with subsequent deletion of the nasal); in Kannaḍa, where the preferred modality is sonorization, except for palatals, which open, the palatals here become voiced stops, not [s]. But in both languages, from the point of view of closure, the result of this lenition (in all categories of Toda, in palatals only in Kannaḍa) is a more occluded segment type than we get in lenition between vowels, with no intervening nasal.

It looks as if what we have operating here is 'protection' again, but this time not the kind of protection that preserves geminates. That is, any less than maximally weak segment in a weakening environment will have a tendency to alter the type of weakening, i.e. to prevent descent down either the opening or sonorization scale from going as far as it would go under 'ideal' conditions. And this suggests that we have to define 'strength' not only in absolute (resistance to airflow) terms, but in terms of power to induce assimilation: so that in this case, for instance, nasals are weaker than vowels in ability to induce lenition, and stronger than vowels in ability to prevent it. So that we might want to set up what amounts to two inverse scales, one of strength per se, i.e. resistance to lenition, and one of sonorancy, i.e. power to induce lenition (cf. Lass 1971a).

In changes other than lenition, however, we may require other hierarchical scales; thus if a change is induced by a consonantal segment, we may find that a situation arises where the change occurs before single obstruents of some type, but if there is no obstruent, then two sonorants are required. Both types of strength may be illustrated by two rules in OE that we have already referred to: breaking and palatal softening. We give the rules (breaking: first version (3.14) and palatal softening (4.29)) again for convenience:

(5.17) *Breaking*

$$\varnothing \rightarrow \begin{bmatrix} V \\ +\text{back} \end{bmatrix} \Big/ \begin{bmatrix} V \\ -\text{back} \end{bmatrix} \underline{\hspace{1.5cm}} \begin{bmatrix} +\text{cons} \\ +\text{back} \\ +\text{cont} \\ \langle -\text{obs} \rangle \end{bmatrix} \langle +\text{cons} \rangle$$

Palatal softening

$$\begin{bmatrix} +\text{obs} \\ \alpha\text{voice} \\ \langle +\text{voice} \rangle \end{bmatrix} \rightarrow \begin{bmatrix} -\alpha\text{strid} \\ \alpha\text{cont} \\ \left\langle \begin{array}{c} -\text{cont} \\ +\text{strid} \end{array} \right\rangle \end{bmatrix} \Big/ \begin{bmatrix} \underline{\hspace{0.8cm}} \\ -\text{back} \\ +\text{high} \end{bmatrix} \Big/ \langle +\text{cons} \rangle \underline{\hspace{1.5cm}}$$

In each case the specification in angled parentheses is an instance of the point we have been discussing: in breaking, a single non-obstruent consonantal segment is insufficient to cause diphthongization unless backed up by another; whereas a single obstruent with the proper features works. Thus one obstruent is equal in strength to two (non-obstruent) consonants. In palatal softening, the agreement between voicing and continuancy fails in the event that the segment involved is preceded by another consonantal segment – precisely the same state of affairs that holds for the PD palatal stop in Kannaḍa, and all the PD stops in Toda. While these examples do not prove anything, they certainly suggest that the concepts we have been trying to frame do have some place in any theory of phonological change – and indeed in synchronic phonology.

We now turn, briefly, to two other classes of environments, and attempt to sketch out the preferred changes: these are (a) word-initial and (b) word-final position. Both of these behave, overall, less regularly than intervocalic or intersonorant position, but there are still some tentative generalizations that can be made.

(a) *Word-initial* (before accented vowels). Insofar as this is a strength-changing position, it seems to favour lenition by opening. Thus in many dialects of English all voiceless stops are aspirated word-initially, but not word-medially: Brit. E. [tʰɔtə] 'totter', etc. In many American dialects /p t k/ aspirate (or affricate) word-initially, but not medially; in this position however /t/ voices. So these dialects treat intervocalic position as 'strong' for non-dentals but dentals behave according to the preferred interpretation of /V_____V/.

It seems word-initial position, if weakening does occur, typically prefers opening to sonorization; and for any language it is usually the case that only certain (positional or articulatory) classes are involved (see further §4).

The suggestion made earlier that what we are calling 'word-initial' position may perhaps be a conflation of 'prevocalic' and 'post-word boundary' will be taken up in §3 of this chapter, where we explore the function of word-boundary in OE; it will become clear that in some cases word-initial (and word-final) positions are 'protected' environments; and these are precisely the cases in which the sequence /# CV-/ is interpreted as a subclass of /CCV/; in the lenition cases, it is interpreted as a subclass of /CV/.

(b) *Word-final*. This is a 'variable' environment, in a rather specific sense, for we find two contradictory processes occurring, often in the same language. As far as the parameter of sonority is concerned, this is by and large a strengthening environment: obstruents typically devoice word-finally, as in German and Russian, and some dialects of English (especially Scots) and some sonorants do also (as in Icelandic and many Scots dialects, where /r/ is [r̥] word-finally).

From the point of view of the 'open'/'close' dichotomy, i.e. in terms of tightness of occlusion, there is a tendency for word-final position to be an opening environment, especially with reference to certain positional classes, notably velars. Thus modern Standard German typically devoices all obstruents at final word-boundary, and spirantizes palatalized velars: [tʰa:k] 'day', gen. sing. [tʰa:gəs], but [kʰø:niç] 'king', gen. sing. [kʰø:nigəs]. This implies two rules, one of devoicing (strengthening), and one of spirantization (weakening). Some northern dialects spirantize unpalatalized /k/ as well, giving [tʰa:x]:[tʰa:gəs] (for details see Lass 1971a). We will return in a later section to the interesting question of strength in the various positional classes, and the problem of language-specific vs. universal strength hierarchies.

2 Historical preliminaries:
weakening and strengthening in the Germanic
obstruent system

The complex history of the Germanic obstruents is relevant to OE in a number of ways: especially since a number of synchronic facts can be seen as reflexions of or versions of earlier sound changes. So we feel that a synchronic study will gain a certain depth from being considered against the historical background. And we think that the development of the Germanic obstruent system is in itself of sufficient interest, in the light of the kinds of issues we have been raising throughout this work, to merit some study.

To begin with, most accounts of the Proto-Indo-European obstruent system (e.g. Streitberg 1963, whom we follow in general) agree that it was of this type:

(5.18)				
	p	t	k	kʷ
	b	d	g	gʷ
	bh	dh	gh	gʷh
		s		

(Some authorities, e.g. Prokosch 1938, §§ 16, 18, consider the 'voiced aspirates' to have been not stops, but 'lenis voiceless fricatives': this is contradicted by much available evidence, including the reflexes of these segments in Modern Indic, and their general Indo-European developments. But the details of their articulation – save for their being noncontinuants – do not concern us here. For details see Lass 1971b, Vennemann 1969, and references therein; and for some commentary on their probable articulation in Classical Sanskrit, see Whitney 1889: §37.)

The system (5.18) underwent some important changes in early Germanic, the first of which is generally described under the heading of 'first Germanic consonant shift' (Grimm's Law, *Erste Lautverschie-bung*). Essentially what happened was this:

$$(5.19) \qquad \begin{matrix} p & t & k & \rightarrow f & \theta & x \text{ (exc. after } s) \\ b & d & g & \rightarrow p & t & k \\ bh & dh & gh & \rightarrow \beta & \eth & \gamma \\ & s & & \rightarrow & s & \end{matrix}$$

(Note that here, as henceforth, we omit the labiovelars, as by and large they collapsed with the velars in Germanic, and the exceptions are, from our point of view, unimportant. *s* remained unchanged.) In effect the process shown in (5.19) was a reorganization of the obstruent system, but without any change in the number of distinctive obstruent types: the voiced aspirates were lost, and a new class, voiced fricatives, developed (in many of the other Indo-European subfamilies, e.g. Baltic, Slavic, Celtic, Italic, the voiced aspirates collapsed with the Indo-European voiced stops, leaving a two-series system, rather than the original three-series one).

Grimm's Law thus involved three shifts in strength of articulation: (a) weakening of voiceless stops to fricatives (opening); (b) strengthening of voiced stops to voiceless (desonorization); and (c) weakening of the voiced aspirates to fricatives (opening). The motivation of this shift is, of course, obscure at best; it seems to us that it is probably essentially typological, i.e. (cf. Lass 1969a, 1971b) for some reason, in Germanic (as in all the Indo-European subfamilies except Indic) voiced aspirates became an 'illegal' category; and the shift may be considered in part a strategy for getting rid of them while at the same time adhering to an output condition forbidding collapse of lexical categories. (For an explanation in terms of the Chomsky-Halle theory of markedness, cf. Vennemann 1969.)

After the operation of Grimm's Law, the obstruent system of Proto-Germanic was as follows (in relation to its historical sources):

$$(5.20) \qquad \left. \begin{matrix} p & t & k \\ \\ f & \theta & x \\ \\ \beta & \eth & \gamma \\ \\ & s & \end{matrix} \right\} < \left\{ \begin{matrix} \text{IE} & b & d & g \\ \\ \text{IE} & p & t & k \\ \\ \text{IE} & bh & dh & gh \\ \\ \text{IE} & s & \end{matrix} \right.$$

We might pause for a moment and ask why, if the motivation for Grimm's Law was to get rid of the voiced aspirates without collapsing the obstruent system, it was necessary to shift the other obstruents as well. After all, if the only change was spirantization of the aspirates, the following result would have met that condition:

(5.21)
$$
\begin{array}{ccc}
\text{p} & \text{t} & \text{k} \\
\text{b} & \text{d} & \text{g} \\
\beta & \eth & \gamma \\
\text{s} & &
\end{array}
$$

A system like this, however, stands in violation of what is apparently a universal constraint: that no system may contain a voiced representative of any obstruent category unless it has the voiceless one – but not vice versa. Voice in obstruents, then, is in the Praguian sense a *Merkmal*, and the 'marked':'unmarked' relation is one of entailment (irreflexive): 'If M, then U' (cf. Jakobson 1941).

If (5.18) were to be regularized, then, in accordance with this restriction, a set of voiceless fricatives would have to develop; and as the discussion in §1 of this chapter suggests, an easy way of doing this is by lenition of voiceless stops, giving:

(5.22)
$$
\begin{array}{ccc}
\text{f} & \theta & \text{x} \\
\beta & \eth & \gamma \\
\text{b} & \text{d} & \text{g} \\
\text{s} & &
\end{array}
$$

But this system also stands in violation of the same universal constraint: because now there is an uncorrelated set of voiced stops. Devoicing these then gives us the well-formed system shown in (5.20). The suggestion is that the apparent 'irrationality' of Grimm's Law is really a problem of rule-generality vs. teleology: the teleological explanation suggests why the peculiar (and otherwise unmotivated) rules arise (see Lass 1971b for details).

Now let us suggest further that there may be (at least for Germanic) a family-specific well-formedness condition that says that the most 'optimal' – i.e. stable, well-formed, what have you – obstruent systems are those which have (in the Praguian sense) no 'uncorrelated' sets: that every category which is manifested as voiceless should be manifested also at some level of representation (not necessarily lexical) as voiced. Then we might expect an evolution such that ultimately representations of this type would appear at some level of the grammar:

(5.23)

p	t	k
b	d	g
f	θ	x
β	ð	ɣ
	s	
	z	

And we will see, as we proceed, that this is precisely the nature of the OE phonetic inventory (with the addition of palatals); though the developments are not terribly straightforward. The historical evolution leading to an output of the type (5.23) will be our next topic.

Following Grimm's Law, the next significant change affecting the Germanic obstruents was the one responsible for the emergence of a new group of voiced fricatives, including [z] (the few original [z] < IE *s contiguous to voiced segments will not concern us here: e.g. Go. *huzd* 'hoard', nor will those in certan inflexional affixes, e.g. Gmc *-az < IE *-os). This is the rule of voicing assimilation in continuant obstruents generally called Verner's Law (cf. Verner 1875). Essentially all voiceless fricatives (< IE *p *t *k *s) were voiced intervocalically if not preceded in IE by an accented vowel. Thus all [f θ s x] > [v (β) ð z ɣ]. (There is considerable fluctuation, even in Modern Germanic, between bilabial and labiodental fricatives; if [β] did in fact result from Verner's Law it sooner or later became [v] in OE. We will however at this stage use [β] as a cover-symbol for a voiced labial fricative of either type.)

The results of Verner's Law are not uniformly recoverable from orthographic evidence; as Prokosch puts it (1938: 63):

...due to later consonant changes and peculiarities of spelling, Verner's Law is not equally traceable in the several...dialects...in general, only Gothic, Old Saxon, and Old High German are apt to give evidence of Verner's Law in all four places of articulation. ON distinguished neither the labial nor the dental spirants; OE did not distinguish the labials.

We can however, taking into account the fairly well-understood spelling conventions and the later changes (which will be discussed below), find OE representatives of the four original alternations:

(5.24)

Original alternation	OE reflex	Gloss
f/v (β)	hebban hōf hōfon hafen	'heave'
θ/ð	cweþan cwæþ cwǣdon cweden	'say'
s/z	cēosan cēas curon coren	'choose'
x/ɣ	tēon tēah tugon togen	'pull'

The original labial alternations especially have been interfered with by later developments–including lexical restructuring – that we will discuss below. But the OE and comparative evidence suggests that we can formulate the original rule in this way:

(5.25) *Verner's Law*

$$[+\text{cont}] \rightarrow [+\text{voice}] / \begin{bmatrix} V \\ -\text{acc} \end{bmatrix} C_0 \underline{\hspace{1cm}} V$$

(We will see later that the process which first occurs here will play, in a generalized form, a crucial role in the synchronic distribution of voice in the OE fricatives.)

After Verner's Law, which is a context-sensitive weakening of a preferred type in this environment, we find the following to be the inventory and historical sources of the Germanic obstruents:

(5.26)

p	t	k	IE	b	d	g
f	θ	x	IE	p	t	k
β	ð	ɣ	IE	bh	dh	gh
			Gmc	f	θ	x (5.25)
	s		IE	s		
	z		IE	s	(5.25)	

with $\left. \begin{matrix} \\ \\ \end{matrix} \right\} < \left\{ \begin{matrix} \\ \\ \end{matrix} \right.$

There are two more major changes affecting this system, and producing the one which is (presumably) input to that of OE: rhotacism, and a general rule of (context-free) strengthening of voiced fricatives. The rhotacism, which seems to be common Germanic (and also occurs in other dialects: cf. L. *honos, honoris* < *honosis) turns all [z] < [s] by Verner's Law (and all other [z]) to some kind of [r]. This accounts for alternations of the *cēosan/coren, wæs/wæron* type. The rhotacism is a lenition; it comes under the heading of what we have called (cf. §1.3.2 of this chapter) 'sonorization', i.e. an increase in the output of periodic acoustic energy. Following Ladefoged's definition (1971), we can interpret this as a change of one major class feature, [+obs] to [−obs]:

(5.27) *Rhotacism*

$$
\begin{bmatrix}
+\,\text{obs} \\
+\,\text{cont} \\
+\,\text{strid} \\
+\,\text{voice}
\end{bmatrix} \rightarrow [-\,\text{obs}]
$$

The Germanic system in (5.26) is rather short lived; after the rhotacism, it no longer has any [z], and in fact is identical in inventory – though not of course in the etymological makeup of that inventory – to the system in (5.20), the output of Grimm's Law.

After Verner's Law and rhotacism, there is a general strengthening of all the voiced fricatives to stops – at least in our interpretation. But we run into a certain difficulty here, if we take as our primary data what might be called 'phonetic continuity', i.e. the apparent 'persistence' of a phone-type in superficial representations. The standard interpretation of the post-Verner developments, however, is based on this: thus Prokosch (1938: 76) on the development of the voiced non-sibilant fricatives (his *ƀ* = [β], and his *ʒ* = [ɣ]):

(1) Gmc. *ð* became *d* in all positions: OE *fæder*, OS *fadar*...

(2) Medial and final *ƀ* remained a spirant...throughout the North: English, Frisian, Saxon...it became a stop in the other German dialects: OE *giefan*, OFris. *ieva* (*geva, jeva*), OS *geƀan*, but OHG *geban*...

(3) The treatment of Gmc. *ʒ* is not altogether certain. For Old English it is certain that medial and final *ʒ* were spirants...

As the following section will make clear, this interpretation lacks insight; and except in a superficial way it is not correct. The OE internal evidence suggests that the fact that Gmc [β ɣ] are stops in some positions, and fricatives in others, is a synchronic property of the grammar: the continuity of phonetic representations is misleading. For it seems clear that the voiced fricatives in early Germanic represented two distinct categories: 'phonemes', i.e. the reflexes of IE **bh *dh *gh*; and 'allophones' by Verner's Law of Gmc /f θ x/ < IE **p *t *k*. The apparent continuity of phonetic representation is made misleading by a later restructuring: all occurrences of [β ð ɣ] of whatever (etymological) origin became lexical stops; and the later occurrences of voiced labial fricatives, let us say, in forms deriving from IE **bh* are due to synchronic intervocalic lenition of the /b/ < Gmc [β]. These cases of weakening occur only where paradigmatic alternations permit the retention of underlying /b/: thus (cf. §3 of this chapter) *habban, hafaþ* < /habban habaþ/. In all forms which had medial labial fricatives which were not in alternation with stops (e.g. *lufu* 'love') there was restructuring to fricatives. So that even though *lufu* has (historically) IE **bh*, it has synchronic /f/. (I.e. any medial [v] in OE which are not in paradigmatic sets that also have [b], and can therefore be represented as stops, are restructured to fricatives.) This will become clearer when we consider the synchronic lenition rules in OE.

So we can say with fair certainty that a rule was added to the grammars of the West Germanic dialects which changed all voiced continuant obstruents to stops; and this resulted in a lexical restructuring where no voiced fricative appears in any lexical forms. We give the rule as follows:

(5.28) *Fricative strengthening*

$$
\begin{bmatrix} +\text{obs} \\ +\text{cont} \\ +\text{voice} \end{bmatrix} \rightarrow [-\text{cont}]
$$

The specification [+obs] is necessary here, as presumably the Germanic liquids were also continuants (as of course were the vowels). For the same reason this specification is not necessary in Verner's Law. Since [z] has become [r] by rhotacism (5.27), there is no need to specify [−strid]. It is clear in fact that rhotacism must precede strengthening: since otherwise [z] would go to [d] by that rule, and we would need a special derivational marker to indicate that these [d] come from [z] rather than [ð], in order to have them rhotacized. Derivational 'tracking systems' of this kind are too powerful to use without very compelling motivation: especially when (diachronic) rule ordering can achieve the same results. (Clearly the sort of problems that arise in a synchronic grammar from arguments for simplicity through ordering do not arise in historical sequences, where ordering occurs in 'real time'.)

After the strengthening, we have the following obstruent system:

(5.29)

$$
\left.\begin{array}{ccc}
p & t & k \\
b & d & g \\
f & \theta & x \\
& s &
\end{array}\right\} <
\left[\begin{array}{cccc}
\text{IE} & b & d & g \\
\text{Gmc} & \beta & \delta & \gamma \\
\text{IE} & p & t & k \\
\text{IE} & s &
\end{array}\right. <
\left\{\begin{array}{cccc}
\text{IE} & bh & dh & gh \\
\text{Gmc} & f & \theta & x
\end{array}\right\}
$$

It now remains, in order for us to get the 'optimally correlated' system suggested in (5.23), to arrange for the voicing of at least some [f θ s x]. As we will see, the ultimate sources of [v ð z] and [ɣ] will not be parallel: in OE, as we showed in chapter III, [x] is deleted intervocalically, and it is this environment that is responsible for [v ð z] < [f θ s]. But [ɣ] arises from continuancy assimilation of /g/ in these same environments. These processes will be discussed in the following section.

For now, let us sum up the rather complex developments leading to the earliest OE obstruent system ((5.30) below). We can see that the crucial changes in this history can be characterized within the framework of strengthening and weakening that we set up in §1 of this chapter.

3   Fricative voicing and continuancy adjustment in OE

We turn now to the assignment of the features [±voice] and [±continuant] to obstruents in certain environments in OE. First, voicing assignment in fricatives. The facts are well known, and amply described in the handbooks, but certain implications – and therefore certain interesting generalizations – have not been observed. (The proposals to follow were first made in a preliminary form in Lass 1971a; we follow that exposition here, with certain modifications.)

A classic formulation of the facts, in terms of the orthography, is given by Sweet (1957: 3):

...*f* and *s*, in addition to their modern values, could represent respectively the sounds of *v* and *z*...These three letters, *f*, *s*, *þ*, had the sounds of *f*, *s*

(5.30) *Development of the Indo-European obstruents:*
       Proto-Germanic to OE

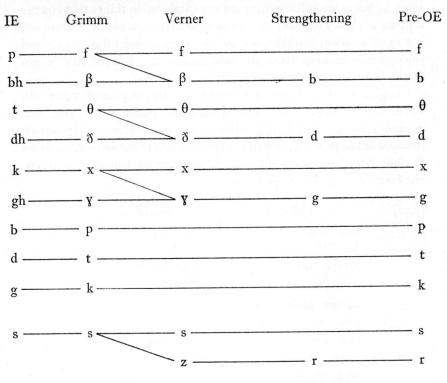

IE	Grimm	Verner	Strengthening	Pre-OE

Rhotacism

and *th* in *thin* ('breathed' or 'voiceless') initially and finally in accented
words; next to 'voiceless' consonants (such as *p, t*); and when double;...
They had the sounds of *v, z*, and *th* in *then* ('voiced') when single between
vowels, or between a vowel and another 'voiced' sound (such as *l, r, m, n*)...

To generalize, we might say that in OE fricatives were voiced between
sonorants, and voiceless in clusters with other obstruents (including
themselves, i.e. in gemination), or contiguous to a word-boundary. One
way of capturing this would be in a rule stating simply that fricatives
are voiced between sonorants, and voiceless elsewhere:

(5.31) *Fricative voicing: first version*

$$\begin{bmatrix} +\text{obs} \\ -\text{cont} \end{bmatrix} \rightarrow \begin{cases} [+\text{voice}] \: / \: [-\text{obs}] \underline{\quad} [-\text{obs}] \\ [-\text{voice}] \end{cases}$$

(This schema abbreviates a pair of simultaneously applicable rules, as set out in Preliminaries, p. 7 n.) The rule given covers the facts well enough; but as we will see there are some interesting things that emerge if we do not lump together all the voiceless environments as 'elsewhere', but examine them in detail. As we will suggest, both the voicing and voicelessness environments are crucial, and the correct rule is not (5.31), but something quite different.

We give a set of forms illustrating the distribution of voice and voicelessness below; for each articulatory position we give one example each of initial, final, geminate, cluster and intervocalic positions (because of accidental distribution gaps, and lack of modern descendants in some cases, we do not illustrate all possible intersonorant contexts, but take 'V_____V' as the type):

(5.32)   *Voiceless*   *Voiced*
        frēo 'free'
        healf 'half'
        offrian 'offer'   ofer 'over'
        æfter 'after'

        smītan 'smite'
        mūs 'mouse'
        assa 'ass'   rīsan 'rise'
        mæst 'mast'

        þēoh 'thigh'
        āþ 'oath'
        moþþe 'moth'   brōþor 'brother'

These distributions can be stated formally as (5.33):

(5.33) *Voice distribution in OE fricatives*

(a) $\begin{bmatrix} +\text{obs} \\ +\text{cont} \end{bmatrix} \rightarrow [-\text{voice}] / \begin{Bmatrix} \# \\ [+\text{obs}] \end{Bmatrix}$

(b) $\begin{bmatrix} +\text{obs} \\ +\text{cont} \end{bmatrix} \rightarrow [+\text{voice}] / [-\text{obs}] \underline{\hspace{1cm}} [-\text{obs}]$

(Note that in (5.33a) we utilize Bach's 'neighbourhood' or 'mirror-image environment' convention once again: suppression of the environment bar indicates an ambisequential syntagm: '/X' expands to '_____X' and 'X_____'.) It may seem at first that this does not take into account voicing in contiguity to voiced obstruents, e.g. in *hæfde* 'had', *lifde*

'lived'; but the segments represented by *f* in these forms are not underlying fricatives, but realizations of lexical /b/, and thus do not participate
in the rule (5.33). We will discuss this later on. Observe also that
(5.33b) is in fact a generalization or 'simplification' of Verner's Law
(5.25); the accent (and vowel) specifications have been deleted. So the
general process of intersonorant voicing is a reflex of the kind of
weakening that first appears in Germanic in Verner's Law.

We now suggest that given the environments as specified in (5.33),
rule (5.31) misses an important generalization. Note first that the
environments in which word boundary /#/ figures group, as far as
voice is concerned, with geminates and clusters. Given intervocalic
position (or more broadly, intersonorant) as a preferred voicing environment, we find that voicing fails there just in case the fricative is protected
by another obstruent. And we find that word-initial and word-final
positions behave in the same way. In fact, as the expansions of (5.33a)
would show, every environment that contains the specification [+obs]
is paralleled by one containing /#/. Here are the three classes of relevant
environments:

$$(5.34)\quad [-\text{obs}] \underline{\hspace{3em}} \# \qquad\qquad\qquad [+\text{obs}] \underline{\hspace{3em}}$$
$$\# \underline{\hspace{3em}} [-\text{obs}] \qquad\qquad\qquad \underline{\hspace{3em}} [+\text{obs}]$$
$$\text{(a)} \qquad\qquad\qquad\qquad\qquad \text{(b)}$$
$$[-\text{obs}] \underline{\hspace{3em}} [-\text{obs}]$$
$$\text{(c)}$$

The word-boundary environments class with the obstruent environments, not with the sonorant ones. Now if we take voicing in (c) to be
assimilatory – as seems obvious – then there seems no particular reason
not to take lack of it to be so in (a) and (b). That is, if the intersonorant
position is the 'goal' of an assimilation, then the 'protected' environment in an obstruent cluster would seem to be the same thing. And if
the protected environment where the protector is an obstruent is the
goal of an assimilation, then the word-boundary environment is too.

Before the argument seems either too involuted or circular, let us
retreat and consider why we assume parallelism. Surely there is no reason
why both feature assignments, [−voice] in (a) and (b) and [+voice]
in (c), must be assimilations; and surely this would not be the case if the
fricatives were specified as [−voice] in the lexicon. And this would be
true, if it were not for the fact that given the environments above, there
are no cases in which the voicing of a fricative is idiosyncratic: there is

total complementary distribution between voiced and voiceless fricatives, and the specifiable contexts (which number only two) exhaust the
total set of contexts where fricatives occur. We assume then that, given
a set of phones which has two members, and a distribution which is
uniquely and exhaustively specifiable for each member, there is no
a priori case for picking one phone as 'basic' and the other as 'derived'.
We will see shortly that an examination of the distribution of the OE
stops will support this analysis on phonetic grounds.

What we are claiming then is that for voice in fricatives, all environments are neutralization environments. That is, there is no lexical
specification; we are dealing with what might perhaps best be called an
'archifeature', i.e. a feature that in one class of segments is always
neutralized in all contexts. (We return to the theoretical implications of
this in chapter VI.)

If we accept voice as neutralizable in toto for fricatives, so that
[+voice] represents voicing assimilation to surrounding sonorants, and
[−voice] represents voicelessness assimilation, then we assume that
/#/ is also the goal of an assimilatory process. And if this is so, we are
in conflict with standard theory, which claims (cf. *SPE*) that boundaries
are [−segment] by convention. And assimilations to nonsegments – or
worse, to features on nonsegments – are perverse. But the facts in (5.34)
seem to us to demand this interpretation: in the light of notions like
'generalization', which we basically accept, it seems wasteful (and
counterintuitive) to deny that there is something generally true about
environments (5.34a, b) that makes them constitute a class. The
sequential syntagms are the same, and the effects are the same. And
certainly rules that devoice at least at final word-boundary are quite
common. (It is of interest in this connexion – cf. Lass, 1971a: 26–7 –
that the rule in German that devoices obstruents at word-boundary
also has a parallel: devoicing of all obstruents in clusters.)

It seems then that – at least in terms of power to inhibit voicing of
fricatives – /#/ is functionally an obstruent, though one with no features, perhaps, but [+obs], or more probably, also [−voice]. This item
behaves as if it is a voiceless obstruent like [p t k f s θ].

So then: if we can say that /#/ is a voiceless obstruent, the voicelessness of fricatives in initial and final positions, and their voicing in
intersonorant position, are both assimilations. The coefficient for
voice on any fricative in OE can then be predicted from the voicing
coefficient of the strongest segment in its immediate environment. That

is, using the kind of strength scale we set up in (5.7) and (5.8), we can see that in the environments (5.34a, b) there is a strong segment, i.e. an obstruent or /#/; in (5.34c) the strongest segment (apart from the 'responding' fricative) is a sonorant.

We can now predict voicing assignment in fricatives by a rule that says: a fricative agrees in voicing with the strongest contiguous segment. We present the revised rule:

(5.35) *Continuant voicing assignment*

$$\begin{bmatrix} +\text{obs} \\ +\text{cont} \end{bmatrix} \rightarrow [\alpha\text{voice}] \, / \, [\alpha\text{voice}]$$

Condition: Agreement is to the strongest segment in the environment. And /#/ = [+obs].

Voice is thus not a lexical feature of OE continuant obstruents, but is entirely predictable by rule.

Let us now examine some further facts about OE that have to do with obstruent distribution, and the behaviour of obstruents in various assimilatory environments. We will see in this investigation also the crucial explanatory role played by considerations of hierarchical strength. We have already seen that fricative distribution is such that it is clear that voicing is crucially responsive to two syntagmatic factors: contiguity to voiceless obstruents of whatever kind (including /#/) and contiguity to sonorants.

Now observe the properties of those obstruents one step higher in the strength scale: the stops. OE seems to have had a symmetrical inventory, of this type:

(5.36) *The OE lexical stops*

	p	b	t	d	k	g
ant	+	+	+	+	−	−
cor	−	−	+	+	−	−
voice	−	+	−	+	−	+

Lexical status seems perfectly clear, on the basis of the apparent non-responsiveness of stops to boundaries, etc. As far as sonorants or boundaries are concerned, we find patterns of this type:

(5.37) pæþ 'path'   bēam 'tree'   trēo 'tree'
       dēop 'deep'   camb 'comb'   fōt 'foot'
       dēop 'deep'   cynn 'kin'   gōd 'good'
       fōd 'food'   āc 'oak'   beorg 'mountain'

We will treat intervocalic contexts separately, for reasons that will shortly become clear. But essentially the distributions in (5.37) suggest that voice is a lexical feature of stops.

There is however one kind of assimilatory process to which at least some stops are sensitive: and this is continuancy assimilation (spirantization) in intervocalic environments. This is not true (as might be expected) of voiceless stops, but only of voiced ones, and not for all these. But we will discuss the exceptions later. For now, consider velars and palatalized velars:

(5.38) lōcian [lōkian] 'look'   æcer [æker] 'acre'
       būgan [būɣan] 'bow'   plēgan [plējan] 'play'
              bucca [bukka] 'buck'
              frogga [frogga] 'frog'

It looks as if (at least for velars) voiceless stops remain noncontinuant between vowels, as do voiced geminates, while voiced stops go to the corresponding voiced fricative. Thus we have a common form of opening in a preferred lenition environment, with resistance determined by inherent strength (for the voiceless stops) and by protection (for the voiced geminates). We might formalize this by saying that the values for continuancy and voice agree in intervocalic velars and palatals (geminates would be excluded by simply not mentioning second segments in the SD of the rule):

(5.39) *Intervocalic continuancy adjustment: first version*

$$\begin{bmatrix} \text{obs} \\ +\text{high} \\ \alpha\text{voice} \end{bmatrix} \rightarrow [\alpha\text{cont}] \; / \; V\underline{\qquad}V$$

(Since palatalized /g/ is already a continuant, the rule will apply vacuously in the case of *plēgan*, etc.)

Now let us consider the distribution of the nonvelar stops. The forms listed below may be considered representative:

(5.40)   *Single*   *Geminate*
           copor 'copper'   cuppe 'cup'
                —   habban 'have'
           mētan 'meet'   mētte 'met'
           hȳdan 'hide'   hȳdde 'hid'

There are two peculiarities in these data: (a) there seems to be a 'gap' in the distribution of *b*; it does not appear single in intervocalic position; (b) there is no evidence for weakening of labials or dentals in this position. We now examine these two facts.

First, there are some suggestive alternations in certain OE weak verb paradigms (those of the so-called class III). Observe the following:

		'have'	'live'
(5.41)	Infinitive:	habban	libban
	Pres. 1 sing.	hæbbe	libbe
	Pres. 2 sing.:	hafast	leofast
	Pres. pl.:	habbað	libbað

Note that in the apparently 'irregular' forms we get a voiced fricative corresponding in point of articulation to the geminate stop of the infinitive, first singular, and plural.

Let us see if this can be explained. To begin with, we observe that there are many forms in OE besides *hæfde*, etc. which are (a) spelt with medial *f* and therefore look like cases to be handled under (5.33b) synchronically; but (b) which have cognates in the other Old Germanic dialects with *b* (and often have a labial stop in the modern dialects); and (c) which were often spelt with *b* in early OE texts (more on this below). In the forms we are interested in, both the OE *f* and the *b* in the other dialects go back to IE **bh*, that is to Gmc [β]. Here are some typical examples:

(5.42) *OE*	*Cognate forms*
gafol 'pitchfork'	OHG gabala, NHG Gabel; Skr. gábhasti-
beofor 'beaver'	OHG bibar, NHG Beber; L. fiber; Skr. babhrú-
nafela 'navel'	OHG nabulo, NHG Nabel; Gr. omphalós; Skr. nābhīla-
wefan 'weave'	OHG weban, NHG weben; Gr. uphaínō; Skr. -vābhi-

There are also numerous OE loans from Latin which have original *b* and show up with *f*: *fefor* 'fever' < *febris*, *tæfl* 'chessboard' < *tabula*, *trifot* 'tribute' < *tribūtum*.

The origins of the OE spellings can be clarified by some suggestive forms from the early (7th–8th century) *Epinal Gloss* (Sweet 1885). In this text the larger number of intervocalic labial fricatives, whether from Gmc [β] < IE *bh or from voicing of [f] < IE *p are spelt *b*: *bebir* 'castorius', *bebr* 'fiber', *hræbn* 'nycticorax', *uuibil* 'cantharis', *gibaen uuaes* 'inpendebatur'. But we also find occasional *f*, e.g. *ifge* 'hedera', and one very curious (unintentional?) *bf* in *nabfogar* 'terebellus'. This last form seems especially to illustrate a tension between two types of representation, which suggests that this text dates from a period following a restructuring of the lexicon in certain respects, and before a reform of the spelling.

What we think happened – historically – was this. After the fricative strengthening (5.28), all Gmc [β] < IE *bh, or from Gmc [f] via Verner's Law, were restructured to /b/. All the forms in (5.42) then had medial lexical /b/, and probably phonetic [b] also. At this point all occurrences of /f/ which had been in the Verner environment were restructured to /b/, but elsewhere intervocalic /f/ < IE *p as in *hræfn* (cf. Skr. *kṛpaté*) was still phonetically [f] and phonologically /f/.

Then we assume the addition of two new rules in OE (and probably in Old Frisian and Old Saxon as well) which (a) weakened intervocalic /b/ to [v], and (b) voiced intervocalic /f/ to [v] (as well as presumably voicing other fricatives). Thus the phonetic reflexes of medial /b f/ overlapped. But there was a long prior tradition of *b*-spellings, so that it became possible for any [v], regardless of origin, to be spelt *b*, in accordance with the principles given at the end of chapter IV.

However, a second restructuring supervened. For observe that while certain occurrences of [v] were in alternation with stops (cf. *libban*, *lifde*, *habban*, *hæfde*), the majority were not; the statistically preponderant alternation was [f] ~ [v]. At this point, then, all [v] < (historical) /b/ which were not in paradigmatic alternation with [b] were restructured to /f/. (It was mistakenly claimed in Lass 1971a that all these IE *bh forms are to be interpreted as having OE /b/; this clearly does not hold in the non-alternating cases.)

This explains the peculiar gap in the distribution of intervocalic stops shown in (5.40): there are no intervocalic [b] in OE because they have all either (a) been restructured to /f/, or (b) weakened by rule, as in *hafað*, etc. We thus have, synchronically, an overlap of this type:

(5.43)   Phonetic   b   v   f

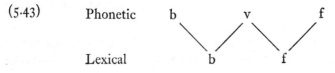

             Lexical   b   f

If we return to our display of the OE stop inventory in (5.36), it then becomes apparent that we can reformulate the continuancy-adjustment rule (5.39) to capture the weakening of both labials and velars, by substituting for [+high] the specification [−coronal]:

(5.44) *Intervocalic continuancy adjustment: final version*

$$\begin{bmatrix} +\text{obs} \\ -\text{cor} \\ \alpha\text{voice} \end{bmatrix} \rightarrow [\alpha\text{cont}] \ / \ V\_\_\_\_\_V$$

(It is of course easier to say that coronals are excluded than to explain it; we will return to this question shortly.) For now let us note that (5.44) accounts for the range of data captured by (5.39), plus the weakening of unrestructured medial /b/. Observe also that there is no motivated ordering relationship between this rule and (5.35), voicing assignment. The latter rule assigns coefficients for voice to lexical continuants depending on environment; but the fricatives produced by (5.44) are by definition both intervocalic and voiced, so that there is no need for (5.35) to apply to them. Thus the specification [+voice] may appear on a (nondental) continuant obstruent as a result either of (5.35) or (5.44). In dentals, only (5.35) applies. To put it another way, voicing in lexical continuants is assigned by (5.35), since its value can be either '+' or '−'; but since continuancy of derived continuants is an automatic consequence of the fact that they are specified [+voice] as input to (5.44), there can be no voiceless ones which are derived from underlying stops.

4 The problem of positional strength-hierarchies: labials and velars as a natural class

The exclusion of coronals from (5.44) raises the problem of 'explanation' or motivation. There is no doubt of the facts: cf. *hȳdan* 'hide', *glīdan* 'glide', not **hȳðan*, **glīðan*. So it is obvious that not all voiced stops in OE belong, with respect to intervocalic lenition, to the same strength rank: velars and labials are weaker than dentals. Another problem that arises is the status of 'noncoronal' as defining any sort of reasonable class. The mere fact that we are able to characterize, with a single feature, the exceptions to a rule does not automatically make that characterization well-motivated: we may have 'captured' it, but we have not 'accounted for' it.

In such literature as has appeared on hierarchical strength, the majority opinion seems to be that universally speaking it is velars that are the weakest, dentals the next weakest, and labials the strongest. Thus Foley (1969) says that there are no languages that delete [b] between vowels that do not also delate [d] and [g], and many that delete [g] and no others: he gives examples from Buriat Mongolian, Kasem, and Czech showing deletion of [g] but not [b d] in certain environments, and from Spanish showing deletion of [d g] but not [b]. The same is true for French (cf. 5.12). It is certainly true that velars (and palatals) are the weakest segments in German (cf. Lass 1971a), and there is some evidence in (Modern) English for a ranking labials–dentals–velars, in a series of decreasing strength (Zwicky 1969).

But further examination falsifies the universal claims that have been made for this particular order, even for intervocalic position, where Foley makes his strongest claims. Thus for instance PD *p *t *c *k are uniformly spirantized intervocalically in Toda, but *ṭ is resistant; sometimes it voices, sometimes it becomes a retroflex trill, but just as often it remains as a voiceless stop (cf. Burrow and Emeneau 1961, any items showing intervocalic -ṭ- in Tamil). Further, consider the Uralic data in (5.14). PU *-k- remains in Hungarian, whereas *-t-, *-p- are weakened, thus showing a hierarchy with weak dentals and labials, and strong velars; *-k- and *-p- weaken in Ostyak, but *-t- remains, thus showing dentals as the exceptional (strong) class, and labials/velars as weak. Cases like this could be multiplied; even the apparent universal weakness of velars is contradicted by Hungarian. This suggests that such hierarchies by positional class are not in fact universals, but statements of statistical probability; and that actual hierarchies by position are language-specific. And certainly OE shows the same grouping we find in Ostyak, rather than what Foley and Zwicky would predict.

If we look at classes not by position in the word, but in terms of all positions, it becomes apparent that again we are faced by considerable variability. Thus to take Hungarian again, while velars are strong intervocalically, they weaken in initial position, as do labials; therefore Hungarian has two different hierarchies for two different positions; while Vogul shows weakening of both initial and intervocalic velars, but no weakening of other segments, etc.

What seems in fact to be characteristic of the resistance of segments to lenition is this: in most languages, for any given word-position, and at any given period in the history of the language, there is usually at least one positional class among the major categories that is idiosyncratic with respect to the other classes. In languages with three or four major positional categories we may find, for instance, that one is weak and three are strong, or vice versa. And sometimes – quite often in fact – the 'odd' category will be even further restricted to a single segment. Thus, as we mentioned above, IE **s* > [h] in Greek, Armenian, Avestan, etc., unless in a protected environment. To take some further examples, IE **p* deletes initially in Celtic (L. *pater, porcus* = OIr. *athir, orc*); Latin *f, h* delete initially in Spanish (L. *homo, filius* = Span. *hombre, hijo*, where *h* = ∅); PD **p* weakens to [h] initially in Kannaḍa (Tamil *pāl* = Ka. *hālu* 'milk', etc.: S. K. Aithal, personal communication). In Japanese, the labials show weakness in most environments: OJ **p-* > [h ç Φ] depending on the following vowel, and **-p-* > [w]; in Modern Japanese it appears that virtually all reflexes of OJ **p* are now interpreted as members of an '/H/-mora' series, and [p] is preserved only in certain protected (word-internal) positions (Takeuchi 1971).

Further, the strength or weakness of a segment may change over time: thus OE clearly shows lenition of labials and velars in intervocalic position, with strong dentals; but as we observed earlier, many (especially U.S.) modern dialects show weak dentals in this position, but strong labials and velars.

The real problem we must approach here, however, is more complex than that of a single weak category; there are two in OE. And this makes us inclined to suspect, at least, that we may be dealing not so much with the idiosyncrasy of a single type (the strength of the dentals), but rather with the naturalness of a class (the weakness of the labials and velars). At least in terms of what the theory leads us to interpret as a 'generalization' (and in view of the fact that such formulations are 'highly valued'), this situation looks as if we should expect one. Certainly it is true that this particular grouping is not unique to OE; we have already seen, briefly, that at least one Uralic language – Ostyak – seems in its historical development to show a similar grouping. And there are other cases, too, which suggest that it is not 'unnatural' for labials and velars to constitute a class; and this is true in phonological rules proper, as well as in general tendencies over time.

Two interesting cases occur in the history of Korean (Lee 1971). The first is a rounding rule that apparently arose in the 15th century, whereby /ɨ/ > [u] before /m p ph k kh/: thus *ətɨp-* 'dark' > *ətup-*, *čɨzɨm* 'at the time' > *čuzum, tǝɨk* 'more' > *tǝuk* (the first *u* in *čuzum* is due to a later regressive vowel-harmony rule). It might be said of course that rounding before labials is natural enough; but certainly this would not be true for velars.

The second rule of interest is called by Lee '*i*-umlaut', and arose in the 19th century. Here /a ǝ o ɨ u/ (the last two not in Standard Korean but in Lee's dialect) became respectively [æ e ø i y] when followed by either a labial or a velar consonant plus /i/. Thus *čaphi-* 'catch' > *cæphi-*, *makhi-* 'prevent' > *mækhi-*, *mǝkhi-* 'eat' > *mekhi-*, *p'ophi* 'choose' > *p'øphi*, *čuki-* 'kill' > *cyki-* (-*hi*, -*ki* are verb-forming suffixes).

In both these changes, the class labials/velars is a crucial part of the environment; in the rounding, they both cause it, and in the *i*-umlaut the rule operates only across a labial or velar consonant or cluster. Lee points out (as we did above) that it is perfectly possible to formulate these rules within the Chomsky-Halle framework: in any obstruent system of the types under consideration, we can specify (at least for stops and nasals) the class labials/velars uniquely as [−coronal]. The question is, however, whether such a specification says anything; after all, vowels are by definition noncoronal also, and the theory has no mechanism, as far as we can tell, that specifies noncoronality as 'explanatory' for consonants, but not for vowels. We might just as well expect a class consisting of labials, velars, and all vowels. That is, the fact that coronality can be distinctive for obstruents but not for vowels does not help in explaining the strength of coronal obstruents or the weakness of noncoronals. It seems to us, that is, that if labials and velars are to constitute a phonologically significant class, there should be some more 'positive' feature defining them; and this should certainly not be a feature that all vowels (redundantly) share.

If we are dealing here with what is in the usual sense of the term a 'natural class', it is surely not a universal one; but there is no particular reason why in fact a category must be universal if it is to have any explanatory value. There are after all different languages, and a theory of language-in-general must be able to accommodate language-specific properties as well as universal ones. If we find that some property is in fact universal – that it belongs to the metatheory rather than to the grammar of a particular language or family, we have found out something important; but it seems on reflexion that if we discover a putative universal to be actually a language-specific option, we have discovered something of equal value. And its value lies not only in the fact that our metatheory is now more adequate; it is useful in itself to have a theory of the differentia of languages, and the typological characteristics of language families. Both types of discovery help us to define language: one defines obligatory properties, and the other defines and delimits optional ones.

On the basis of the limited amount of data we have looked at here – and considering the (avowed) topic of this book and the limitations of space and the reader's patience – we cannot make a really firm statement on this matter. But we can suggest at least that it looks very much as if – at some level – there are certain kinds of natural classes that are natural only for certain languages. For Korean, Ostyak, and English, it is a fact that at certain periods of their history there exists a natural class (insofar as that is synonymous with the domain of regular phonological processes) which includes labials and velars, and excludes dentals. Whether this is because of certain properties of these segments like 'peripherality' or its acoustical cognate 'graveness', or whether it is simply an unmotivated typological peculiarity, we cannot say, though the acoustic explanation seems most likely. It does seem likely, however, that in order for a language to specify a class, there must be some objective features shared by that class – though exactly how they are to be accounted for is another question. But we doubt whether even the definition of a 'language-specific natural class' is circular, i.e. that a class is natural because it occurs repeatedly in rules. We prefer a stronger hypothesis. It may be the case that what seem to be, let us say, 'Chomsky-Halle' languages, with velars and labials unrelated, may at certain periods or at certain grammatical levels choose a 'Jakobsonian' option, where peripherality or graveness is a stronger classifier than some other feature which is a classifier at other levels or at other times. (For further discussion of this point see Lass 1973a.)

It is of interest, however, that even though dentals are the strong intervocalic class in OE, and the weak one in Modern English, they are still separate in certain significant ways, for certain rules, from labials and velars. In the absence of any stronger statement than we have so far made, we leave this matter unsolved: as far as OE continuancy adjustment (5.44) is concerned, the feature excluding dentals is [−coronal]. But we think that more work on this and related matters is in order.

VI Epilogue: historical implications; the phonological inventories; some afterthoughts on theory

1 The long vowels: historical implications of the geminate vowel hypothesis

1.1 'Change of typology' and the Great Vowel-Shift

Beginning with our treatment of the ablaut alternations in chapter 1, we have operated on the assumption that the 'long'/'short' vowel dichotomy in OE is a single/double dichotomy, with all long vowels (and diphthongs) being at some stage of their derivation clusters, with identical or non-identical members. The possibility of there being underlying double vowels in OE raises some serious and interesting historical questions: for one thing, it suggests that we ought to look again at some similar proposals about 'length' in the history of English – e.g. those of Vachek (1959) and Martinet (1955) who assumed that the long vowels were bimoric; and like those of Stockwell (1958, 1961), who analysed the long vowels and diphthongs in OE and Middle English as 'complex nuclei', of the Trager-Smith types, consisting of vowel plus 'offglide' (/y w h/). We may in fact have to consider seriously the possibility that something very like a Trager-Smith type of analysis of the English vowel system (at least at certain points in its history) may turn out to be well motivated (though not in the original terms).

If our claim for a single-vowel/cluster organization in OE is tenable, it raises anew some of the same questions that prompted Stockwell to adopt the Trager-Smith analysis for OE in 1958, and for Middle English in his (1961) paper on the 'open' and 'close' long mid vowels. That is: if the living form of a language seems to be a particular structural type, is it not uneconomical (at least) to posit, on rather uncertain evidence, a major typological break at some point in the history, just to support a putatively canonical view of the older stages? For instance, if Modern English turns out to be a vowel/vowel + offglide language (as Stockwell was convinced in 1958 was the case), then should we not try at least to see if a similar analysis will hold for earlier stages? Otherwise, we are forced to introduce a typological shift somewhere in the vast wasteland of 'Early Modern English' (as in fact nearly all traditional scholars – as well as Vachek and Martinet – do). At least there ought to be pretty strong evidence to make us posit such a shift; and it might, in the absence of such evidence, be instructive to try and extrapolate the synchronic characterization of Modern English as far back as possible. And on the other hand – as we will try to show – it can be equally profitable to try and project forward from our OE analysis, and see what consequences, and what explanatory yield, this analysis might have for later periods.

But it does seem in some ways very hard to get around the notion of a typological break; in fact, a very profound one, involving in an important way the features responsible for the differentiation of the two underlying vowel sets. At least this problem arises if two conditions hold: (a) that our analysis of the OE vowel system is correct; and (b) if the now well-known proposals of *SPE* concerning the Modern English and the early Modern English (immediately post-Middle English) vowel systems are also correct. For in the Chomsky-Halle analysis, a set of rules very similar to those constituting the (historical) Great Vowel-Shift are claimed to play a crucial part in the synchronic grammar of Modern English; and this analysis rests on a lexicon divided into two classes of vowels – lax vs. tense – with all diphthongs produced by rules acting on single tense vowels. It is at least clear that by using this form of organization they have worked out rather impressive explanations of such alternations as those in *divine/ divinity*, *abound/abundance*, and so on. (We will return to some problems connected with this and similar analyses – including our own – in §3 of this chapter.)

Now it may well be, of course, that at some point in the history of English a typological break did occur, and the original single/double dichotomy was reanalysed as a tense/lax one. There is surely no reason in principle to rule out such changes, since there are many well attested cases such as the loss of lexical length in Vulgar Latin, Modern Scots, and the modern Scandinavian languages, and the development of the non-tonal early Lolo-Burmese dialects into languages with lexical tone (cf. Maran 1971).

But it might also be the case that such a shift never occurred: what for instance would be the consequences of assuming this, and extending our analysis of OE into the Middle English and early Modern English periods, even including the Great Vowel-Shift? Let us explore this possibility with reference to the vowel system of the first witness that Chomsky and Halle invoke for the vowel-shift: John Hart. According to their analysis (*SPE*: ch. 6, §2), Hart (1569) shows a vowel system with three types of vocalic nuclei in underlying representations: lax vowels, tense vowels, and diphthongs consisting of a tense vowel plus a 'glide' (/w/ or /y/). We will examine their account of Hart, and then show that even for this dialect a system of underlying representations in terms of single vowels and clusters is possible, and yields ultimately the same superficial reflexes of the vowel shift.

According to Chomsky and Halle, Hart's underlying 'tense' vowel and diphthong system is:

(6.1)   ī   ū

                        ē   ō

                        ǽ   ɔ   ā

      ēw   ǽw   ǽy   āw   ɔw   ɔy

We will devote ourselves first to the tense vowels, as the diphthongs behaved ultimately in a quite similar fashion, their first elements shifting the same way as the corresponding tense vowels. We will return to them briefly in §1.2.

The phonetic reflexes of the system (6.1), which is the same as the late Middle English vowel system, are said to have been, on Hart's evidence:

(6.2)   ī → ey   ū → ou

                  ē → ī   ō → ū

                  ǽ → ē   ɔ → ō

                        ā → ā

That is, all nonhigh tense vowels which are also $\begin{bmatrix} \alpha\text{back} \\ \alpha\text{round} \end{bmatrix}$ raise one height, and the high vowels diphthongize, with the first elements dropping one height, to mid. The result is the familiar pattern:

(6.3)

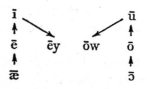

(A later rule 'laxes' the [ē ō] in [ēy ōw].)

Chomsky and Halle visualize this process as occurring in three stages (i.e. by the addition to the grammar of late Middle English of three rules): first, there is a rule of 'glide-insertion' which inserts a homorganic glide after high tense vowels, so that:

(6.4)   ī → īy   ū → ūw

This is followed by an alpha-switching rule, which switches the highness values on nonlow vowels, so that the high ones go to mid and the mid ones to high. This has the effect of simultaneously raising [ē ō] to [ī ū], and converting [īy ūw] to [ēy ōw]:

(6.5)
$$\begin{bmatrix} V \\ \alpha high \\ -low \end{bmatrix} \rightarrow [-\alpha high] \ / \ \begin{bmatrix} \underline{\quad\quad} \\ +tense \\ +stress \end{bmatrix}$$

A third rule raises the low vowels which agree in backness and rounding, i.e. [æ ɔ], to [ē ō], thus completing the pattern shown in (6.3).

Now let us consider what would happen if Hart's 'tense' vowels, like the OE 'long' ones, were underlying geminates. This would then give us, instead of the system (6.1), the system (6.6):

(6.6)   ii   uu
               ee   oo
               æinæ   ɔɔ   aa

Observe that if this were the case, we could still formulate the vowel-shift quite easily. We could say then that the proper analysis to be met for the relevant rules is not the presence of a feature [+tense] in the matrix for a vowel, but rather the presence of an immediately following vowel, with no intervening boundary. So that, schematically, the environments for the vowel-shift under the two interpretations are as follows:

(6.7)   *Tense/lax*   *Single/double*

$$/ \begin{bmatrix} \underline{\quad\quad} \\ +tense \end{bmatrix} \qquad /\underline{\quad\quad}V$$

We can now sketch out the shift as follows: first, we can dispense with a rule of high vowel diphthongization, since the high vowels are already double. Instead, we begin as follows: first, an alpha-switching rule

like Chomsky and Halle's, which reverses the height coefficients on
nonlow vowels followed by another vowel:

(6.8) *Vowel-shift*

$$\begin{bmatrix} V \\ \alpha\text{high} \\ -\text{low} \end{bmatrix} \rightarrow [-\alpha\text{high}] \, / \text{\underline{\hspace{1cm}}} V$$

This rule will have the following effect on the system (6.6):

(6.9)   ii → ei   uu → ou
              ee → ie   oo → uo

(It is interesting that the effect of this rule on /ee oo/ is precisely the same
as the first stage of the High German vowel-shift, where pre-OHG
$\bar{e}$, *$\bar{o}$* diphthongize to [ie], [uo]: cf. *hier* 'here' < PGmc *$h\bar{e}r$, *fuoʒ* 'foot'
< PGmc *$f\bar{o}t$*, etc. See further the discussion in Lass 1969b.)

We then have a rule which raises low vowels that agree in backness and
rounding in the same environment:

(6.10) *Vowel raising*

$$\begin{bmatrix} V \\ -\text{low} \\ \alpha\text{back} \\ \alpha\text{round} \end{bmatrix} \rightarrow [-\text{low}] \, / \text{\underline{\hspace{1cm}}} V$$

The results of (6.10) will be:

(6.11)   ææ → eæ   ɔɔ → oɔ

Finally, we introduce a constraint which says in effect that the only
permissible two-vowel sequence is one in which the second of the two
vowels is either the same as the first, or higher than the first; if the second
vowel is not either the same or higher, it raises to the same height as the
first. We might formulate it this way:

(6.12) *Double nucleus constraint*

$$\begin{bmatrix} V \\ -\text{high} \end{bmatrix} \rightarrow \begin{bmatrix} \alpha\text{high} \\ \beta\text{low} \end{bmatrix} \, / \begin{bmatrix} V \\ \alpha\text{high} \\ \beta\text{low} \end{bmatrix} \text{\underline{\hspace{1cm}}}$$

(Observe that this appears to be a restricted form of DHH (3.15).) The
application of (6.12) will have the following effects:

(6.13)   ie → ii   eæ → ee
                uo → uu   oɔ → oo

In combination, then, the effects of the two rules – vowel-shift (6.8) and vowel raising (6.10) – plus the double nucleus constraint (6.12) will be, overall:

(6.14)

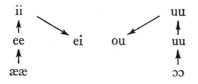

It turns out, then, that given the differences in the two interpretations of what Hart's underlying nuclei are, the process shown in (6.14) is exactly the same as that shown earlier in (6.3).

If we look at the two accounts of the early vowel-shift as a whole, Chomsky and Halle's and ours, we can compare them in this way:

(6.15)   *Chomsky and Halle*   *Lass and Anderson*

	Chomsky and Halle	Lass and Anderson
1.	Glide insertion	Vowel-shift
2.	Vowel-shift	Vowel raising
3.	Vowel raising	Double nucleus constraint

Both accounts require three rules; or perhaps ours requires two rules and a sequence structure condition. Chomsky and Halle's rules require reference to a feature [+tense], ours reference to another segment marked [−cons]. On the face of it, it does not look as if one account is notably 'simpler' or 'more economical' than the other; and if we consider further any other possible processes involved in the generation of surface representations from underlying forms, the same kind of relative similarity will become apparent. Wherever Chomsky and Halle need a rule 'tensing' a vowel, we need an epenthesis rule; where they need a 'laxing' rule, we need a deletion rule (cf. the treatment of 'lengthening' and 'shortening' of vowels in the history of English in appendix II).

The purpose of this exposition is not to show – necessarily – that a double vowel rather than a tense/lax analysis is a better account of Hart's dialect; we only want to show that it is possible to handle the same facts, with no additional complication, using the same analysis we used for OE. It will take far more investigation than we have yet carried out to make the empirical decision as to which analysis is

7

preferable for Hart, or for Modern English. All we have tried to do here
is to suggest that, if our claims for OE are well-founded, it is possible
that the traditional shift in typology might not have occurred as early
as it has been assumed to have done; and it now remains to see if in fact
it ever occurred at all. (The possibility has been proposed that in some
cases both treatments of 'length', (a) that it is a segment, and (b) that
it is a feature, may even apply to the same language at one point in
time, depending on the level of analysis, and the types of rules involved:
for some interesting arguments to this effect for Modern Lithuanian,
see Kenstowicz 1970.)

1.2   Monophthongization and the 'New Middle English diphthongs'

We suggested at the end of chapter III that it would be possible to account
for the Middle English developments of the OE diphthongs in a quite
simple and natural way, even assuming that 'long' and 'short' *ea, eo*
were phonetically identical. Very simply, with the loss of breaking and
velar umlaut, the 'short' diphthongs revert to short vowels, and the
long ones 'monophthongize', i.e. their second elements become
identical to their first elements. We will now extend this proposal, and
consider its implications for other Middle English developments, and
see if there is any explanatory value in extending the two-vowel hypothesis into at least early Middle English.

Following the traditional accounts, we assume that the OE 'long'
diphthongs in general developed this way in Middle English:

(6.16)

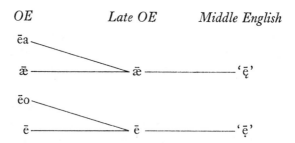

Following our analysis of the structure of the diphthongs, and assuming
that Middle English 'long open' *e* was at least systematically a low
vowel, i.e. long [æ], we can restate (6.16) this way:

(6.17)

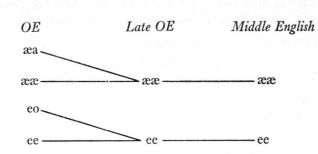

That is, we arrive at a point in the history of the language where there are no longer any diphthongs of the characteristically OE type, i.e. sequences like this: $\begin{bmatrix} V \\ +\text{syll} \\ \alpha\text{high} \end{bmatrix} \begin{bmatrix} V \\ -\text{syll} \\ \alpha\text{high} \end{bmatrix}$. Any new diphthongs that arise after this point are of a new type, characteristic of ME and (the non-northern dialects of) Modern English: whatever the height of the syllabic vowel, the nonsyllabic is high: this type can be represented as $\begin{bmatrix} V \\ +\text{syll} \end{bmatrix} \begin{bmatrix} V \\ -\text{syll} \\ +\text{high} \end{bmatrix}$. (There seem to be no particular constraints on back-ness relations: thus we find in Modern English the types [ʊ̯i], [aɪ̯], [aʊ̯], [ɔɪ̯], and so on. This is of course applicable mainly to the 'standard' dialect types: but we limit ourselves to these for the sake of convenience, and because those dialects with diphthong-types like e.g. [eə] in environments not before /r/ are in the minority.)

This change of diphthong-type is first apparent in the development of a rich new series of diphthongs in Middle English, which arise basically from two sources: (a) what is traditionally called 'vocaliza-tion' of OE [j w ɣ], and (b) a process very much like breaking: epen-thesis of a high back vowel before [x] and a high front vowel before [ç] ($<$ /x/). The most characteristic developments are of the types shown below in (6.18), which basically follows the account given by Mossé (1952: §31). We include here only the most significant developments, and begin from a point in late OE where [æ] has fallen together with [a] ('loss of AFB'), and the original OE diphthongs have either reverted to their corresponding short vowels (if from breaking), or 'monophthongized' to long vowels. We also assume that OE [aa] has undergone rounding to [ɔɔ] (ME /ǭ/), i.e. that we are dealing with the

developments of non-northern dialects. The basic types of diphthong-
formation in early Middle English are then as follows:

(6.18) *The new Middle English diphthongs*

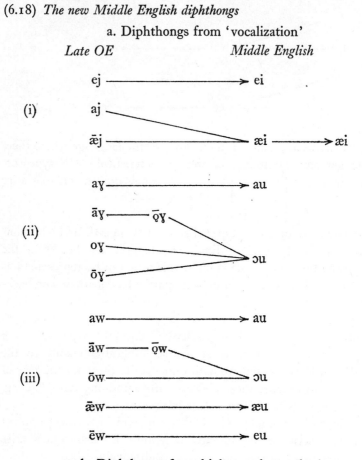

a. Diphthongs from 'vocalization'

| Late OE | Middle English |

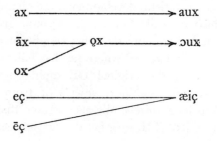

b. Diphthongs from high vowel epenthesis

| Late OE | Middle English |

Now observe that in a number of cases, both before 'vocalized' [j w ɣ] and before [x ç], the OE long and short vowels fall together. This is crucial, and in fact makes the whole set of developments quite easy to explain. We will not go into a full and detailed treatment, because of the complications involved in dialect-differences, exceptions, chronology, and so on; and also because these details are not really relevant here. What is of interest is the overall picture, and (6.18) is an accurate representation of that. We will now proceed to indicate briefly what we think happened, as it lends some support both to the two-vowel hypothesis, and the characterization of [j w] that we proposed in the Preliminaries.

To begin with, it is clear that the processes involved in (6.18) involve two different kinds of rules: the first, (6.18a) produces a change of one major class feature on [j w ɣ], from [+cons] to [−cons]; the second involves epenthesis of a high vowel between some other vowel and a voiceless velar or palatal fricative. The first change, 'vocalization', affects three segments that share the specifications $\begin{bmatrix} +\text{cons} \\ +\text{high} \\ +\text{cont} \\ +\text{voice} \end{bmatrix}$. It seems that all these features must be specified: [+voice] to exclude [x], and [+cont] to exclude [g]. However, it may be that (if [j w] are liquids, for instance) there is a rule weakening intervocalic [ɣ] to [w], thus collapsing sets (a. ii–iii) in (6.18). We will not consider this here. At any rate, the developments under (6.18a) are apparently the result of a single rule of this type:

(6.19) *Continuant vocalization*

$$\text{SD:} \ [-\text{cons}] \ \begin{bmatrix} +\text{cons} \\ +\text{high} \\ +\text{cont} \\ +\text{voice} \end{bmatrix} \qquad \text{SC:} \ 1, 2 \rightarrow [-\text{cons}]$$

$$\quad\ \ 1 \qquad\qquad 2$$

Since the rule leaves the point of articulation features unchanged, it will presumably convert [j] to [i], and [ɣ w] to [u].

Now if we assume the double-vowel analysis for the Middle English long vowels, then the rule (6.19), operating on the forms in (6.18a), will give these results:

(6.20)

	a.i	*a.ii*	*a.iii*
	ej → ei	aɣ → au	aw → au
	aj → ai	aaɣ → ɔɔu	aaw → ɔɔu
	ææj → ææi	oɣ → ɔu	oow → ɔɔu
		ooɣ → ɔɔu	ææw → ææu
			eew → eeu

Now let us assume that in Middle English, as well as in OE, there was still operative some rule like trimoric nucleus simplification (3.22). If this is so, then the ultimate results of vocalization will be comprehensible in the same way that the outputs of breaking of the OE geminate vowels are. A sequence like [ææj] or [ææw] in OE was allowable, because [j w] were [+cons], and these sequences were thus /VVC/. But if a rule like (6.19) arises while trimoric nucleus simplification is still a well-formedness constraint on vocalic nuclei, then the forms it produces – like [ææi] or [ææu] – are /VVV/, and thus not canonical. They would therefore be converted to the proper two-vowel sequences. So once again all underlying three-vowel sequences are reduced by one, and in phonetic representation we have only a two-way contrast – single vs. double. (Notice however that since the effect of trimoric nucleus simplification is to neutralize length distinctions in certain environments – cf. ch. III, §5 – it is likely that in these cases the underlying length distinctions were rapidly lost, and the new diphthongs reinterpreted as lexical.)

The same thing happens of course in diphthongization by epenthesis before [x ç] (6.18b). Since both velars and palatals are [+high], we can formulate the rule – which we call, for obvious reasons, Middle English breaking – in this way:

(6.21) *Middle English breaking*

$$
\varnothing \rightarrow \begin{bmatrix} V \\ +high \\ \alpha back \end{bmatrix} / V \underline{\hspace{1cm}} \begin{bmatrix} +obs \\ +high \\ \alpha back \\ +cont \end{bmatrix}
$$

(The particular formulation here assumes that some rule fronting /x/ to [ç] has applied first; therefore we have backness agreement depending on the value of the consonant. But it is equally likely that backness agreement is later, and that at the stage at which this rule applies, /x/ is still [x] after both front and back vowels. If that is the case, then the rule could be formulated in such a way as to show agreement of the epenthesized vowel with the original one. Since we have no information on this matter, we will simply make the arbitrary choice shown above.) The rule (6.21) will then give us developments like these, of the forms in (6.18b):

(6.22) *b.i* *b.ii*

ax → aux eç → æiç

aax → ɔɔux eeç → ææiç

ox → ɔux

oox → ɔɔux

Once again, if we assume trimoric nucleus simplification, the outputs will be as expected, all three-vowel clusters being reduced to two, and underlying length neutralized. The collapse of the sequences of OE long vowels plus [x ç j w ɣ] with the short vowels plus these same segments is thus precisely parallel with the OE diphthongs. We can exemplify the four types of development by looking at the derivational histories of four cases out of (6.18): [ow oow] to illustrate continuant vocalization (6.19), and [ox oox] to illustrate Middle English breaking (6.21):

(6.23)

Input	ow	oow	ox	oox
Continuant vocalization	ou	oou	—	—
Middle English breaking	—	—	oux	ooux
Diphthong lowering	ɔu	ɔɔu	ɔux	ɔɔux
Trimoric nucleus simplification	—	ɔu	—	ɔux
Output	ɔu	ɔu	ɔux	ɔux

(A few words of commentary are in order here. First, the rule that we call 'diphthong lowering' needs more investigation; it is essentially an extrapolation back from the results of the Great Vowel-Shift, the modern forms like *grow*, *glow* suggesting that the diphthongs in these forms contained [ɔ] rather than [o]. Second, continuant vocalization and Middle English breaking are listed in that order merely for expository convenience; they could obviously apply in either order or simultaneously.)

If the account up to now is substantially correct, it suggests strongly that the Middle English diphthongs – and hence the diphthongs in

Hart's underlying representations – were not, as Chomsky and Halle claim, of the type /ēy/ (as opposed both to /e/ and /ē/). That is, instead of there being in Middle English three types of vocalic nuclei, /V/, /V̄/, and /V̄y/, /V̄w/, there were only two: /V/ and /VV/. And this would further make it impossible for there to be in Hart's dialect contrasting diphthongs of the type [ow] vs. [ōw], [ey] vs. [ēy], which Chomsky and Halle claim are respectively the reflexes of ME /ū/, /ɔ̄w/, /ī/, and /ǣy/. (It might be of interest here to note that the same arguments that Stockwell and Barritt put forth against there being two types of diphthongs in OE would also hold in the case of Hart.) The one thing that is clear from the discussion above is that a Middle English vowel system built along the same lines as the OE one could not yield all the surface reflexes proposed for Hart by Chomsky and Halle. Unless that is there was a typological break, which as far as we can tell is still debatable.

The entire Middle English long vowel and diphthong system, then, as we see it having developed along the lines proposed above, would be as follows (cf. (6.1)):

(6.24)   ii   uu
     ee   eu   oo
       æær   æu   æi   ɔi   ou   ɔɔ   aa   au

And this entire system, in Hart's dialect, would yield as far as we can tell the set of reflexes shown below:

(6.25)

Middle English	ii	ee	eu	æær	æi	æu	uu	oo	ɔɔ	ou	ɔi	aa	au
	|	|	|	∨	|	|	|	∨	|	|	|
Hart		ei	ii	iu	ee	eu	ou	uu	oo	oi	aa	au

The monophthongization of /æi/ and /ou/, and their phonetic merger with /æær/ and /ɔɔ/ respectively, are denied by Chomsky and Halle (*SPE*: 261–2); and indeed, it does not square with the later developments in most dialects of English. Normally, ME /æi/ falls together with /aa/ (cf. *day, name*), though the other merger is historically correct. But Hart's evidence – despite certain vacillations – does show just this merger; and wanting further knowledge we can only assume that Hart represents, in this particular, a line of development that is not parallel to those which eventuated in the 'standard' dialects.

1.3   The phonetic realization of vowel 'length'

We have established fairly well, it seems to us, that the final outputs of
the phonological rules of OE contain representations of the type [aa],
[ee], [oo], etc. But what do such objects mean in actual (not 'systematic')
phonetic terms? How, in other words, might such sequences have been
realized, i.e. 'pronounced'? Or is this even an askable question? There
are of course a large number of possibilities here, and the evidence for
one solution or another is far from compelling. We will however look
at some possible analyses of the distinction between the OE 'long' and
'short' vowels, and see if we can determine at least what the limitations
are on the recovery of this kind of phonetic detail, and what sorts of
proposals – if any – can intelligently be made.

First of all, it is often assumed that in OE the surface length distinction was matched by a quality distinction for the most part, so that
the high short vowels were lower and/or more central than the long
ones, the mid short ones lower than the long ones, and the low ones
distinct only with respect to length. Thus a frequent sort of proposal
involves values like these:

(6.26)

ī	[iː]	i	[ɪ]
ē	[eː]	e	[ɛ]
ǣ	[æː]	æ	[æ]
ū	[uː]	u	[ɷ]
ō	[oː]	o	[ɔ]
ā	[ɑː]	a	[ɑ]

The assignment of IPA symbols here is based on the key words given
by Moore and Knott (1955: 13), which is fairly typical. The same
analysis is found in Quirk and Wrenn (1957: §15). Sweet (1957: §2)
gives much the same values, but suggests [a] for *a*. Mossé (1945: §11)
is similar, except that *e* is given the value [e], thus creating an asym-
metry: he otherwise balances [iː]/[ɪ], etc.

There are a number of complex (and usually unstated) assumptions
behind this sort of reconstructed 'pronunciation' of a dead language,
which assume considerable importance if one tries to balance the
claims for one reconstruction as against another. Basically these
assumptions are closely tied up with notions about the present-day
phonetic systems of particular dialects of English – more or less (as
far as we can tell) in the following way. First, as the typical lists of key

words show, the tendency is to use pairs like *sit/seat, bet/bait*, to illustrate 'short *i*' vs. 'long *i*', 'short *e*' vs. 'long *e*'. The long/short dichotomy in OE is thus assumed to have been parallel to what is usually thought of as the same dichotomy in Modern English. So that if one thinks of the vowel in *sit* as 'short', and that in *seat* as (the corresponding) 'long', a Daniel Jones type of transcription – and hence reconstruction – like [ɩ]/[iː] suggests itself.

Now it is clear that such reconstructions involve the extrapolation back into history of an ethnocentric – or perhaps better 'linguacentric' notion: that the history of English eventuated, by a fairly direct line of progression, in one's own dialect. At least if that dialect happens to be a 'Kenyon-Knott' American English, or RP. And if one's own dialect is not of that type (as neither of ours is), the prestigious (or perhaps merely well known) form is still the model for phonetic reconstruction, and in general for the study of the history of the language. It is certainly the fact that up until very recently, both of us operated on this kind of assumption, though it was not conscious.

But what would happen if we took as our point of departure say a typical Lowland Scots (e.g. Edinburgh) urban dialect? If we used *seat* and *sit*, *bait* and *bet*, *boat* and *pot* as bases, we would be tempted to reconstruct OE *ī/i* as [i]/[ɛ̈], *ē/e* as [ẹ]/[ɛ̣], and *ō/o* as [o]/[ǫ]. For in these dialects there is no synchronic dichotomization of the vowel system in the same sense that it occurs in non-Scots, and the spread of vowel qualities over the quadrilateral is quite different. Particularly, the historical 'short' high front vowel is now lower than the mid one. And if we were on the other hand to take a typical New York City dialect as our basis, a reconstruction of *ē/e* as [ɛɩ]/[ɛ̣], and *ō/o* as [əɷ]/[ä] would be quite reasonable. And almost any Scots dialect would make one wonder if a *ū/u* distinction ever existed. (Most of these difficulties are of course due to differential reflexes of the Great Vowel-Shift: but that is not the way scholars in general proceed.)

This merely goes to show that attempts to reconstruct the 'pronunciation' of a dead language are (a) usually doomed from the first to circularity by a bias in favour of certain (usually spelling-based) norms, and (b) are therefore based on oversimple and often rather naive notions of what Modern English phonetic systems are really like. After all, why should any dialect of OE have been phonetically more like RP than Midlothian urban? And further, such reconstructions are based in the nature of things on so little hard evidence that the attempt seems hardly worth making, and is likely to lead either to vacuous or irresponsible statements when it is made.

This last pessimistic note is inspired not only by the preceding matters, but by the kind of claims which, though pure and unsupported guesswork, often find their way into otherwise sober works. For instance, consider the following, from Campbell (1959: §33): '*o* (except when it is a variant of *a* before a nasal) represented a rounded back vowel, probably rather less open than that of NE *not*, more like that of NHG *Gott*.' True, there is that hedging 'probably': but the putative authority of Campbell's work masks the fact that there is no basis whatsoever for claiming that some vowel in OE was 'rather less open' than some Modern English vowel. First of all 'NE *not*' in our experience occurs with at least the vowels [æ a ɑ ɔ ɒ], in various dialects; and second even speakers of RP often fluctuate in words of this type between rounded and unrounded vowels; and third, since obviously the range of variation cited above represents outputs of derivations in different dialects from a vowel which is phonologically mid, back, and round (at least insofar as we assume stressed vowels of the same height in the lexical forms of *cone/conical*, etc.), all we can say about 'OE *o*' is that it seems not unreasonable to suppose that it might have had a phonetic value like one of the five cited above.

As far as we can tell, historical investigation does not permit us to recover much more than grossly binary (i.e. classificatory) specifications. This does not mean of course that we can permit ourselves the luxury of a purely 'algebraic' approach to historical phonology, where only 'oppositions' and not their content count. We must attempt, as we have all along here, to achieve reasonably full specification at the phonological and systematic phonetic levels; but when it comes to 'pronunciation', i.e. the specification of what would have to be n-ary feature coefficients, we must simply say that we have no relevant information, and cannot even conceive how we might get it, short of a time machine.

This holds true, in fact, not only for reconstructions based on written texts, but even of those based on the apparently precise observations of orthoëpists. Even in the description of a good impressionistic phonetician like John Hart (and he was certainly one of the very best), there are many indeterminacies: in Hart (1569) it is for example impossible to tell whether his reflex of ME /ā/ is a front [a] or a back [ɑ]; whether his *e* is [e] or [ɛ]; or whether his short *o* is [o] or [ɔ]. This is of course why we have used wherever possible fairly neutral symbols, assuming that *e* can cover a range of at least [e] to [ɛ], and so on.

To return to our primary aim, the characterization of phonetic length in OE: it does seem possible in principle to suggest what might be reasonable possibilities, even though we cannot specify the exact qualities of the vowels in question. We proceed on the following assumption: since it seems that long vowels are at some stage of their derivation vowel clusters (as 'long' consonants are consonant clusters: see appendix ii); and since the behaviour of the diphthongs seems to be parallel to that of the long vowels, both historically and synchronically, we can say that 'length' is a mora. The long vowels may be assumed to be 'double', i.e. bimoric, in surface as well as phonological representation, and the long consonants the same.

This means that a representation at the systematic phonetic level like [ee] can be mapped directly into an output phonetic string [ee] with no change: as long as the vowels are not in hiatus, each underlying segment in an input sequence will be mapped into one mora of length in an output sequence. Phonetic realization will then depend on a function which maps any segment in a systematic phonetic representation into one mora of length in phonetic realization, characterized by the same features as the underlying segment.

If any systematic phonetic vowel is a set of features $\{F_1, \ldots F_n\}$ and any output phonetic vowel is a set $\{F'_1, \ldots F'_n\}$, then phonetic actualization may be defined as a one-to-one mapping:

$$(6.27) \qquad \textit{Input} \quad \{F_1, \ldots F_n\} \quad (\{F_1, \ldots F_n\})$$
$$\textit{Output} \quad \{F'_1, \ldots F'_n\} \quad (\{F'_1, \ldots F'_n\})$$

This may be formalized simply by a function that maps phonological features into phonetic ones, with no special treatment of two-vowel sequences as opposed to single vowels. Thus if, as in (6.27), we say that some phonological segment $S = \{F_1, \ldots F_n\}$, and some phonetic segment $S' = \{F'_1, \ldots F'_n\}$, then if there is some function f such that $f(S \to S')$, this will guarantee the one-to-one mapping described above. In terms of a representational system like that of the IPA, such a function will map a systematic phonetic sequence [VV] into [V:], where [:] represents a mora of length, i.e. a continuation of the articulation specified by the left-hand symbol over some period beyond that normally associated with [V] alone. Thus a representation [e:] is equivalent to [ee], and [t:] to [tt], and so on.

This is certainly the simplest, most neutral interpretation of what [VV] might mean; and one which is not out of line with the situation in many Modern English dialects, where the difference between the vowels of *bet* and *bait*, say, is not of the type [ε] vs. [εɪ], but rather [ε] vs. [ɛ̣:] (this is a rather common northern English type). There is a similar type of distribution in many dialects of German, and in Norwegian and Swedish also (cf. appendix II, §6). So we can assume that direct mapping of bimoric underlying sequences into bimoric phonetic ones is not unreasonable. But neither of course are many others. We might assume that the OE pattern was more like that of RP and most American dialects, where 'long' vowels are realized as diphthongal nuclei with a fairly high nonsyllabic element (as opposed to e.g. short vowels before sonorants, which are diphthongal, but have a central nonsyllabic: thus some Midwestern U.S. dialects have pairs like [bɛ̣ɪt] 'bait' vs. [bɛ̣ənd] 'bend'). Another possibility is the type that one finds in some dialects of Swedish, where long high vowels are followed by a homorganic fricative, long mid vowels are simply bimoric, and long low vowels have a centring glide. And so on. The point is that there is really no principled reason, given the phonetic diversity to be found among Modern English and other Germanic dialects, to choose one alternative over another. We thus suggest that direct bimoric mapping is the simplest, least idiosyncratic possibility, keeping in mind that further investigation might conceivably prove us wrong, but is unlikely to prove us right.

So we will make no further attempt to specify a 'pronunciation' for the surface realization of any OE segment; except to say that it seems likely that such pronunciations – if they are of any interest – probably fell somewhere within the 'natural' range suggested by the symbols we have chosen.

2   The phonological inventory

2.1   The vowel system

2.1.1   *The simple nuclei.* We shall return below to the question of the precise form of lexical representations for 'long' vowels and diphthongs. But we must begin by establishing the set of lexical simple vowels, a proper subset of whose combinatorial possibilities constitutes the set of long or diphthongal nuclei.

At the systematic phonetic level we find the following set of stressed single vowels:

(6.28)

i	y	u
e		o
æ		a

These may be exemplified by *fisc* 'fish', *feld* 'field', *dæg* 'day', *styrian* 'stir', *full* 'full', *dohtor* 'daughter', *dagas* 'days'. The phonetic vowels are specified distinctively in terms of the features [±high, ±low, ±back, ±round], as shown below:

(6.29)

	i	e	æ	y	u	o	a
High	+	−	−	+	+	−	−
Low	−	−	+	−	−	−	+
Back	−	−	−	−	+	+	+
Round	−	−	−	+	+	+	−

We showed earlier (ch. II) that [æ] is not a lexical segment, but is in alternation with [a]. The distribution of these two phones depends on the operation (and 'failures') of AFB: thus *dæg* (with AFB), but *dagas* (retraction before a back vowel), and *bær*, but *band* (nasal influence (b)). Similarly, [y] derives from *i*-umlaut of [u]: *cyme* 'coming, n.' with umlaut before a final underlying /-i/, but *cuman* 'come'. Further, many surface [e] have their source in either [o] or [a]: from the former via *i*-umlaut and nonhigh unrounding, and from the latter via AFB and *i*-umlaut. Thus the stressed vowel in *dehter*, pl. of *dohtor*, derives as follows: /o/ → [ø] (*i*-umlaut) → [e] (nonhigh unrounding); that in *sellan* 'give' (cf. Go. *saljan*) derives this way: [a] → [æ] (AFB) → [e] (*i*-umlaut). The [a] in those forms which are exceptions to AFB provide a further source for phonetic [æ] by umlaut without AFB: the first person singular present indicative of *faran* is *fare* (it has, exceptionally, not undergone AFB). We find, however, second and third person *færst*, *færð* (< [farist], [fariÞ]), once again presumably with no AFB, but with umlaut.

Apart from these alternations, there are also notably cases of [i] < /e/ and [o] < /u/ by highness harmonization: thus *rignan*, vb. vs. *regn* n. 'rain', *gold* 'gold' vs. *gylden* 'golden' (with *i*-umlaut of /u/). We can indicate these various lexical-to-surface relations diagrammatically in this way:

(6.30)

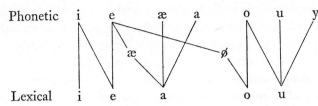

Thus we need only five short vowels, /i e u o a/, at the lexical level. We can then represent the underlying stressed nuclei of the forms we have mentioned so far as follows:

(6.31)

	rignan	sellan		cuman
	regn	dæg	dohtor	cyme
fisc	feld	dagas	dehter	gold
/i/	/e/	/a/	/o/	/u/

2.1.2 *Vowel clusters*. Let us turn now to the two-vowel clusters. We have allowed for the following long vowels and diphthongs at the phonetic level:

(6.32)
    [ii] fīf 'five'   [uu] hūs 'house'
    [ee] hēr 'here'   [oo] bōc 'book'
    [ææ] hǣr 'hair'   [aa] hām 'home'
    [yy] cȳþan 'make known'
        [iu] cīest 'he chooses'
        [eo] þēof 'thief'
        [æa] bēam 'tree'

Of the long vowels (two-vowel sequences with identical members), only [ææ] and [yy] are not also phonemic. The examples with non-low long vowels (which are not from ablaut), indeed, have the same sequences phonemically, i.e. [fiif] < /fiif/, and so on. However, we argued in chapter 1 that surface [ææ] in words like *hǣr* derive from phonemic /aa/ by backness switching (1.8), whereas the [aa] in *hām* is from /ai/ by DHH (3.15), AFB (2.11), and backness switching. Other instances of [ææ] and [oo] are derived geminates. Thus [ææ] in *cwǣdon* comes from [ee] by lowness assignment (1.28), which is from [e] by quantitative ablaut (1.27), which is ultimately from /V/ by qualitative ablaut (1.19). And *nōmon* shows a similar derivation, but with the addition of nasal influence (b) followed by a second application of lowness assignment.

The only permissible lexical long vowels, then, are geminates involving the simple vowels we have already established as lexically distinct. We must now decide how these sequences are to be represented in the lexicon. To take the simplest case, let us suppose (falsely) for the moment that there are no lexical two-vowel sequences whose members are not identical. If this were the case, it would be possible to enter the second vowel in each sequence with unspecified articulation. For instance, the nucleus of *fīf* would be given this way:

(6.33)
$$\begin{bmatrix} V \\ +\text{high} \\ -\text{back} \end{bmatrix} \begin{bmatrix} V \\ o[\text{artic}] \end{bmatrix}.$$

(This would assume a redundancy rule specifying that nonback vowels are nonround.) We have of course already allowed in chapter 1 for an unspecified radical vowel in the strong verbs, where the articulatory features are predictable from the phonological and syntactic environments. And this unspecified vowel must be added to the set of simple lexical vowels that we established above: the inventory is now /i e u o a V/. If there were no non-identical two-vowel sequences in the lexicon, we could simply extend the notion 'unspecified vowel' in such a way as to allow for unspecified articulations following specified ones, with a convention that the second of any two vowels in sequence is redundantly identical to the first. This would make [o[artic]] on a vowel after another vowel simply the lexical equivalent of phonetic [:]. But things are not so simple: there are underlying diphthongs as well as long vowels in OE.

We mentioned above that we had argued earlier for a derivation of the [aa] in *hām* from /ai/. We must now determine what other underlying diphthongs are necessary, and how they will affect the representation of the long vowels: in other words, under what circumstances is the second vowel of a two-vowel sequence predictable, and how do we rule out inadmissible sequences like *[ou] or *[ie]?

Of the three surface diphthongs exemplified in (6.32), the [iu] in *čīest* is derived by *i*-umlaut from [eo]; and indeed all surface [iu] are so derived, either from [eo] or [æa]. There is further no reason to suppose that the other two forms, *þēof* and *bēam*, with phonetic [eo] and [æa] respectively, do not contain 'lexical divocalic nuclei: though of course there are many instances of [eo] and [æa] like *feoh*, *lēoht*, *bearn*, *nēah*, which come from [e], [ee], [æ], [ææ] respectively by back

umlaut. However, the surface specifications for the diphthong in
bēam are the result of AFB and DHH; the sequence here has its source
in /au/, and develops in the same way as the [au] produced (in strong
verbs of class II) by qualitative ablaut. Thus /au/ → [æu] (AFB) → [æa]
(DHH). We thus require two lexical diphthongs with initial /a-/. There
remains the question of what the lexical nucleus is in forms like *þēof*.
Observe that we have argued earlier that it is unnecessary to allow for
a lexical /ei/ which subsequently becomes [ii] by highness harmonization: it seems less costly to enter all [ii] apart from those deriving from
qualitative ablaut in class I PRES as lexical /ii/.

It might appear that there is similarly little motivation for a claim
that the nucleus of *þēof* is lexically anything other than /eo/ (or perhaps
/eu/ becoming [eo] by DHH). This cannot of course be ruled out
a priori; but it is interesting to note that if the diphthong here is /eu/
or /eo/, it is the only one of the series which has as its first member
a mid vowel: the others, /ai au/, all begin with low vowels. (If we were
operating in terms of markedness theory, a diphthong in /e-/ would be
the only one that has a first element which is [*m* high]; but see appendix IV.) It is also worth noting that given /ai au/, these diphthongs
contain all and only the vowels belonging to the 'minimal' natural
vowel system /i u a/: a subset of the OE vowel inventory that we have
already seen playing a role in the operation of the nasal influence conventions (ch. II). Since it is clear that OE has at no point diphthongs in
/u-/, but does have a surface diphthong in /i-/, viz. [iu], might there be
a third combination of the set /i u a/ available in lexical representations,
i.e. /iu/?

If, let us say, there is an /iu/ diphthong underlying what we have
assumed to be lexical diphthongs of the /eo/ type, then we would need
a rule to collapse such /iu/ with the [eu] from ablaut in class II PRES,
and from back umlaut. Now observe that we have already discussed
(ch. III, §7) the possibility that we might need just such a rule to
account for the surface vocalism of verbs like class I *wrēon* and class III
þēon. In that earlier discussion we decided that these forms in themselves did not provide enough evidence for such a synchronic rule:
the new forms involved could be handled more simply by exception
features. But it seems, if the discussion above in terms of a 'minimal'
inventory has anything to it, that there might be stronger evidence for
such a rule. We will see in fact that such a process, collapsing sequences
of the type [iu]/[eo] in [eo], has interesting implications for the phonology

as a whole. Accordingly, we will propose such a rule, and then explore its consequences:

(6.34) *Nonlow diphthong collapsing*

$$
\text{SD:} \begin{bmatrix} V \\ \alpha\text{back} \end{bmatrix} \begin{bmatrix} V \\ -\alpha\text{back} \end{bmatrix} \quad \text{SC: } 1 \ 2 \rightarrow [-\text{high}] \\
\phantom{\text{SD:}} \quad 1 \qquad\quad 2 \qquad\qquad\qquad\quad 1 \qquad\quad 2
$$

(This will apply vacuously to [eo] and [æa].) The rule (6.34) must apply before the development of [iu] from *i*-umlaut of [eo] (as in *cīest*), or [æa] (as in *ieldra*), since this does not undergo collapse. We will see that this is of some interest in the light of the historical developments of the diphthongs.

It is, further, not necessary to assume that forms like *meox*, etc., which historically show breaking of /i/, have that /i/ synchronically. The simpler derivation involves underlying /e/, and we suppose that such restructuring has taken place in all non-crucial cases – i.e. except where avoiding back umlaut of [i] requires the introduction of exception features (cf. ch. III, §7).

Observe now that the existence of a rule like (6.34) has interesting consequences for some arguments already broached – and provisionally concluded – earlier on: particularly that concerning the form and ordering relations of DHH (cf. particularly ch. I, §3). We concluded earlier that DHH was essentially a redundancy rule, requiring agreement in highness and lowness between two vowels differing in backness. It thus operates as shown below in (6.35) in the derivation of the root vowels in forms like *bēodan, bēad* and *bād*:

(6.35)

Input (post-ablaut)	eu	au	ai
DHH (3.15)	eo	—	aæ
AFB (2.11)	—	æu	æaæ
DHH (3.15)	—	æa	—
Backness switching (1.8)	—	—	aa
Output	eo	æa	aa
Spelling	bēodan	bēad	bād

The backness disagreement condition is required if [ei] in *bīdan*, etc. is to be excluded from DHH. The fact that DHH can apply as an 'anywhere' rule, both before and after AFB, means that it accounts for both the shift from [ai] to [aæ] in the derivation of *bād* (before AFB), and the development of [æa] in *bēad* from [æu] (after AFB).

We did however consider another possible interpretation of DHH in chapter 1, §3. This involved removing the condition that the two vowels disagree in backness, and excluding [ei] from DHH by ordering. DHH is then a straight phonological rule, ordered after the highness harmonization rule that shifts [ei] to [ii]. If this were the case, then the derivations of *bēad*, *bād* and *bīdan* would be:

(6.36)

Input (post-ablaut)	au	ai	ei
Highness harmonization (1.11)	—	—	ii
AFB (2.11)	æu	æi	—
DHH (3.15)	æa	ææ	—
Backness switching (1.8)	—	aa	—
Output	æa	aa	ii
Spelling	bēad	bād	bīdan

The main objection to this proposal was that the post-ablaut [eu] in *bēodan*, etc. (< /-Vu/) would shift to [iu] by highness harmonization, and DHH would fail to apply. But we now have two independent motivations for a rule lowering the [i-] in such sequences to [e-] – i.e. nonlow diphthong collapsing (6.34). This particular impediment, involving the derivation of *bēodan*, etc., would seem to be removed. And since the interpretation of DHH we have just outlined has the merit of removing the need for a (somewhat ad hoc) condition of backness disagreement, it would seem to be preferable. We must now consider whether there are any further objections.

The other area where we suggested that DHH might apply both before and after the application of a particular rule was discussed in chapter IV, §3. There we argued that DHH might affect diphthongs in an *i*-umlaut context both before and after umlaut. Consider the derivations of the root vowels in *bierhto* 'brightness' (cf. *beorht*) and *ieldra* 'older' (cf. *eald*):

(6.37)

Input	e	a
AFB (2.11)	—	æ
Breaking (3.35)	eu	æu
DHH (3.15)	eo	æa
I-umlaut (4.15)	io	ia
DHH (3.15)	iu	iu
Output	iu	iu
Spelling	bierhto	ieldra

It is however also clear, from the discussion in chapter IV, §3, that this is really no more strongly motivated than a derivation in which DHH simply follows umlaut. The derivational history in (6.37) was preferred on the basis of the discussion in chapter I, §3 concerning the derivation of the vowels of the PRES and PRET of strong verbs of classes I and II. And we showed immediately above that there is good reason to reject the conclusion reached there, in view of the motivations for a rule of Nonlow diphthong collapsing, and the attendant simplification of DHH.

Accordingly, the backness disagreement condition can be removed from DHH, and it can simply be ordered after umlaut. The revised rule is as follows:

(6.38) *Diphthong height harmony: revised*

$$V \rightarrow \begin{bmatrix} \alpha\text{high} \\ \beta\text{low} \end{bmatrix} \Big/ \begin{bmatrix} V \\ \alpha\text{high} \\ \beta\text{low} \end{bmatrix} \underline{\hspace{2cm}}$$

(This will apply vacuously to all geminates.) One further observation is in order: notice that this interpretation of DHH somewhat weakens the argument for [iu] rather than [iy] as the value for *ie* from umlaut, since this depended in part on the existence of the backness disagreement condition (cf. ch. IV, §3).

We now present here, as a resumé of the preceding discussion, the derivations of the vowels in the six crucial forms we have been looking at. We assume here that DHH takes the form in (6.38), and is ordered after umlaut:

(6.39)

Input	ei	ai	eu	ai	e	a
Highness harmonization	ii	—	iu	—	i	—
AFB	—	æi	—	æu	—	æ
Breaking	—	—	—	—	iu	æu
Nonlow diphthong collapsing	—	—	eu	—	eu	—
i-Umlaut	—	—	—	—	iu	iu
DHH (6.38)	—	ææ	eo	æa	—	—
Backness switching	—	aa	—	—	—	—
Output	ii	aa	eo	æa	iu	iu
Spelling	bīdan	bād	bēodan	bēad	bierhto	ieldra

The preceding has been something of a digression – though a necessary one – from our discussion of the lexical vowel inventory. We want to consider now the consequences of our suggestions about the lexical diphthongs for the representation of geminates exemplified in (6.33). This proposal can no longer stand as a characterization of /ii/ and /aa/ (unless we use the zero specification distinctively), since the element following /i-/ or /a-/ in a two-vowel sequence is no longer predictably /-i/ after /i-/ and /-a/ after /a-/. We must allow for /ii/, /iu/, /aa/, /au/, and /ai/. We can, however, retain representations of the type shown in (6.33) for /uu/, /ee/, and /oo/:

(6.40)   *Representation*   *Example*

$$\begin{bmatrix} V \\ +\text{high} \\ +\text{back} \end{bmatrix} \begin{bmatrix} V \\ 0[\text{artic}] \end{bmatrix} \qquad \text{hūs /huus/}$$

$$\begin{bmatrix} V \\ -\text{high} \\ -\text{back} \end{bmatrix} \begin{bmatrix} V \\ 0[\text{artic}] \end{bmatrix} \qquad \text{hēr /heer/}$$

$$\begin{bmatrix} V \\ -\text{high} \\ -\text{low} \\ +\text{back} \end{bmatrix} \begin{bmatrix} V \\ 0[\text{artic}] \end{bmatrix} \qquad \text{bōc /book/}$$

The vowel specifications here would presuppose two redundancy rules of the following types:

(6.41)   (a) $[+\text{high}] \rightarrow [-\text{low}]$

$$(b)\ V \rightarrow \begin{cases} [\alpha\text{round}] \ / \begin{bmatrix} \underline{\qquad} \\ \alpha\text{back} \\ -\text{low} \end{bmatrix} \\ [-\text{round}] \ / \begin{bmatrix} \underline{\qquad} \\ +\text{low} \end{bmatrix} \end{cases}$$

(Rule (6.41a) is presumably a universal condition dictated by the definition of the features involved: (6.41b) is similar to Chomsky and Halle's marking convention XI for vowel-roundness (cf. appendix IV), but we assume it to be simply a condition on lexical representations in OE, and to have no universal status; therefore it must be stated.)

We can now suggest the following preliminary representations for divocalic sequences in /i-/ and /a-/:

(6.42)   *Representation*   *Example*

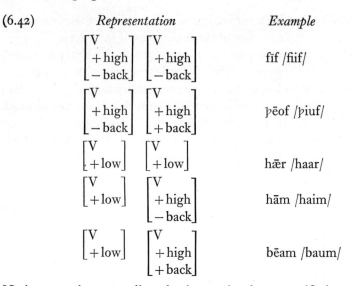

$$\begin{bmatrix} V \\ +\text{high} \\ -\text{back} \end{bmatrix} \begin{bmatrix} V \\ +\text{high} \\ -\text{back} \end{bmatrix} \qquad \text{fīf} \ /\text{fiif}/$$

$$\begin{bmatrix} V \\ +\text{high} \\ -\text{back} \end{bmatrix} \begin{bmatrix} V \\ +\text{high} \\ +\text{back} \end{bmatrix} \qquad \text{þēof} \ /\text{þiuf}/$$

$$\begin{bmatrix} V \\ +\text{low} \end{bmatrix} \begin{bmatrix} V \\ +\text{low} \end{bmatrix} \qquad \text{hǣr} \ /\text{haar}/$$

$$\begin{bmatrix} V \\ +\text{low} \end{bmatrix} \begin{bmatrix} V \\ +\text{high} \\ -\text{back} \end{bmatrix} \qquad \text{hām} \ /\text{haim}/$$

$$\begin{bmatrix} V \\ +\text{low} \end{bmatrix} \begin{bmatrix} V \\ +\text{high} \\ +\text{back} \end{bmatrix} \qquad \text{bēam} \ /\text{baum}/$$

Notice too, that as well as having a simple unspecified vowel, as in *helpan*, we must also allow for /Vi/ and /Vu/ in the strong verbs of classes I and II respectively:

(6.43)   *Representation*   *Example*

$$\begin{bmatrix} V \\ \text{o[artic]} \end{bmatrix} \begin{bmatrix} V \\ +\text{high} \\ -\text{back} \end{bmatrix} \qquad \text{bīdan} \ /\text{bVidan}/$$

$$\begin{bmatrix} V \\ \text{o[artic]} \end{bmatrix} \begin{bmatrix} V \\ +\text{high} \\ +\text{back} \end{bmatrix} \qquad \text{bēodan} \ /\text{bVudan}/$$

It is now clear that the second element in any divocalic sequence must be either /i/, /u/, or identical to the first. This brings up a rather interesting fact about the typological relations holding between the OE lexical nuclei and the surface nuclei of later periods. The previous discussion, and the examples given in (6.40), (6.42), and (6.43) show that OE had different sets of constraints on phonetic vowel clusters from those holding for lexical ones. This is shown below in (6.44):

(6.44) (a) *Lexical vowel clusters*

  i. $\begin{bmatrix} V \\ \alpha\text{[artic]} \end{bmatrix} \begin{bmatrix} V \\ \alpha\text{[artic]} \end{bmatrix}$: uu ee oo ii aa

  ii. $[V] \qquad \begin{bmatrix} V \\ +\text{high} \end{bmatrix}$: Vi Vu iu ai au

(b) *Phonetic vowel clusters*

$$\begin{bmatrix} V \\ \alpha\text{high} \\ \beta\text{low} \end{bmatrix} \begin{bmatrix} V \\ \alpha\text{high} \\ \beta\text{low} \end{bmatrix} : \quad \text{(a)} \quad \text{iu} \quad \text{eo} \quad \text{æa}$$

$$\text{(b)} \quad \text{ii} \quad \text{ee} \quad \text{uu} \quad \text{uu} \quad \text{oo} \quad \text{aa}$$

In the lexicon, that is, all vowel clusters are either identical or have the second member marked [+high]; in phonetic representation, all vowel clusters, whether identical or not, have elements that agree in height. All identical clusters (e.g. (6.44(a)i)) are properly included in the type allowed in phonetic representation; and all non-identical clusters (6.44(a)ii) have been subject to DHH, so that there is only one phonetic type.

If we return to the discussion of the vowel-shift and the ME diphthongs in §1 of this chapter, we will see that the same conditions holding for the OE lexicon – not those holding for phonetic forms – hold for the phonetic long vowel and diphthong systems. Thus the system given above in (6.24), for Middle English, can be characterized as containing the same types only that were allowed in the OE lexicon:

(6.45) *The Middle English long vowels and diphthongs*

i. $\begin{bmatrix} V \\ \alpha[\text{artic}] \end{bmatrix} \begin{bmatrix} V \\ \alpha[\text{artic}] \end{bmatrix} : \quad \text{ii} \quad \text{ee} \quad \text{ææ} \quad \text{uu} \quad \text{oo} \quad \text{ɔɔ} \quad \text{aa}$

ii. $[\text{V}] \qquad \begin{bmatrix} V \\ +\text{high} \end{bmatrix} : \quad \text{eu} \quad \text{æi} \quad \text{æu} \quad \text{ɔi} \quad \text{ɔu} \quad \text{au}$

It looks as if rules of the DHH type represent a rather short-lived episode in the history of English. If we are right in our interpretation of the vowel shift, such a rule did in fact, in a restricted form, play a part in the derivation of the phonetic nuclei in John Hart's dialect: that is, rule (6.12), the double nucleus constraint. This seems to be, as we mentioned above, a restricted version of DHH in the form given in (6.38). But it is noteworthy that the restriction in effect permits the generation of vowel clusters of a type which are obligatory for the OE lexicon but phonetically inadmissible. There may well have been an even greater typological uniformity throughout the history of English than we suggested in §1 of this chapter: the constraints on lexical types may actually have come through unchanged from Proto-Germanic to early Modern English.

2.2   The nonvowels

2.2.1   *The phonetic inventory.* Our study so far has suggested that OE had the following consonantal segments in phonetic representations:

(6.46)

	Labial		Dental		Alveolar		Palatal		Velar		Uvular	Glottal
Stops	p	b	t	d					k	g		
Fricatives	f	v	θ	ð	s	z		ʃ	x	ɣ		h
Affricates							c	ɟ				
Nasals	m		n						ŋ			
Liquids	w		ł				j		(w ł)	R		

(There are some problems of classification here which we will attempt to resolve in the next few sections: especially the status of [h] and [ʃ], and the reason for calling [w j] 'liquids'. The dual assignment of [w ł] is due to the fact that they were probably coarticulated: [w] is labiovelar, and [ł] is a velarized dental.)

The lexical inventory is of course quite different from this: among other things it is in most respects smaller; though it does contain one segment – the 'laryngeal' /A/ – which never appears phonetically. Because of the various problems of classification we will not attempt to give a phonetic feature representation here, but we will proceed directly to a discussion of the various phonological classes, and their surface realizations.

2.2.2   *Noncontinuant obstruents.* The OE lexical stop system seems to have been of the very common symmetrical type:

(6.47)   p   t   k
              b   d   g

As we showed in chapter v, /b g/ are subject to intervocalic lenition (continuancy adjustment (5.41)), which /d/ resists. Further, /k g/ are subject to palatalization in front environments, as described in chapter IV (backness accommodation (4.27), palatal softening (4.29)). There is also, in all probability, spirantization of /k/ before /t/ (velar spirantization (3.29b)), and in some cases – though this is not certain, and is probably optional when it does occur – final devoicing of /g/ (velar devoicing (3.29a)). Leaving aside the last somewhat doubtful rule, the lexical stops and their phonetic realizations can be visualized this way:

(6.48)

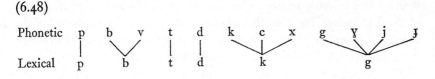

These relations may be exemplified as follows: /p/, *piċ* 'pitch'; /b/, *beran* 'bear', *hafað* 'they have'; /t/, *tīma* 'time'; /d/, *dēman* 'judge'; /k/, *catt* 'cat', *ċinn* 'chin', *tǣhte* 'he taught'; /g/, *gōd* 'good', *āgan* 'own', *ġieldan* 'yield', *senġean* 'singe'.

Some of these phonetic reflexes overlap with those of other segments: [j] < /g/ overlaps with [j] < /j/, [v] < /b/ overlaps with [v] from voicing of an underlying labial fricative, and [x] < /k/ overlaps with [x] from an underlying velar fricative. We will discuss these relationships in the next two sections.

2.2.3   *Continuant obstruents, I: fricatives.* These segments pose significant theoretical problems, which we touched on to some extent in chapter v, but which require some further comment. In that chapter we proposed that the distribution of voiced and voiceless surface phones – [f θ s] vs. [v ð z] – should be accounted for by having these segments unspecified for voice in the lexicon. We made this claim on the basis of their crucial responsiveness to other contiguous segments – including word-boundary. Briefly, voiced fricatives appear only in intersonorant position, and voiceless ones only in contiguity to other obstruents, including / # /, which we provisionally assigned to that category. This claim raises a serious problem: what is the status of segments lexically specified for all features but one?

For instance, the only other segment we have that is not fully specified in the lexicon – the [o[artic]] vowel /V/ – is unspecified, not for one feature, but for a whole submatrix; and if we represent fricatives as [o voice], we might seem to be getting ourselves into the classic difficulties associated with zero as a 'third value' in lexical entries (cf. discussion in *SPE*: ch. 9, and Stanley 1967). Actually, however, this is not a problem here: because the 'value' [o voice] is not in fact being used at any point to specify even a spurious distinctiveness: the fricatives are $\begin{bmatrix} +\text{obs} \\ +\text{cont} \end{bmatrix}$, which defines them against all other obstruents, and all other continuants. And further, it is perhaps misleading to say in any case that we really have a 'third value' here: what we have is better defined as a missing feature. Our claim is not in fact that fricatives are marked [o voice], but that there is no feature 'voice' in their matrices at all (for a similar proposal in regard to certain other features in other instances see Chafe 1970, and discussion in Lass 1971b).

The essential point, in our discussion in chapter v, was that it would be totally arbitrary for us to mark the fricatives as either [+voice] or [−voice] in the lexicon, since the values for this feature are totally determined by context – and by very natural rules in each context as well. Since the two values are in absolute complementation, the only insightful claim would seem to be that for voicing in fricatives all environments are neutralization environments: the OE fricatives are genuine 'archiphonemes', in the Praguian sense.

It might be said, of course, that if a language has only one (phonemic) set of fricatives, these are 'naturally' to be taken as voiceless; i.e. the 'unmarked' value for voice in obstruents is 'minus'. And this does certainly reflect what appear to be genuine implicational universals (cf. Jakobson 1941): that no language will have a voiced obstruent of a given type unless it also has the corresponding voiceless one. But even if this is true, such an implicational statement says only that if there is one phonetic type it will be voiceless; we see no reason for projecting such distributional facts into the lexicon of a language that has both phonetic types, especially when by doing so we lose an obvious generalization (see further appendix II, §2).

So we will assume that the OE fricatives are archisegments of a particular type: essentially with no specification for voice. (Or, in another sense, that they are not [o voice], but [−[+voice]] and [−[−voice]], i.e. that the 'voice' cell in their matrices is absent.) We will indicate this special status here by using 'neutral' upper-case symbols to represent them. Given this analysis, OE has four lexical continuant obstruents: labial, dental, dental strident (or alveolar), and velar, which we shall represent respectively as /F Þ S X/. Although /Þ/ is probably a 'pure' dental and /S/ postdental or alveolar, we shall assume that their distinctiveness in this case is the same as for most languages that have [s] and [θ] in contrast: they are both specified as $\begin{bmatrix} +\text{ant} \\ +\text{cor} \end{bmatrix}$, but [θ] is [−strid] and [s] is [+strid].

The phonological behaviour of /F Þ S/ is in general quite straight-forward (with one problem which we will come to shortly); but there are some difficulties with /X/. First of all, although it might appear that in accordance with the continuant voicing assignment rule, (5.35), it should have a voiced reflex [ɣ] as well as voiceless [x], this is not the case. The reason here is not some intrinsic property of /X/, but the fact that it is deleted from the environments in which a voiced reflex would appear before (5.35) applies. Thus the expansion of that rule which assigns [+voice] is always vacuous. (The rule in question here, which deletes /X/, is the one we called loss of *h* (3.26)). In all other contexts, /X/ is either word-initial or word-final (and therefore contiguous to /#/, which makes it [−voice]), or in gemination: *hǣlan* 'heal', *feoh* 'cattle', *hliehhan* 'laugh'.

A further complication arises in the fact that /X/ has two quite different types of surface realizations: [x] (and possibly [ç] after front vowels); and [h]. We are assuming, since there seems to be no convincing counterevidence, that the OE scribal practice of writing *h* in all these contexts was morphophonemically justified, as was suggested earlier by Stockwell (1958). Early Middle English evidence, such as omission of initial *h* and the occurrence of excrescent *h*, suggests the 'weak' value [h] in this position, rather than [x]. Thus we posit a rule that turns [x] < /X/ to [h] after word-boundary. As we see it, this rule is simply one that erases the articulatory (supraglottal) gesture of [x], leaving only 'breath'. That is, we characterize [h] as the minimally specified voiceless continuant obstruent, one which is $\begin{bmatrix} +\text{obs} \\ +\text{cont} \\ -\text{voice} \end{bmatrix}$, but has no articulatory features whatsoever.

The rule producing [h] then deletes the entire [artic] submatrix of [x], leaving only the [phon] submatrix, i.e. obstruency, continuancy, and voicelessness. Assuming that it is possible to represent any segment (see the formal proposal in appendix II, §2) as a conjunction of two submatrices, $\begin{bmatrix} [\text{articulation}] \\ [\text{phonation}] \end{bmatrix}$, each of which may be independently the domain of a rule, we can state the generation of [h] as a 'dearticulation' (see chapter V, §1), i.e. a submatrix deletion:

(6.49) *Velar dearticulation*

$$\text{SD: } \# \begin{bmatrix} [+\text{back}] \\ \begin{bmatrix} +\text{obs} \\ +\text{cont} \\ -\text{voice} \end{bmatrix} \end{bmatrix} \qquad \text{SC: } 1\ 2 \rightarrow \begin{bmatrix} +\text{obs} \\ +\text{cont} \\ -\text{voice} \end{bmatrix}$$

$$\qquad\quad 1 \qquad\quad 2 \qquad\qquad\qquad\qquad 1 \qquad\quad 2$$

As we mentioned above, there may also be some rule that converts [x] to [ç] after front vowels, as in *niht* 'night', etc. We have in fact assumed such a rule in our discussion of the Middle English diphthongs in § 1.2 of this chapter; but it is by no means a certainty. It is true that a rule of this type is to be found in many Germanic dialects, e.g. the *ich/ach* rule in German, and the similar one in Scots, where we get [x] in *loch* and [ç] in *fecht* 'fight'. But some other dialects, for example most forms of Yiddish, do not have this: in various Russian and Polish Yiddish dialects we find [näxt] 'night' and [ɪx] 'I' – sometimes even when the fricative is not velar, but a uvular [χ]. In other cases we find an assimilation, but this time a modification of the vowel, e.g. rather than [ɪx] we get a centring glide, [ɪəx]. This is a matter of detail too fine to recover historically; and as we showed earlier, nothing crucial, at least as far as the ME diphthongization is concerned, depends on it. If there is such a fronting rule, it might very well be handled as a minor modification of the post-vocalic subpart of backness accommodation.

There is one further matter bearing on the fricatives which we must deal with: and this is the undoubted presence in surface forms of a fricative of the type [ʃ], e.g. in *scieran* 'shear', *fisc* 'fish', *fiscas* 'id. pl.'. What is the status of this segment? If it is a phonemic fricative, we must somehow prevent it from being subject to voicing assignment, otherwise we get *[fiʒas] instead of [fiʃas] for *fiscas*; and in fact there is no evidence at all for [ʒ] in OE, though the [ʃ] in the form above and in many others stands in the proper position for assimilation.

Historically, of course, we know that [ʃ] derived from a cluster [sk] (cf. Go. *fisks*, ON *fiskr*, etc.). But can this be the case synchronically? If it were, we could simply have a rule converting [sk] to [ʃ] ordered after voicing assignment. There would thus be no need of any special machinery to block voicing. Actually, there is such evidence; not very much, to be sure, but enough to suggest that such a rule is probable, and to avoid the problem.

This evidence is primarily in the form of metathesized [sk] clusters, i.e. [ks], which occur in all positions in words of this type, but especially before back vowels. These are recognizable in graphic representation by the fact that they are spelt with *x*, rather than *sc*. If we were, for instance, to find forms of the same word in which *sc* ~ *x*, this would go some way toward supporting a claim for a synchronic derivation. In his discussion of OE *sc* (1959: §440), Campbell cites a number of suggestive forms: especially cases where an *sc* spelling is found in early West Saxon, and an *x* spelling in late WS. For this to be the case, it would be necessary for the /sk/ clusters to remain in underlying representations; since a derivation /sk/ → [ks] is clearly more likely than /ʃ/ → [ks]. Further, the fact that the [ks] forms are commoner in back-vowel environments also suggests a synchronic derivation, since clearly a change /sk/ to [ʃ] is a palatalization, and we would expect such a process to fail in back environments. Some typical examples of the alternant spellings are: *frosc ~ frox* 'frog', *fiscas ~ fixas* 'fish, pl.', *tusc ~ tux* 'tusk' (cf. NE *tusk/tush*), *þerscan ~ þerxan* 'thresh', and so on.

In the *x*-forms we can assume an optional metathesis of /sk/ word-finally and before back vowels; and following this (in the synchronic ordering at least) an obligatory rule converting /sk/ to [ʃ] if it has not been metathesized.

(6.50) sk-*metathesis*

$$\text{SD}: \begin{bmatrix} +\text{obs} \\ +\text{cor} \\ +\text{strid} \end{bmatrix} \begin{bmatrix} +\text{obs} \\ +\text{back} \\ -\text{voice} \end{bmatrix} \left\{ \begin{bmatrix} \text{V} \\ +\text{back} \end{bmatrix} \atop \# \right\} \quad \text{SC: } 1\ 2\ 3 \rightarrow 2\ 1\ 3$$

$$\quad 1 \qquad\qquad 2 \qquad\qquad 3$$

(The specification of /k/ does not require [−cont], as /X/ does not appear in this position.)

(6.51) sk-*Palatalization*

$$(a) \begin{bmatrix} +\text{obs} \\ +\text{cor} \\ +\text{strid} \end{bmatrix} \rightarrow [-\text{ant}] / \underline{} \begin{bmatrix} +\text{obs} \\ +\text{back} \\ -\text{voice} \end{bmatrix}$$

$$(b) \begin{bmatrix} +\text{obs} \\ +\text{back} \\ -\text{voice} \end{bmatrix} \rightarrow \emptyset / \begin{bmatrix} +\text{obs} \\ -\text{ant} \\ +\text{cor} \end{bmatrix} \underline{}$$

(We are assuming here that [ʃ] is a 'palato-alveolar', i.e. in terms of Chomsky and Halle's features it is specified distinctively as non-anterior and coronal.)

We can now display the lexical fricatives and their phonetic reflexes:

(6.52)

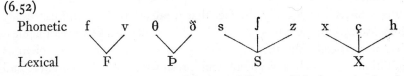

These relations can be exemplified as follows: /F/, *faran* 'go', *ofer*

'over'; /Þ/, *þēoh* 'thigh', *ōþer* 'other'; /S/, *sellan* 'sell', *rīsan* 'rise', *fisc* 'fish'; /X/, *nēah* 'near', *niht* 'night', *hālig* 'holy'.

2.2.4 *Continuant obstruents, II: the 'laryngeal' /A/.* This segment,which we discussed in some detail in chapter 1, is problematical: in that (if it really exists) it never appears in phonetic representations. We inferred its existence, in fact, from its usefulness in enabling us, with no obvious hyperingenuities, or an overuse of exception features, to account for the peculiarities in the vocalism of class VI and VII strong verbs by means of rules well-motivated for the other five classes. Actually of course we are in one sense no worse off in this matter than those scholars who are concerned with the purely diachronic problems posed by the Indo-European laryngeals: in this area too the fact is that otherwise 'aberrant' forms – ones with unexpected quality-shifts, lengthenings, etc. – can be accounted for in a reasonable way by positing some segment that once was there. (This is certainly a time-honoured procedure in purely diachronic – i.e. projective, extrapolative – reconstruction: there is still, in a sense, no better example than Saussure's brilliant 1887 study of the Indo-European vowel system, which is where all the 'laryngeal' trouble really began.)

But in cases where the only remnant of a segment in phonetic representation is its assimilatory or quasi-assimilatory effect on other segments, there are severe problems in deciding on feature-specifications (as well as the more serious epistemological problem of whether such segments may be properly imputed to synchronic grammars at all: see our earlier discussion, and §3 of this chapter). Assuming that we want to claim a phonological reality for such a segment, we can specify it only insofar as its effects are left to us: in Puhvel's words (1960: 4) 'the uncoverable remnants may be the *disiecta membra* of a phoneme'. (On the problems involved see Watkins 1960, Lehmann 1955, 1960; and perhaps most importantly, Sapir 1938.) In this case we can recover with some certainty, as we indicated in chapter 1, only the class features $\begin{bmatrix} +\text{obs} \\ -\text{cons} \end{bmatrix}$, and the articulatory features $\begin{bmatrix} +\text{back} \\ +\text{low} \end{bmatrix}$. On consideration of the effects of /A/ – especially the fact that it affects vowels, and can easily be vocalized, the features [+voice] and [+cont] also seem reasonable – but not crucial. But this is as far as we can go, except the obvious addition that such a segment will presumably also be $\begin{bmatrix} -\text{ant} \\ -\text{cor} \end{bmatrix}$, and

$\begin{bmatrix} -\text{strid} \\ -\text{nas} \end{bmatrix}$ as well. As for what it might really have been, we can only guess, and not too intelligently at that: if it were not for the typological problems that this would raise, the most logical choice in every way would be a pharyngeal 'fricative', like Arabic [ʕ]. But there is little point to such speculation.

2.2.5   *The sonorants.* Two members of this group, /j w/, raise some problems. We have already referred to /j/ as a 'palatal fricative'; but in the light of our discussion in §2.2.3 it seems that there is a certain lack of congruity. There is no doubt that it is [+cons]; but its other major class feature is disputable. For instance, there are some arguments in favour of its being an obstruent, e.g. it merges in phonetic representations with [j] from palatalized /g/, and there seems to be no particular motivation for extending the rule of palatal softening any further, i.e. weakening the resulting voiced palatal continuant from its presumable [+obs] value to [−obs]. So on grounds of 'simplicity' it might seem that /j/ should be an obstruent.

But against this there is the fact that, unlike the other continuant obstruents /F Þ S X/, neither /j/ nor [j] < /g/ show the characteristic assimilatory response to boundaries: there is no evidence at least for a change like [j] to [ç] initially or finally. Perhaps the best solution, and the one we provisionally adopt here, is to take lexical /j/ as a sonorant, i.e. as a palatal liquid, with the major class features $\begin{bmatrix} -\text{obs} \\ +\text{cons} \end{bmatrix}$, i.e. as a palatal liquid, and the articulatory features of a palatal fricative, i.e. $\begin{bmatrix} -\text{back} \\ +\text{high} \end{bmatrix}$. The latter specification is of course shared with [i], which accounts for the fact that both induce *i*-umlaut; and the fact that it is [+cons], in opposition to [i], specifies it as the environment for the West Germanic gemination (appendix II). Certainly an analysis of this sort, as we pointed out in the Preliminaries, would be plausible for NE /j/: it behaves in many dialects parallel to the undoubted liquid /r/, for instance devoicing and developing friction at word boundary and after voiceless obstruents. (I.e. 'liquid' is a cover-term, phonetically, for 'nonvowel approximant'.)

So we suggest that /j/ in OE is a liquid; and that [j] from palatalized /g/ becomes one also at some point in derivation after palatal softening, so that up until this point [j] < /g/ and [j] < /j/ differ in the features

[±obs]; but phonetic [j] from whatever source is [−obs]. If this is the case, then the rule might well be of this sort:

(6.53) *J-weakening*

$$[+\text{obs}] \rightarrow [-\text{obs}] \Big/ \begin{bmatrix} -\text{back} \\ +\text{high} \\ +\text{voice} \end{bmatrix}$$

We will treat /w/ as symmetrical to /j/, i.e. as a labio-velar liquid. We have developed sufficient detail to schematize the reflexes of the whole obstruent system (minus /A/), plus the liquids /j w/, so that the total pattern of overlapping and nonoverlapping is clear:

(6.54)

Phonetic	p	b	v	f	t	d	θ	ð	s	z	ʃ	h	ç	x	k	c	g	ɣ	ɟ	j	w
Lexical	p		b	F	t	d		Þ		S			X		k			g		j	w

As far as the other liquids are concerned, there is little to be said here. The feature specifications of /r/ (or /R/) and /l/ have been discussed in some detail in chapter III. To recapitulate briefly, we claimed that (at least in the environment where we have useful evidence) /r/ was a uvular continuant, and /l/ was a velarized dental lateral. Any 'allophonic' variations in the surface realizations of these segments are too fine to be recovered historically.

For the nasals, we can say with some confidence that OE had two at the systematic phonemic level: a dental /n/ and a labial /m/. At least there is no evidence for any other lexical nasals, though it seems probable that [ŋ] occurred phonetically for /n/ before velars. At various points in this book (especially ch. III, §6) we have used the 'neutral' representation /N/ for a postvocalic, preconsonantal nasal; this is not to be taken as a claim for an archi-nasal, parallel to the unspecified vowel /V/, but as a cover-symbol for any nasal in that environment. We have done this to indicate that we are not sure at what point assimilation of /n/ to velars takes place. It does seem likely, given the Modern English evidence, that it was extremely low-level; certainly in many modern dialects [n] and [ŋ] are in free variation before [k g] in certain forms. We are familiar with speakers who have characteristically both [bæŋkwɪt] and [bæŋkwɪt] 'banquet', [pɛngwɪn] and [pɛŋgwɪn] 'penguin', etc. Further, the fact that /n/ clearly appears as [n] before [ɟ] in forms like *sengean* 'singe' < /sangjan/ suggests that it is still [+ant] at this point: it would seem superfluous to suppose a derivation like [ngj] → [ŋgj] → [nɟj].

We can now give a table showing the feature specifications for the lexical consonant inventory of OE.

(6.55) *The OE lexical consonant inventory*

	p	b	F	m	Þ	n	t	d	S	j	l	k	g	X	w	r	A
obs	+	+	+	−	+	−	+	+	+	−	−	+	+	+	−	−	+
cons	+	+	+	+	+	+	+	+	+	+	+	+	+	+	+	+	−
ant	+	+	+	+	+	+	+	+	+	−	+	−	−	−	+	−	−
cor	−	−	−	−	+	+	+	+	+	−	+	−	−	−	−	−	−
high	−	−	−	−	−	−	−	−	−	+	+	+	+	+	+	−	−
low	−	−	−	−	−	−	−	−	−	−	−	−	−	−	−	+	+
back	−	−	−	−	−	−	−	−	−	−	+	+	+	+	+	+	+
round	−	−	−	−	−	−	−	−	−	−	−	−	−	−	+	−	−
lat	−	−	−	−	−	−	−	−	−	−	+	−	−	−	−	−	−
nas	−	−	−	+	−	+	−	−	−	−	−	−	−	−	−	−	−
cont	−	−	+	−	+	−	−	−	+	+	+	−	−	+	+	+	+
strid	−	−	−	−	−	−	−	−	+	−	−	−	−	−	−	−	−
voice	−	+	o	+	o	+	−	+	o	+	+	−	+	o	+	+	+

These specifications are presumably those of fully specified systematic phonemic matrices; the redundancies in the consonant inventory are quite simple and straightforward, and do not raise the kind of problems we met with in the vowels; we have therefore not given any formal statement of segment-structure conditions.

3 Some afterthoughts on theory

3.1 The problem of 'productiveness': how extensible are rules?

In looking back over these studies, a year after having completed the basic work, we are struck by the extent to which the structure of our arguments has been determined by implicit presuppositions. And even more, by the lack of genuine empirical support for many of them. The most disturbing thing, ultimately, is the immense power of 'standard' generative phonological theory, and the somewhat ad hoc and even circular nature of portions of the theory that enshrine this powerful machinery as canonical. In this light, one of the most difficult problems is that of finding a principled definition of 'productiveness': particularly with respect to paradigm-forming rules, and their legitimate extension to forms outside the paradigms the rules are apparently 'recovered' from.

Take for instance what seems to be the most far-reaching claim we have made: that the complex mass of vowel-alternations in the OE strong verb system is in the now usual sense of the term 'rule-governed'. Except for certain minor lexical specifications (e.g. for class II verbs in -*ū*- and some class VII verbs – cf. appendix I), we have assumed that the whole strong verb system is a rule-governed paradigm, i.e. that the 'solution' (considering it a 'problem' to be 'solved') is 'phonological' rather than 'morphological'. We do not, that is, posit features like [+class III], etc., in order to generate the surface vowel-alternations. Except for the ablaut alternations themselves, the vowel qualities (and quantities) are generable, by and large, by 'independently necessary rules', e.g. lowness assignment, AFB, DHH, and so on.

But is the mere fact that a phonological solution works any guarantee that it is correct? In the light of our present knowledge this would seem to be at least arguable. In fact, since even the internalized grammar of a speaker of a living language (let alone one like OE) is not available for direct inspection, we cannot tell whether its internal organization is anything at all like what the theory (whose framework is largely aprioristic) makes it out to be. How do we know, for instance, that the ablaut alternations are not stored in a look-up table with columns headed 'Class II PRES', and so forth? (Certainly something very like this must be the case for certain aspects of 'addressing' of lexical items in performance grammars: cf. Fromkin 1971.) We *think* we know because our theory is so constructed that it values more highly grammars that are not of this type; consequently we have developed a kind of inverse discovery-procedure, which is not to find such grammars, but rather find sets of rules that generate the paradigms.

In terms of empirical 'cost' (which must ultimately be associated with some as yet ill-defined notion like 'expense of cognitive energy') we have no way of testing, in a case like this, which grammar is in fact 'cheaper': as Chomsky has repeatedly pointed out (notably 1965), one cannot test two grammars against each other by the same evaluation measure if the theories are not comparable. Our only firm point of reference, in judging a phonological analysis, is the metatheory as defined by what we, as practising generative linguists, take to be the canon; but the metatheory is itself an axiomatic-deductive system, and its primitives are related only in a very indirect way to even the most tenuous of observables (cf. the comments on markedness and 'evaluation' in appendix IV, §2).

It is clear that in the preceding sections of this book, we were working, despite certain objections in detail to the theoretical canon as set out for instance in *SPE*, within the 'standard' generative paradigm (using this latter term here in the sense of Kuhn 1962). Our principles were not substantially different from those motivating the bulk of recent work in the field. Now, however, we have begun to think along slightly different lines: our views and concerns have shifted toward a greater preoccupation with the task of constraining the theoretical machinery much more closely than has been done in the past.

We are not, however, convinced that the position we are working toward at this point (1973) is in the long view necessarily correct, or that we will not have cause in the future to shift gears again. For this reason, rather than trying to revise what we have done up to now, we will let it stand on its own merits, and discuss here some possible alternative solutions, based on a different conception of what's wrong and what's right with the theory, and on some notions about the direction that we think theoretical revision might profitably proceed in.

Let us begin by looking at one example of the kind of claims that the theory has led us to make, and suggest a possible alternative. Recall that in our discussion of the *i*-umlaut (ch. IV) we came to the conclusion that in alternating pairs like *cūþ/cȳþan* 'know/make known' it was reasonable to derive both phonetic representations from a single lexical base, i.e. /kuuþ-/. The same thing was true of short vowel pairs like *trum/trymman* 'strong/strengthen', and so on. Because of the existence of many such pairs – in fact for all the OE vowels and diphthongs – we considered it justified to propose a rule of *i*-umlaut (which we know of course to be the historical cause of the alternations) as a synchronic property of the OE grammar.

But we went a step further: on the basis of the obvious derivation of [y(y)] in such pairs as those given above from [u(u)], we then claimed that there is no need, at the lexical level, for front round vowels – even in those forms that are not members of an alternating set. What held for *trymman* holds also for *cyning*, what held for *cȳþan* holds also for *hȳdan*. This is not, given the structure of current phonological theory, at all out of line; it is a simply an application of the 'free ride' principle. Exactly the same kind of thinking holds for the claim in *SPE* for a synchronic vowel shift in NE.

Let us look briefly at the line of argument in *SPE*. After establishing with great care the basis for a claim that a single lexical base underlies each paradigmatic pair of the type *divine/divinity*, etc., Chomsky and Halle propose that the same vowel – in this case /ī/ – underlies not only forms like *divine*, but all words with surface [ai]. Schematically, we might outline the argument as follows:

(a) It is a fact that pairs like *divine/divinity, crime/criminal*, etc., share a lexical base – at least on intuitive grounds.

(b) For various (generally well-motivated) reasons, it can be argued that this base has a nuclear /ī/.

(c) Therefore these paradigmatic alternations can be produced by rules operating on underlying representations in /ī/, such that all /ī/ are converted (ultimately) to [ai]. But there is also a rule – ordered prior to vowel-shift – which laxes antepenultimate tense vowels. Thus the root vowels in trisyllabic derivatives are lax at the point where the vowel-shift rules – which specify tenseness – apply. This produces the surface [ɪ] ~ [ai] alternations.

(d) Since the paradigms motivate such a rule-set, let us extend the vowel-shift to all occurrences of [ai], so that *night, mine, time, desire, bite, drive*, etc. all have underlying /ī/.

If the rules in (c) above constitute a 'significant generalization' about a paradigm, then the extension (d) is an even greater generalization, since it applies to the whole phonology. We can now say that all superficial [ai] are [ī] at some point in their derivation, whether lexically, as in *crime* < /krīm/, or derived, as in *right* < [rīt] < [rīxt] < /rixt/. The rules originally devised to account for a restricted group of paradigmatic phenomena are now 'central' to the phonology; and if all non-alternating [ai] can be derived, with no ad hoc rule-extensions, from the same segment as the alternating ones, we can 'save a phoneme', by eliminating [ai] from underlying representations. (In this way, in fact, Chomsky and Halle eliminate all diphthongs from the Modern English lexicon, through a series of restructurings over time: see their account of the development of the Modern English vowel system, especially the sections on Cooper and Batchelor, ch. 6, §§4–5.)

We have of course done much the same thing in our derivation of OE [y(y)]. There is no possibility, as far as we can tell, of eliminating

/i e u o a/ from the lexicon; but since all [y(y)] derive (historically) from *i*-umlaut of Gmc *ŭ, and there seems to be good evidence that many [y(y)] in alternant pairs derive the same way synchronically, we can then derive all [y(y)] from [u(u)] at some stage, and eliminate a segment from the lexical inventory. And this inventory is now the 'optimal' five-vowel system /i e u o a/. And most crucially, since the rule deriving at least some [y(y)] is 'independently necessary', we have captured an even bigger generalization than the one we set out after.

According to currently accepted criteria, such as 'generality', 'simplicity', and so on, we have effected a genuine saving, by 'proving' that a given vowel is derived; the rule deriving it is needed for some forms anyhow, so by extending it, in the absence of clear indications to the contrary, we have achieved a simplification that the theory rewards us for making. But is it in fact a good decision on other grounds? Is an account which can do things like this really a psychologically valid or insightful one, or does it merely show how powerful the theory – divorced from any real accountability to anything but itself – can be? Especially, as here, divorced from accountability to the speaker. The real question about such an analysis (and this holds for Chomsky and Halle's Modern English vowel-shift too) is this: given the fact that a child might assign a single lexical base to pairs like *cūþ/cȳþan*, etc., is this sufficient grounds for claiming that he will assign the same base-form to other instances of the same vowel which are not in alternating forms? Take cases like *fȳr* 'fire', *ȳð* 'wave', *cyning* 'king', *yfel* 'evil'. These forms do not fit into paradigms like *cūþ/cȳþan, cuman/cyme, mūs/mȳs, trum/trymman*. Why not assume then that these non-alternating forms in fact have phonemic /y(y)/?

Compare for instance these two sets of possible underlying forms selected according to this criterion, and their justifications:

(6.56) (i) (a) *cȳþan* /kuuÞjan/   because of *cūþ* /kuuÞ/

     (b) *mȳs* /muusi/   *mūs* /muus/

     (c) *trymman* /trumjan/   *trum* /trum/

     (d) *cyme* /kumi/   *cuman* [kuman] < /kVman/

   (ii) (a) *fȳr* /fyyr/   because it alternates with nothing

      (b) *ȳð* /yyÞ/

      (c) *cyning* /kyning/

      (d) *yfel* /yFel/

If a proposal of this sort is taken seriously, it means that we have complicated the lexicon by making it two segments longer (or one, if we count only the simplex vowel); further, it is no longer possible to make the fairly neat generalization about the feature composition of the underlying simplex vowels that we stated in (6.41b). The presence of a front round vowel makes it impossible to state any conditions holding for both front and back nonlow vowels; all we can say is:

(6.57)

$$
V \rightarrow \begin{Bmatrix} [\alpha\text{round}] \ / \ \begin{bmatrix} \underline{\hspace{1.5em}} \\ \alpha\text{back} \\ -\text{high} \\ -\text{low} \end{bmatrix} \\ [-\text{round}] \ / \ \begin{bmatrix} \left\{ \begin{matrix} \overline{[+\text{low}]} \\ \begin{bmatrix} -\text{back} \\ -\text{high} \end{bmatrix} \end{matrix} \right\} \end{bmatrix} \end{Bmatrix}
$$

Such revision, however, even if we wanted to do it, would not be possible in all cases; certainly not, for example, with respect to AFB. We would not want to posit a lexical /æ/, because in just about every case the environments triggering the [a] ~ [æ] alternation remain in phonetic representations. Thus the metaphonic blocking of AFB is clear in *faran*, *dæg* ~ *dagas*, etc., and the pre-nasal 'failure' in *band* as opposed to *bær*, and so on. But the umlaut vowels are a different case – because there the crucial environments are deleted or otherwise modified in surface forms. (Except for a few cases, notably the class I weak verbs with *r*-final stems, like *nerian* 'save', *herian* 'praise', and so on, and some scattered items like *cyning* 'king'.) But notice that in a verb like *nerian* it is by no means obvious that the *-i-* represents a mutation-causing affix: because the deverbal noun *nerġend* 'saviour' does not show the corresponding back vowel, but has the same root (the fact that there is probably a historical thematic *-j-* in these forms is not to the point, if we are considering the recoverability of underlying structure from surface alternations). Further, to take verbs of the *nerian* type again, the class II weak verbs show a superficially similar structure, but often with unmutated vowels before *-ian*: *lufian*, *macian*, etc.

In the light of the foregoing, it might be necessary to set some fairly powerful constraints on the permissible abstractness of lexical representations, from this point of view (the following is based in part on some suggestions of Robert Stockwell, personal communication). We might want to define the constraints on permissible lexical abstractness and extra-paradigmatic rule extension somewhat in this way:

(a) Let there be a class P of formatives containing the phones p_i, p_j (where $p_i \neq p_j$), of which it is true that $p_i \sim p_j$; and the rule R which produces the alternation $p_i \sim p_j$ is well-motivated.

(b) Let there be potential classes, P_i, P_j, in which any morpheme $m_i \in P_i$ contains p_i, and any morpheme $m_j \in P_j$ contains p_j, and it is not true that $p_i \sim p_j$ in either class.

(c) If the classes P_i, P_j are empty, i.e. it is always the case that $p_i \sim p_j$, then there is only one lexical representation $/p/$ occurring in all formatives that are members of P, and the rule R is a function $R\,(p \rightarrow p_i)$ for some contexts, and a function $R\,(p \rightarrow p_j)$ for the others. (Taxonomically, two phonetically similar phones in absolute complementation are allophones of the same phoneme.)

(d) If either P_i or P_j or both are non-empty, i.e. there is at least one class where p_i or p_j appears, but it is not true that $p_i \sim p_j$, then the nonempty class or classes must have separate lexical representations $/p_i/$ or $/p_j/$. And this is so even if the rule R which is well-motivated for the alternation-class P could map some segment $/p/$ into p_i or p_j with no complication of the grammar.

The effect of the limiting condition (d) is to disallow bi-unique relations based on alternating forms in the case of non-alternating ones. That is, if any phone appears always and only as a member of an alternation, it must derive from some one segment underlying the alternation (e.g. AFB); but if any phone appears in a non-alternating form, it must be lexical in that form. No segment then which appears in non-alternating forms may *not* be lexical.

The conditions proposed above, if acceptable, would make it the case that paradigm-forming rules are restricted in their scope solely to the paradigms they produce, and do not constitute 'generalizations' about the phonology of a language beyond the paradigms which are their domains. In a sense then we are stating the converse of Kiparsky's 'strong alternation condition' (1968a), which says that no segment which never appears phonetically may appear in a well-formed lexical representation (see further §3.2 of this chapter). We are in essence stating a 'strong non-alternation condition', which says that no phone which appears in non-alternating surface forms may be excluded from the lexicon, even if it is technically derivable from some other segment by extension of a paradigm-generating rule.

It may seem that a constraint of this sort simply undoes a lot of what has been gained in phonology over the past decade or so; we are deliberately 'complicating' the grammar, and appear to be losing generalizations that are very naturally stated within a theory to which we – overall – subscribe. But our claim here is that it just might be the case that generalizations achieved by extraparadigmatic extension are specious. Certainly on intuitive grounds they are at least suspect: it seems relatively natural for instance to accept the same underlying nuclear vowel in *crime* and *criminal*, but a mere artifact of the theory to extend that vowel to *night* and *desire*. The possibility of doing this may just be a property of the model, rather than of the reality that it purports to be a model of. If this should turn out to be so, then any 'reward' given by the theory for the discovery of 'optimal' grammars in this sense would be vacuous. What seems uncertain at this point is whether the form of a grammar – with respect to issues of this sort – is in fact an empirical question at all, or whether in the light of our restricted knowledge all such discussion is empty. Obviously we cannot make a firm statement one way or the other, but the alternatives are clearly worth considering.

Let us go a bit further along this line now, and look at some other facts which suggest that a 'classical' generative solution, with its attendant theoretical and formal commitments, may not be entirely appropriate to some of the phenomena we have treated in this way. Consider the theoretical status of paradigms, such as that of the strong verbs (for any or all classes). In accordance with current theory, we have assumed that paradigms of this type do not have any independent status, but are rather automatic consequences of the operation of grammatical rules. Paradigms, like inventories, and so on, are 'epiphenomena', derivable from rule-outputs at certain derivational points; but they are not, per se, independent entities (cf. further Stanley 1967, and Ruwet 1968: 51, who says 'les inventaires d'éléments ne sont qu'un sous-produit du système de processus recursifs sous-jacents à la formation des phrases'). This originally well-motivated attempt to make linguistics an explanatory rather than a taxonomic science has tended, as major reforms often do, to become monolithic and polarizing; it has removed taxonomy from the realm of even subsidiary goals of linguisitic theory, and thrown some good babies out with a lot of expendable bath-water.

There has recently been a revival of interest, however, in the status of paradigms as primes of the theory; generative-oriented Romance scholars like Harris (1970) have followed up the kind of emphasis on paradigmatic phenomena that used to be stressed by linguists of the Martinet-Malkiel persuasion. As Harris says (1970: 1) in this connexion:

Neither paradigmatic relations nor analogy has any official status in current generative phonological theory. The material to be covered here [in a study of the development of certain Spanish verb forms: RL/JMA] suggests, however, that paradigms are a real part of language, not an artifact of the linguist; and that paradigmatic relationships, or analogy if you like, play a role in the organization of grammars, both synchronically and diachronically, and therefore must be incorporated into linguistic theory.

Similar proposals have been made by Shopen and Konaré (1970) and Shopen (1971) with respect to syntactic paradigms. We will return to some of these proposals later.

Let us consider some evidence from OE suggesting that we might be losing babies as well as bath-water by not granting paradigms an independent status. If our analysis of the ablaut alternations in chapter 1 is correct, within the definitions of current theory, this means that, as we tried to show in detail, such categories as 'Class 1 PRES', or 'PRET$_2$' are essentially expository cover-symbols for sets of forms produced by the operation of phonological rules under a very broad overall syntactic specification; in fact, if the strong verbs have a nuclear /V/, there is practically no place in which the rules deriving the surface alternations are anything but purely phonological. If this is the case, if something like 'PRET$_2$' has no theoretical status, then such a specification, or the form which embodies it, should presumably not be available to a speaker as an independent lexical item. And this is rather troublesome, because it appears that a fairly extensive class of derived forms in OE requires the selection of just such forms as inputs to rules.

Let us look at two classes of such phenomena: deverbal nouns which appear to have their sources in strong verbs, and deverbal (usually causative) verbs of the same type. The table below gives some characteristic examples of the first type, deverbal nouns, which are semantically nominalizations of the actions of the verbs (e.g. *cuman* 'come', *cyme* 'a coming', *cēosan* 'choose', *cyre* 'choice', and so on).

Taking the class II deverbal nouns as the most clearcut example, for the moment, it seems obvious that forms like *cyre, lyre, hryre,* etc., if they are (as must be the case) derived from the corresponding strong verbs, must be derived from the PRET$_2$ stems, with an umlauting suffix added, which turns up as surface -*e*. Both the vocalism and the consonantism make this clear. (We have of course already suggested that the class II *s* ~ *r* alternation is suppletive, so that there is already some evidence for lexical specification of at least some parts of these paradigms.) What must happen, then, is this: to the PRET$_2$ stem, e.g. [kur-], there is added an affix [-i], which causes in the usual way *i*-umlaut of [u] to [y], and is later lowered to [e]. These *s* ~ *r* examples are crucial for the claim that there is selection of particular parts of the paradigm, since there is no other possible source for both the vocalism and consonantism.

(6.58)

Class	PRES	PRET$_1$	PRET$_2$	PART	Deverbal noun	Verb gloss
I	bītan	bāt	biton	biten	bite	bite
I	grīpan	grāp	gripon	gripen	gripe	grip
I	stīgan	stāg	stigon	stigen	stige	climb
I	blīcan	blāc	blicon	blicen	blice	glitter
II	brūcan	brēac	brucon	brocen	bryce	use
II	ċēosan	ċēas	curon	coren	cyre	choose
II	hrēosan	hrēas	hruron	hroren	hryre	decay
II	lēosan	lēas	luron	loren	lyre	lose
II	scēotan	scēat	scuton	scoten	scyte	shoot
II	drēopan	drēap	drupon	dropen	drype	drop
II	lēogan	lēag	lugon	logen	lyge	lie
II	ġēotan	ġēat	guton	goten	gyte	pour
II	flēogan	flēag	flugon	flogen	flyge	fly
IV	cuman	c(w)ōm	c(w)ōmon	cumen	cyme	come

If it were the case that only verbs with suppletive consonantism, like the class II 'Verner'-verbs, participated in this process, then we could say that the prior necessity (in just these cases) for some lexical differentiation makes it possible. But observe that in the case of all the class I and IV verbs, and in the non-Verner class II verbs, this is not so. There are no suppletive forms here. So for *brūcan, scēotan, flēogan, cuman*, etc., there is no possible derivational source for deverbal nouns other than an isolation of the PRET$_2$ form, with its specific vowel grade, and affixation of a nominalizing suffix to that form.

The derivational sources are less determinate in the case of class I: there the grade could be either PRET₂ or PART; and in class IV there is a similar problem, in that the source there could be either PRES or PART. But in both cases, even in the face of some indeterminacy, we can still separate out impossible vs. possible sources, and we are forced to specify by syntactic category the paradigmatic sources of the derivatives.

Now consider another group of cases: causative verbs formed in a similar way (by *-jan* suffixing) from noncausative strong verbs.

(6.59)

Class	PRES	PRET₁	PRET₂	PART	Causative	Glosses
I	drīfan	drāf	drifon	drifen	drǣfan	drive/herd
III	springan	sprang	sprungon	sprungen	sprenġan	spring/cause to spring
III	windan	wand	wundon	wunden	wendan	wind/turn
III	drincan	dranc	druncon	druncen	drenċan	drink/drown
V	sittan	sæt	sǣton	seten	settan	sit/set
V	licgan	læġ	lǣgon	leġen	lecgan	lie/lay
VI	faran	fōr	fōron	faren	fēran	go/carry
VII	feallan	fēoll	fēollon	feallen	fiellan	fall/fell

In class I, the causative shows *i*-umlaut of the surface root-vowel ([æǣ] < [ai] < /Vi/); in class III, the causative shows *i*-umlaut of [æ], i.e. the PRET₁ grade has apparently been selected before the application of the nasal influence conventions; in class V there is direct umlaut of the surface [æ]. Classes VI and VII display a certain indeterminacy: in VI, the root for causativization could be either PRET₁ or PRET₂ (though congruity with the first five classes suggests PRET₁), and in class VII, at least in this example, the indeterminacy is theoretically complete, since umlaut of any of the root vowels will give the same result.

These cases suggest that the process of causative-formation depends crucially on the singling out of individual members of strong verb paradigms, and attaching affixes to them. And the necessity for specifying individual forms holds whether the affixation is assumed to occur before or after the phonetic specification of vowel qualities.

We now find ourselves in the following situation: on the grounds of generality, within the framework of standard generative phonological theory, it is the case that the individual members of the strong verb paradigms (the 'principal parts') do not have to be specified syntactically (except for the two general cover-specifications '[SV]' in qualitative ablaut (1.19) and '[PP]' in pre-Germanic accentuation (1.17) – and these both represent the unions of paradigmatic sets, not individual members). The derivations, beyond these specifications, are purely phonological. And yet it is also the case that given such derivations, the members of the paradigms are not available as such, and there is thus no way of selecting the proper forms for causative-formation to act on at the point in the grammar where it must.

So generality considerations and the theory they are part of demand phonological derivation of the principal parts of the strong verb, without their (redundant) specification as being 'principal parts'; and the evidence from causatives (and deverbal nouns, as shown earlier) seems to demand that precisely these phonologically derivable forms be available also as independent, syntactically specified entities: i.e. virtually as separate lexical items.

This problem is not unique to OE, and in fact it is not unique to phonology either; there are similar cases in syntax, and these have been the subject of a number of recent studies, notably Shopen (1971) and Shopen and Konaré (1970). We will consider one of these here in some detail, as its conclusions are relevant to the doubts we have been raising about the theory behind our own analyses. Shopen (1971), in a paper on a class of 'quasi-modal' verbs in English, demonstrates that there is considerable evidence for the independent (and 'psychologically real') status of paradigms – in this instance, especially the 'defective' modal paradigms. His argument hinges on the fact that certain verbs which formerly occurred only as main verbs (i.e. propositional heads) are now beginning to occur in syntagmatic association with other main verbs of the type characteristic of the so-called modals. For instance, in Shopen's dialect the following are grammatical sentences:

(6.60) (a) The cabinet members *go eat* every day at 12:15.
   (b) No one should *go complain* to the headmaster unless there is good reason.
   (c) We will *come swim* in your pond one of these days.
   (d) Please *come pick* up your laundry.

In addition the paradigms for expressions like *go eat* show a remarkable defect in distribution:

(6.61)   (a)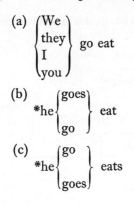

$$\left.\begin{matrix} \text{We} \\ \text{they} \\ \text{I} \\ \text{you} \end{matrix}\right\} \text{go eat}$$

(b) $*\text{he}\left\{\begin{matrix} \text{goes} \\ \\ \text{go} \end{matrix}\right\} \text{eat}$

(c) $*\text{he}\left\{\begin{matrix} \text{go} \\ \\ \text{goes} \end{matrix}\right\} \text{eats}$

And further:

(6.62)   (a) *He goes eat.
            (b) Does he go eat?
            (c) He doesn't go eat.
            (d) He does too go eat.
            (e) Did he go eat?
            (f) *He went eat.

Thus (1971: 254) 'expressions such as *go eat* have conjugations that are incomplete in all and only those cases where inflection is required within the two-verb sequence itself.' And as noted above, in (6.62), the two-verb constructions with quasi-modals are acceptable, regardless of tense, if *do*-support has operated. The point then is that this distribution is clearly related to the inflexional paradigm of modals; the only cases in which *go eat* and the like are acceptable are just those where they are not required to carry third-person (or other) inflexions: in other words, just where they coincide with the modals, which also occur as invariable heads of two-verb clusters.

That this restriction is in fact paradigmatic (inflexional), is clearest in those cases where the base and participial forms of a verb are homophonous: *they often come sleep at our house* vs. *they have often come sleep at our house*. Shopen's comment here is of some interest (1971: 254): 'Despite the fact that the past participle of *come* is homophonous with the base form, only the latter is acceptable in this kind of construction, interesting support for the claim that an inflection is an inflection whether or not it has phonetic consequences.'

Without going into the rest of the arguments here, the paper as a whole makes a good case for the psychological reality of inflexional paradigms, such as (in this particular instance) the two following (1971: 262):

(6.63)

    (*a*) *Main verb paradigm*

a. Base	b. Base+Z	c. Base+D
d. Base+ING	e. Base+EN	

    (*b*) *Modal paradigm*

a. Base	b. Base+D

(The shaded portion for modal past tense relates to the rather tenuous paradigmatic and semantic connexions of *will/would, may/might,* etc.) In terms of the specifications for acceptable quasi-modal constructions in English, then, the intersection of the two paradigms defines what is well-formed; and in this case the intersection consists only of Base.

Paradigms of this type (not necessarily formally, but shall we say 'practically') can be taken to be something like lexical redundancy rules or implicational statements: in terms of Shopen and Konaré (1970) 'word-structure conditions', parallel to Stanley's (1967) morpheme structure conditions. What happens in the case of a paradigm, simply, is that – even though the actual forms which are members are in fact generated by rules – the paradigms serve as a further (subordinate) structure of which they are members. We then reach the somewhat paradoxical – but seemingly empirically motivated – position that certain rule-generated forms must also be independent lexical entries. As Shopen concludes (1971: 262–3) 'we need distinct lexical entries for inflected forms and base forms, even though most often they would be redundant. The main verb and modal paradigms would serve as redundancy statements making inflectionally related forms of low cost as lexical entries.'

If a proposal like this is accepted, it requires, from the point of view of principle, a substantial modification of the standard theory (both in syntax and phonology): basically, that 'simplicity' is not a mechanical or algorithmic notion, definable in purely formal (and grammar-internal) terms. It must be defined also in terms of what we might, for want of a better label at the moment, call 'function'. A (notationally) more complex grammar may be psychologically 'simpler', in terms of availability of necessary material to the speaker, than a notationally simpler one, which may render inaccessible material required for certain processes in the language (for similar comments on 'simplicity' in phonology see Ohala 1971).

Where does all this leave us in relation to our ablaut alternations? In principle, it leaves the rules, as far as we can see, unchanged: they are (presumably) a correct statement of why the paradigms have the particular phonological/phonetic content they do, and are in that sense explanatory. But in another way they are now quite different, since they no longer represent 'sequential' derivations ordered in the sequence after the assignment of syntactic specifications. Categories like $PRET_1$ can no longer be derived notions, but must be syntactic primitives. What the rules now say is that given a strong verb of root structure X, the individual vowel specifications will be related in certain ways, *within* a labelled paradigmatic structure. And the members of this set will be available – as such – at the point of lexical insertion (in a 'standard' transformational grammar, which we will use here as an exemplificatory *point d'appui*).

Take for instance the case of a strong-verb-derived causative, as in the italicized verb in these lines from *The Battle of Maldon* (136–7: Sweet 1969, no. XXI):

(6.64)

hē scēaf þā mid þām scylde, þæt se sceaft tōbærst, / and þæt spere *sprengde*, þæt hit sprang ongēan...'He shoved then with his shield, so that the shaft broke, and (he) caused the spear to spring, so that it sprang back.'

At some point we may imagine an underlying structure for the crucial proposition 'he...þæt spere sprengde' like (6.65) below (according, say, to a proto-Lakoffian model). Then let us say that in the event that a configuration where the 'abstract verb' *cause* commands a verb in a lower S which is realizable as a (derived) causative, there will be a series of rules producing the derived structure (6.66) (the syntactic details are not at issue here). Concord rules will then select the proper form of the causative affix, in this case /-ide/, and the pre-umlaut form of the verb, in accordance with the ablaut regularities, will be [sprang + ide], which gives in the usual way the phonetic representation [sprenǰde].

(6.65)

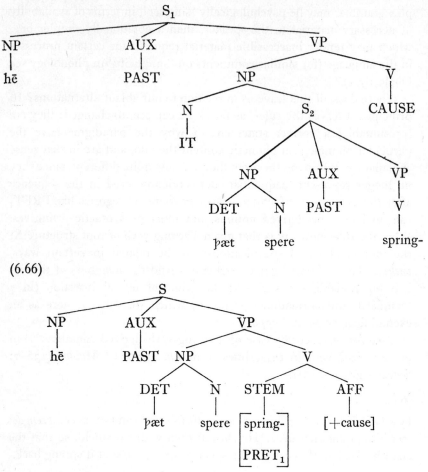

(6.66)

If this is anything like what happens, it may very well be the case that while the specification [PRET$_1$] is unnecessary for the derivation of the next sentence – *þæt hit sprang ongēan* – it is in the one that we have been discussing. The PRET$_1$ member of the paradigm must be chosen as input to causativization regardless of syntactic tense. So these specifications may be, like those for modals and main verbs in Shopen's framework, partly redundant and partly necessary. The basic point, both in Shopen's examples and in ours, is that it may be necessary to loosen the framework of the grammar somewhat, to ensure a closer fit with the actual behaviour of speakers. If these and similar arguments have any force, they may possibly point towards a less monolithic theory, in the sense that only those aspects of competence that are correctly formulable within a unitary framework (i.e. sequential-generative) will have to be captured within it, while other aspects will be handled by formally rather different kinds of structures. It is after all only an assumption – and not clearly an empirical one – that grammars are strictly 'generative' in the usual sense, and do not contain 'taxonomic' inventories. It may prove to be, after all, the right one; but as far as we know now, it might just as likely not. There is certainly no principled reason why a grammar – even a competence grammar – should not contain both look-up tables and generative rules. There is as yet nothing that would consitute 'proof' one way or the other.

We might add here that another solution, not involving paradigms as primitives, is available if we want to keep a 'classical' solution to the ablaut problem and still account in some way for causatives. This would be to enter the entire causative as a full lexical item in its own right: then the lexicon would contain, not the paradigm for *springan* plus the ablaut rules plus the PRET$_1$, etc., specifications, but only the rules and /sprVng-/ and /sprangjan/. While we are not entirely happy with either, the awkward rule-plus-paradigm model seems preferable in some ways; it may add a good deal of redundant material, but the other one obscures the relation between *springan* and *sprengean*. It seems on the face of it that a grammar incorporating the relation between a strong verb and its deverbal causative captures a more desirable and important generalization than a grammar that fails to represent that relationship. But this is an area which is certainly in need of further work, and we will not explore it any further here. Our intention in this section has been only to examine a potential problem (or what we feel to be one: not everybody does); it would take (at least) another book to put forth anything like a solution, and this section is a set of after-thoughts, not a new monograph.

3.2 On 'absolute neutralization': How are 'non-segments' acquired?

There is one final problem associated with the one we have been dis-cussing, which revolves around the general notion of 'abstractness': what is the status of phonetic 'nonsegments' which we posit phonologi-cally? We discussed this in chapter 1, and came to the conclusion that the case for their admission into the theory was stronger than the case that had been made against them by Kiparsky (1968a). We would like to explore this a bit further here.

In chapter 1, we posited an 'absolutely neutralized' segment, the 'laryngeal' /A/ (much as had been done in Anderson 1970). We did so on the grounds that:

(a) We had a set of rules that generated the vowels in strong verb classes I–V in what appeared to be an insightful and plausible way; and many of these rules were also required for phenomena that we found in other grammatical categories.

(b) Given paradigms like *faran/fōr/fōron* vs. *beran/bær/bǽron*, we claimed that overall the verbs were quite similar; we had to account for two main differences: a $\begin{bmatrix} +\text{low} \\ +\text{back} \end{bmatrix}$ vowel in PRES where we expected $\begin{bmatrix} -\text{low} \\ -\text{back} \end{bmatrix}$; and long (and back) vowels in PRET_1 and PRET_2, where we expected that both would be nonback, and only PRET_2 would be long, unless there was a following vowel in the root sequence, as in classes I and II.

(c) If we posited a segment which could (i) retract and/or lower a following vowel, or (ii) vocalize and make a vowel long, we could derive class VI by the same rules that we used to derive I–V, merely adding rules which registered the effects of this extra segment. And more important, even with this new segment in the lexical representations, the derivations of class VI were not different in principle from those of classes I–V: they still depended on segments in the root, not on morphological specifications, exception features, or the like.

We thus achieved a solution that was 'pure phonological', as one might say, i.e. one in which nothing depended on diacritical devices, but all divergences from the other paradigms were accounted for by segmental properties. The rules involved in the derivations were in addition 'phonetically natural': they were assimilatory for the most part, and at least did not involve unattested or odd processes. Nor did we have to invoke any ad hoc or idiosyncratic properties. Our derivations for class VI are thus in this way 'explanatory' derivations, rather than ones that merely work.

But it turns out on closer scrutiny that our solution is perhaps not so impressively 'natural' as it seemed at first. We find ourselves involved in a number of serious questions, which are intimately related to some of the most basic issues in contemporary phonology. These are, particularly, (a) the suspension of the Saussurian dichotomy, and (b) the implications of any phonological claims for a model of language acquisition.

Let us begin with the question of 'naturalness', and its bearing on the persistence of underlying representations over time. When we say that a rule is 'natural', we presumably mean two (interconnected) things: first that it is a common type, found in many languages, and so does not need special justification; and second, that it is a physiologically or perceptually plausible rule, i.e. that in a sense the wide distribution of a rule type implies a closeness-of-fit with the neurophysiological properties of the speech apparatus. Certainly this holds with particular force in the domain of low-level phonetic rules: it is not at all surprising to find vowel-lengthening before voiced obstruents, lowering of tone after breathy-voiced stops, raising of tone before voiceless stops, and so on. In each of these cases the process taking place is correlated with properties of the glottal configuration associated with the consonant in question. But how legitimate is it to project this kind of naturalness-judgement into pre-phonetic stages of derivations? When we describe some rule as natural on phonetic grounds, we do so in terms of physical configurations: but can this be extrapolated back into the domain of what are by common consent 'mental representations'? It would seem perhaps to be stretching the notion of a 'natural relation' between the phonetic and phonological levels to assume that a property like 'raised glottis: adducted vocal bands' can legitimately be part of the content of a feature at the pre-output level. If this is in fact stretching things, then it may not be possible to define 'naturalness' in precisely the same way at all grammatical levels. After all, a 'phonetic representation', in current theory, must be assumed to have as one of its functions the specification of a neural programme for the speech apparatus: and it seems difficult to accept the possibility that such purely physical facts are incorporated into the sequence of psychological operations that precede the formulation of this programme. This argues for the possibility that the content of phonological and phonetic features may be different, not just in degree of specificity (binary vs. n-ary), but in kind.

From this point of view – which is not necessarily ours, but is certainly a possible one – there is nothing particularly 'natural' about the rules involving the class VI 'laryngeal', since they function at a point in the grammar where the larynx itself is irrelevant. We might sum this

line of questioning up as follows: yes, it is true that a rule where a segment with the specifications of our /A/ retracts a front vowel is natural
in the mouth: but what does it mean in the cortex? We will however
abandon this line of inquiry for now, as it must impinge on the province
of some area of neurolinguistics which has not even been defined as yet.

Let us return however to /A/ from another point of view. We said
above that a solution to the aberrancy of class VI, involving /A/, is a
'pure phonological' or nondiacritical solution. But this is not really so:
it is 'inferential phonological', and this is not at all the same thing. And
it is precisely because of our reliance on inference (albeit a theoretically
sanctioned form of inference) here that we come up against a rather
thorny epistemological paradox. We set out to construct a synchronic
grammar of the OE strong verb system, but we have no sure way of telling
whether or not we have done that. We may in fact have actually constructed a diachronic account – without meaning to – and incorporated
it into the synchronic one, because of a certain property of our model.
This property is rule-ordering: even though as linguists we know perfectly well that a sequence of rules has only 'abstract order', i.e. it does
not proceed stepwise in real time, the metaphor of order apes historical
sequence. This means that in the absence of certain kinds of con-
firmatory phonetic evidence we cannot tell whether we have constructed
a synchronic derivation, or recapitulated an historical sequence – or both.

Here is a concrete if slightly oversimplified example. In one dialect
of central Panjabi (Ranvir Bakshi, personal communication), the
nominative singular form of the first person pronoun is [mɛ̃:], and the
corresponding objective form is [mɛnu]. On the basis of a large set of
alternations of which this is only one example, we might want to
assume for the first person pronoun a base form of the type /mɛn-/, and
the following rules:

(6.67)

(a) $V \rightarrow [+\text{nas}] / \underline{\qquad} \begin{bmatrix} C \\ +\text{nas} \end{bmatrix} \begin{Bmatrix} \# \\ C \end{Bmatrix}$

(b) $\begin{bmatrix} C \\ +\text{nas} \end{bmatrix} \rightarrow \emptyset / \begin{bmatrix} V \\ +\text{nas} \end{bmatrix} \underline{\qquad}$

(c) $\begin{bmatrix} V \\ +\text{nas} \end{bmatrix} \rightarrow [+\text{long}] / \underline{\qquad} \#$

These three rules – in this order – state a synchronic generalization about this Panjabi paradigm (and other similar ones). It is also reasonable to suspect that this sequence of rules represents the actual historical sequence by which (superficially) distinctive nasalized vowels arose in Panjabi. But consider the case of nasalized vowels before consonants, which do not alternate with full nasals: e.g. [pũʧ] 'tail', objective [pũ ʧnu]. If we were to construct for this form an underlying representation /punʧ/, it would then be subject to rules (6.67a, b) above, giving the intermediate stage [pũnʧ] by (a) and finally [pũʧ] by (b).

If it is true that [mɛ̃:] and [mɛnu] give evidence for synchronic rules of nasalization and nasal-deletion, and the sequence /mɛn/ → [mɛ̃n] → [mɛ̃] → [mɛ̃:] can be considered, on paradigmatic grounds, a synchronic derivation, this is still not necessarily the case with /punʧ/ → [pũnʧ] → [pũʧ]. We can say with some justice, perhaps, that /mɛn/ is the lexical base of [mɛ̃:]; but we cannot determine in any sure way whether our lexical /punʧ/ is a synchronic form, or whether what we have really done is reconstructed a proto-Panjabi *punʃ. If we take the latter view, the rules (6.67) are merely paradigmatic relics of earlier sound changes in the personal pronoun system, but *punʃ, a non-alternating formative, has been restructured to /pũʧ/. (This would then constitute another objection to the extension of paradigm-forming rules to nonparadigmatic forms.)

The point is that the notions of 'sequence', 'order', 'derivation' have very different meanings in synchronic and diachronic grammars; in synchronic grammars they are 'abstract' concepts, but their operations are not distinguishable from those of their analogues in real time. It seems, on epistemological grounds, to be possible that a given 'derivation' may be indeterminate with respect to whether it is synchronic or merely pseudo-synchronic; in other words, it may be that there is no principled way of telling whether our processes of inference have resulted in a synchronic generalization, or whether we have inadvertently constructed an account of how a set of forms came about in time, and then de-historicized it by asserting it to be a property of a synchronic grammar.

If this is a genuine indeterminacy, it means that we can no longer be sure of the status of our lexical entries for class VI verbs. Is /fAVr-/ in fact the OE underlying root for the paradigm of *faran*, or have we unwittingly reconstructed a pre-OE *fAVr-, from which the attested paradigm has descended over time? If there is an answer to this, it can come, finally, from only one source: a much better knowledge than we have now of the constraints on abstractness involved in language-acquisition. A definition of these constraints will give us the information we need for a principled account of the stability of underlying representations; because in this way we can say that some derivation D_i is too abstract and complex for a child to construct in acquisition, while some other derivation D_j is not. And thus we must reject D_i, even if it is 'insightful' and 'general' according to the requirements of the theory that sanctions it, because the constraints on the power of the language-acquisition device disconfirm that theory. As of now, unfortunately, this is not an empirical question in any reasonable sense. (But for some interesting evidence bearing on this matter see Skousen 1973.)

Let us focus specifically on the hypothetical OE child acquiring *faran*, in the rather crude and speculative way that our current ignorance forces on us. Does this child, on hearing *faran/fōr/fōron*, construct in his internalized grammar a set of underlying forms and rules such that the derivation of this paradigm is as much like *beran/bær/bæron* as possible? If he does – if the ability to construct such derivations is a part of the innate *faculté de langage* – then we imagine the child (metaphorically) asking himself something like this (a crude expository version of Chomsky's notion of the child as hypothesis tester): 'What do I need to get [a] instead of [e] in PRES, a long back vowel in PRET₁, and [ō] instead of [æ] in PRET₂?' If the child can (unconsciously) ask himself such a question, then he can construct a root in /-AV-/ for class VI verbs. In these terms, of course, the question is ludicrous: children are not linguists. But, we might add, if they are not, then it is somewhat difficult to conceive how something like /A/ could remain as an underlying segment when it has ceased to exist phonetically; it exists only 'anaphorically' as it were, in terms of its effects on a putative 'norm'. The crucial question is whether absolute neutralization of this kind is in the technical sense a recoverable deletion. The claim that it is, requires the child to recognize 'paradigmatic aberrancy' as a property, and to be capable of sufficiently powerful inference to reconstruct a cause for it. Very simply, he must construct, not on the basis of auditory input per se (the simplest type of 'primary linguistic data'), but on the basis of an aberrancy in one proper subset of a given morphological class, a non-phonetic segment with the appropriate feature specifications.

The obvious solution, if we choose not to admit segments like /A/ on principle, is an exceptional paradigm. Either all verbs of class VI are marked 'minus' for the regular ablaut rules, and 'plus' for a set of minor rules; or the aberrant paradigms are merely sets of suppletive lexical entries. At this stage it is not possible to choose in any very informed way; but in closing we might raise the question of whether in fact all three solutions – absolute neutralization, minor-rule-generated paradigm, and lexical suppletion – are, if not notational equivalents, at least, in the current state of our knowledge, empirical ones. In what way, for example, given the limitations of our ability to recover the facts about the behaviour and intuitions of OE speakers, and our abysmal ignorance of the mechanisms of acquisition, is reconstruction of a nonphonetic (absolutely neutralized) segment really different from lexical suppletion pure and simple?

Appendix I
Class VII strong verbs

The vowel alternations in class VII strong verbs appear to present even greater difficulties for a unitary view of ablaut than the superficial series in class VI. We have been able to suggest that the verbs in class VI are basically either class IV or class V and thus obey the ablaut processes we formulated for classes I–V. However, class VI verbs differ from 'normal' class IV and V verbs in the underlying presence of a prevocalic glide, with whose specification (in particular $\begin{bmatrix} +\text{back} \\ +\text{low} \end{bmatrix}$) the differences in the surface series are associated. Thus either the vowel is assimilated to the glide in backness and lowness (as in PRES, $PRET_2$ and PART forms) or the glide is vocalized if the vowel is already $\begin{bmatrix} +\text{back} \\ +\text{low} \end{bmatrix}$ by qualitative ablaut (as in $PRET_1$).

These assimilations (together with the loss of the glide where not vocalized, and lowness assignment in $PRET_1$ and $PRET_2$) account for the surface series $a\text{-}\bar{o}\text{-}\bar{o}\text{-}a$: *faran, fōr, fōron, faren*. The uniformity of the membership of class VI and the uniformity of the results of whatever processes have disrupted the 'normal' ablaut series thus enabled us to extend the unitary hypothesis in a fairly obvious way.

However, neither of these kinds of uniformity exist in class VII. 'Membership' of class VII does not imply a particular surface series (or several obviously related series). Consider the paradigms in (1.1):

(1.1) *Class VII verbs*

PRES	$PRET_1$	$PRET_2$	PART	
blandan	blēnd	blēndon	geblanden	'mix'
healdan	hēld[1]	hēldon[1]	gehealden	'hold'
bēatan	bēot	bēoton	gebēaten	'beat'
lācan	lēc	lēcon	gelācen	'play'

---

[1] In addition to the preterites with $\bar{e}$, we also find the spellings *hĕold, hĕoldon*. Sievers (1903 :§81) is uncertain whether this represents 'levelling' with verbs like *bēatan* or an exceptional breaking before $l+C$. We presume that the $\check{e}o$ alternative can be allowed for by marking such verbs as optionally undergoing breaking.

Observe too that the vowels taking part in intra-paradigmatic alternations are not related in the same rather obvious way that we found to be the case in class VI, in which there is a close-to-surface series [a-aa-aa-a]. However, there are some similarities to class VI, and these suggest an approach to the analysis of these verbs. The alternations, in the first place, show the same overall pattern as occurs in class VI, with (superficially) the same vowel in PRES and PART, and $PRET_1$ and $PRET_2$, respectively. Further, in all of the PRES and PART forms we can once more discern an underlying [a]. Our analysis will depend crucially on these two observations.

Suppose, then, that once again we suggest a prevocalic /A/ in such forms as *blandan* and *feallan*. This will permit derivations for the PRES and PART forms which require only rules which we have already shown to be independently necessary.

(1.2)

Input	/AV/	/AV/
Qualitative ablaut (1.19)	Ae	Ae
Vowel-glide assimilation (1.24)	Aa	Aa
Glide deletion (1.25)	a	a
AFB (2.11)	æ	æ
Breaking (3.35)		æa
Nasal influence (b) (2.16)	a	
Output	a	æa
Spelling	*blandan*	*feallan*

Thus, these class VII verbs are merely class III verbs – such is the root structure – with prevocalic glide, just as class VI verbs differ in the same way from 'ordinary' class IV and V.

Now consider *bēatan*, with *ēa* in both PRES and PART. We know that [æa], if not from breaking, derives usually from a [au] diphthong. This, together with the pattern that is now emerging for classes VI and VII, suggests that such verbs may belong to class II, again with prevocalic glide. We have then the derivation: /-AVu-/ → [Aeu] → [Aau] → [au] → [æu] → [æa]. Similarly, in the case of verbs like *lācan*, it is clear that the root structure can be interpreted as including /AVi/ – i.e. they are class I verbs with prevocalic glide. *Lācan* has the following derivation: /-AVi-/ → [Aei] → [Aai] → [ai] → [aæ] → [ææ] → [aa]. Thus, in both these instances, no new rules are involved. We merely extend the analysis already proposed for class VI, involving a prevocalic glide, to what are the majority of the members of VII. The differences between classes VI and VII and among the members of class VII are due to the same factors that underlie the divisions among the first five classes that we have discussed above in some detail. Class VI and (most of) class VII are merely ordinary members of one of the classes I–V, in terms of their post-vocalic root structure; the differences (from 'ordinary' members of I–V) in their development derive from the presence of the prevocalic A-glide.

However, such an explanation breaks down in the case of the preterite forms. By simply extending the interpretation we have given for the PRES and PART forms, we would expect the following derivations for $PRET_1$:

(1.3)

Input	/AVi/	/AVu/	/AVR/
Qualitative ablaut (1.19)	Aai	Aau	AaR
Glide vocalization (1.23)	aai	aau	aaR
Trimoric simplification (3.22)	ai	aa	
DHH (3.15)	aæ		
Lowness assignment		ʔoo	oo
AFB (2.11)	ææ		
Backness switching (1.8)	aa		
Output	aa	oo	oo
Actual form	lēc	bēot	hēld/hēold

That is, in each case, where we would expect by the posited derivation in (1.3) that the result would be a long back vowel, we find instead a nucleus with a mid front vowel as first element. The only point that comes out partly right is the surface identity for the verbs belonging to classes II and III. Further, for verbs of classes I–III, we would expect the $PRET_2$ forms to coincide with the PART in its vocalism, since they do not have the proper structure for lengthening in $PRET_2$. Clearly, there is something else involved here.

One possibility is suggested by the fact that the Gothic cognates for many such verbs show reduplication. Compare OE *healdan* 'hold' with $PRET_1$ *hēld*, and Go. *haldan*, $PRET_1$ *haíhald*. Further, there are a few verbs usually included in class VII in OE which, it is traditionally said, show relics of reduplication in the preterite, for instance *heht* from *hātan* 'order' or *leolc* from *lācan* 'play'. However, they are very few, and doubts have been cast (by e.g. Lehmann 1954) on a reduplication analysis even of them. Whatever the virtues and defects, from a historical point of view, of an account of the preterite forms we have been considering which involves reduplication, there appears to be little synchronic motivation for such a derivation in OE. Certainly, we could interpret the mid front vowel in these preterite forms as coming from the reduplicated syllable by loss of the intervening segment. But there are perhaps less devious solutions.

Consider the following possibility. These preterite forms must be derived in such a way as to block those processes that produce $\begin{bmatrix} +\text{back} \\ +\text{low} \end{bmatrix}$ vowel segments. Instead, we get initial sequences of mid front vowels. Thus, both the presence of a $\begin{bmatrix} +\text{back} \\ +\text{low} \end{bmatrix}$ prevocalic glide and the operation of part (b) of qualitative ablaut (which renders PRET_1 forms $\begin{bmatrix} +\text{back} \\ +\text{low} \end{bmatrix}$) are undesirable. Accordingly, we suggest that there is associated with such verbs (a) a rule shifting the prevocalic laryngeal in quality and (b) an exception feature indicating that part (b) of qualitative ablaut is inapplicable. Neither of these involves additions to the lexical entries for such verbs; they are associated by rule with verbs of classes I–III (i.e. with two postvocalic radical segments) which contain a prevocalic glide. We propose the following readjustment rules, to account for the exception to qualitative ablaut part (b):

(1.4) *Class VII preterite exception*

$$V \rightarrow [-(1.19)] / \begin{bmatrix} +\text{obs} \\ -\text{cons} \end{bmatrix} \underline{\quad\quad} \text{SC}$$

and the shift in the quality of the glide:

(1.5) *Glide-shift: first version*

$$\begin{bmatrix} +\text{obs} \\ -\text{cons} \end{bmatrix} \rightarrow \begin{bmatrix} -\text{low} \\ -\text{back} \end{bmatrix} / \underline{\quad\quad} \begin{bmatrix} [-(1.19\text{b})] \\ [\text{PRET}] \end{bmatrix}$$

This will result in an initial derivation for *blēnd*: $/\text{-AV-}/ \rightarrow [\text{-EV-}]$ (by glide-shift) $\rightarrow [\text{Ee}]$ (by qualitative ablaut). ('E' represents a mid front glide.) Now we need a rule to vocalize [E] before a vowel which is also $\begin{bmatrix} -\text{back} \\ -\text{low} \end{bmatrix}$. We already have a rule of glide vocalization (1.23), which vocalizes the glide [A] before a vowel which is also $\begin{bmatrix} +\text{low} \\ +\text{back} \end{bmatrix}$. This rule can be generalized to affect the present case:

(1.6) *Glide vocalization: revised*

$$\begin{bmatrix} +\text{obs} \\ -\text{cons} \\ \alpha\text{low} \end{bmatrix} \rightarrow [-\text{obs}] / \underline{\quad\quad} \begin{bmatrix} \text{V} \\ \alpha\text{low} \end{bmatrix}$$

After (1.6), the PRET_1 form of *blandan* will contain the desired superficial divocalic sequence [ee]. Similarly, *bēot*, the PRET_2 of *bēatan*, will be derived as follows: /-AVu-/ → [EVu] → [Eeu] → [eeu] → [eu] (the final step by trimoric nucleus simplification). Thus too *lēc* from *lācan*: /-AVi-/ → [EVi] → [Eei] → [eei] → [ee].[1]

But this does not yet allow for the PRET₂ forms. In 'normal' verbs of classes I–III, these have the 'reduced' grade: the root vowel is deleted in classes I and II and appears as *u* in class III. If we merely extend the glide-shift in some way to the PRET₂ forms of such verbs, we would therefore expect the following superficial vocalic sequences: for *blēndon*, [eo]; for *bēoton*, [eo]; for *lēcon*, [ii] (by highness harmonization). Of these, only the representation for *bēoton* is correct; and, in its derivation, the nucleus has not undergone trimoric simplification, as we would expect of a 'long' diphthong. This suggests that, in the case of such verbs, not only part (b) of qualitative ablaut but also part (b) of quantitative ablaut (1.16) is suspended. Accordingly, we reformulate (1.4), amalgamating it now with (1.5):

(1.7) *Glide-shift: revised*

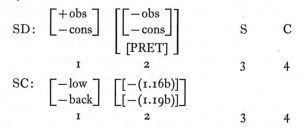

In terms of this modification, the nuclei in *blēndon*, *bēoton* and *lēcon* will have identical derivations to the vowel sequences in *blēnd*, *bēot* and *lēc*, respectively.

However, one problem remains. Forms like *blēnd/blēndon* etc. do not undergo lowness assignment (1.28), by which the nucleus would shift to [ææ] – as [ee] shifts to [ææ] in the derivation of, say, *cwǣdon*. Yet, as derived geminates, they meet all the conditions (including, in particular, the derivational constraint) for the operation of (1.28); only 'original' divocalic nuclei are excluded from (1.28) (even though they otherwise meet the appropriate SD). Apparently, another exception feature is involved. (1.7) is re-formulated as follows.

---

[1] Simplification from [eei] to [ee] requires that trimoric nucleus simplification (3.22) be expanded not in the order represented in (3.23) but one in which part (b) or part (c) precedes (a). In that case, [eei] would be simplified to [ei]. The generalization is simply that the last of three vowels drops (*sčoh* 'shoe', *sčōs* 'id. gen. sing.' <[ʃooes]) unless it is [+back] and the preceding is [−back], in which case the latter drops (*hēah* <[hæææax]). See app. v.

(1.8) *Glide-shift: second revision*

$$\text{SD:} \quad \begin{bmatrix} +\text{obs} \\ -\text{cons} \end{bmatrix} \quad \begin{bmatrix} -\text{obs} \\ -\text{cons} \\ [\text{PRET}] \end{bmatrix} \qquad \text{S} \qquad \text{C}$$

$$\qquad\qquad 1 \qquad\qquad\quad 2 \qquad\qquad 3 \qquad 4$$

$$\text{SC:} \quad \begin{bmatrix} -\text{low} \\ -\text{back} \end{bmatrix} \quad \begin{bmatrix} [-(1.16\text{b})] \\ [-(1.19\text{b})] \\ [-(1.28)] \end{bmatrix} \qquad \text{S} \qquad \text{C}$$

$$\qquad\qquad 1 \qquad\qquad\quad 2 \qquad\qquad 3 \qquad 4$$

The addition of this one rule (1.8) to those we have already formulated and motivated enables us to account for the majority of the members of class VII[1] in a way which shows in what sense they are 'strong verbs' and yet provides for their idiosyncrasies vis-à-vis the 'ordinary' strong verbs. We have been able to provide a unitary account of ablaut in the strong verbs, such that all 'regular' strong verbs contain lexically an unspecified radical vowel, and the 'members' of classes v and VII are reinterpreted as belonging to one of classes I–v and differing from the other members of the appropriate class only in terms of the presence vs. the absence of a prevocalic glide. The question of course remains – as it does in any account of this type – whether the elaborate machinery of exception features needed in a formulation like (1.8) is 'higher-valued' than a statement in terms of lexical suppletion. As yet, no evaluation metric has been developed which can, with algorithmic precision, weigh apples against pears – which seems to be the case here.

---

[1] There remain three groups of 'members' of class VII which we assume must be marked as exceptional in various ways. At least, we have been unable to devise for them any obvious extension of the analysis found to be appropriate for the 'members' of class VII represented in (1.1). Included in the exceptions are *slǣpan* 'sleep' (PRET₂ *slēp*) and the like, *blōtan* 'sacrifice' (PRET₂ *blēot*) and the like (including the 'weak present' *wēpan* 'weep' and *būan* 'cultivate').

Appendix II

The West Germanic gemination and the history of Germanic syllable structure

1 Preliminaries

The majority of the OE 'geminate' consonants (i.e. those spelt with double graphs) are historically the results of a sound-change called the West Germanic gemination (*Konsonantendehnung, -verdoppelung*). Its name derives from its function as a (partial) isogloss apparently separating West Germanic from the other major dialect groups: cf. OE *biddan*, OS *biddian* vs. Go. *bidjan*, ON *biðja*, OE *settan*, OS *settian* vs. ON *setja*, etc.[1]

This gemination (henceforth WGG) is traditionally described as either a 'lengthening' or a 'doubling' of a single consonant before a following sonorant. Streitberg (1963: 148) sums it up (and has it both ways): 'Vor *j w r l n m* wird ein vorausgehender Konsonant...verdoppelt (gedehnt).' Actually, as we will see, the OE manifestations are more restricted; the effects of the WGG show up consistently just in case (a) the vowel preceding the consonant in question was short, and (b) the consonant was not /r/.

The WGG is in many ways a rather odd process – at least at first glance – and whatever its precise synchronic relevance to OE may be, it is sufficiently interesting to warrant a fairly detailed discussion. As we will see, its peculiarity has been noticed by others, and there is no dearth of conflicting opinions about what it was and how it came about. We hope that our offering will not be just another in the series, but will be reasonably insightful. In particular – and in line with the emphasis we have placed in this book on the relation of aspects of OE phonology to the later history of the language – we think that the WGG should be interpreted, not as an isolated oddity, but as a foreshadowing of a rather important typological trend in Germanic. Though we will of course deal in detail with the relevance of the WGG to the synchronic phonology of OE, our emphasis will be (as in chs. v and vi) largely historical: especially with reference to the question of what the

---

[1] To be strictly correct, the WGG accounts for the majority of geminate consonants only word-medially; the final geminates in *eall*, *full*, etc. are not from this source, as will become apparent later – though those in *cynn* and all *ja*-stem and *jō*-stem nouns are. Further, there is a certain amount of gemination (especially of velars) that does show up in *-jan* verbs in other dialects: cf. ON *leggja* = OE *lecgan*. (These two points were suggested by David Tittensor.)

motivation of this change was, and its relation to earlier and later events in the history of the Germanic dialects.

We will begin with the question of synchronic status: is there evidence in OE that the WGG – or something very like it – is a productive process? As far as we can see, one aspect certainly seems to fit this description: The WGG does seem to be responsible for significant morphophonemic (specifically, paradigm-forming) alternations. These involve the environment before historical (and if our arguments in chapter IV are accepted, synchronic) /j/ in certain morphological categories. The evidence for gemination before **m *n *w*, even in non-alternating forms, is not (for OE at least), very firm: cf. Campbell (1959: 167 n. 1). And gemination before **r *l*, while it does appear in some forms (e.g. *æppel, bitter, snottor*), is sporadic: there are just as many cases like *æcer* (< **akr-*: cf. L. *ager, agr-*, etc.). So (despite the arguments to the contrary of Kurath 1956, which we find unconvincing), we will take the WGG proper as an historical sound-change whose basic environment in OE is restricted to positions before (suffixal) /j/.

There are many forms which show, in isolation, the historical results of the WGG; but we cannot really take any of them as being synchronically so derived until we have adduced those which clearly support a synchronic rule, in the particular sense of exhibiting alternations clear-cut enough to be called real generalizations. The actual number of such forms is somewhat restricted, especially with regard to the morphological/syntactic category they belong to; but they are widespread and basic enough to suggest synchronic productiveness in other parallel cases as well.

The locus classicus for paradigmatic gemination is the weak verbs of class I: those which (historically) show a present system with a **-j-* formative (probably derived – ultimately – from the Indo-European forms underlying the Sanskrit 4th and 10th verb classes: cf. Prokosch 1938: 147). The verbs showing the effects of WGG are in fact a proper subset of class I weak verbs: those which have historically a 'short' stem-syllable (i.e. /-VC-/). A typical conjugation for a verb of this type is that of *fremman* 'do':

(II.1)

	Present		*Preterite*
Sing.	1. fremme	1.	fremede
	2. frem(e)st	2.	fremedest
	3. frem(e)þ	3.	fremede
Pl.	fremmaþ	Pl.	fremedon
Infinitive:	fremman	*Pres. participle:*	fremmende

Similar patterns appear in many common verbs like *cyssan* 'kiss', *swebban* 'kill', *trymman* 'strengthen', *wennan* 'accustom' *dynnan* 'din', *gremman* 'provoke', *sceppan* 'injure', *wecgan* 'agitate', *wreppan* 'support'. We also find them in the so-called 'weak-present' strong verbs, like *biddan* 'ask', *sittan* 'sit', *licgan* 'lie' (see further Campbell, 1959: §§748–49).

The crucial fact about these verbs is that they show both gemination and umlaut in the present 1 sing. and pl., and in the infinitive and present participle, and umlaut alone in the pres. 2–3 sing. and the whole preterite system. (For evidence of umlaut cf. *gram* 'angry': *gremman*, *trum* 'strong': *trymman*, etc. Observe further that no verbs of this group have unmutated vowels in their present systems.) The usual historical explanation for this is the assumption of a stem-final or 'thematic' *-j- element in the present stem, preceding the endings, and a thematic *-i- in the past; thus in the present there is umlaut even before endings which do not themselves have umlaut-causing vowels: so *fremman* < **fram-j-an*, *fremme* < **fram-j-ō*. In the pres. 2–3 sing., the usual assumption is that *-j- 'was lost before *i* in West Germanic before causing consonant doubling' (Campbell 1959: §750). Thus we have *fremeþ* < **fram-iþi*, where the earlier (putative) form **fram-j-iþi* would give incorrect **fremmeþ*.

Another important group is those verbs of weak class I which show alternations involving WGG and umlaut in the present system, but neither in the past: historically these verbs seem to have had athematic preterites, i.e. with no *-i- or *-j- linking root and suffix. One particular class of these verbs, as we will see, is important for establishing the ordering relations in OE between WGG and other rules, especially breaking. Typical examples are *sellan* 'sell', *tellan* 'tell', pret. *sealde*, *tealde*, where the present shows *i*-umlaut of [æ] < WGmc **a* (by AFB), and the preterite shows AFB and breaking. A similar verb, with a special consonantal development in the past system which is not relevant here is *bycgan* 'buy', pret. *bohte*. The pres. 2–3 sing. of these verbs shows the same pattern as *fremman*, e.g. *telest*, *selest*, *byġest*.

Further geminate/nongeminate alternations, with special complications of different sorts, but a nonetheless clear pattern, are found in two weak verbs of 'class III': *secgan* 'say', *hycgan* 'think' pres. 3 sing. *sæġeþ*, *hyġþ* (cf. Campbell 1959: §762).

At this point, let us formulate a preliminary version of the WGG rule. Since at the outset we have no way of telling whether the rule will ultimately be a '*Verdoppelung*' (epenthesis) or a '*Dehnung*' (marking with some feature like [+long]), we will use the ad hoc cover-specification '[+geminate]' in our first version:

(11.2)

$$C \rightarrow [+\text{geminate}]/ \; XV \underline{\hspace{1.5cm}} \begin{bmatrix} C \\ -\text{back} \\ +\text{high} \end{bmatrix}$$

Condition: C ≠ /r/, X ≠ V

We must now decide: (1) what (if any) is the motivation for this rather odd rule? Is it just a rule that happens to have occurred, or is it related in any way to other facts about the grammar? (2) Why should /r/ alone resist gemination; and further, why should just those cases where the SD for gemination is met – except for /r/ – be also just those cases where some reflex of the /j/ is retained, e.g. *herian* 'praise', *nerian* 'save', *erian* 'plough', *byrian* 'pertain to', *snyrian* 'hasten', *styrian* 'stir'? (That the -*i*- in these forms represents [j] is quite clear from the frequent spellings of the type *herg(e)an*, and so on; for the class I, rather than class II status of these verbs, cf. Go. *harjan, nasjan*.) And, finally (3), what does the specification '[+geminate]' mean?

Let us first approach the solution of (2). It is clear that whatever happens in the WGG, the conditioning segment can be minimally specified as $\begin{bmatrix} +\text{cons} \\ -\text{back} \\ +\text{high} \end{bmatrix}$. And if this is so, what is there (if anything) about /r/ which would make it a motivated exception? If, as we argued in chapter III, OE /r/ was a uvular, then we can see the beginning of a possible motivation. A uvular would have at least the specification $\begin{bmatrix} +\text{back} \\ +\text{low} \end{bmatrix}$: and it would thus be the only nonvowel segment in OE with this specification, except for the 'laryngeal' element /A/, which does not anyhow appear in gemination environments. If any feature specification is going to 'interfere with' (i.e. characterize an exception to) some rule whose crucial context is the present of a $\begin{bmatrix} -\text{back} \\ +\text{high} \end{bmatrix}$ segment, then $\begin{bmatrix} +\text{back} \\ +\text{low} \end{bmatrix}$ seems to be a reasonable choice.

This is – admittedly – not a terribly convincing answer; although in conjunction with the evidence for a uvular *r* in OE in chapter III it does seem to have some force. But from the overall Germanic point of view of course this proposes uvular *r* not only for OE but for West Germanic in general. Actually this is not an entirely unattractive idea; nor is the extension of this to Proto-Germanic. We are not prepared, however, to argue this here; though the geographical distributions cited in chapter III furnish some support.[1]

Fred Householder (personal communication) has suggested that it would be quite possible to handle the exceptional behaviour of /r/ in gemination environments even if it were not uvular, in a quite natural way; and this does, if true, weaken our claims both here and in chapter III, since both uvular-*r* arguments are mutually reinforcing (or constitute a circularity, if you prefer). Since our conclusions in this area are extremely tentative anyway, and since the bulk of our exposition would be unaffected anyhow if we should be wrong on this point, it seems worthwhile to quote Householder's comments. Even without the uvular-*r* assumption, he says, 'alternative ways out of the gemination bind are available. For instance you could have a rule producing geminate palatalized consonants...then a rule converting the second plaatalized [r] to [i], then one depalatalizing all geminates. Exactly this sort of thing

With this assumed, let us reformulate rule (11.2) without the ad hoc condition; or let us incorporate the ad hoc condition into the rule, and at least give it a representation in terms of phonological, rather than merely exceptional, properties. (The variable 'X' must remain, however, to exclude a preceding vowel; this position must be filled either by word boundary or a consonant):

(11.3)

$$\begin{bmatrix} C \\ -low \end{bmatrix} \rightarrow [+geminate]/ XV \underline{\hspace{2cm}} \begin{bmatrix} C \\ -back \\ +high \end{bmatrix}$$

Condition: $X \neq V$

We cannot now proceed any further without answering question (3) above: are we dealing here with addition of a segment or a feature? It will be recalled that in our treatment of ablaut (ch. I) we began with the assumption that 'long' and 'short' vowels were distinguished by some feature [±long]; and in the course of our discussion we had reason to revise this, not only for ablaut, but for other processes (e.g. breaking, ch. III) as well; and we were led to claim that 'length' is the presence of another segment, i.e. that 'long' vowels are /VV/ (as are diphthongs), as against 'short' vowels, which are /V/. This suggests that there might be some parallelism in the case of consonants, that 'geminate' vs. 'nongeminate' might be a contrast of the type /C/ vs. /CC/. This would be especially the case if it could be shown that geminates behave like other consonant clusters. We will return to this below.

If this is the case, we might ultimately expect to be able to set up a series of parallel structures, perhaps on this order:

(11.4)   Short vowel: V   Single consonant: C
           Long vowel: V_1V_1 Geminate: C_1C_1
           Diphthong: V_1V_2 Cluster: C_1C_2

                    i.e.

        V vs. VV   C vs. CC

This kind of symmetry does not in fact appear in a clear, across-the-board fashion in English; though there are cases in which some such parallelism seems to operate, i.e. where 'length' of vowels and consonants is in complementary distribution. We will look at some of these cases in the final section

happens elsewhere on a smaller scale, and in many languages *-ry-* segments tend to *-ri-* though all others palatalize (e.g. Modern Greek). The physiological difficulty of combining palatalization with apical flap or trill is some sort of explanation.' If this is the right tack, then our problem again is one of features: what is the distinctive characterization of an [r]-type segment?

of this appendix, not only in English but in other Germanic dialects, and at various historical periods.

At any rate, since we have made at least something of a case, in chapters I, III and VI, for the usefulness of the 'long' = double analysis for vowels, and since the environment in which geminate consonants arise depends on a pre-consonantal 'short' (i.e. nongeminate) vowel, we will assume the kind of parallelism referred to above. We will see in §3 how useful this assumption is. For now, then, we assume that the WGG is epenthesis of an identical segment to the right of a nonvowel marked [−low] in the environment shown in (II.2). In other words, the rule, when finally given its full formulation, will be of this type:

(II.5) *Gemination: preliminary version*

$$\varnothing \rightarrow C / \, XV \begin{bmatrix} C \\ -\text{low} \end{bmatrix} \underline{\hspace{2em}} \begin{bmatrix} C \\ -\text{back} \\ +\text{high} \end{bmatrix}$$

Condition: $X \neq V$

2   A convention for segment-identity

An object like (II.5) above, if we consider it carefully, is not really a 'gemination' rule at all; at least in the sense that it is interpretable as an instruction to insert anything more specific than 'some consonant'. It is nothing more than a generalized schema for consonant-epenthesis. How do we ensure the generation of a segment identical in all particulars to the first one? It might seem initially that this could be handled by means of variables: but a little consideration will show that in order to effect identical epenthesis, we would really need a specification like (II.6) below for each segment involved:

(II.6)

$$\begin{bmatrix} \alpha\text{obs} \\ \beta\text{cons} \\ \gamma\text{ant} \\ \delta\text{cor} \\ \cdot \\ \cdot \\ \cdot \\ \omega F_n \end{bmatrix}$$

That is, there must be agreeing variables for every feature; and the status of 'F_n' would depend on one's notion of how fully specified a fully-specified matrix has to be. This is of course wildly uneconomical and, what is more, it misses the point: what defines identity, as far as we can see, is not pairwise agreement of arbitrary features, but rather total identity of all features in two (or more) matrices. We are concerned, that is, with the possibility of only two options; given a pair of segments (X, Y), either X = Y or X ≠ Y. And if this is the case, then it seems over-concrete and undergeneral to list the individual features when a rule is concerned only with the set of all pairs (X, Y) such that X = Y, and nothing else.

One solution – notationally the simplest – is to represent processes like gemination by indexing (as for example we did in our formulation of quantitative ablaut A (1.16)). Thus we could restate rule (11.5) in the format usually used for transformational rules, and this way ensure a correct output for gemination:

(11.7)

$$\text{SD: X V} \begin{bmatrix} \text{C} \\ -\text{low} \end{bmatrix} \begin{bmatrix} \text{C} \\ -\text{back} \\ +\text{high} \end{bmatrix} \text{SC: } 1\ 2\ 3\ 4 \rightarrow 1\ 2\ 3\ 3\ 4$$
$$\quad\ 1\quad 2\qquad 3\qquad\qquad 4$$

We can interpret this correctly by assuming the convention that replication of an integer in the structure index means replication in all particulars of whatever that integer refers to.

Even though this is adequate, however, we propose a more complicated notation, which we feel captures certain kinds of details that (11.7) does not, and which in fact makes rather different theoretical claims about the nature of the items involved in phonological rules. We have already utilized this convention in some places (notably in the representation of the archi-vowel in the strong verb stems, and the two parts of the nasal influence convention (2.15)). We now propose to explain its motivation in slightly more detail.

This particular solution is suggested in a preliminary form in Lass (in preparation a); and though it is not at this point fully developed, we present it here in outline. In the above-mentioned paper, the primary aim is to show that [ʔ h] are not 'glides', as Chomsky and Halle claim, but rather minimally specified obstruents; and in the course of the discussion a case is made for a rather different kind of representation of phonological matrices than is customary. In essence, the claim is that the proper form of a matrix is not merely an unordered (or even hierarchized) set of features, but rather two (potentially) disjoint sets of specifications, each capable of being invoked in rules independently of the other.

For instance: if [ʔ] is, as Chomsky and Halle claim, specified as $\begin{bmatrix} -\text{obs} \\ -\text{cons} \\ -\text{voc} \end{bmatrix}$,

then a rule such as the rather common one in many English dialects that turns /t/, or /t k/, or occasionally /p t k/ to [ʔ] in certain environments (e.g.

at word-boundary or preconsonantally) becomes exceedingly complex and 'costly' to state. It involves, among other things, a change of two major class features, and a completely new articulatory specification. And if the rule is restricted, say, to /t/, then every feature except [−voc] must be changed by the rule. And yet the rule is common, widespread, and intuitively highly natural.

But what if we were to separate, in our representations, glottal from supraglottal articulation? It is clear that the articulatory properties of [ʔ] – adducted vocal bands, raised glottis, complete stoppage of airstream – are in fact also the minimal properties of postvocalic voiceless (unaspirated) stops: minus the oral articulation. If this is so, then a rule turning such a stop to [ʔ] can be conceived as erasing the supraglottal articulation entirely, leaving behind as a kind of 'relic' only the gesture characterizing the general type of the affected segment.

Actually the basic division turns out not to be strictly between glottal and supraglottal articulation, but between what might be called the two component gestures of any phone: the general defining one, characterizing essentially the degree of resistance to airstream passage of the vocal tract as a whole, and a specifying gesture, i.e. the localizing articulator-target relationship that characterizes the positional type. Thus properties like obstruency, consonantality, and so forth belong to the first gesture, and localized properties like dentalness, etc., belong to the second. We use the cover terms 'phonation' for the first gesture, and 'articulation' for the second.

We then represent any matrix as composed of (at least) two submatrices, one defining the general configurational vocal-tract properties, and the other the localization – if any – of an articulatory gesture in the sense defined above. The proposed matrix will then be of the type:

(II.8)
$$\begin{bmatrix} [\text{articulation}] \\ [\text{phonation}] \end{bmatrix}$$

A segment of the type [t] will then be represented this way:

(II.9)
$$\begin{bmatrix} \begin{bmatrix} +\text{ant} \\ +\text{cor} \end{bmatrix} \\ \begin{bmatrix} +\text{obs} \\ -\text{cont} \\ -\text{voice} \end{bmatrix} \end{bmatrix}$$

In this case, a rule turning [t] to [ʔ] would then simply erase the articulation submatrix, leaving only a segment marked as a (further unspecified) voiceless noncontinuant obstruent – nothing more. (This is tantamount to claiming that there are derived as well as yet-to-be-specified 'archisegments', which seems a worthwhile idea to follow up.)

Let us then adopt the convention that we represent identity of complete gestures (rather than pairwise feature-agreement) by Greek-letter variables standing outside the proper submatrix brackets. Thus we would state the schematic sequence '(any) nasal followed by a homorganic obstruent' this way:

(II.10)
$$
\alpha\begin{bmatrix} \begin{bmatrix} \text{artic} \\ +\text{nas} \end{bmatrix} \\ [-\text{obs}] \end{bmatrix}
\begin{bmatrix} \alpha[\text{artic}] \\ [+\text{obs}] \end{bmatrix}
$$

(where the phonatory gestures are non-identical, and the articulatory gestures are identical except that one is [+nas]).

In this case 'α' is a variable ranging over any combination of the values '+' and '−' on any features in the inner brackets: the only condition being that as usual all values covered by any given pair of variables agree, so that:

(II.11) $[\alpha[\text{artic}]] [\alpha[\text{artic}]] =$
$$
\begin{bmatrix} \alpha\text{ant} \\ \beta\text{cor} \\ \gamma\text{back} \\ . \\ . \\ . \end{bmatrix}
\begin{bmatrix} \alpha\text{ant} \\ \beta\text{cor} \\ \gamma\text{back} \\ . \\ . \\ . \end{bmatrix}
$$

This convention allows a clear statement of the gemination rule. With the same basic format as in (II.5) above, we can now give the rule as an identical epenthesis:

(II.12) *Gemination: second version*

$$
\varnothing \rightarrow \begin{bmatrix} \alpha[\text{artic}] \\ \beta[\text{phon}] \end{bmatrix}
\Big/ \text{X V} \begin{bmatrix} \alpha\begin{bmatrix} \text{artic} \\ -\text{low} \end{bmatrix} \\ \beta\begin{bmatrix} \text{phon} \\ +\text{cons} \end{bmatrix} \end{bmatrix}
\underline{\qquad}
\begin{bmatrix} +\text{cons} \\ -\text{back} \\ +\text{high} \end{bmatrix}
$$

Condition: X ≠ V

This is now – essentially – correct; there is however one more revision necessary, which we shall get to in §4. But first we must survey some traditional explanations of the WGG, and propose our own interpretation. We will then attempt to establish its synchronic status in OE, and explore some other historical developments that seem relevant.

3 The traditional explanations

There seem to be two major types of explanation for the (historical) origins of the WGG. One is that it is an assimilation process of some kind, in which the inducing segment (/j/ or any other) loses its distinctiveness and takes on the features of the preceding consonant; and the other is that what is primarily involved is syllable structure: the cause of the WGG is a '*Verschiebung der Silbengrenze*'.

The assimilation theory is rejected outright by Streitberg (1963: 148): 'Von einer Assimilation des zweiten Lautes an den ersten ist keine Rede; hierdurch hebt sich die westger. Konsonantendehnung scharf von der urgerm. Assimilation ab.' After this rejection he goes on to give an excellent summary of two major variations of the *Verschiebung der Silbengrenze* theory. We quote the summary in full:

'Nach Kauffmann [*Paul-Braunes Beiträge*, 12.520 ff: RL/JMA] beruht die westger. Konsonantendehnung auf dem Unterschied, der in der Silbentrennung zwischen (schematischem) *ta-la* und *tal-ịa*, *na-ka* und *nak-ụa*...bestanden habe. Dieser soll ausgeglichen worden sein, indem der Typus *ta-la* auf den Typus *tal-ịa* einwirkte, und ihn zu *tal-lịa* umbildete.

'Diese Erklärung unterliegt, wie Sievers [*PBB*, 16.262 ff: RL/JAM]... hervor hebt, schweren bedenken. Vielmehr ist mit Sievers anzunehmen, daß die Gesamtquantität der Silbe spontan gesteigert sei. Die Folge dieser Quantitätssteigerung ist die Verschiebung der Silbengrenze. Die Konsonantendehnung ist nur das Mittel, die Quantitätssteigerung zur Ausführung zu bringen. Da im urgermanischen die Trennung *ta-lịa* und nicht *tal-ịa* bestanden hat, so muß Kauffmanns Ausgangspunkt verworfen werden.' (1963: 148–9)

The question of 'boundaries' is indeed important here: but as we will see, the boundaries in question are those between morphemes, not syllables: though the notion 'syllable' itself is critical. But one point in Sievers's view, as summarized by Streitberg, is particularly interesting: it amounts, we think, to a correct statement of what the WGG was really 'about'. And this is that the significance of the rule itself is 'instrumental', as it were, that it is 'nur das Mittel, die Quantitätssteigerung zu Ausführung zu bringen'. We will develop this further in the next section, and explore the importance of what Streitberg calls the 'Gesamtquantität der Silbe' – both in the WGG and in other aspects of Germanic phonology.

Between the Streitberg-Kauffmann-Sievers claim that in one way or another syllable-structure is the prime factor, and the idea that the WGG is purely an assimilation, lies a no-man's-land inhabited by Prokosch (1938: 87). He claims that both factors are involved:

'Phonetically the process is not entirely clear, but it is apparently connected with a difference in syllable-division: in a word like Go. *hal-dan*, *l* belongs clearly to the first syllable: but *ð* in *bidjan* belongs to the second syllable as well as the first; this may have led to lengthening of articulation.

The type *bidjan*, with a *j*-suffix, is by far the most common. The palatal spirant palatizes the preceding consonant, and a palatal consonant is in its very nature a long consonant.'

While a case can certainly be made for 'amphisyllabic' segments (cf. Anderson and Jones 1972), dual membership of this type does not seem to be critically involved here. (The usual case of 'syllable overlap' is in clusters like medial /st/ or /pl/, which when postvocalic after the first syllable of a polysyllabic word can be interpreted either as 'closing' the first syllable or 'opening' the next.)

The palatalization explanation seems equally dubious. Aside from the fact that labials and dentals show no palatalization in WGG environments (*hebban*, *clyppan*, *settan*, *biddan*), the claim that palatals have inherent length rests on no phonetic reality that we know of.

This leaves us then with assimilation alone as a possibility; and here the clearest statement that we know is Kurath (1956: 152):

> 'Most long consonants in this position [V̆__V: RL/JMA] result from assimilation of /j/ to the preceding consonant, as in *settan* < **satja-nam*... since /j/ was assimilated to a consonant without lengthening it if the consonant was preceded by a long vowel, a diphthong, or a short vowel plus consonant (as in *sēcan* 'seek', *hwǣte* 'wheat', *sendan* < **sōkja-*, **hwaitja-*, **sandja-*) long consonants could occur only after short vowels in OE...'

This description (though we do not agree with the explanation that Kurath proposes, particularly his rather odd and ambiguous use of 'assimilation') raises some points which will help us to arrive at a relatively natural and well-motivated description of the process, and to explain why it operated only on concatenations of a certain restricted type.

4   The motivation

Recall that (in Kurath's version) /j/ was 'assimilated to a consonant without lengthening it if the consonant was preceded by a long vowel, a diphthong, or a short vowel plus consonant'. We can best approach the problem of why this limitation should obtain if we consider the total set of possible outputs if gemination were to occur in both the excluded environments, and those where it actually took place. Using Kurath's key words as examples, and starring phonotactically ungrammatical outputs (i.e. configurations which West Germanic languages do not permit), let us see what would happen – schematically – if gemination occurred before all /j/:

(11.13)	*Type*	*Result*
	(i) sōkja-	VVCj → *VVCCj
	(ii) hwaitja-	VVCj → *VVCCj
	(iii) sandja-	VCCj → *VCCCj
	(iv) satja-	VCj → VCCj

That is, of the three possible types of environment before /j/ (since (i) and (ii) are really the same), (i–ii) and (iii) will both yield 'overlong' clusters of four members (/VVCC/ or /VCCC/) before /j/: only (iv) gives the three-member cluster /VCC/, which judging from the historical results is one of the two sequences permitted in this environment: the other being /VVC/ as in *sōkja-. And – except if C = /r/ – the sequence /VCj/ is also rejected: this one is 'overshort'.

Now it is worth observing, before we go any further, that it is the clusters /VVCCj/ and /VCCCj/ in particular which are noncanonical: not /VVCC/ or /VVCCC/. Certainly in superficial forms in OE we find both types: *rǣdde* 'he counselled', *rītst* 'thou ridest', respectively /-VVCCV/ and /-VVCCC/. What is crucial here is the presence of a following /j/: and what is more, this /j/ is always the first segment of a suffix: it is preceded by morpheme boundary. To clarify the sequences involved:

(11.14)   (i) sōkja-, hwaitja-   VVC+j → *VVCC+j
          (ii) sandja-   VCC+j → *VCCC+j
          (iii) satja-   VC+j → VCC+j

The result of gemination in (11.14.iii) is then one of the three acceptable concatenations: /VCC+j/, the same as in *sandja-. (The other two are of course /VVC+j/, and in the special case, /Vr+j/.) It is worth noting here that the 'overlong' sequences in forms like *rǣdde* and *rītst* have a quite different structure: /-VVC+CV/ in the first case and /-VVC+CC/ in the second: we do not have sequences of more than three segments to the left of a morpheme boundary.[1]

The exceptions to the gemination in OE are of two types; in both of these, in superficial forms, sequences of /VC+j/ appear:

(a) Class I weak verbs in radical -r, either original or from *s via Verner's Law and rhotacism. Thus *herian* 'praise' (cf. Go. *harjan*), *nerian* 'save' (cf. Go. *nasjan*). In these and similar verbs, as we mentioned above, frequent spellings of the type *herg(e)an*, etc. strongly suggest that *i* in these cases represents [j].

(b) Class II weak verbs: *lufian* 'love', *macian* 'make', and so on.

We have already given some account of the type (a) exceptions; but those of type (b) are to be explained rather differently. As we showed earlier (ch. IV), these verbs derived from an underlying type /-VC-ojan/ (historically *-ōjan), where /o/ is a theme vowel that appears in some surface forms (*lufode, lufod*), or else apparently influences the form of the superficial desinences (e.g. pres. 2

---

[1] There are actually some intramorphemic /VVCC/ sequences in OE; but these are all of the type with 'ambiguous' clusters (i.e. clusters which can be both syllable-initial and syllable-final: Anderson and Jones 1972). The commonest cluster of this kind is /st/: thus *rǣste* 'rest', *prēost* 'priest', with the structure /VVst(V)/.

sing. *-ast* vs. class I *-est*). The fact that these verbs do not show umlaut in the root vowel, or palatalization in velar-final stems like *stician*, *prician*, *macian*, suggests that at the time when these rules apply the thematic /o/ is still present, and blocks them. So when WGG applies (whether we consider it from a synchronic or a diachronic viewpoint), the class II weak verbs do not exhibit the uncanonical /-VC+j/ sequence.

We now turn to a more precise characterization of what the WGG actually does; and we will approach this historically. Below are some representative class I weak verbs, chosen to illustrate the various possible stem-types. We give first a Gothic form, to illustrate the (putative) earlier shape, and then its OE cognate; and we also give a schematic representation of the canonical shapes at various major historical periods: Proto-Germanic, Proto-West-Germanic, and (attested) OE. In each of these cases we are citing presumed phonetic – not underlying – forms:

(11.15)

	Examples			*Sequences*	
	Go.	OE	PGmc	PWG	OE
(a)	bugjan	bycgan	$-$VC$+$jan	$-$VCC$+$jan	$-$VCC$+$an
(b)	sandjan	sendan	$-$VCC$+$jan	$-$VCC$+$jan	$-$VCC$+$an
(c)	sōkjan	sēcan	$-$VVC$+$jan	$-$VVC$+$jan	$-$VVC$+$an
(d)	hausjan	hīeran	$-$VVC$+$jan	$-$VVC$+$jan	$-$VVC$+$an
(e)	harjan	herian	$-$Vr$+$jan	$-$Vr$+$jan	$-$Vr$+$jan

This display reveals two interesting facts: (a) that there is a definite connexion between the WGG and the loss of (superficial) /j/ in OE; and (b) that there is a definite change over time in the permissible concatenations of stem-final and suffix-initial clusters in these verbs. The result is that there is a decrease in the number of sequences allowed from Proto-Germanic to OE; and this runs in a clear direction. To represent this schematically, we shall consider each cluster type, both phonologically and phonetically; in the display below, /PWG/ etc. = 'underlying' and [PWG] etc. = 'superficial':

(11.16)

	Sequence	PGmc	/PWG/	[PWG]	/OE/	[OE]
(a)	$-$VC$+$jan	yes	yes	no	yes	no
(b)	$-$VCC$+$jan	yes	yes	yes	yes	no
(c)	$-$VVC$+$jan	yes	yes	yes	yes	no
(d)	$-$Vr$+$jan	yes	yes	yes	yes	yes

Of the four phonetic sequence-types acceptable in Proto-Germanic, all are acceptable underlyingly in Proto-West-Germanic and OE, three are acceptable phonetically in some West Germanic dialects (cf. OS *biddian*, *settian*, etc.), and only one is acceptable in surface forms in OE. All the others are changed in OE, either by WGG, or by deletion of suffix-initial /j/. Thus (unless C = /r/), the canonical Proto-Germanic sequence /–VC+jan/ is apparently 'overshort' for West Germanic: the WGG produces /–VCC+jan/. So that forms of the original *bugjan* type now have – phonetically – the same root structure as those of the *sandjan* type. And in a clear sense, in fact, they have the same kind of root structure as the *sōkjan* type, too. Consider the structures of the forms given in (11.16) now, not from the point of view of the type of segments that are involved in the sequences, but simply in terms of the number of segments occurring in postvocalic root position, before a morpheme-boundary and a suffix /+jan/. In this schematization 'S' = 'segment' (of whatever type):

(11.17)	Type	PGmc	WG	OE
(a)	bugjan	–VS+jan	–VSS+jan	–VSS+an
(b)	sandjan	–VSS+jan	–VSS+jan	–VSS+an
(c)	sōkjan	–VSS+jan	–VSS+jan	–VSS+an
(d)	harjan	–VS+jan	–VS+jan	–VS+jan

If we take Old Saxon as representative of the earlier West Germanic type, and OE as the later (e.g. OS *settian*, OE *settan*), it is now fairly clear what has happened: the only general Proto-Germanic sequence-type that survives into West Germanic in this context is /–VSS+jan/, except in the case of stems in *-r*; in OE, while this latter type is permitted still, the /VSS+jan/ sequences are reduced to [VSS+an]. But at the phonological level at least the sequences are unchanged from Proto-West-Germanic, as suggested in (11.16). So as far as underlying sequences in OE are concerned, we have a restriction of stem-final postvocalic clusters such that they may have neither more nor less than two members; and phonetically, we have a deletion of a suffix-initial consonant just in case the preceding cluster is /VSS/.

The implications of this are rather interesting; among other things, this analysis in terms of segment-numbers rather than segment-types suggests that we are dealing here with a rather abstract matter of syllable typology. The number of segments in a given configuration seems to be a determining – or at least influential – factor in a sound-change. It might be interesting to see whether this same kind of typology has effects in other contexts as well, perhaps in terms of the structural descriptions of other rules. Let us recall now that we are dealing with two separate phenomena: (a) increase of /S/-final weak verb stems to /SS/-finals; and (b) deletion of /j/ after /SS/.

In §1 of this appendix we suggested a possible parallelism between sequences of the types /VV/ and /CC/; we are now in effect suggesting a further one, between /VVC/ and /VCC/, which the WGG seems, on the face of it, to bear out. On strictly logical grounds this is plausible; but it is also empirically supported as well. There are other processes in the phonology of OE that bear out this equation.

Consider these typical nom. sing. and nom. pl. forms of OE neuter *a*-stem nouns:

(11.18)	*Nom. sing.*	*Nom. pl.*	*Gloss*
(a)	scip	scipu	ship
	god	godu	god
	hof	hofu	dwelling
(b)	word	word	word
	hors	hors	horse
	bold	bold	dwelling
(c)	dēor	dēor	animal
	wīf	wīf	woman
	bǣl	bǣl	pyre

Schematically, these three groups are representable as:

(11.19)	*Sing.*	*Pl.*
(a)	−VC (−VS)	−VC+u (−VS+u)
(b)	−VCC (−VSS)	−VCC (−VSS)
(c)	−VVC (−VSS)	−VVC (−VSS)

Not only is it clear once more that 'long' vowels and diphthongs are phonologically parallel, but also that – with regard to the presence or absence of plural inflexion – nouns with stems in /−VCC/ and nouns with stems in /−VVC/ constitute a class, as opposed to those with /−VC/ stems; and further, that the two classes are reducible to /−VS/ vs. /−VSS/.

A similar situation holds with the nominative singulars of ō-stem feminine nouns: thus *faru* 'journey', *lufu* 'love', *nafu* 'nave' vs. *lār* 'learning', *lēah* 'lea', *wund* 'wound'. The same thing can be seen, though a bit less clearly, in *wō*-stem feminines, where back umlaut has interfered with the historical situation: thus *sinu* 'sinew', *sceadu* 'shade' (where back umlaut is historically later than phonetic loss of -*u*) vs. *lǣs* 'meadow', *hrēow* 'penitence'.

In other noun classes we find a similar distinction in terms of stem types between forms with and without nom. sing. suffixes: thus among the *i*-stems *wine* 'friend', *mere* 'lake' vs. *dǣl* 'part', *ent* 'giant' (masculine); *spere* 'spear', *sife* 'sieve' vs. *flǣsc* 'flesh', *(ġe)byrd* 'birth' (neuter). Among the *u*-stems we find the same pattern: *sunu* 'son', *wudu* 'wood' vs. *flōd* 'flood', *feld* 'field'. There are also traces of this among the 'athematic' nouns: *studu* 'post', *hnutu* 'nut' vs. *bōc* 'book', *turf* 'turf', etc.

It is evident by now that this is the familiar distinction between forms with 'long' stems and forms with 'short' stems ('heavy' vs. 'light', *langsilbig* vs. *kurzsilbig*). We give all these forms merely as a reminder that this is not an arbitrary or meaningless distinction, but one that has important repercussions in OE phonology (and indeed in the phonology of other Germanic dialects).

The crucial fact is that 'stem-type' is a notion that can be appealed to by phonological rules. And the terms of the appeal – in these cases – are not entirely different from the terms of appeal involved in the WGG, though they are by no means identical in detail. What is of interest, though, in connexion with the idea of a possible 'numerical' constraint underlying certain sound changes, is the fact that: (a) /VVC/ and /VCC/ sequences are under some circumstances equivalent; and (b) /VVC/, /VCC/ sequences may under some (morphological) circumstances be 'equivalent' to /VCV/. This latter claim at least suggests some overall motivation for the retention of nom. sing. affixes only in short-stem nouns, and the behaviour of the *a*-stem neuter plurals. A nucleus of the type /VC/ is simply, to put it rather crudely, 'too short' for certain specific morphological contexts. In the final section of this appendix we will look at some evidence suggesting that the short/long syllable dichotomy has a long and important history in Germanic, and is involved in some of the major transformations from what we might call phonologically 'conservative' languages like English, and to some extent German, to the more 'advanced' types like Swedish and Norwegian.

If these arguments hold, then we can see the abstract shape of the WGG, its teleology as it were, in this way: it is the reflex of a well-formedness condition arising in West Germanic, which restricts morpheme-final sequences in certain environments to only the long (/VVC/, /VCC/) type.[1]

Now that we have established the significance of the morpheme boundary preceding /j/ for the WGG, we can incorporate this into the rule, and give it in its final form:

(II.20) *Gemination*

$$
\varnothing \rightarrow \begin{bmatrix} \alpha[\text{artic}] \\ \beta[\text{phon}] \end{bmatrix} \Big/ V_1^1 \begin{bmatrix} \alpha \begin{bmatrix} \text{artic} \\ -\text{low} \end{bmatrix} \\ \beta \begin{bmatrix} \text{phon} \\ +\text{cons} \end{bmatrix} \end{bmatrix} - + \begin{bmatrix} +\text{high} \\ -\text{back} \end{bmatrix}
$$

The output of (II.20) will be subject to some rule deleting the post-boundary /j/; this essentially morphological rule (which also presumably deletes other suffixal /j/ except after /r/) will be among those processes we have called 'affix modification' (cf. ch. IV, §4 above): we will not formulate it here.

The effects of the WGG also appear in nouns and adjectives, specifically those of the *ja*- and *jo*- declensions (which are equivalent to the so-called 'pure' *a*- and *o*-stems, except for the presence of a thematic *-j*- before the affix vowel). Thus *dæg* < *dag + a*- vs. *cynn* < *kun + ja*-, *lufu* < *luð + o* vs. *synn* 'sin' < *sun + jo*. For further details cf. Campbell 1959: §§ 575–9, 590–3, 644–8).

5 Gemination, breaking, and *i*-umlaut

It is fairly certain that WGG is historically (as a 'sound-change') earlier than breaking: that is, clearly a pre-OE development, prior also to *i*-umlaut. But the synchronic sequence – if these three rules are synchronic rules – is rather different. We consider now the ordering relations apparently holding between these three processes.

To begin with, we note that there must be at least two kinds of geminate consonants in OE: those in which the gemination is induced by a following /j/, and those in which there seems to be no reasonable synchronic environment. Since the environments for WGG are obviously a proper subset of the *i*-umlaut environments, it follows that any form showing an unmutated vowel before a geminate consonant must not be an example of the WGG. Thus *full* 'full', *catt* 'cat', *eall* 'all' (cf. ON *fullr, kǫttr, allr*). So we must assume that forms of this type have their geminates in lexical representation, e.g. /full/, /katt/, /all/, and so forth. These then are lexical geminates, as opposed to the type *sellan, bycgan*, which are derived geminates.

Now consider the relation between gemination and breaking. As we mentioned earlier, there are weak verb paradigms in class I which show the effects of umlaut and WGG in their present system and AFB and breaking in their preterites. Thus *sellan* shows umlaut and gemination (underlying /saljan/), while *sealde* 'he gave' shows AFB and breaking (underlying /salde/).

It is particularly interesting in cases of this sort that breaking occurs only in the preterite system, before [ld], and not in the present, before [ll]; and yet [ll] is undoubtedly a breaking cluster, as witness *eall, feallan* 'fall'. There are two possible explanations for this disparity. The easier and less interesting is that the [ll] clusters in *sellan, tellan* and the like are marked with some idiosyncratic feature like [−breaking], and that this feature is (circularly) a property of all forms which have [ll] but are not subject to breaking. The second possibility, which we prefer on grounds of principle, and which contradicts no known synchronic facts, is that at the point in the grammar where breaking applies, the present-tense forms of these verbs do not satisfy the proper analysis of the rule; but at this point the [ld] clusters are present in the preterite forms, so that the rule applies.

This means that whatever the historical order might have been, gemination is synchronically a later rule than breaking. It must follow it, to avoid an ad hoc and unmotivated explanation of *sellan*. So WGG must follow breaking, and may either precede or follow umlaut. Since the products of AFB and breaking are acted upon by umlaut, it follows that umlaut is the later rule; but since umlaut and WGG have partially joint environments, it follows that there is no really motivated way of deciding on ordering in terms of the form of the rules themselves.

We did however show in chapter IV, §8 that WGG must precede palatal softening (4.29), since it provides the crucial environment for the development of /g/ to a strident stop in *secgan*, etc., rather than to a fricative. But palatal softening is not crucially ordered with respect to umlaut itself; it must merely precede any second (i.e. post-umlaut) application of backness accommodation (4.27) (cf. ch. IV, §5). However if backness accommodation is an 'everywhere' rule, operative whenever its proper analysis is met, then the way to block post-umlaut palatal softening is by ordering that rule before umlaut, and thus before the conditions for backness accommodation are created in forms like *cēne*. So it would seem that the proper order is: AFB, breaking, gemination, backness accommodation, palatal softening, *i*-umlaut, and (again) backness accommodation.

We can derive forms like *sellan*, *sealde* as follows:

(II.21)

Input	sal+jan	sal+de
AFB	sæl+jan	sæl+de
Breaking	————	sæul+de
Gemination	sæll+jan	————
Umlaut	sell+jan	————
DHH	————	sæal+de
Affix modification	sell+an	————
Output	sellan	sæalde
Spelling	*sellan*	*sealde*

It is of some interest in this connexion that the particular relationship between breaking and WGG that we have been discussing here has been used by others as an example of nonchronological rule addition (see Postal 1968: 263).

6   Gemination and the history of Germanic syllable-structure

We turn now to some relations between the WGG and various other processes – both before it and after it – in the history of Germanic phonology. We are particularly concerned here with two matters: the extension that the WGG effects of long or heavy stem-syllables to positions formerly occupied (or occupiable) by short ones; and the fact that it does not make long syllables longer, at least phonetically, in OE. A further aspect of this last point is that /j/ is deleted in cases where, after WGG, we would otherwise have an 'overlong' sequence. In other words, there is a clear relation between vowel length and consonant length in at least this limited case, and a kind of upper limit on cluster size in certain positions.

The earliest instance in Germanic, as far as we know, of an important role being played by the long/short syllable dichotomy, is the set of phenomena associated with the *vokalischen Auslautsgesetz* ('law of vocalic finals'), now usually called 'Sievers's Law', or the 'Sievers–Edgerton Law'. The first relatively formal statement of this is Sievers (1878). The basic problem Sievers attacked was the origin of the differences in the endings of certain types of Gothic *ja*-stem nouns and other forms, e.g. *harjis* vs. *hairdeis*, where the comparative evidence suggests a thematic **-ja-* in both cases. Various explanations had been proposed, none of which held up; and Sievers, in short, proposed that the ancestral (Proto-Germanic) forms had shown an alternation between **-ja-* and **-ija-*: the former after short syllables and the latter after long. Thus *harjis* goes back to **harja-* (with **a > i* by an umlaut-like assimilation), and *hairdeis* goes back to **herðija-*, where Go. *ei* (= *ī*) is from vocalization of **j* after **i*. (See further Campbell 1959: §355.3.) Sievers compared this to a similar Vedic Sanskrit alternation, where *i ~ y* and *u ~ v* under similar conditions. The 'Law' for Sanskrit may be briefly stated this way (see Sievers's examples): in certain morphological contexts, unaccented high vowels are consonantal after short stem syllables and vocalic after long ones.

The relation between this Indo-European alternation and the circumstances of the WGG is quite obvious: if **j* and **i* were respectively [+cons] and [−cons], but otherwise the same, then **harja-* has a root structure /-VCCV-/ and **herðija-* has a structure /-VCCVCV-/ (we assume that both **-ja-* and **-ija-* were at this period purely thematic, i.e. there was no morpheme boundary before **j*; thus the Proto-Germanic nominative singular forms would be /harja+z/ and /herðija+z/ respectively). But if there were a root **herðja-*, this would contain a sequence /-VCCC-/, which would be 'overlong' in precisely the same way in which sequences derived from WGG after a long vowel would be: the result in the latter case would be /-VVCC-/. The problem is four-member clusters, or three-member postvocalic clusters, in stem-final position. In Proto-Germanic, the stem-final cluster includes **j*; in OE, it seems likely that the morphological structure of many forms had been reinterpreted, so that the /j/ was suffix-initial rather than root-final.

So the alternation defined by the law of vocalic finals is the same in essence as that defined by the WGG: both the forms that undergo it, and those that do not. In later West Germanic, it seems to be the case that, except for *r*-finals, no cluster smaller than /VCC/ or /VVC/ is permitted in stem-final position in certain contexts: and none longer, either. In this way Sievers's law is an earlier instance of the same general type of motivation as that of the later WGG: a constraint on the length of stem-syllables, setting, for the cases in which it applied, both an upper and lower limit.

One aspect of both Sievers's Law and the WGG, which is of considerable interest in the light of later historical developments, concerns the precise nature of the change effected by blocking – or promoting – certain stem-final sequences on the basis of their clustering properties. And this is that all such processes are in essence neutralizations. In any language with a long/short distinction in its vowel system, the end result of rules like the WGG (and the later deletion of /j/) is partial complementation in a given environment. Thus after the WGG consonant length and vowel length are in complementary distribution in stem-final position. What has happened, in a sense, is that there has been a decrease in the functional load of the (underlying) length distinction: or to put it another way, an increase in the total predictability of length-relations in the system. We will shortly see the implications of this fact.

In the history of English (as well as the other dialects) there have been numerous instances in which rules operate – apparently in 'conspiracy' – to bring about just such partial (context-restricted) complementations as those we have been looking at. One case in point, interesting because of its relation to the long/short syllable dichotomy, is a set of rules that arose at various points in the history of Old and Middle English. We will discuss them here very briefly, as their overall shape, rather than the details, is what we are interested in; for fuller discussion see e.g. Jordan (1934: §§22–6).

The first rules of this type seem to have arisen in about the 8th century, and their effects were: (a) to shorten long vowels before three-consonant clusters; and (b) to shorten long vowels before two consonants in the antepenult of trisyllabic words. The first rule is illustrated by developments like *gŏdspell* < *gōdspell*, and the second by *hlămmæsse* < *hlāfmæsse* (Campbell 1959: §285). These rules can be roughly abbreviated by a schema of this type:

(II.22) *Pre-cluster shortening I; trisyllabic shortening I*

$$V \to \emptyset \;/\; V \underline{\hspace{2em}} C \begin{Bmatrix} CC \\ CVCVC_0 \,\# \end{Bmatrix} \begin{matrix} \text{(a)} \\ \text{(b)} \end{matrix}$$

Thus all sequences of the type /VVCCC/ were disallowed, as well as all /VVCC/ in the antepenults of trisyllables. In a trisyllabic word, long vowels occurred only in the sequence /VVC/, and in all other words both /VVCC/ and /VVC/ were acceptable.

At a slightly later period (possibly as early as the 10th century: Jordan 1934: §23), both of these rules had simplified: (II.22a) now operated before two-consonant clusters, and (II.22b) before single consonants in the antepenults of trisyllables: thus *kept* < *kĕpte* OE < *cēpte, southern* < ME *sŭþerne* < OE *sūþerne*. The simplified schema for shortening is now:

(II.23) *Pre-cluster shortening II; trisyllabic shortening II*

$$V \to \emptyset \;/\; V \underline{\hspace{2em}} C \begin{Bmatrix} C \\ VCVC_0 \,\# \end{Bmatrix} \begin{matrix} \text{(a)} \\ \text{(b)} \end{matrix}$$

These two rules thus effected, as they were simplified by the change from (11.22) to (11.23), an increasing neutralization of length, in these two environments. And this neutralization was increased still further by another rule, probably roughly contemporaneous with (11.22) or even a bit earlier, which lengthened vowels before clusters of sonorant plus homorganic voiced obstruent: thus *field* < ME *fĕld* < OE *fĕld*, *climb* < ME *klīmb(en)* < OE *clĭmban*. The rule might be formulated this way:

(11.24) *Pre-cluster lengthening*

$$\emptyset \to V \;/\; V \underline{\hspace{2em}} \begin{bmatrix} \alpha[\text{artic}] \\ \beta\begin{bmatrix} \text{phon} \\ -\text{obs} \end{bmatrix} \end{bmatrix} \begin{bmatrix} \alpha[\text{artic}] \\ \beta\begin{bmatrix} \text{phon} \\ +\text{obs} \\ +\text{voice} \end{bmatrix} \end{bmatrix}$$

After the implementation of the schemata (11.23) and (11.24), long and short vowels were in absolute complementation before virtually all /CC/ clusters, and length was neutralized in the trisyllabic antepenult. The only places where (on the whole) length was still lexically distinctive was (a) in the stressed open syllables of disyllabic words (since already in late WGmc vowels were long – if stressed – in absolute finality: Campbell 1959: §125); and (b) before single final consonants. All of these processes, however, show a certain variability before certain clusters, particularly /st/; in Jordan's words (1934: §23), 'vor solchen Konsonantengruppen, welche ihrer Natur nach den Anlaut der zweiten Silbe bilden konnten, so daß der vorhergehende Vokal den Silbenauslaut bildete'. Thus there is no shortening in French loans like *coast*, *feast*, *roast*, and in native words like *most*, *east*; though there is shortening in *breast*, *blast*. But it is to be remembered that absolute regularity of application is not our concern here; these are rules that illustrate a tendency, and they would probably be equally significant if they only affected a few lexical items at any one time: at least in an essentially typological argument.

One of the environments in which free length still occurred at this point was later removed, probably in about the 13th century: this is the first stressed open syllable in a disyllabic word. Here again, as in the case of (11.22)–(11.23), the development was in two stages.

The first stage lengthens and lowers mid vowels, and lengthens low vowels, thus giving *over* < ME *ǭver* < OE *ŏfer*, *name* < ME *nāme* < OE *năma*, etc. This stage involves these rules:

(11.25) *Open-syllable lengthening I*

$$\text{(a) SD:} \quad \# \quad C_0 \quad \begin{bmatrix} V \\ -\text{high} \\ -\text{low} \end{bmatrix} \quad C \; V \; C_0 \; \# \qquad \text{SC:} \; 3 \to [+\text{low}] \, [+\text{low}]$$

$$1 \qquad 2 \qquad\quad 3 \qquad\quad 4\;5\;6\;7$$

(b) SD: $\#$ C_0 $\begin{bmatrix} V \\ +\text{low} \end{bmatrix}$ C V C_0 $\#$ SC: $3 \to 3\ 3$

$\quad$ 1 $\quad$ 2 $\quad\quad$ 3 $\quad\quad$ 4 5 6 7

The second was a lengthening and lowering of high vowels in the first open syllables of disyllabic words:

(11.26) *Open-syllable lengthening II*

$\quad$ SD: $\#$ C_0 $\begin{bmatrix} V \\ +\text{high} \end{bmatrix}$ C V C_0 $\#$ SC: $3 \to [-\text{high}]\ [-\text{high}]$

$\quad\quad$ 1 $\quad$ 2 $\quad\quad$ 3 $\quad\quad$ 4 5 6 7

From this stage we get *wood* < ME *wōde* < OE *wŭdu*, *weevil* < ME *wĕvel* < OE *wĭfol*. (For detailed discussion and justification of the fact that these rules involve lowering of both high and mid vowels, see Lass 1969b.)

The overall effects of these rules may be summed up this way: even though Middle English was a language with two distinct underlying vowel sets (as indeed Modern English still is), the larger number of phonetic long and short vowels represented neutralizations, not direct mappings of underlying vowels of one type into surface vowels of the same type. (A number of rules of this type – if the claims made in *SPE* are correct – are still operative: for instance trisyllabic shortening in paradigms of the *sign–signify*, *cone–conical*, *obscene–obscenity* type.)

Thus Middle English, from this point of view, appears to represent a logical intermediary between a language with no neutralization of underlying length contrasts (or, if there is no such thing, one like Latin with practically none) and one with full neutralization, i.e. with totally predictable phonetic length. At least this is true in the abstract; but from our point of view, which is as it were 'evolutionary' here, it would be more interesting if this logical intermediary could be seen as an historical transition-phase. This would be clearest if there were Germanic languages which have (a) long and short (phonetic) vowels, and (b) total complementation of the two types, i.e. no lexical length at all. And the whole sequence we have been trying to establish would be even better attested by a language with both long and short vowels and long and short consonants (as well as non-identical clusters), and total complementation of both types of length. A language of this sort would be the end phase of a sequence in which languages like early OE or Old Norse stood at one end, and languages like Middle or Modern English stood in the middle.

Two such languages come to mind immediately: Modern spoken Norwegian and Swedish. Consider for instance the following Swedish forms (from transcriptions of native speakers; but cf. Björkhagen 1948: §7, Teleman 1969: 168). These represent characteristic superficial distributions of vowel and consonant length for six selected vowels (not the whole system); primary stress is marked with an acute accent.

(11.27)	$V\#$	$VC\#$	VCV	VC_1C_1	VC_1C_2
(a)	ví:	ví:n	çí:na	flík:a	víst
(b)	sé:	bré:v	ré:sa	pén:a	fést
(c)	fέ:	vέ:g	lέ:sa	vég:	hέst
(d)	bú:	bú:k	rú:lig	blúm:a	mústər
(e)	fó:	bó:t	mó:la	ɔ́t:a	mɔ́stə
(f)	brɑ́:	glɑ́:s	bɑ́:ra	glás:	lámpa

(*Orthographic forms and glosses:* (a) *vi* 'we', *vin* 'wine', *Kina* 'China', *flicka* 'girl', *visst* 'certainly'; (b) *se* 'to see', *brev* 'letter', *resa* 'to travel', *penna* 'pen', *fest* 'party'; (c) *fä* 'beast', *väg* 'road', *läsa* 'to read', *vägg* 'wall', *häst* 'horse'; (d) *bo* 'to dwell', *bok* 'book', *rolig* 'entertaining', *blomma* 'flower', *moster* 'aunt'; (e) *få* 'to take', *båt* 'boat', *måla* 'to paint', *åtta* 'eight', *måste* 'must'; (f) *bra* 'good', *glas* 'glass', *bara* 'only', *glass* 'ice cream', *lampa* 'lamp').

The distributional patterns shown in (11.27) suggest that – as far as primary-stressed syllables are concerned – there is no length at the lexical level in Swedish. And this cuts two ways: not only are long vowels and long consonants (or clusters) in complementary distribution, but every syllable bearing primary stress contains either a long vowel plus at most one consonant, or a short vowel plus a long consonant or cluster. Certainly this is not the kind of distribution characteristic of Old Swedish or any other Old Germanic language. How it arose is a complex historical question that we will not go into here, but it did involve some familiar types of rules: certainly lengthening in open syllables, and just as certainly some kind of compensatory gemination after short vowels. But we do find the same kind of set-up in Norwegian (cf. the detailed discussion in Haugen 1967), and to a certain extent in Icelandic (cf. Einarsson 1945: 4–6). And it is in a sense what we might call the 'ultimate' development of the sort of tendency we have been suggesting has been operative throughout the history of Germanic.

That is, the tendency, as manifested in recurring rules – even though each may in fact have covered only a minority of forms – has been to neutralize length distinctions, both vocalic and consonantal, in an increasingly large set of contexts, until finally the neutralization holds true for the whole language, and length ceases to be phonological but becomes purely phonetic. Within this trend there has been a subtendency, most clearly exemplified by the WGG, to generalize long syllables of either the /VVC/ or /VCC/ type to stress-bearing positions, at the expense of short syllables. In Modern Norwegian and Swedish this tendency has reached its apogee: not only are vocalic and consonantal length, in major lexical categories, in complementary distribution, but primary stress occurs only on those syllables in which the complementation is operative, i.e. long ones. So if we can say that something like an 'entelechy' is determinable over time with reference to the development of Germanic syllable-structure, it seems to be an entelechy with two characteristics: (a) loss of phonological length, and (b) generalization of phonetically long syllables to stress-bearing positions. In this light Sievers's Law, the WGG, and a host of other phenomena can be seen as partial implementations of this overall trend. (For a detailed discussion of this 'length conspiracy' in the history of English, see Lass 1973c.)

Appendix III
The status of 'diphthongization by initial palatals'

Even if we accept the proposal that the *gi-*, *ge-* forms from Gmc /j/ (cf. ch. III) before back vowels represent only [j], with the *e*, *i* functioning merely as palatality diacritics, we are still faced with the problem of those which show the so-called 'palatal diphthongization'. According to Campbell (1959: 69) 'One of the most regular changes in the West Saxon dialects is the diphthongization of front vowels after palatal consonants. This change is caused not only by original palatal *i̯*, but by the new palatals which arose from Prim. Gmc. *k* and *g*...By the diphthongization *ē* became *īe*, and *ǣ* became *ēa*.' The following are examples of this process:

(III.1)

(a) *e* > *ie: scieran* 'cut', *ġiefan* 'give', *ġieldan* 'pay', *-ġietan* 'get', *ondġiet* 'sense', *ġielpan* 'boast'.

(b) *ē* > *īe: ġīet* 'yet', *ġīeta*, *ġīena* 'id.', *ġīe* 'ye' (poetical).

(c) *æ* > *ea: sceaft* 'shaft', *sceabb* 'scab', *sceal* 'he shall', *scear* 'he cut', *ċeaster* 'city', *ġeat* 'gate', *ġeaf* 'he gave'.

(d) *ǣ* > *ēa: scēap* 'sheep', *scēaron* 'they cut', *ċēace* 'jaw', *ġēar* 'year', *ġēafon* 'they gave'.

The interpretation of these spellings as representing diphthongs was challenged (along with the whole diphthongization hypothesis for breaking and velar umlaut) by Stockwell and Barritt (1951: 14). While we do not accept (as should be clear from ch. III) their detailed proposals, we do accept their basic claim that the relation *æ*/*ea* is predictable (in their terms that *ea* represents an 'allophone' of /æ/). In this light we consider their claims about palatal diphthongization.

They first state that the 'results of the phenomenon called diphthonging after a preceding palatal...cannot be considered analogous to' the results of the processes occurring in the breaking and velar umlaut environments (1951: 14). They go on to defend this statement first (and we think most importantly) on the grounds of phonetic plausibility: 'There is no phonetic basis for assuming that *æ* and *ea* were here [after palatals: RL/JMA] different allophonically (and certainly they were not different phonemically).'

[279]

They then suggest that the occurrence of the *ea* forms can be explained on purely graphic grounds, as follows. First, they assume that both *æ* and *ea* are acceptable writings for (at least some) realizations of some /a/. Then they add to this the well-known fact that there are many cases in which an *e* after a *c* or *g* or *sc* stands unambiguously for palatality (which even those who believe in palatal diphthongization accept): e.g. *fisceas* 'fish', *heriġean* 'praise'. Then they make a statement which, though perhaps rather controversial in 1951, is now much less so, owing to the work of McIntosh (1956, 1963) and Samuels (1963): that 'purely graphic characteristics can be as much dialectal as can phonemic characteristics'. And further that:

> '...The WS scribes had a tradition in which *e* was written to indicate that a preceding *c*, *g*, or *sc* was palatal. Ideally, they should have written something like *geæt* or *geaet* for *geat*, but they did not for two good reasons: graphic triphthongs were not permitted except very early in the OE scribal tradition and they already had a perfectly satisfactory way of spelling the phoneme /a/ which included an *e* in the right position, namely *ea*.' (1951: 16)

Their treatment of *ie* < *e* after a palatal is not quite so clear. They seem to claim that there are two kinds of entities represented by this spelling. In the case of forms like *ġiest* 'guest' < **gasti* they see the *i* apparently as a palatal marker, with a preceding development **gasti* > **gæsti* > **gesti* by AFB and *i*-umlaut (1951: 23–24). That is, *ie* was simply a spelling for all *e* after palatals, whatever their historical origins (cf. *scieran* < **skeran*): that is, even when there was no umlaut involved. So that forms like *ġiest* do not show, as tradition would have it, the *i*-umlaut of *ea* which is *ie*, but rather the *i*-umlaut of *æ* which is *e*, plus a spelling modification whereby [e] is spelt *ie* after palatals.

The second type of *ie* is a spelling for a 'back allophone' of /i/, resulting from a secondary umlaut of *ea* (1951: 21). We will not concern ourselves with this any further here. The essential point is that Stockwell and Barritt see all the instances of 'diphthongization by initial palatals' as essentially non-phonetic, that is, as governed by 'graphotactic' constraints. The crux seems to be that certain sequences of letters are not permissible.

We might sum up the graphic permissibility problem by saying that we can account for the *ea*, *ie* forms as follows:

(III.2)   (a) $\begin{Bmatrix} g \\ c \\ sc \end{Bmatrix}$ *ea:* because $\begin{Bmatrix} g \\ c \\ sc \end{Bmatrix}$ *eæ*, $\begin{Bmatrix} g \\ c \\ sc \end{Bmatrix}$ *eae* are not permitted

and *e* must follow $\begin{Bmatrix} g \\ c \\ sc \end{Bmatrix}$ if they represent palatals.

(b) $\left\{\begin{matrix} g \\ c \\ sc \end{matrix}\right\}$ *ie*: because $\left\{\begin{matrix} g \\ c \\ sc \end{matrix}\right\}$ *ee* are not permitted, and *e* must

follow $\left\{\begin{matrix} g \\ c \\ sc \end{matrix}\right\}$ if they represent palatals.

Under this interpretation there was no 'diphthongization' as a sound-change at all, but only a graphic modification. (The spellings of [ju] as *geo-* are similar in origin: in the West Saxon tradition *geu-* was not allowed, so all [u] after [j] were written with *o*.)

Stockwell and Barritt's denial that palatal diphthongization was a sound-change was challenged during the long controversy over the OE digraphs (cf. ch. III), but the only objection of any substance at all seems to have been the one brought up by Kuhn and Quirk (1953), concerning the WS form *ċȳse* 'cheese'. Stockwell and Barritt had claimed that palatal diphthongization could safely be assumed to be a graphic development *following* umlaut, not a phonological change preceding it. But Kuhn and Quirk claimed that Stockwell and Barritt had ignored

> '...the well-known test word for the relative dating of palatal diph-thongization and *i*-umlaut. Latin *cāseus* was borrowed early by the English and underwent both changes, resulting in a late WS *ċȳse*. The development here must have been *ā* > *ǣ* (fronting) > *ēa* (pal. diph.) > *īe* (*i*-umlaut) > *ȳ* (late WS). If *i*-umlaut had preceded palatal diphthongization...the development would have been *ā* > *ǣ* (fronting) > *ǣ* (*i*-umlaut had no effect upon *ǣ*) > *ēa* (pal. diph.), resulting in a form *cēase.' (1953: 146–7)

Stockwell and Barritt in their answer (1955) claim, we think rightly, that since *ċȳse* is a unique item, it does not have sufficient status to prove either (a) that there was a certain ordering relation between two sound changes, or (b) that palatal diphthongization was a sound change at all. As they say (1955: 382–3):

> 'If *ċȳse* is a test case, it is a curiously circular one, since no matter how often it appears in the MSS, it is an isolated item which has no etymological parallels throughout every stage of its reconstruction. Unique etymologies are not ordinarily used to establish sound laws if the sound laws thus established contradict laws which are needed to describe a set of nonunique items. There is no question but that *ċȳse* is a bona fide WS form. The question is whether items like *giest*, *cietes*, *cietel*, and *scieppan*, which in the traditional frame have been explained by placing *i*-umlaut EITHER before or after diphthonging by the initial palatal...do not outweigh the evidence of *ċȳse* in a frame where *i*-umlaut must be stated to precede

diphthonging...leaving *cȳse* without parallels. Our position is that by describing certain phonological patterns more rigidly we necessarily find that a few items traditionally easy to explain become difficult, but that such difficulties are justified by the precision with which the phonological structure can be described and related to its living derivative.'

They point out further that the problem with *cȳse* is that the only attested forms are L. *cāseus* and the various OE forms, and that there is a good deal of evidence for divergent developments from a single ancestor, some of which have no distinct etymological parallels. They cite as one example the various shapes of *room* in American English (in their notation: /rúm/, /rúwm/, /rówm/): these presumably have the same Middle English ancestor, but divergent developments; and the third is probably without parallel (1955: 383). There are, that is, clearly such things as exceptional items in languages, and it is fallacious to assume that every word has an 'etymology' in the usual sense of that term. It is even more fallacious to set up a chronology – or in fact to set up a phonological process – which is actually needed for one item only, and then to extrapolate this to the entire history of the language.

As far as we can see, *cȳse* is simply an exception to the expected historical development of L. *ā* under *i*-umlaut in English, and either develops from an unattested Latin form, or is subject to some minor rule, operative only in this form.[1] It seems proper to treat it as an exceptional item rather than as a 'test word'. (It is of some interest perhaps in this connexion that the Modern English word *cheese* is exactly what one would expect from an OE form with the underlying representation /kaasi-/.) Without the supposed history of *cȳse*, palatal diphthongization does not seem to be necessary as part of the (diachronic or synchronic) phonology of OE, and the lack of compelling phonetic motivation makes it even less necessary. It seems to us that the purely graphotactic explanation proposed by Stockwell and Barritt can be accepted as the correct one.

---

[1] Within the synchronic phonology, it may have been reinterpreted as having underlying /-au-/, which would yield the appropriate surface form as follows: /au/ → [æu] (AFB) → [iu] (*i*-umlaut) (→ [yy] eventually, by roundness attraction and monophthongization (ch. III, §8)).

Appendix IV

Some reflexions on the theory of markedness

1 Marking theory and historical 'prediction'

At various points in this study we have referred to the possibility of employing the Chomsky-Halle theory of markedness, for one purpose or another. In chapter II we suggested that it would – assuming the values assigned by the marking conventions to be the correct ones – be possible to state the nasal influence convention (2.16) in those terms. And in chapter IV we considered the possible effects that a marking convention for vowel-roundness would have on our statement of the umlaut rule. In both these cases, and in some others, we have considered markedness theory as an alternative – and rejected it. And in fact we rejected it in some cases even at the expense of clumsier, more complex, or vaguer formulations. This appendix will we hope clarify some of our reasons for doing so.

It is certainly not true at present that marking theory (despite the inflated claims in Postal 1968: ch. 8, and the more temperate ones in *SPE*) is an integral part of 'standard' phonological theory; but since the appearance of a formal statement of the theory, enough has been written to make us comment on why we should, by and large, choose to ignore it. In Lass (1972) detailed arguments are brought to bear against markedness, mainly on historical grounds; but in this appendix (which largely follows that exposition) we can do no more than point out some of the primary failures which make it impossible for us to accept it – at least in anything like its present form.

In this section we will consider certain facts bearing on the choice of 'marked' and 'unmarked' values for features, and look in detail at one of Chomsky and Halle's marking conventions, especially with regard to its implications for the history of English. In the second section we will consider some of the general properties of the theory, and attempt to show that the 'predictive' difficulties brought up in the first section are due largely to logical faults in the theory itself: that it is ad hoc and circular, and because of this, and a serious methodological error, it fails in its primary aim, which is to describe the 'intrinsic content' of phonological features.

In its current formulation, marking theory embodies a set of proposals

concerning 'marked' and 'unmarked' values for features in lexical representations, and a projective device (the 'linking' principle) which ties marking
conventions to the outputs of phonological rules; in other words, which
makes it clear that the principles behind the theory may be considered to
operate at all levels of a grammar. If a value 'u' attaches to some specification
[αF] for some feature 'F', and the value 'm' to some specification [βF]
(where 'α' and 'β' are variables over the values '+' and '−', and 'α' $\neq$ 'β'),
then a lexical representation containing [αF] is 'cost-free' with respect to that
feature, while a 'cost' attaches to [βF]. An inventory approaches 'optimal-
ness' insofar as the number of [m F] specifications for any features approaches
zero, and becomes 'more complex' or 'less optimal' in proportion to the
number of [m F] entries it contains. Marking theory is thus a cost-assigning
algorithm, which (putatively) defines 'highly valued' as against 'less highly
valued' configurations. We will explore this in more detail in §2.

The decision as to what values for what features are 'marked' or 'unmarked'
is supposed to reflect, in some way, the 'intrinsic content' of those features,
in other words to explain why certain configurations are more 'natural' than
others. There is then some property of any conjunction of feature specifications that makes it either 'simple' or 'complex'. For instance, let us take
roundness as a feature on vowels. *SPE* (405, XI) gives the following marking
convention:

(IV.1)

$$[u \text{ round}] \rightarrow \left\{ \begin{array}{l} [\alpha\text{round}] \ / \ \begin{bmatrix} \underline{\hspace{1em}} \\ \alpha\text{back} \\ -\text{low} \end{bmatrix} \\ [-\text{round}] \ / \ \begin{bmatrix} \underline{\hspace{1em}} \\ +\text{low} \end{bmatrix} \end{array} \right\}$$

Thus a vowel like [i] is 'simple' as compared with [y] or [ɯ], and so on.
Decisions of this type are justified mainly, as far as we can tell, on the grounds
of frequency of appearance in natural languages (a fact whose implications we
will discuss in §2). Statements detailing this are to be found with special
clarity in Postal (1968: 166), where he says that (to give his example)
glottalized consonants are 'nonnormal' compared to non-glottalized ones,
and therefore 'they are not found in many languages, are a minority in those
where they are found, etc.'. With reference to vowel roundness, it is certainly
true that vowel systems of a type that would be described in terms of (IV.1)
as 'maximally unmarked', e.g. /i u a/ or /i e u o a/, are quite common, whereas
those of the type /i y e u o a/ or /i y e ø u o a/ are less so. Thus, for instance,
among the 170 vowel systems surveyed by Sedlak (1969), only 28 (a little
more than 15%) have front round vowels (there are a number of systems
known to us that Sedlak does not mention, but the type of distribution would
be similar, regardless of details).

Further, there appear to be implicational universals with respect to the relation of 'marked' to 'unmarked' vowels: e.g. no language will have [y] which does not also have [i u], and so on (this is not true, by the way, for many Modern Scots dialects, which have [y] but no [u]: see below). On the basis of such distributions and implicational relations, Chomsky and Halle claim that languages without the 'complex' vowels are 'more optimal' than those with them. But this raises a serious empirical problem: what reality does this evaluative judgement correspond to? If systems are 'complex', then within a theory that takes 'optimization' as a prime, such systems should 'simplify' over time. The convention (IV.1) should predict (a) that front round vowels should not arise as innovations (since this represents an increase in markedness, i.e. a 'complication' of the grammar), and (b) that if they should arise they will be unstable, and tend to disappear over time, especially by merger with similar 'unmarked' vowels (for an explicit claim of this sort, see Postal 1968: 170). These predictions, however, are with respect to English and the other Germanic languages, consistently wrong.

To begin with, vowels of the [y ø] types arose as innovations in (relatively) late Germanic; there is no evidence for them in Gothic, though they appear indicated in the earliest OE texts. And in later times they have been remarkably stable. Of all the Germanic languages, to our knowledge, there is only one – Yiddish – that does not have such vowels in at least some of its dialects. In the history of Icelandic, it can be shown that, in terms of convention (IV.1), about 50% of the major changes in the vowel system from Old Icelandic to modern times are in the 'marked' direction (e.g. /au/ > /øi/, /u/ > /y/) and about 50% in the opposite direction (e.g. /ey/ > /ei/, /y/ > /i/). And the modern language has both types. This 50:50 split is not a very good record for a 'predictive' algorithm; and it is unfortunately rather typical.

Let us however give a rather detailed illustration of the problems with such a marking convention, based on the history of front round vowels in English. We will trace briefly some of the major processes that have led to both the origin and loss of such segments over the span of the history of the language. To begin with, these vowels, as we showed in chapter IV, originated, not only in OE, but in all the Germanic languages, as a result of the *i*-umlaut. The first major transformation involved a change of this type (we will revert here to the practice of marking 'long' vowels with a macron, for expository clarity):

(IV.2)	(a) *Pre-umlaut*				(b) *Post-umlaut*					
	ī	i	u	ū		ī	i	ȳ	y	u	ū
	ē	e	o	ō		ē	e	ø̄	ø	o	ō
	ǣ	æ	a	ā		ǣ	æ			a	ā
		æa	eo				æa	eo	iu		

A phonetic inventory of the type (IV.2b) is characteristic, we may assume, of early West Saxon, just prior to the period in which texts like the *Cura Pastoralis* were set down; and indeed such texts show vestiges of the [ø]-type vowels that were shortly to vanish.

At a slightly later stage, we find that the mid front round vowels disappear phonetically, probably through the operation of the rule we have called nonhigh unrounding (4.17). This rule unrounds all prephonetic [ǒ] in West Saxon, thus effecting, from the surface-phonetic point of view, the merger:

(IV.3)

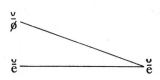

This unrounding does not affect [ỹ]; so we are left with a phonetic system containing one front round vowel-type, not two. But at a somewhat later stage, in the period usually known as 'late West Saxon', there was extensive monophthongization of the diphthong [iu] (graphic *ie*): as we showed in chapter IV, this tended to go to [ī] before palatals and to [ỹ] before nonpalatals. Thus while the [ø]-type vowels disappeared, the number of forms containing [y]-type vowels increased, so that the total functional load of the 'complex' [ỹ] was greater than before, and certainly greater relative to the 'simple' [ū]. And the rule itself, of course, involves a feature-specification that must override the convention (IV.1), since it produces a marked vowel.

In late OE or early Middle English (certainly by c. 1100–50), we find that in the West Saxon-derived dialects the *eo* diphthongs have monophthongized, with regressive assimilation, to [ø]-type vowels (cf. ch. III). This gives us the following sequence:

(IV.4)

	Period	Front round vowels	
(a)	Pre-OE	none	
(b)	Early WS	ỹ, ǒ	(*i*-umlaut)
(c)	Later WS	ỹ	(nonhigh unrounding)
(d)	Late WS	ỹ	(incl. earlier *iu*)
(e)	Early ME	ỹ, ǒ	(from *eo*)

In terms of directionality with respect to markedness, (a) to (b) represents an increase in markedness, (b) to (c) a decrease, (c) to (d) an increase, and (d) to (e) another increase. The sequence (IV.4) represents the addition of four rules to OE, three of which involve the generation of 'marked' vowels. And in particular, the merger of [ěʼ] and [ǒ] effected by (c) is undone by (e).

In later periods (probably late 14th or early 15th century), the West Saxon-derived dialects lost both sets of front round vowels by merger, but not before their ranks had as it were been swelled by the addition of new forms from French containing both short and long vowels of these types; so there was a period before the final loss when the functional load on these vowels was even higher than it had ever been in OE. In a sense then, we might say that convention (IV.1) has predicted the ultimate loss of front round vowels in certain dialects of English; but it has counterpredicted their development in the first place, the retention of the high one into Middle English, and the development of new high ones, and new mid ones to 'replace' the earlier ones. An 'explanatory' theory that can account for two stages in the development of a language, but none of the intervening ones, does not seem to explain very much. And as we will see there are cases in Modern English where the record is not even this good; for only certain dialects have no front round vowels even now.

Let us turn now to some developments in those dialects descending not from West Saxon but from Old Northumbrian; particularly the Middle English dialects of Scotland and the North of England, and some modern dialects of the Scottish Borders and Lowlands.

In Old Northumbrian, unlike West Saxon, both sets of front round vowels – high and mid – remain until quite late in OE (cf. Campbell 1959: §§6, 196, 198). But instead of the asymmetrical persistence of [ỹ] and loss of [ő] that characterized the later stages of West Saxon, we find a symmetrical loss, through merger, of both sets:

(IV.5)

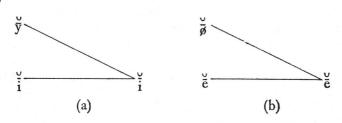

(a)   (b)

This is as expected, a change from marked to unmarked, in fact an 'optimization' of the system. But now observe what happens. First, in the 14th century, the northern dialects underwent a change whereby for the most part all long [ō] are fronted and raised to [ỹ] (by way of [ø̄]: cf. Jordan 1934: §54). This means that the change (IV.5) above is brought about by a rule that effects a reduction in the overall markedness of the system, but the new change by one that increases it. We now have a change from a long vowel system of the type (IV.6a) below to one of the type (IV.6b):

(IV.6)

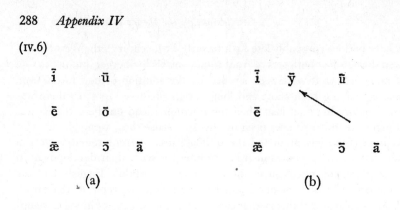

(a)   (b)

(All [ō] do not vanish; there are sporadic persistences, especially before labial continuants and [s]: for distributions see the data under ME *ō*[1] in Kolb 1966, and Orton and Halliday 1962, especially the responses to Questionnaire items v.2.4 *roof*, III.2.8 *hoof*, IV.6.15 *goose*, vs. v.5.6 *tooth*, VII.6.3 *moon*.)

Dialects that underwent the change from (IV.6a) to (IV.6b) have thus in effect undone half the merger (IV.5b); they have added a new 'marked' vowel, one that they had earlier lost. And most interesting, they have drastically reduced (in some cases even to zero) the functional load on the unmarked [ō]. (For the representation of the Middle English vowels see *SPE* 52, and Lass 1969b.)

The intersection of markedness and functional load becomes even more suggestive in a certain subset of these dialects, for the following reason: in general, those dialects in which ME [ō] was lost by the fronting (IV.6b), show an 'incomplete' realization of the Great Vowel-Shift. In particular, they tend to have high back monophthongs of the [ū] type as the reflex of ME [ū] in *house*, etc., rather than the [au]-type diphthong found in most other dialects (for details see Lass 1969b, Carter 1967). But at a period after the vowel-shift, when the reflexes of ME [ō] were generally distinguished as [ȳ] in distinction to the [ū] reflexes of ME [ū], some of these dialects, especially in southern Scotland, show a new development: another fronting, this time of [ū], so that all [ȳ] < [ō] merge with the new [ȳ] < [ū]. (The date of this shift is uncertain, but there seems to be a description of this pronunciation in Hart 1569: 32v.) These dialects have then greatly increased the functional load on [ȳ], by drawing into its orbit nearly all the representatives of two major etymological categories. This may be summed up by saying that in such dialects *loose* < ME *lōs* and *louse* from ME *lūs* are homophones. So in the history of these dialects (which are fairly characteristic of types we have observed in the Lothians, Fife, and the Borders) we have, from late OE on, the developments of (IV.7) below. (The symbol [y] for modern dialects covers a phonetic range from a rather advanced [ʉ] to phones of the type [y].) The macron indicates etymological length, as

(IV.7)

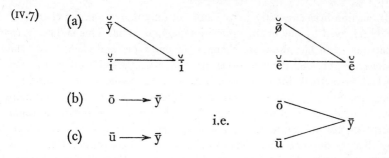

i.e.

synchronic length has been lost in Scots. For details of these developments see Lass (1973c).

Now let us proceed from bad to worse. Consider the developments of the vowel systems of certain northern English dialects, mainly in Northumberland and Durham, as exemplified by the Survey of English Dialects areas 1.1 (Lowick, Nb.) and 3.2 (Wearhead, Du.). These dialects generally show the reflexes of the (IV.6a)–(IV.6b) transition; a front nucleus for ME [ō], and a non-shifted ME [ū]. But there are two other developments: first [ȳ] < [ō] has been unrounded, usually giving a diphthong of the type [ɪə]; and long [ɔ̄] and short [o] have become front round vowels, of the type [ø œ] (cf. Orton and Halliday 1962, s.v. VII.6.3 *moon*, III.8.8 *hog*, VIII.8.1 *bogey*). The sequence of changes here, then starting from the OE mergers (IV.5), is as follows: first development of [ȳ] < [ō], then unrounding of [ȳ], then fronting of [ɔ̄] and [o], so that we are left with only scattered (lexically specified) instances of mid back round vowels, and a high functional load on the mid front round ones. And the final system, which has mid front round vowels but no high ones, is of an exceedingly rare (and therefore 'marked') type: of the 170 systems surveyed by Sedlak (1969), only 3 show this type of distribution; Sedlak did not consider the English type, so this now makes 4 out of 171.

If we look back at the sequence involved in these northern changes, in terms of directionality, we find the following:

(IV.8)   *Change*   *Direction*

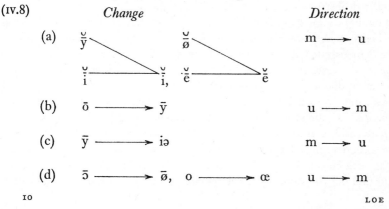

The proportion here is exactly 50:50; and not only that, we find a change o one type followed by one of the opposite type, and so on. This is, however, ʳ peculiar only if in fact these are changes 'of one type' and changes of 'the opposite type', i.e. that the categories 'marked to unmarked' and 'unmarked to marked' are actually involved here. Otherwise, the sequence is unrounding, fronting, unrounding, fronting; and surely rules of these types are common enough throughout the history of the language that neither should occasion any surprise; nor for that matter should a sequence of one and then the other.

The changes discussed here seem to show that the convention (IV.I) is of no explanatory value in discussing the history of the English vowel system; that in fact an assumption of unroundness of front vowels as 'normal' does not hold for English at any period, except for certain dialects. And when taken in connexion with the overwhelming preponderance within Germanic of languages with vowels of this type, such a convention makes the assertion that Germanic is a 'nonoptimal' or 'costly' family, with respect to its vowel system. And if there are less than optimal families, the notion seems to have no empirical content whatever. We will discuss this further, in connexion with the theoretical basis of markedness theory, in the following section.

2   Further empirical problems: the statistical fallacy

The discussion in §1 has demonstrated clearly, we think, that if a marking convention like (IV.I) is used to 'evaluate' grammars of English at various historical periods, the judgements of 'value' that it imposes do not correlate with any empirical properties. In particular, the assignment of 'cost' is vacuous, because the more 'costly' grammars do not in general behave particularly as if they are 'less optimal' than the others. In fact the pattern of fluctuation between loss and origin of front round vowels, and stages with and stages without them, suggests that no particular value – either positive or negative – attaches to them. They are simply a fact about English, the way glottalized obstruents are a fact about Korean.

It might be argued at this point that actually we have – so far – said nothing that bears on the empirical validity of marking theory, but that we have at most demonstrated that one particular convention is incorrect. This is not however the case: given the assumptions on which marking theory is based, there is no doubt that the convention (IV.I) is correct. It is in fact the only possible one; vowels like [y ø] are (to use Postal's phrase) 'not found in many languages'. In the survey of Sedlak (1969) that we referred to earlier, 85% of an extensive and well-distributed sample did not have them. So front round vowels, under any interpretation of the term, are 'marked'. The only thing wrong with convention (IV.I) is that it does not say anything more than one could find out by counting vowel systems in Sedlak's list, or any other such survey. (It is of interest, however, that among the 15% or so vowel systems that show front round segments, the majority belong to two families: Ural-Altaic and Indo-European, particularly Germanic. In a sense the absence of such vowels is 'marked' for these families.)

The crucial problem, overall, seems to be that while the theory purports to represent 'intrinsic content', it is actually no more than a body of statistical generalizations based on likelihood of occurrence given our prior experience of natural languages. It is quite clear, from the available literature, that the basis of marking theory is a logical progression something like this:

(a) Some configurations, segment-types, etc. are relatively common, and others not so.

(b) Therefore 'common' or 'usual' = 'unmarked', and (relatively) 'uncommon' = 'marked'.

(c) Since what is commonest must be clearly 'most natural', 'unmarked' = 'natural', and 'marked' = (relatively) 'unnatural'.

(d) Since something is common and 'natural' only if it is (relatively) 'simple' (cognitively? physically?), then, given the underlying assumption that speakers 'optimize', and that 'optimality' = 'simplicity' (shades of Zipf!), it follows that 'natural' = 'simple', because things would not be common and 'natural' if they were not also 'simple'.

Thus what started out as a statement of a rather simple descriptive sort, based on statistical frequency, is elevated into a 'naturalness'-metric, and therefore also, in terms of the theory's presuppositions, into a 'simplicity'-metric as well. The basic properties are set up on a statistical basis, and then extrapolated to whatever realm these quantities are ultimately to be measured in.

This seems to make explicit the essentially circular and ad hoc nature of the theory; as well as falsifying the claim that markedness represents anything 'intrinsic' other than statistical distribution. If some value [βF] is 'marked' because that configuration is rare, then what is 'intrinsic' is the marking 'm', as a property of a matrix containing [βF] instead of [αF]. There is no 'explanation' of anything here, only the assertion that on (ultimately) statistical grounds the interpretation [u F] → [αF], or conversely, that [m F] → [βF], is true. 'Intrinsic content' thus reduces to the assertion that an 'm' or a 'u' appears in the matrix; and this is just about as 'intrinsic' as an exception-feature or any other diacritic of this essentially post facto sort. If it can be shown that the 'm' and 'u' markings really equate with anything other than statistical distribution, then the theory might be of interest; but at present it seems to be merely an instance of the 'naming fallacy'.

Stated in this way, the premises seem to be indefensible. In what way are glottalized obstruents (which Postal, on statistical grounds, says are 'nonnormal') in fact 'nonnormal' in Korean? Or to take some other cases, clicks in Hottentot, voiceless laterals in Welsh and Nahuatl, laryngealized voicing in Danish or Panjabi? Surely these things are relatively uncommon, given the whole universe of discourse; but by the same token so are Koreans and Nahuatls.

Clearly the assertion of 'naturalness' as a function of distribution is a mis-interpretation of the nature of statistical frequencies: by analogy, we might assert that since marsupials are relatively rarer than placental mammals, it is 'unnatural' (and 'complex') to be a marsupial; and the prediction would be that marsupials would be on their way out vis-à-vis placentals. Which might be the case in Australia, due to human intervention, but is not in the U.S., where the opossum has increased its range from Virginia to Canada in less than a century. The real point is that it is obviously perfectly 'natural' for marsupials to be marsupials, because they are that kind of beast; and similarly it is natural for Korean to have glottalized obstruents and Germanic languages to have front round vowels, and so on. What is not 'natural' should – if the theory is to have any content – have restrictions on its viability; and the various segment-types that are singled out as 'marked' in the current theory show as far as we are aware no particular signs of such reduced viability in a large enough number of cases for it to be meaningful. It is a fact that some things are less common than others; it is an assertion (and probably not a testable one) that this is due to 'intrinsic' properties; and it is even more of an assertion that these properties correlate with some kind of quantifiable 'cost'.

The final difficulty we wish to explore is the nature of the principle of 'evaluation' which is the ultimate goal of marking theory; and our main contention is that the notion of 'value', as presently conceived, is essentially pseudomathematical. Markedness theory – like other aspects of generative metatheory which are concerned with 'evaluation', asserts the principle that it is possible to quantify various properties of language; but it is by no means at all clear – given our present knowledge of languages – that such quantification is even possible in principle. For instance, Chomsky and Halle say (*SPE*: 334) that 'the "value" of a sequence of rules is the reciprocal of the number of symbols in its minimal representation.' This is highly explicit, and within any one grammar, arithmetically definable: that is the 'value' is a real one, an integer arrived at by a formulable operation. But it has yet to be shown that such a numerical value has any precise arithmetical connexion with any fact in a natural language; and as long as this cannot be shown, as long as there are no principles which enable us to frame an experiment that might test such an assertion, the value '$1/n$' for a rule sequence whose minimal representation has n symbols is vacuous. And this is an important issue, because such state-ments as the one quoted above lend to statements in linguistics a spurious glamour, imitative of the properties of analogous statements in the physical sciences.

We are, it seems to us, so far at this point from a psychological (or any other empirical) definition of 'value' that any such quantification is both arbitrary and circular. Since 'value' can only be defined in terms of a formula that tells us what 'value' is, it has no concrete correlates outside the defining formula. In this sense 'value' of a rule-sequence, the 'cost' of a feature specification, are vacuous notions, except within the model. They cannot be related to any empirical properties of natural language – in the precise sense in which they are formulated. The same thing is true of quantitative definitions in terms of markedness. If, as Chomsky and Halle propose, the 'complexity of a system is equal to the sum of the marked features of its members' (1968: 409), then, according to their marking conventions, a system /i e u o a/ has 'a complexity of six', while one of /i e u o æ/ has a 'complexity of eight'. But how does one tell? What do languages which are two degrees more complex than others do? And so on. To be fair, in this case Chomsky and Halle do not claim that the values they give are 'the real' ones; but they do set up an apparently quantifiable set of properties, which turn out on examination not to be quantifiable at all in any empirical sense.

And in fact there does not seem to be any particular reason why they should be. There is after all no very compelling evidence (other than perhaps a desire that it should be so) for us to believe that the internal structure of a grammar is 'lawful' in precisely the same sense as the internal structure of an enclosed volume of gas. And to look for 'laws' in linguistics of the same *form* as Boyle's Law is probably a mistaken endeavour. At least the idea that we should find 'constants' in language like the speed of light does not show signs of being very fruitful, as the example of lexicostatistics might have taught us.

This is not intended to be a denial of the 'scientific' nature of linguistics, nor even of the possibility of correct formal grammars (and therefore of evaluation-procedures that define 'correctness'). But it is important to distinguish between pseudoarithmetical (or better perhaps metaphorically mathematical) metrics of value and other formal criteria for explanatory theories. Numerical measures are not of the same status as evaluations based for instance on the weak or strong generative capacity of grammars. We can test whether a given grammar generates a well-formed string with a correct structural description, at least up to a point; but we cannot test 'value' or 'optimality' against anything external, since for all we know such things may be only properties of our models, not of the empirical universe our models purport to represent.

Of course this pessimism may not be justified; the mathematical or arithmetical properties of our models may represent something external to them. It is logically possible – and probably even likely – that 'optimization' of various kinds is possible, that there are relatively 'costly' and 'noncostly' grammars; but such properties seem to be of a very different type from the numerical ones that the present theory supposes to exist. (We are thinking here of entailment relations between segment types in a system, considerations of symmetry, and so on.) It is important, however, that we avoid confusing procedural imperatives and formal desiderata with empirical facts; and that we recognize the absence of facts in those cases where they are lacking.

We have not in fact achieved this goal in this book; since we have been operating largely within the 'standard' paradigm of generative phonology, with all its assumptions and theoretical machinery. And in fact it does seem to us that by and large this is a fruitful paradigm, and that most of its assumptions are not fundamentally mistaken. But markedness is surely not, as yet anyhow, a part of this paradigm, in any firm sense; and from the evidence available we see no particular reason why it should be.

Appendix V
The rules

A Readjustment rules

1. *Glide-shift* (app. *1.8*)

$$
\text{SD:} \quad
\begin{bmatrix} +\text{obs} \\ -\text{cons} \end{bmatrix}
\begin{bmatrix} -\text{obs} \\ -\text{cons} \\ [\text{PRET}] \end{bmatrix}
\quad \text{S} \quad \text{C}
$$

$$
\phantom{\text{SD:}} \qquad 1 \qquad\qquad 2 \qquad\quad 3 \quad 4
$$

$$
\text{SC:} \quad
\begin{bmatrix} -\text{low} \\ -\text{back} \end{bmatrix}
\begin{bmatrix} [-(1.16\text{b})] \\ [-(1.19\text{b})] \\ [-(1.28)] \end{bmatrix}
$$

$$
\phantom{\text{SC:}} \qquad 1 \qquad\qquad 2 \qquad\quad 3 \quad 4
$$

2. *AFB exception* (*classes VI, VII*)

$$
\text{V} \rightarrow [-(2.11)] \,/\, \begin{bmatrix} +\text{obs} \\ -\text{cons} \end{bmatrix} \underline{}
$$

B Redundancy rules ('everywhere' rules)

(These are not necessarily morpheme-structure conditions, but rules which apply at no particular (delimited) point in the sequence of P-rules proper.)

1. *Syllabicity assignment* (*Preliminaries 13*)

    A. $[+\text{obs}] \rightarrow [-\text{syll}]$

    B. $[-\text{obs}] \rightarrow \begin{cases} [+\text{syll}]/[+\text{cons}] \underline{} [+\text{cons}] \\ [-\text{syll}] \end{cases}$

    C. $[-\text{cons}] \rightarrow \begin{cases} [-\text{syll}]/[-\text{cons}] \underline{} \\ [+\text{syll}] \end{cases}$

2. *Lowness assignment* (*for derived geminates*) (*1.28*)

$$
\text{SD:} \quad
\begin{bmatrix} \text{V} \\ -\text{high} \\ \alpha\text{back} \end{bmatrix}
\begin{bmatrix} \text{V} \\ -\text{high} \\ \alpha\text{back} \end{bmatrix}
\quad \text{SC:} \quad
\begin{bmatrix} -\alpha\text{low} \\ \alpha\text{back} \end{bmatrix}
\begin{bmatrix} -\alpha\text{low} \\ \alpha\text{back} \end{bmatrix}
$$

$$
\phantom{\text{SD:}} \qquad 1 \qquad\quad 2 \qquad\qquad\quad 1 \qquad\quad 2
$$

3. *Trimoric nucleus simplification (3.22)*

$$V_1 \rightarrow \emptyset \;/\; V_2 \underline{\qquad} \;//\; V_3$$

Condition: If $V_1 < V_3$ then $\begin{bmatrix} V_1 \\ -\text{back} \end{bmatrix}\begin{bmatrix} V_3 \\ +\text{back} \end{bmatrix}$ (where '$<$' is to be read as 'immediately precedes').

Note: This embodies the modification of (3.22) suggested in appendix I, p. 253 n.

4. *Backness accommodation (4.27)*

$$\begin{bmatrix} +\text{obs} \\ -\text{back} \\ \langle\,-\text{voice}\,\rangle \end{bmatrix} \rightarrow [-\text{back}] \;/\; \left\{ \begin{array}{ll} \underline{\qquad} \left[\begin{array}{l} -\text{back} \\ \left(\begin{array}{l}[-\text{cons}] \\ \left[\begin{array}{l}+\text{cons} \\ +\text{high}\end{array}\right]\end{array}\right) \end{array}\right] & a \\[2em] \begin{bmatrix} -\text{cons} \\ -\text{back} \\ \langle\,+\text{high}\,\rangle \end{bmatrix} \underline{\qquad} \cdot \langle\,X\,\rangle & b \end{array} \right.$$

$$\textit{Condition: } X \neq \begin{bmatrix} -\text{cons} \\ +\text{back} \end{bmatrix}$$

C Major (non-cyclic) phonological rules

1. *Qualitative ablaut (1.19)*

$$\begin{bmatrix} +\text{syll} \\ [\text{SV}] \end{bmatrix} \rightarrow \begin{bmatrix} \begin{bmatrix} -\text{back} \\ -\text{low} \end{bmatrix} \\[1em] [+\text{low}] \;/\; \left[\overline{\text{[PP]}}\right] (S)\, C\, \# \end{bmatrix} \begin{array}{l} \text{(a)} \\[1.5em] \text{(b)} \end{array}$$

2. *Glide vocalization (1.23)*

$$\begin{bmatrix} +\text{obs} \\ -\text{cons} \\ \alpha\text{low} \end{bmatrix} \rightarrow [-\text{obs}] \;/\; \underline{\qquad} \begin{bmatrix} V \\ \alpha\text{low} \end{bmatrix}$$

Note: This is the version proposed in appendix 1.6.

3. *Vowel-glide assimilation (1.24)*

$$V \rightarrow [+\text{low}] \;/\; \begin{bmatrix} +\text{obs} \\ -\text{cons} \end{bmatrix} \underline{\qquad}$$

4. *Pre-Germanic accentuation (1.17)*

$$\begin{bmatrix} V \\ -\text{low} \\ [\text{PP}] \end{bmatrix} \rightarrow \left\{ \begin{array}{ll} [-\text{acc}] & \text{(a)} \\[1em] [+\text{acc}] \;/\; \underline{\qquad} C\,V\,(C)\,\# & \text{(b)} \end{array} \right.$$

Note: [−low] on the left-hand side was not included in (1.17): see the discussion following (1.19).

5. *Quantitative ablaut (1.16 and 1.27)*

      (a) SD: [+acc]   SC: $1 \rightarrow 1\ 1$

$$\text{(b)}\quad \begin{bmatrix} V \\ -\text{acc} \end{bmatrix} \rightarrow \left\{ \begin{matrix} [\alpha\text{back}] \ / \ \underline{\hspace{1cm}} \begin{bmatrix} C \\ -\alpha\text{obs} \end{bmatrix} \\ \varnothing \ / \ \underline{\hspace{1cm}} \ V \end{matrix} \right\}$$

6. *Glide deletion (1.25)*

$$\begin{bmatrix} +\text{obs} \\ -\text{cons} \end{bmatrix} \rightarrow \varnothing$$

7. *Strong verb highness assignment (1.10)*

$$\begin{bmatrix} V \\ +\text{syll} \\ \alpha\text{back} \\ -\text{low} \\ [\text{SV}] \end{bmatrix} \rightarrow [\alpha\text{high}]$$

8. *Nasal influence convention (a) (2.15)*

$$\begin{bmatrix} V \\ \langle\alpha[\text{artic}]\rangle \end{bmatrix} \rightarrow [u\ \text{high}] / \begin{bmatrix} \underline{\hspace{1cm}} \\ -\text{low} \end{bmatrix} \ / \ \underline{\hspace{1cm}} \ \left\langle \begin{bmatrix} V \\ \alpha[\text{artic}] \end{bmatrix} \right\rangle [+\text{nas}]$$

9. *Highness harmonization (1.11)*

$$\begin{bmatrix} V \\ \alpha\text{back} \\ -\text{low} \end{bmatrix} \rightarrow [-\alpha\ \text{high}] / \underline{\hspace{1cm}} S_0^3 \begin{bmatrix} V \\ -\alpha\text{high} \end{bmatrix}$$

Note: In (1.11), the rule was not restricted to strong verbs: but see ch. III, §7.

10. *Anglo-Frisian brightening (2.11)*

$$\begin{bmatrix} V \\ +\text{low} \end{bmatrix} \rightarrow [-\text{back}]$$

11. *Nasal influence condition b (2.15)*

$$\begin{bmatrix} V \\ \langle\alpha[\text{artic}]\rangle \end{bmatrix} \rightarrow [u\ \text{back}] / \begin{bmatrix} \underline{\hspace{1cm}} \\ +\text{low} \end{bmatrix} \ / \ \underline{\hspace{1cm}} \ \left\langle \begin{bmatrix} V \\ \alpha[\text{artic}] \end{bmatrix} \right\rangle [+\text{nas}]$$

12. *Nasal vocalization (3.28)*

$$[+\text{nas}] \rightarrow \begin{bmatrix} -\text{nas} \\ -\text{cons} \\ \alpha[\text{artic}] \end{bmatrix} \Big/ \begin{bmatrix} V \\ \alpha[\text{artic}] \end{bmatrix} \underline{\quad\quad} \begin{bmatrix} +\text{obs} \\ +\text{back} \\ +\text{cont} \end{bmatrix}$$

13. *Back umlaut (3.36)*

$$\emptyset \longrightarrow \begin{bmatrix} V \\ +\text{back} \end{bmatrix} \Big/ X \begin{bmatrix} V \\ -\text{back} \\ \langle -\dot{\text{low}} \rangle \\ 1 \quad 1 \end{bmatrix} \underline{\quad\quad} \begin{array}{cc} \langle +\text{cons} \rangle \\ 1 \quad 1 \end{array} \begin{bmatrix} +\text{back} \\ +\text{cont} \\ \left\{ \begin{array}{c} \left\langle \begin{array}{c} -\text{cons} \\ -\text{low} \end{array} \right\rangle \\ 1 \quad 1 \end{array} \right. \\ \left. \begin{array}{c} \langle -\text{obs} \rangle \\ 2 \quad 2 \end{array} \right\} \end{bmatrix} \begin{array}{c} \langle +\text{cons} \rangle \\ 2 \quad 2 \end{array}$$

Note: This incorporates the addition to (3.36) proposed in the immediately following discussion.

$$\text{Condition on} \quad \langle \ldots \rangle$$
$$ \text{I} \quad \text{I}$$

$$\langle +\text{cons} \rangle = \left\{ \begin{array}{c} [-\text{obs}] \\ \begin{bmatrix} +\text{ant} \\ -\text{cor} \end{bmatrix} \end{array} \right\}$$
$$\text{I} \quad\quad \text{I}$$

$$\text{or} \quad X = Y\,[w]$$

14. *Velar devoicing (3.29a)*

$$\begin{bmatrix} +\text{obs} \\ +\text{back} \\ -\text{cont} \end{bmatrix} \rightarrow [-\text{voice}] \Big/ \underline{\quad\quad} \#$$

15. *Velar spirantization (3.29b)*

$$\begin{bmatrix} +\text{obs} \\ +\text{back} \end{bmatrix} \rightarrow [+\text{cont}] \Big/ \begin{bmatrix} V \\ +\text{back} \end{bmatrix} \underline{\quad\quad} \left\{ \begin{array}{c} \begin{bmatrix} +\text{obs} \\ +\text{cor} \end{bmatrix} \\ \# \end{array} \right\}$$

16. *Non-low diphthong collapsing (6.34)*

$$\text{SD:} \begin{bmatrix} V \\ \alpha\text{back} \end{bmatrix} \begin{bmatrix} V \\ -\alpha\text{back} \end{bmatrix} \quad\quad\quad \text{SC: } 1 \; 2 \rightarrow [-\text{high}]$$
$$ \text{I} \quad\quad\quad 2 \text{I} \quad\quad\quad 2$$

17. *Continuant voicing assignment (5.35)*

$$\begin{bmatrix} +\text{obs} \\ +\text{cont} \end{bmatrix} \rightarrow [\alpha\text{voice}] \,/\, [\alpha\text{voice}]$$

Condition: Agreement is to the strongest segment in the environment; and $/\#/ = [+\text{obs}]$.

18. *Intervocalic continuancy adjustment (5.44)*

$$\begin{bmatrix} +\text{obs} \\ -\text{cor} \\ \alpha\text{voice} \end{bmatrix} \rightarrow [\alpha\text{cont}] \,/\, \text{V}\_\_\_\_\_\text{V}$$

19. *Gemination (appendix 11.20)*

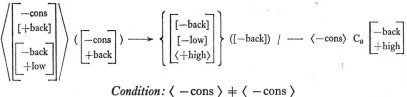

20. *Palatal softening (4.29)*

$$\begin{bmatrix} +\text{obs} \\ \alpha\text{voice} \\ \langle +\text{voice} \rangle \end{bmatrix} \longrightarrow \begin{bmatrix} -\alpha\text{strid} \\ \alpha\text{cont} \\ \left\langle \begin{matrix} -\text{cont} \\ +\text{strid} \end{matrix} \right\rangle \end{bmatrix} \,/\, \begin{bmatrix} \\ -\text{back} \\ +\text{high} \end{bmatrix} \,/\, \langle +\text{cons} \rangle \_\_\_\_\_$$

21. *Stridency assimilation (4.31)*

$$[-\text{cont}] \rightarrow [+\text{strid}] \,/\, \_\_\_\_\_ \, [+\text{strid}]$$

22. *I-umlaut (4.15)*

$$\left\langle \begin{bmatrix} -\text{cons} \\ [+\text{back}] \\ -\text{back} \\ +\text{low} \end{bmatrix} \right\rangle \left(\begin{bmatrix} -\text{cons} \\ +\text{back} \end{bmatrix} \right) \longrightarrow \left\{ \begin{bmatrix} [-\text{back}] \\ [-\text{low}] \\ \langle +\text{high} \rangle \end{bmatrix} \right\} ([-\text{back}]) \,/\, \_\_ \, \langle -\text{cons} \rangle \, C_0 \begin{bmatrix} -\text{back} \\ +\text{high} \end{bmatrix}$$

Condition: $\langle -\text{cons} \rangle \neq \langle -\text{cons} \rangle$

23. *Nonhigh unrounding (4.17)*

$$[-\text{cons}] \rightarrow [-\text{round}] \,/\, \begin{bmatrix} \\ -\text{high} \\ -\text{back} \end{bmatrix}$$

24 *Diphthong height harmony (6.38)*

$$V \rightarrow \begin{bmatrix} \alpha high \\ \beta low \end{bmatrix} \Big/ \begin{bmatrix} V \\ \alpha high \\ \beta low \end{bmatrix} \underline{\quad\quad}$$

25. *Loss of h (3.26)*

$$\begin{bmatrix} +obs \\ +back \\ +cont \end{bmatrix} \rightarrow \varnothing \ / \ [-obs] \underline{\quad\quad} [-obs]$$

26. *Backness switching (1.8)*

$$SD: \begin{bmatrix} V \\ +low \\ \alpha back \end{bmatrix} \begin{bmatrix} V \\ +low \\ \alpha back \end{bmatrix} \qquad SC: 1 \ 2 \rightarrow \underset{1}{[-\alpha back]} \ \underset{2}{[-\alpha back]}$$

$$\qquad\qquad\quad 1 \qquad\quad 2$$

Condition: 1, 2 constitute a lexical two-vowel nucleus.

27. *Retraction of æ before back vowels (2.10)*

$$\begin{bmatrix} V \\ +low \end{bmatrix} \longrightarrow [+back] \ / \ \underline{\quad\quad} \begin{bmatrix} C \\ \langle \alpha[artic] \rangle \end{bmatrix} \Big\langle \begin{bmatrix} C \\ \alpha[artic] \end{bmatrix} \Big\rangle \begin{bmatrix} V \\ +back \end{bmatrix}$$

D Minor rule

1. *Class II monophthongization (1.14)*

$$SD: \begin{bmatrix} V \\ +high \\ -back \end{bmatrix} \begin{bmatrix} V \\ +high \\ +back \end{bmatrix} \qquad SC: 1 \ 2 \rightarrow 2 \ 2$$

$$\qquad\qquad\quad 1 \qquad\quad 2$$

References

Anderson, John M. (1970). '"Ablaut" in the synchronic phonology of the Old English strong verb', *Indogermanische Forschungen* 75. 166–97.

Anderson, John M. and Jones, Charles (1972). 'Three theses concerning phonological representations', *Edinburgh Working Papers in Linguistics* 1. 92–115.

Anderson, Stephen (1968). 'The Faroese vowel system and the Faroese Verschärfung', *Quarterly Progress Report of the Research Laboratory of Electronics* 90. 228–40. Cambridge, Mass: M.I.T.

Bach, Emmon (1968). 'Two proposals concerning the simplicity metric in phonology', *Glossa* 2. 128–49.

and Harms, R. T. eds. (1968). *Universals in linguistic theory.* New York: Holt, Rinehart and Winston.

Bach, Emmon and Harms, R. T. (1969). 'How do languages get crazy rules?' Unpublished MS.

Bailey, Charles-James N. (1969). 'The integration of linguistic theory.' Unpublished MS.

Bennett, W. H. (1955). 'The Southern English development of Germanic initial [f s þ]', *Language* 37. 367–710.

Bird, Charles (1969). 'Initial consonant-change in south-western Mande.' Duplicated. Bloomington: Indiana University Linguistics Club.

Björkhagen, Im. (1948). *Modern Swedish grammar.* Stockholm: Svenska Bokförlaget Norstedts.

Blake, N. F., ed. (1964). *The Phoenix.* Manchester: Manchester U. P.

Braune, Wilhelm, ed. E. A. Ebbinghaus (1966). *Gotische Grammatik*, 17th ed. Tübingen: Niemeyer.

Brown, Gillian (1970). 'Syllables and redundancy rules in generative phonology', *Journal of Linguistics* 6. 1–18.

Brunner, Karl (1965). *Altenglische Grammatik, nach der angelsächische Grammatik von Eduard Sievers*, 3rd ed. Tübingen: Niemeyer.

Burrow, T. and Emeneau, M. (1961). *Dravidian etymological dictionary.* Oxford: Oxford U. P.

Campbell, Alistair (1959). *Old English grammar.* London: Oxford U. P.

Carter, Richard J. (1967). 'Theoretical implications of the Great Vowel Shift.' Unpublished MS.

Chafe, Wallace (1970). 'Review of Postal (1968)', *Language* 46. 116–125.

Chen, Matthew (1972). 'The time dimension: contribution toward a theory of sound change', *Foundations of Language* 8. 457–98.

Chomsky, Noam (1965). *Aspects of the theory of syntax*. Cambridge, Mass.: M.I.T. Press.

 (1967). *Current issues in linguistic theory*. The Hague: Mouton.

Chomsky, Noam and Halle, M. (1968). *The sound pattern of English* (*SPE*). New York: Harper.

Collinder, Björn (1960). *Comparative grammar of the Uralic languages*. Stockholm: Almqvist & Wiksell.

Danielsson, Bror (1963). *John Hart's works on English orthography and pronunciation*, vol. II. Stockholm: Almqvist & Wiksell.

Daunt, Marjorie (1939). 'Old English sound changes reconsidered in relation to scribal tradition and practice', *Transactions of the Philological Society*, 108–37.

Dickins, Bruce and Ross, A. S. C., eds. (1954). *The Dream of the Rood*. London: Methuen.

Dobbie, E. V. K. (1942). *The Anglo-Saxon Minor Poems*. The Anglo-Saxon Poetic Records, VI. New York: Columbia University Press.

Einarsson, Stefán (1945). *Icelandic: Grammar, texts, glossary*, Baltimore: Johns Hopkins Press.

Foley, James (1969). 'Morphophonological investigations, II.' Unpublished MS.

Fromkin, Victoria (1961). 'The non-anomalous nature of anomalous utterances', *Language* 47. 27–52.

Garmonsway, G. N., ed. (1947). *Ælfric's Colloquy*. London: Methuen.

Gimson, A. C. (1965). *An introduction to the pronunciation of English*. London: Edward Arnold.

Gordon, I. L., ed. (1960). *The Seafarer*. London: Methuen.

Hall, Robert, A., Jr (1950). 'The reconstruction of Proto-Romance', *Language* 26. 6–27.

Halle, Morris and Keyser, S. J. (1967). 'Review of Danielsson (1963)', *Language* 43. 773–87.

Harms, Robert T. (1968). *Introduction to phonological theory*. Englewood Cliffs: Prentice-Hall.

 (1973). 'How abstract is Nupe?', *Language* 49. 439–46.

Harris, James W. (1970). 'Paradigmatic regularity and naturalness of grammars.' Unpublished MS.

Hart, John (1569). *An orthographie*. Repr. 1969, as vol. 209 in *English Linguistics 1500–1800*. Menston: The Scolar Press.

Haugen, Einar (1967). 'On the laws of Norwegian tonality', *Language* 43. 185–202.

Hockett, Charles F. (1958). *A course in modern linguistics*. New York: Macmillan.

(1959). 'The stressed syllabics of Old English', *Language* 35. 575–97. Reprinted in Lass (1969a: 108–32).

Holthausen, F. (1963). *Altenglisches etymologisches Wörterbuch*. Heidelberg: Winter.

Howren, Robert (1967). 'The generation of Old English weak verbs', *Language* 43. 674–85.

Hyman, Larry M. (1970). 'How concrete is phonology?', *Language* 46. 58–76.

(1973). 'Nupe three years later', *Language* 49. 447–52.

Jakobson, Roman (1941). *Kindersprache, Aphasie, und allgemeine Lautgesetze*. Uppsala: Almqvist & Wiksell.

Jakobson, Roman, Fant, G. and Halle, M. (1951). *Preliminaries to speech analysis*. Cambridge, Mass.: M.I.T. Press.

Jespersen, Otto (1961). *A modern English grammar on historical principles*. 7 vols. Reprint. London: George Allen & Unwin.

Jones, Charles (1972). *An introduction to Middle English*. New York: Holt, Rinehart & Winston.

Jones, Daniel (1964). *An outline of English phonetics*, 9th ed. Cambridge: Heffer.

Jordan, Richard (1934). *Handbuch der mittelenglischen Grammatik*, 1: *Lautlehre*, rev. W. Mathes. Heidelberg: Winter.

Kenstowicz, Michael J. (1970). 'On the notation of vowel length in Lithuanian', *Papers in Linguistics* 3. 73–114.

Kim, Chin-wu (1970). 'Two phonological notes: A$\sharp$ and B$\flat$.' Duplicated. Bloomington: Indiana University Linguistics Club.

King, Robert D. (1969). *Historical linguistics and generative grammar*. Englewood Cliffs: Prentice-Hall.

Kiparsky, Paul (1968a). 'How abstract is phonology?' Duplicated. Bloomington; Indiana University Linguistics Club.

(1968b). 'Linguistic universals and linguistic change', in Bach and Harms (1968: 170–202).

Kirk, Arthur (1923). *An introduction to the historical study of New High German*. Manchester: Manchester U. P.

Kisseberth, Charles (1969). 'On the role of derivational constraints in phonology.' Duplicated. Bloomington: Indiana University Linguistics Club.

(1970a). 'On the functional unity of phonological rules', *Linguistic Inquiry* 1. 291–306.

(1970b). 'The treatment of exceptions', *Papers in Linguistics* 2. 44–58.

(1970c). 'The Tunica stress conspiracy.' Duplicated. Urbana: University of Illinois.

ed. (1973). *Studies in Generative Phonology*. Champaign: Linguistic Research, Inc.

Klaeber, Fr. (1950). *Beowulf and the Fight at Finnsburg*, 2nd ed. Boston: D. C. Heath.

Kolb, E. (1966). *Phonological atlas of the Northern region*. Bern: Francke.

Koutsondas, A., Sanders, G. and Noll. C (1971). 'The application of phonological rules.' Duplicated. Bloomington: Indiana University Linguistics Club.

Kuhn, Sherman M. (1961). The syllabic phonemes of Old English', *Language* 37. 522–38.

ed. (1965). *The Vespasian Psalter*. Ann Arbor: University of Michigan Press.

Kuhn, Sherman M. and Quirk, R. (1953). 'Some recent interpretations of Old English digraph spellings', *Language* 29. 372–89.

(1955). 'The Old English short digraphs: a reply', *Language* 31. 390–401.

Kuhn, Thomas S. (1962). *The structure of scientific revolutions*. Chicago: University of Chicago Press.

Kurath, Hans (1956). 'The loss of long consonants and the rise of voiced fricatives in Middle English', *Language* 32. 435–45. Reprinted in Lass (1969a: 142–53).

Kuryłowicz, Jerzy (1956). *L'apophonie en indo-européen*. Wrocław: Polska Akademia Nauk.

Ladefoged, Peter (1971). *Preliminaries to linguistic phonetics*. Chicago: University of Chicago Press.

(1973). 'The features of the larynx', *Journal of Phonetics* 1. 73–83.

Lakoff, George (1965). 'The nature of syntactic irregularity'. Bloomington: Indiana University Ph.D. Dissertation.

Lass, Roger, ed. (1969a). *Approaches to English historical linguistics*. New York: Holt, Rinehart and Winston.

(1969b). 'On the derivative status of phonological rules: the function of metarules in sound change.' Duplicated. Bloomington: Indiana University Linguistics Club.

(1970). 'Palatals and umlaut in Old English', *Acta Linguistica Hafniensia* 13. 75–98.

(1971a). 'Boundaries as obstruents: Old English voicing assimilation and universal strength hierarchies', *Journal of Linguistics* 7. 15–30.

(1971b). 'Sound shifts as strategies for feature-erasing: some evidence from Grimm's Law.' Duplicated. Bloomington: Indiana University Linguistics Club. (Revised version (1974): 'Strategic design as the motivation or a sound shift: the rationale of Grimm's Law', *Acta Linguistica Hafniensia* 15. 51–66.)

(1972). 'How intrinsic is content? Markedness, sound change, and "family universals"', *Edinburgh Working Papers in Linguistics* 1. 42–67.

(1973a). 'On the non-universality of "natural classes", and how some of them get that way.' Duplicated. Bloomington: Indiana University Linguistics Club.

(1973b). 'What kind of vowel was Middle English /a/, and what really happened to it?', *Work in Progress (Dept. of Linguistics, Edinburgh University)* 6. 60–84.

(1973c). 'Linguistic orthogenesis: Scots vowel quantity and the English Length Conspiracy', *York Papers in Linguistics* 4. 7–25.

(in preparation a). 'On the phonological characterization of [ʔ] and [h].'

(in preparation b). *English phonology and phonological theory: synchronic and diachronic studies.*

Lee, Byung-Gun (1971). 'A reconsideration of NC/MH's feature system.' Unpublished MS.

Lehmann, W. P. (1954). 'Old English and Old Norse secondary preterites in -*r*-', *Language* 30. 202–10. Reprinted in Lass (1969a: 276–86).

(1955). *Proto-Indo-European phonology.* Austin: University of Texas Press.

(1960). 'The Germanic evidence for laryngeals', in Winter (1960: 1–12).

Lehnert, Martin (1965). *Altenglisches Elementarbuch.* Berlin: de Gruyter.

Levin, Samuel R. (1964). 'A reclassification of the Old English strong verbs', *Language* 40. 156–61. Reprinted in Lass (1969a: 251–7).

Luick, Karl (1964). *Historische Grammatik der englischen Sprache*, 2 vols. Reprint. Oxford: Basil Blackwell.

Malmberg, Bertil (1963). *Phonetics.* New York: Dover Publications.

Maran, La Raw (1971). *Burmese and Jingpho: a study in tonal linguistic processes.* Occasional papers of the Wolfenden Society, IV. Urbana: Center for Asian Studies.

Martinet, André (1955). *Economie des changements phonétiques.* Bern: Francke.

McIntosh, Angus (1956). 'The analysis of written Middle English', *Transactions of the Philological Society*, 26–55. Reprinted in Lass (1969a: 35–57).

(1963). 'A new approach to Middle English dialectology', *English Studies* 44. 1–11. Reprinted in Lass (1969a: 392–403).

Meillet, Antoine (1964). *Introduction à l'étude comparative des langues indo-européennes.* Reprint. Alabama: University of Alabama Press.

Moore, Samuel and Knott, T. A. (1955). *The elements of Old English.* Ann Arbor: Wahr.

Moore, Samuel and Marckwardt, A. H. (1964). *Historical outlines of English sounds and inflections.* Ann Arbor: Wahr.

Mossé, Fernand (1945). *Manuel de l'anglais du moyen âge:* 1, *Viel anglais,* 2 vols. Paris: Aubier.

(1952). *Handbook of Middle English.* Baltimore: Johns Hopkins Press.

Moulton, William G. (1954). 'The stops and spirants of early Germanic', *Language* 30. 1–42.

Needham, G. I., ed. (1966). *Ælfric's lives of three English saints.* London: Methuen.

Ohala, John J. (1971). 'The role of physiological and acoustic models in explaining the direction of sound change.' Paper delivered at the 1st Annual All-California Linguistics Conference, Berkeley, 1–2 May 1971.

Orton, Harold and Halliday, W. J. (1962). *Survey of English dialects. B: The basic material,* 1: *The six Northern counties and the Isle of Man.* Leeds: E. J. Arnold.

Penzl, Herbert (1947). 'The phonemic split of Germanic *k* in Old English', *Language* 23. 34–42. Reprinted in Lass (1969a: 97–107).

Pike, Kenneth L. (1943). *Phonetics.* Ann Arbor: University of Michigan Press.

Postal, Paul M. (1968). *Aspects of phonological theory.* New York: Harper.

Prokosch, Eduard (1938). *A comparative Germanic grammar.* Baltimore: Linguistic Society of America.

Puhvel, Jaan (1960). 'The present state of laryngeal studies', in Winter (1960: 1–12).

Quirk, Randolph and Wrenn, C. L. (1957). *An Old English grammar,* 2nd ed. London: Methuen.

Ruwet, N. (1968). *Introduction à la grammaire générative.* Paris: Plon.

Samuels, M. L. (1952). 'The study of Old English phonology', *Transactions of the Philological Society,* 15–47.

(1963). 'Some applications of Middle English dialectology', *English Studies* 44. 81–94. Reprinted in Lass (1969a: 404–18).

Sapir, Edward (1938). 'Glottalized continuants in Navaho, Nootka and Kwakiutl (with a note on Indo-European)', *Language* 14. 248–74.

Saussure, Ferdinand de (1887). *Mémoire sur le système primitif des voyelles dans les langues indo-européens.* Paris: Vieweg.

Schane, Sanford A. (1968). 'On the non-uniqueness of phonological representations', *Language* 44. 709–16.

(1973). *Generative phonology.* Englewood Cliffs: Prentice-Hall.

Scriven, Michael (1959). 'Explanation and prediction in evolutionary theory', *Science* 130. 477–82.

Sedlak, Philip (1969). 'Typological considerations of vowel quality systems', *Working Papers on Language Universals,* 1. Stanford: Language Universals Project.

Shopen, Tim (1971). 'Caught in the act: an intermediate stage in a would-be historical process providing syntactic evidence for the reality of para-digms.' Duplicated. Bloomington: Indiana University, Department of Linguistics.

Shopen, Tim and Konaré, M. (1970). 'Sonrai causatives and passives: transformational vs. lexical derivations for propositional heads', *Studies in African Linguistics* 1. no. 2.

Sievers, Eduard (1878). 'Zur Accent- und Lautlehre der germanischen Sprachen. III, Zum vokalischen Auslautsgesetz', *Beiträge zur Geschichte der Deutschen Sprache und Litteratur* 5. 63–163.

(1903). *An Old English Grammer*, 3rd ed. Boston: Ginn.

Sivertson, Eva (1960). *Cockney phonology*. Oslo: Oslo U. P.

Skonsen, Royal (1973). 'Evidence in phonology', in Kisseberth (1973: 72–103).

Sledd, James (1966). 'Breaking, umlaut and the southern drawl', *Language* 42. 18–41.

Stanley, Richard (1967). 'Redundancy rules in phonology', *Language* 43. 393–436.

Stockwell, Robert P. (1958). 'The phonology of Old English: a structural sketch', *Studies in linguistics* 13. 13–24.

(1961). 'The Middle English "long close" and "long open" mid vowels', *Texas Studies in Literature and Language* 2. 259–68. Reprinted in Lass (1969a: 154–63).

(1962). 'On the utility of an overall pattern in historical English phono-logy', in *Proceedings of the ninth international congress of linguists*, 663–71.

Stockwell, Robert P. and Barritt, C. (1951). 'Some Old English graphemic-phonemic correspondences: æ, ea, e', *Studies in Linguistics*, Occasional Papers, 4.

(1955). 'The Old English short digraphs: some considerations', *Language* 31. 373–89.

(1961). 'Scribal practise: some assumptions', *Language* 37. 75–82. Reprinted in Lass (1969a: 133–41).

Streitberg, Wilhelm (1963). *Urgermanische Grammatik*, 3rd ed. Heidelberg: Winter.

Sweet, Henry (1871). *King Alfred's West Saxon version of Gregory's Pastoral Care*. EETS, 45. London: Trübner.

(1877). *A handbook of phonetics*. Oxford: Clarendon Press.

(1885). *The oldest English texts*. EETS, 83. London: Oxford U. P.

(1957). *Anglo-Saxon Primer*, rev. N. Davis. Oxford: Clarendon Press.

(1969). *Sweet's Anglo-Saxon reader*, rev. D. Whitelock. Oxford: Clarendon Press.

Takeuchi, Michiko (1971). 'Appearance of the /H/-phoneme in the Japanese phonemic pattern.' Unpublished MS.

Teleman, Ulf (1969). 'Böjningssuffixens form i nusvenskan', *Arkiv för Nordisk Filologi* 84. 164–208.

Teleman, Ulf (1970). 'Stavning och fonologi. Om ortografins plats i en generativ svensk grammatik.' Meddelanden från Forskningsgruppen för Talsyntax, 27. Duplicated. Lund: Talsyntax.

Trager, George L. and Smith, H. L. (1951). *An outline of English structure.* Washington: American Council of Learned Societies.

Traugott, Elizabeth (1969). 'Simplification vs. elaboration in syntactic change.' Unpublished MS.

Vachek, Josef (1959). 'Notes on the quantitative correlation of vowels in the phonematic development of English', in *Mélanges de linguistique et de philologie: Fernand Mossé in memoriam*, 444–56. Paris: Didier.

Vago, Robert M. (1973). 'Abstract vowel harmony systems in Uralic and Altaic languages', *Language* 49. 579–605.

Vaiana, Mary E. (1972). 'A study in the dialect of the southern counties of Scotland.' Bloomington: Indiana University Ph.D. thesis.

Vennemann, Theo (1969). 'Historical German phonology and the theory of marking.' Unpublished MS.

Verner, Karl (1875). 'Eine Ausnahme der ersten Lautverschiebung', *Zeitschrift für vergleichende Sprachforschung auf dem Gebiete der Indogermanischen Sprachen* 23. 97–130.

Wagner, Karl Heinz (1969). *Generative grammatical studies in the Old English language.* Heidelberg: Groos.

Wang, William S-Y. (1969). 'Competing changes as a cause of residue', *Language* 45. 9–25.

Watkins, Calvert (1960). 'Notes on componential analysis of laryngeals', in Winter (1960: 232–8).

Whitney, William Dwight (1889). *Sanskrit grammar*, 2nd ed. Cambridge, Mass.: Harvard U. P.

Winter, Werner, ed. (1960). *Evidence for laryngeals: Work papers of a conference in Indo-European linguistics on May 7 and 8, 1959.* Austin: Dept. of Germanic Languages, University of Texas.

Wrenn, C. L. (1933). 'Standard Old English', *Transactions of the Philological Society*, 65–88.

Wright, Joseph and Wright, E. M. (1925). *An Old English grammar.* Oxford: Oxford U. P.

Zwicky, Arnold (1969). 'A note on a phonological hierarchy in English.' Unpublished MS.

Subject and author index

Word index

Members of inflexional paradigms are listed alphabetically, each as a separate entry; but they are keyed to a head-word or 'lexeme-representative': in the case of nouns this is the nominative singular; for verbs it is the infinitive. Individual forms will be no further specified (as to specific morphosyntactic properties), but this information will normally be available in the first text reference. Thus an entry like *rād* (< *rīdan*) means that *rād* is a member of the paradigm whose head-word is *rīdan*.

Alphabetization will follow the usual English conventions; but *æ* follows *ad*, and *þ/ð* follow *t*.

Variant spellings (archaic or non-WS) are alphabetized separately, with an indication equivalence: e.g. *ald* (= *aeald*) The head-word here is the most usual WS spelling.

ARMENIAN

hin 163

AVESTAN

hanō 163

DANISH

ja 11

DUTCH

a 11

CZECH

prst 5, 14

FRENCH

avoir 160
croire 160
lire 160
majeur 160

GERMAN

ach 220
alt 60
Beber 181
Gabel 181

Gott 203
Haar 36
ich 220
ja 11
Kiene 113
Nabel 181
weben 181

GOTHIC

andeis 271
aukan 75
baiþ (< *beidan*) 34, 35
bauþ (< *-biudan*) 34, 35
beidan 27, 34, 35
bidjan 264–5
bidum (< *beidan*) 34
bidans (< *beidan*) 34
-biudan 27, 34, 35
-budans (< *-biudan*) 34
-budum (< *-biudan*) 34
bugjan 267, 268
dags 60
fisks 220
haihald (< *haldan*) 251
hairdeis 273
haldan 251, 264
harjan 258, 266, 267, 268
harjis 271, 273
hausjan 267

huzd 170
-ima 30
-ina 30
-is 25
-iþ 25, 30
jaind 138
juk 138
kuni 270, 271
nasjan 258, 266
reiki 271
saljan 206
sandjan 267, 268
sōkjan 267, 268
tiuhan 93
twaddjē 160
þiuda 75
-um 30
-un 30
-uþ 30

GREEK

esti 163
hénē 163
hépta 155
léipō 59
le-lóipa (< *léipō*) 59
omphalós 181
spaínō 163
stásis 163
upháimō 181
zugón 138

OLD ENGLISH (*cont.*)
tǣhte (< *tǣċan*) 100,
    217
tēah (< *tēon*) 93, 94, 100,
    171
tealde (< *tellan*) 257
telest (< *tellan*) 257
tellan 85, 257, 271
tēon 93, 94, 95, 100, 171
tielung 123
tīma 217
-togen (< *tēon*) 100, 171
trēo 179
trifot 181
trum 227, 229, 257
trymman 227, 229, 256,
    257
tugon (< *tēon*) 100, 171
turf 269
tusc 221
tux (= *tusc*) 221
þǣah 75n
þǣċċ 145
þāh (< *þēon*) 99
þēah (< *þēon*) 99
þenċan 99, 100
þēod 75, 121
þēof 207, 208, 209, 214
þēoh 176, 222
þēon 98, 99, 100, 107,
    209
þēow 69
þerscan 221
þerxan (= *þerscan*) 221
-þigen (< *þēon*) 99
þigon (< *þēon*) 99
þīn 124
-þogen (< *þēon*) 99
þōhte (< *þenċan*) 99
þugon (< *þēon*) 99
þūhte (< *þynċan*) 99
-þungen (< *þēon*) 98
þungon (< *þēon*) 98
þynċan 99, 100
underþīedan 121
ūre 8
ūt 8
ūþe 8
uuibil (= *wifol*) 182
wǣron (< *wesan*) 101, 172
wǣs (< *wesan*) 101, 172
wand (< *windan*) 235
wearþ (< *weorþan*) 25, 29,
    34, 74, 75
wearþ (< *weorþan*) 59, 90,
    101

wecgan 256
wefan 181
weġ 130, 142, 143
wendan 235
wennan 256
weoloras (< *we(o)lor*) 102
weorada (= *weoruda*) 102
weoruda 102
weorpan 25, 27, 29, 74,
    75
weorþan 59, 90, 101
wēpan 254n
weras 103
wēriġ 110
wesan 101
wīf 269
windan 235
wine 269
wierpst (< *weorpan*) 25
wierpð (< *weorpan*) 25
wifol 276
witan 74, 123
wlite 9, 71
woeġ (= *weġ*) 130
word 269
-worden (< *weorþan*)
    101
-worpen (< *weorpan*) 25,
    30
wrāh (< *wrēon*) 93, 97,
    107
wrēah (< *wrēon*) 97, 100,
    107
wrēon 93, 97, 100, 107
wreþþan 256
-wrigen (< *wrēon*) 97
wrigon (< *wrēon*) 97
wrītan 9
-wrogen (< *wrēon*) 97,
    100
wrugon (< *wrēon*) 97,
    100
wucu 8
wudu 8, 269, 276
wulf 8
wund 8, 269
-wunden (< *windan*) 235
wundon (< *windan*) 235
wundor 8
wurdon (< *weorþan*) 8,
    101
wurpe(n) (< *weorpan*)
    30
wurpon (< *weorpan*) 25,
    30
yfel 229

yldra (= *ieldra*) 124
yrmþu (= *iermþu*) 124
ȳð 229

OLD FRISIAN

deg 60
flecht 93
geva 172
ieva 172
iung 138
jeva 172
jogethe 138

OLD HIGH GERMAN

bibar 181
-fehan 93
fuoʒ 192
gabala 181
geban 172
hier 192
-is 25
-it 15
lahan 93
līhan 93
magatīn 63
nabulo 181
rihan 93
salbōn 62, 142
tag 60
weban 181

OLD IRISH

athir 185
drui 119
orc 185

OLD NORSE

allr 271
biðja 255
dagr 60
fiskr 220
Frigg 160
fullr 271
galgi 136
gata 136
gefa 136
geta 136
Hreinn 160
kǫttr 271
leggja 255
ǫllum 160
rekkr 73n